D1557333

CLAIMING CRIMEA

CLAIMING CRIMEA

A HISTORY OF CATHERINE THE GREAT'S

SOUTHERN EMPIRE

KELLY O'NEILL

New Haven and London

Yale UNIVERSITY PRESS

Published with assistance from the foundation established in memory of Amasa Stone
Mather of the Class of 1907, Yale College.

Yale University Press books may be purchased in quantity for educational, business, or
promotional use. For information, please e-mail sales.press@yale.edu (U.S. office) or
sales@yaleup.co.uk (U.K. office).

Set in Sabon and Berthold City Bold types by Westchester Publishing Services.
Printed in the United States of America.

ISBN 978-0-300-21829-9 (hardcover : alk. paper)
Library of Congress Control Number: 2017937440
A catalogue record for this book is available from the British Library.

This paper meets the requirements of ANSI/NISO Z39.48-1992 (Permanence of Paper).

10 9 8 7 6 5 4 3 2 1

For my daughters,
Saoirse, Aoibhin, and Fiona

Petersburg, situated upon the Baltic, is Russia's northern capital; Moscow is its central, and may Kherson or Akhtiar be my Sovereign's southern capital. Let them see which Sovereign made the best selection.

—Prince Grigorii Potemkin to Empress Catherine II, June 13, 1783 (translated by Douglas Smith)

Contents

Preface

When I began this project, the Russian annexation of Crimea was a singular occurrence in world history, and very few of my friends, family members, or casual acquaintances could do more than feign interest in this unfamiliar and seemingly insignificant fragment of Eurasia. But in late February 2014, Russian forces seized the local parliament in Simferopol. In a matter of days a new government took the reins, declared independence from Ukraine, and held a referendum. Then, on March 18, 2014, President Vladimir Putin brought an end to months of political upheaval and controversial military intervention by formalizing the annexation of Crimea, an autonomous republic of Ukraine, to the Russian Federation. The move sent shock waves across Europe, waves that continue to ripple through deliberations over the value of Ukrainian sovereignty and the shape of geostrategic policies toward a resurgent Russia. A nonbinding United Nations resolution was put in place, affirming the territorial integrity of Ukraine and rejecting the legitimacy of the Russian move, yet interest in the fate of Crimea itself vanished from the front pages and blogrolls of Western media almost as quickly as it had materialized. With the peninsula safely ensconced within the federated structure of the Russian state, Putin has a free hand to deal with those who refuse to accept Russian rule. The most vocal resistance has come from Crimean Tatars—an ethnic minority whose legislature has been banned and whose leaders have been exiled and arrested.

The Crimean Tatars have largely failed to mobilize sustained support from Western audiences. Meanwhile, Putin's government succeeded almost immediately in rallying strong domestic support for the reclamation of the Black Sea peninsula. The Kremlin deployed a range of soft-line tactics. The Boris Yeltsin Presidential Library organized new collections celebrating "the unique historical-cultural preserve" that is the (newly established) Republic of Crimea. The Tretyakov Gallery is mounting a major exhibition of the work of Ivan Aivazovskii, the great landscape painter and native Crimean. The State Hermitage Museum has convened international conferences and poured funding into moribund dig sites from Kerch to Chersonesos. Annexing Crimea is, the state would have its people believe, a simple matter of restoring ancient legacies, reinvigorating primordial connections, and remembering, above all, that Crimea is an integral part of Russia's sprawling political and cultural terrain.

To be fair, it wasn't a hard sell. For as bold as Putin's annexation maneuver might have been, it was not terribly original. Russia's relationship with Crimea has evolved over half a millennium; the peninsula and its hinterland have figured prominently in the development of the east Slavic world for twice that long. The moment in which this long trajectory truly took shape came not in the spring of 2014 but one morning late in the autumn of 1782, as Empress Catherine II sat in her study in the Winter Palace drinking coffee. In her hand was a carefully crafted letter from Prince Grigorii Potemkin, president of the War College, commander-in-chief of the armed forces, and grand admiral of the Black Sea and Caspian fleets. For some months Potemkin had been urging his sovereign to declare an end to the independence of the Crimean Khanate (an interlude that began in 1774). Catherine was reluctant. With mounting frustration, Potemkin informed her that she should act soon, else "there will come a time when everything that we might now receive for free, we shall obtain for a high price." What, exactly, was at stake? Potemkin's list was short but compelling: the security of the empire's borders, the allegiance of its Russian inhabitants, and unimpeded access to the Black Sea. "Believe me," wrote Potemkin, "with this acquisition you will achieve immortal glory such that no other Sovereign in Russia has ever had."

Such were the contents of the handwritten note shuttled from one palace to another in the bone-chilling cold of St. Petersburg. The significance of Crimea is now, as it was then, as much about security as it is
about symbolism. And it is as much about Crimea itself as it is about
the projection of Russian power well beyond the peninsula. As Potemkin's letter suggests, annexing Crimea would allow the empress, and
those who succeeded her, to assert influence over even broader swaths
of territory than those constituted by modern-day Ukraine. By virtue
of its geography, Crimea is a portal to the world of the Black Sea. As
a former vassal of the Ottoman Empire and home to some 300,000
Muslims, Crimea gave tsarist Russia entrée into the fractious politics
of the Sublime Porte. And as the last remnant of the Mongol commonwealth in the west, Crimea provided grounds for Russia to reclaim the
imperial mantle of the Eurasian steppe.

There are echoes of these grandiose claims in the discourse now emanating from Moscow. Putin has gestured toward the idea of Russia as
a Eurasian power—a global player both apart from and, to a significant extent, opposed to the rest of Europe. In this context Crimea is a
critical axis for the economic and geopolitical projection of Russian
power. But Crimea is more than just a portal into other, more strategically significant terrain. It is, in the minds of government officials and
private citizens alike, for a host of complex and often contradictory
reasons, a significant terrain in its own right. Above all, it is a crucial
site for exploring and articulating Russian identity.

As proof of this one need only consider the government's extraordinary ideological investment. In 1783—in the wake of the *first* annexation of Crimea—Catherine set about renaming the towns and rivers
of her southern province and thus imbuing what many perceived as an
unstable and threatening Turko-Islamic landscape with classical Greek and
Orthodox Christian civilization. She ordered the planting of groves of
olive and citrus, and vineyards full of grapes imported from Tuscany
and the Greek islands. She built Orthodox churches and sprawling vil-
las. She spent outrageous amounts of money choreographing her 1787
tour from Petersburg through Kiev to Bahçesaray, the capital of the
khanate—a tour designed for the express purpose of taking possession
of Crimea through ritual and ideology. Her successors followed suit, con-
secrating the southern coast with palaces and botanical gardens, and
crafting their own southward passages from St. Petersburg to the place

where Russia met the mountains and the sea in appealingly spectacular fashion.

It was my friend Alexei Petrov, a marine biologist from Sevastopol, who showed me something of Crimea's sedimentary nature. It was a dusty, shabby place when I first saw it in 1995, with a distinct Soviet patina. When I returned for a summer in the archives in 1999, Alexei and his wife, Marina, took it upon themselves to show me what (or perhaps where) Crimea really was. We followed grass-covered paths and climbed broken, rusty gates in order to explore the remnants of ruined churches. We bushwhacked through low-growth forests (always with an eye out for wild boar) on the way to Ai Petri, the 4,000-foot peak above Alupka. We swam in the turquoise water at Laspi (long before the construction of the impossibly high-end Bay of Dreams Hotel). We ate enormous quantities of cherries—Crimeans are fiercely proud of their fruit—and, every once in a while, drank a glass of watered wine in the way of the ancient Greeks. One afternoon, during one of our many excursions through the grounds of Chersonesos, I noticed two small ceramic fragments dislodged by heavy rain the previous night. One was green, the other blue. When I showed them to Alexei and his friend, a local historian, they shrugged. "Well you see," explained the historian, "these are not such special things. They are, well, fifteenth century probably," dismissing my treasures with a sweeping gesture meant to remind me of our surroundings, which included the whitewashed columns of a fourth-century basilica and piles of amphora dating back to the second century BCE.

The historian—his name was also Alexei—carried a satchel at all times, and at one point toward the end of that first summer he pulled out a set of photographs. They were images of the Cathedral of St. Vladimir at Chersonesos, a church originally conceived by an admiral of the Black Sea Fleet to celebrate the supposed site of a Kievan prince's baptism into the Christian faith back in the late tenth century (archaeologists have long argued that St. Vladimir's is built on a temple to Apollo rather than the baptismal basilica of the city). Tsar Alexander II attended the ceremonial foundation of the cathedral in 1861 and it functioned as a church until 1926, perched atop—and thus preventing excavation of—one of the most important areas of the ancient Greek city. The German army (or the Soviet army, depending on whom you ask) bombed St. Vladimir's in 1942, converting the site into a hulking, shattered mass of Inkerman stone and Italian marble. At some point thereafter, someone took the series of black-and-white photographs that ended up in Alexei's satchel. They are remarkable images, filled with brooding stone and sky. A few men and women pick their way through the rubble, some gazing up at the protruding ribs of the ninth-century church that had been swallowed up by cathedral walls in the nineteenth century. Contrary to what one might expect, the images speak of a relentlessly dynamic place—a ruin demanding restoration or, perhaps, reinvention.

From the very beginning, the fate of the cathedral has depended on the relationship between Russia and Crimea. When the Presidium of the Supreme Soviet announced in 1954 that the Crimean oblast' would henceforth be part of the Ukrainian Soviet Socialist Republic, it added a layer of complexity to an already volatile situation. Archaeologists and advocates of the Orthodox Church had been clashing since the 1870s over whether the cathedral had any right to exist at all, located as it was on a crucial archaeological site. To the delight of the former group, Chersonesos acquired the status of "historic-archaeological preserve" in 1978, though that did not deter church officials. In the aftermath of 1991 the archbishop of Crimea and Simferopol pressed the Ukrainian government to restore the cathedral as property of the Orthodox Church. Religious services began in 1992 and, with Kiev's decision to transfer the cathedral to the diocese of Crimea and Simferopol in 1994, restoration work got under way. The new cathedral stands, gilded and gleaming, under the jurisdiction of the Ukrainian Orthodox Church.

Meanwhile, in 2013 UNESCO awarded the Chersonesos Archaeological Preserve status as a World Heritage Site under the jurisdiction of Ukraine's Ministry of Culture. UNESCO has not acknowledged Russia's annexation of Crimea. Then again, it has not satisfied the requests of Ukraine's Permanent Delegation, which has called for an investigation of the current state of conservation at the site—a site that, in practice, is now located in the Russian Federation. The newly launched website of the preserve, officially known as the State Historical-Archaeological Preserve at Khersones-Tavricheskii, displays the country code top-level domain of the Russian Federation (.ru) rather than that of Ukraine (.ua) in its URL. The preserve's interactive map acknowledges St. Vladimir Cathedral, but does not identify it or explain the presence of this monumental attestation of Ukrainian (ecclesiastical) authority.

Crimea, I have concluded after countless sojourns, is its own deep map. It is a material world inscribed with meaning, rich with stories that are legible one minute and indecipherable the next. It is a dense web of religious and political symbols, but also an accretion of intensely physical experiences and the knowledge they produce. It changes according to scale and perspective, but remains one of the micro-terrains of the former Russian Empire in which historical memory and national identity have been worked out over the last two decades.

And it remains a contested place. In the late eighteenth century, Catherine and Potemkin tried to shore up their claim through settlement, bringing tens of thousands of Slavic peasants as well as Bulgarian, Mennonite, and Lutheran immigrants to settle the steppe. By contrast, settlement of the peninsula proceeded slowly. Finally, with the debacle of the Crimean War in the rearview mirror, the imperial government oversaw the resettlement of two-thirds of the Crimean Tatar population (some 300,000 people) to Ottoman lands—a move that radically altered the landscape of local society and allowed Russian officials and subjects to begin reinventing Crimea. Of course, the events of the 1860s pale in comparison to the trauma of the deportation of roughly a quarter million Crimean Tatars in May 1944—an event that continues to shape political dialogue, ethnic relations, and socioeconomic institutions. But demographic change was never enough. Taking a cue from Catherine (though I doubt he thought of it that way), Stalin channeled exorbitant amounts of money to Crimea so that Sevastopol, the hero city destroyed during German occupation, could rise again, clad this time in elegant neoclassical architectural stylings. The former mayor of Moscow, the patriarch of the Russian Orthodox Church, and countless oligarchs have continued the tradition of sponsoring the construction of elite residences, improved infrastructure, and gleaming upscale maritime oases as part of the work of staking Russia's claim to Crimea.

In a sense, it all comes down to place names. "Crimea" (Krym in Russian, Krim in Ukrainian, Qırım in Crimean Tatar) is a shorthand reference to countless cultural, ideological, and geospatial entities. It refers to a peninsula that juts southward into the Black Sea, connected to the mainland by the perilously narrow isthmus of Perekop, but also to a Tatar state that extended across the Pontic steppe, its borders moving along with the nomadic Nogay tribes that embodied the range of the khan's authority. Imperial officials drew on that amorphous geography when they established their new southern province in 1784. Then again, they channeled the Greek legacy of the Black Sea as well, creating toponyms—Tavrida (Tauride), Sevastopol, Feodosiia, Evpatoriia—that would reinscribe the region with an entirely different ideological meaning. Oddly enough though, mapmakers, governors, and inhabitants alike remained ambivalent about this new toponymy. Eighteenth- and nineteenth-century documents often refer to Sevastopol, the naval port, as Aktiar, Simferopol, the provincial town, as Akmeçet, and Feodosiia, the preeminent port, as Kefe or Caffa.

It is difficult to avoid the politics of place names in a project like this. In the rare case where a standard English spelling exists, I gladly use it. For example I use St. Petersburg rather than Sanktpeterburg, and Crimea rather than any of the alternatives. I refer to members of the Tatar ruling dynasty as Giray rather than Geray (Crimean Tatar), and the architect of the first annexation as Catherine rather than Ekaterina. Because the vast majority of the archival record that I used exists in Russian, Russian names and toponyms do occur throughout this book. But for the most part I have tried to default to Turkish spellings. In so doing I follow in the footsteps of historians such as Alan Fisher and Michael Khodarkovksy: scholars on either side of the Black Sea, so to speak, but who have both done excellent work on various aspects of steppe history. Thus in this book the (former) Tatar capital appears as Bahçesaray instead of Bakhchysarai (Ukrainian), Bakhchisarai or Bakhchisaray (Russian), or Bağçasaray (Crimean Tatar). To the extent that it is possible, I identify individuals by transcribing the names they bore in their native languages (Şirin rather than Shirin, for example). But it is not always possible. It seems that either most Russian clerks had a poor ear for Turkic languages, or they did not care terribly much about consistency, let alone legibility. To my chagrin, a single man can appear in the records as Megmetsha Mirza, Megmet Mirza, and Megmedcha. And in an environment in which roughly three-quarters of the population did not have surnames, the task of piecing together identity across document collections was extraordinarily challenging. Along the way, I compiled a database of one thousand *mirzas* (clan leaders and members of the Crimean Tatar elite), painstakingly cross-checking landholding records, birthdates, and service records in an effort to understand the shape of both individual lives and clans. Even then, I would say I am no more than reasonably confident about the accuracy of my work. I can say with confidence, though, that my motivation was not to assert the legitimacy of Russian—or Tatar, or Ukrainian—claims to Crimea and its history. If anything, I advocate for embracing the rich and flexible system of names in this part of the world. I suggest that you attempt to hold Caffa, Kefe, and Feodosiia in your mind and, rather than identify one as "right," ponder the ways in which each toponym describes, evokes, possibly even creates historical space.

Truth be told, even if they had no talent for spelling Tatar names, I have a soft spot for the scribes and scriveners whose efforts produced the archives in which I have been immersed for years. I can't help thinking of them, hunched over their tables, writing mindlessly hour after hour in the raw damp of the provincial offices, in the flickering shadow of the southern sun, making it possible, however unintentionally, for me to imagine what it meant to inhabit Crimea in the aftermath of Russian annexation.

☆

One final note. Many of the maps, images, and spatial arguments found here are presented in a different, and hopefully complementary way, in a digital history project I call *Beautiful Spaces*. The site offers additional data visualizations, source documentation, and a curation system that reveals the often surprising connections between people, places, and power. In a sense, it is a boutique "deep" gazetteer of the places mentioned in this book. You are most welcome to explore it here: http://dighist.fas.harvard.edu/projects/beautifulspaces/.

Acknowledgments

The research for this book would not have been possible without generous support from a number of institutions. I have been the beneficiary of grants from the Fulbright-Hays Doctoral Dissertation Research Abroad program, the IREX Regional Scholar Program, the Davis Center for Russian and Eurasian Studies, and the Weatherhead Center for International Affairs.

I have benefitted from the expertise and generosity of librarians and archivists at the Harvard Library, the National Library of Russia, the Tavrika Library in Simferopol, the Harvard Map Collection, the Davis Center Collection at the Fung Library, the George Gordon Library at Worcester Polytechnic Institute, the John Hay Library at Brown University, the New York Public Library, the Boston Athenaeum, the Russian State Historical Archive, the Russian State Military History Archive, the Russian State Archive of Ancient Acts, and particularly the State Archive of the Autonomous Republic of Crimea in Simferopol. I think it is worth pointing out that this last archive was liquidated in October 2014 and reconstituted as the State Archive of the Republic of Crimea, under the umbrella of RosArkhiv.

My colleagues are a constant source of insight, inspiration, and guidance. The list of fellow Harvard historians to whom I am indebted is long, but includes Terry Martin, Serhii Plokhii, Alison Johnson, Dan

Smail, David Armitage, Cemal Kafadar, Roman Szporluk, Ian Miller, Andy Jewett, Kirsten Weld, and the late Ned Keenan. For sharing their incomparable knowledge of, and devotion to, Russia's history and culture I am deeply grateful to Julie Buckler and John LeDonne, both of whom have been sources of inspiration from my earliest days as a graduate student. Special thanks go to Eric Lohr, John Randolph, Valerie Kivelson, Jane Burbank, Nancy Shields Kollmann, Dominic Lieven, Erika Monahan, Nick Breyfogle, Paul Werth, Catherine Evtuhov, and Elise Wirtschafter for providing valuable perspective, feedback, words of wisdom, and a bit of sanity during long slogs in the archives. It is a true joy to work in a field so chock-full of generous souls that I can't begin to name them all here. I am deeply grateful as well to my blind reviewers, whose comments proved invaluable from start to finish.

Happily, part of any historian's work takes place in a classroom. Many of the thoughtful comments and questions posed by my students— undergraduate and graduate alike—have helped shape the way I think about the past. I am particularly grateful to Greg Afinogenov, Megan Duncan Smith, Erin Hutchinson, Marysia Blackwood, Rachel Koroloff, Philippa Hetherington, Johanna Conterio, Jessica Peyton Roberts, Jordan Bryant, and Eren Tasar. Some are students, some have become scholars or professionals in their own right; all are tremendous credits to the discipline.

Finally, writing a book is difficult work, but it is work made easier by the support and encouragement of friends and family. So to the friends I've held dear since kindergarten and to those I've collected much more recently, thank you from the bottom of my heart. To my parents, my sister, my husband, my daughters, and the rest of my wonderful family: please know that my love for you is bigger than the Russian Empire ever was.

CLAIMING
CRIMEA

Introduction

Locating Crimea in Russian History

> The Kaima-Kan is the Khan's first minister; he is totally ignorant of the
> geography of his own country; and says that England and Petersburgh are
> the same thing.
> —Elizabeth Lady Craven, *A Journey Through the Crimea
> to Constantinople*

EARLY IN THE spring of 1783, as the rivers of the south began to swell
and rush toward the Black Sea, Empress Catherine II announced that
Russia had at long last annexed the Crimean Khanate.[1] Although it had
been a major player in eastern European and steppe politics since coming into existence in the middle of the fifteenth century—and one
enjoying something of a cultural renaissance in the middle of the
eighteenth—the khanate's power had diminished noticeably. The treaty
of Constantinople (1700) brought a formal end to the annual tribute
delivered to the khan, rather grudgingly, by the tsars, and in 1768
Crimean horsemen conducted their last slave raids into Russian territory. The khanate was weakened by internal political strife as much as
by Russia's meteoric rise, but it was nevertheless an enviable prize for
the empress to claim. Inhabited by Tatars, Greeks, Armenians, Karaites,
and Roma, supported by a mixed economy, and ruled by a dynasty that
grounded its legitimacy in its descent from Chingis Khan, Crimea offered Catherine a strategic stretch of coastline close enough to the
Ottoman capital—so she liked to imagine—that she could bathe in full
view of the sultan.

This book explores what happened in the aftermath of annexation.
It is a book about how empires are built and about how they are experienced by the subjects who come to inhabit them. It is a book about

the world of the Black Sea, about the experience of Muslim peoples in Russian society, and about Crimea itself. The story of Crimea's transition from khanate to Russian province has eluded the attention of most historians. It did not, after all, involve the bloody glories of wars of conquest like those that unfolded in the Caucasus or Central Asia; nor did the annexation manifesto wrest people, resources, and property from a European power, as was the case with the nearly contemporaneous partitions of the Polish-Lithuanian Commonwealth. Unlike many other borderland territories, Crimea seemed to go quietly into the fold, quickly subsumed within the administrative terrain of the empire.

I argue that the incorporation of the Crimean Khanate—a process that unfolded over seventy years stretching between 1783 and the outbreak of the Crimean War in 1853—was in fact a complicated and prolonged iteration of empire building. In Crimea, Russian officials confronted the challenge of administering a predominantly Muslim population. They had done so before, but not since Catherine's reinvention of Russia as a state saturated in Enlightenment principles such as religious toleration and rational, equitable rule. Russia had annexed coastal territory before as well, though it was possession of Crimea that gave it a substantive presence on the Black Sea. Crimea was neither the biggest nor the most lucrative of the empire's acquisitions. Its significance rests instead in the combination of cultural, chronological, and geographical conditions that made it an object of intense fascination and anxiety in distant St. Petersburg. Crimea lay on the imagined meridian between Muslim and Christian civilization, between old and new modes of constructing imperial society, and between terrestrial and maritime worlds. As the Crimeans had been vassals of the Ottoman sultans for nearly three hundred years, finding themselves part of an empire was nothing new (though swearing allegiance to a Christian sovereign certainly was). But the khanate presented a novel opportunity to Catherine and the "viceroy of Southern Russia," Prince Grigorii Potemkin. Surveying the steppe, the mountains, the rivers, and the sea, they saw an opportunity not simply to integrate a new province, but to build a new empire—a southern empire.

A New Russia—*Novorossiia*—was on the map long before 1783. Established in 1764 and reorganized in 1775, its territory stretched from the Bug River in the west to the Donets River in the east. Unencumbered by serfdom, settled by a mixture of foreign colonists, military, and free peasant settlers, graced with rich soil and a profusion of rivers, Novorossiia was a region unlike any other in the empire. The addition of the khanate in 1783 (and Bessarabia in 1812) lent it ideological as well as geographical coherence. Indeed, Apollon Aleksandrovich Skal'kovskii, a prolific historian and indefatigable statistician from Zhitomir, exclaimed with great enthusiasm that just as the Spanish, Dutch, and British had their respective "New Worlds," so too Russia, "having captured the abandoned steppes and territories of the enemy Tatar hordes, and having made out of them a European-style region, had full right to name its own new world . . . 'New Russia.'"[2]

Was it truly a colonial possession? Was Russia a colonial empire? Some of the scholars who examined the Crimean case have framed their work within the colonial paradigm, and not without reason.[3] A substantive body of work on the policies and practices implemented from Vilnius to Tashkent provides us with a more nuanced understanding of the tensions, both productive and destructive, between the Russian center and the non-Russian periphery. Without doubt the core-periphery dynamic is both relevant and revealing. Historians have deployed it to great effect to reconstruct the histories of the geographical, social, and cultural margins and to show the extent to which empire could be a negotiated, adaptable process. But the most striking result of the "imperial turn" initiated by Andreas Kappeler's influential work has been the reemergence of one of the most fundamental and bedeviling questions in Russian history: where did "interior Russia" (*vnutrennaia Rossiia*) end and the empire begin? To put it another way, what constituted the core of the imperial project? In this multiethnic, contiguous, dynastic entity is it possible to discern static, or more or less stable, geographic or cultural boundaries? How well can we understand the peripheries if we cannot locate the center?[4]

Mapping the boundaries of the Russian core is an extraordinarily difficult proposition. It might also be a misleading proposition. In an effort to contend with all of this, some scholars have carefully reconstructed the conceptual geographies that defined Russia in various phases of its history. Others have developed the argument that the imperial core was located not in geographical space but in the social space of the ruling elite—a dispersed, organic metropolis that lent coherence to lands inhabited by Russian-speaking peasants and Turkic-speaking pastoralists alike.[5]

But what if we shift the terms ever so slightly and seek instead to identify the connective tissues that lent the imperial project coherence? Scholars working along these lines have produced a series of innovative studies of the empire's financial architecture, its confessional policy, and its implementation of legality and citizenship as tools for shoring up an increasingly fissured population. This body of work does not reject the "core" as the ultimate source or arbiter of power in the imperial narrative, and neither do I. I am interested in approaching the empire as a continuous space, though a differentiated one.[6]

This is, after all, how a great many tsarist officials and subjects conceived of their country. Even Catherine II, whose vision of the south was informed by Enlightenment ideals and the imperial pursuits of fellow sovereigns, did not see Novorossiia as foreign terrain in the way that her Hanoverian, Hapsburg, and Bourbon peers did the Americas and Indian subcontinent. From the perspective of St. Petersburg, Novorossiia—which eventually became the provinces of Kherson, Ekaterinoslav, and Tavrida, as well as parts of Poltava and Kharkov—was many things at once. It was a land threatened by Turks, Poles, Tatars, and Zaporozhian Cossacks. It was "wild and unpossessed," and devoid of European civilization. It was distinctly evocative—"as wide as the sea" that separated Spain from its colonies—and yet intrinsically part of Russia. As one travel guide explained, "For the Russian traveler with a true poetic soul, it would be impossible to find a better place in all the world than Crimea." Here the "radiant light" of tsarist rule conjured cities and farms, creating a comfortingly familiar landscape of cultivation and habitation, but even if imperial officials had failed in that project the exotic nature of the region was something in which any true Russian could exalt, for Crimea was, at root, Russian land, "inhabited by Russians, then known as European Scythians, from the most ancient of times." In the minds of those who followed this logic, 1783 marked not the expansion of the organic boundaries of the Russian core but a moment of reclamation or restoration.[7]

Of course, the scholars, writers, and officials who pondered such matters advanced varying interpretations of Crimea and its status as interior province or borderland, exotic Orient or integral piece of the Russian core. Tavrida's place in the empire remained open to interpretation over subsequent generations, and this book attempts to explore and explain the remarkable persistence of these ambiguities. One of the central contentions of this book is that those ambiguities, and the competing perspectives that created them, mark Crimea, and the south more broadly, not as an imperfectly integrated territory but as a space in which the Russian brand of empire thrived. That brand of empire was an effective mechanism for securing order, allegiance, and stability. It was complex, in terms of the arrangement of political, social, and cultural relationships that defined it. And it was flexible, evolving over time and across space. Most important, it was of a piece in ways that distinguished it from its British, Dutch, and Spanish counterparts. To be sure, the Russian Empire looked one way when viewed from Tashkent and another when viewed from Warsaw; the idea is not to downplay the significance of regional variation or to dismiss the validity of the core-periphery binary. Instead I want to emphasize the idea that while Russian policies and practices—what Jane Burbank and Fred Cooper refer to as "imperial repertoires"—can and should be examined from a number of different vantage points, the empire itself had an enduring topology: a set of properties that maintained their inner logic despite the relentless stretching, straining, and bending of an expansionist, multiethnic, multicultural state.

This book tests the concept of imperial topology, though its scale is far more humble than that of the tsarist state. I focus on what I call Russia's "southern empire," using that concept to pull together three ideas. First, I see the region as a system not fully contained by political boundaries or administrative institutions. This was space defined by overlapping imperial interests and legacies. It was shaped by post roads and black earth but also by riverine networks, salt flats, harbors, and maritime passages that flowed not north toward Petersburg but south toward Constantinople. Second, understanding the southern empire requires paying attention to the role of place: the sites within the natural and built environments in which life is experienced and meaning and memory are generated. Third, I approach the southern empire not as the product of a binary relationship (linking St. Petersburg to Simferopol, for example) but as an arrangement of interrelationships—a topology capable of stretching and bending, growing compact or attenuated, defined by connection rather than rupture. In other words, this is an attempt to transcend the language of core and periphery, metropolis and borderland, and to reconsider the spatial structure of the Russian Empire. It is an attempt to play with the scale of empire and the viewsheds of those who experienced it.

Crimea is at the heart of this project. The book therefore has an undeniably local flavor; it is not, however, a local history. There is a well-entrenched history of studying the local in Russian scholarship. *Kraevedenie* (local or regional studies) spread tentative roots in the late eighteenth century, blossomed in the 1860s, and thrived in the late imperial era. In recent decades it has enjoyed a resurgence both as a mechanism for reclaiming the past from dominant Soviet narratives, and as a topic of study in and of itself—a productive way to reconsider the importance of science, history, and local agency. The Russian Geographical Society has a branch devoted to "local studies and scholastic geography," and there are local-studies museums in at least two dozen Russian cities, including Perm, Novosibirsk, Saratov, Minsk, Rostov, Omsk, Tomsk, Irkutsk, Barnaul, Krasnoiar, Voronezh, Cheliabinsk, Murmansk, Sukhumi, Arkhangel'sk, Astrakhan, Tambov, and Sakhalin. Practitioners of kraevedenie have published countless "sketches" of villages, towns, and regions, as well as toponymical dictionaries, collections of songs and legends, conference proceedings, and family histories. *Krymovedenie*—Crimean studies—is booming as well. Its leading light is Andrei Anatol'evich Nepomniashchii, professor of regional history at the Tavrida Academy of the Federal University of Crimea in Simferopol, chairman of the Crimean Union of Local Studies Specialists, and author of annotated bibliographies as well as studies of luminaries in the field, the preservation of cultural monuments, and the role of travel writing and guidebooks in the development of Crimean studies. The Russian Society for the Study of Crimea, reestablished in 2011 (it had existed from 1920 to 1930) and headquartered in Moscow and Simferopol, organizes conferences and publishes *The Crimea Almanac*—an "illustrated historical–local studies almanac" devoted to the study and popularization of Crimea in Russia.[8]

While some scholars—particularly those in the west—disparage the genre for producing uncritical recitations of facts about territorial units (provinces, more often than not) created to suit the interests of the state, Susan Smith-Peter has insisted that we look with fresh eyes at what she describes as "an interdisciplinary study of the local." Certainly there was no shortage of enthusiasm for kraevedenie in the eighteenth and nineteenth centuries, when it drove the generation of descriptive geographies which in turn served as the foundation of historical scholarship. Echoing that enthusiasm, Catherine Evtuhov has expressed confidence that "the elevation of local studies from a more or less anecdotally oriented kraevedenie to a genuine engagement with regional specificity in an imperial framework" has the potential to generate "a substantially new portrait of the empire as a whole."[9]

Whether ultimately productive or simply myopic, the boundaries within which kraevedenie functions draw attention to an aspect of the tsarist system that is often overlooked: the ruling elite's distinctly spatial approach to ordering and administering its domains. John LeDonne examined the territoriality of Russian authority in a series of articles published over more than two decades. In the course of documenting the seemingly ceaseless rearrangement of jurisdictions between 1708 and 1825, LeDonne reminds us that by their very nature administrative boundaries created artificial cleavages through "natural and historical regions . . . which retained much of their old unity despite the new administrative-territorial fragmentation." While their ability to redefine society was limited, these cleavages were meaningful. The reorganization of the state into eight administrative units in 1708, LeDonne argues, heralded the implementation of a new vision of the geography of governance, though it was the fragmentation of the empire wrought by Catherine's 1775 territorial reforms that was the conceptual watershed. By carving her domain into a proliferation of relatively uniform *gubernii* (provinces) and *uezdy* (districts), Catherine effected "the abolition of the distinction between core and periphery and the creation, from an administrative point of view, of a unitary state" in one fell swoop.[10]

Historians will argue for a long time to come over whether the tsars ultimately desired a unitary state or something that more closely resembled an empire (composed of a core and a constellation of dependent units associated more closely with the core than with each other). But the importance of spatial thinking is clear. After all, decrees and policies could create certain kinds of space, but they could not control the full space of the empire. For example, Peter I and Catherine II brought about radical redistributions of Russia's administrative geography. At the same time, they witnessed the reinvigoration of spatial entities capable of holding their own against the totalizing intent of top-down reform. As early as the 1720s influential figures such as the renowned scholar Vasilii Tatishchev advocated for the utility of grouping provinces according to region in recognition of the seeming inescapability of supra-provincial connections expressed in terms such as "Siberia" and "the steppe." Decades later, Catherine II addressed the persistence of supra-provincial connections by creating governor-generalships along with the reconfigured gubernii and uezdy. The office of governor-general brought two or sometimes three provinces under the same jurisdiction in an effort to mitigate the localizing effect of the new administrative architecture, and to strike the elusive balance between local and central authority.[11]

Region, meanwhile, became a powerful spatial concept and an essential attribute in the definition of administrative policies from the reign of Alexander I onward. It makes sense then that regions and other sub-imperial spaces are increasingly used as analytical tools for uncovering the subtle connections between territoriality, state-ascribed identity, and locally generated meaning. Mark Bassin's work gave the field a necessary push in this direction. His studies of the "invention" of Siberia and development of its imagined geography as a foil for the construction of Russian identity have been deeply influential. The crux of Russia's identity problem, Bassin explains, was not always and everywhere the tension between empire and nation but rather the challenge posed by "the Europeanization of Russia's imperial image" in the eighteenth century. This ideological shift demanded "a basic perceptual rebounding and rebranding of its domestic geographical space"—a rebounding and rebranding that would make clear the distinction between the metropolitan and colonial space of the empire.[12]

When Tatishchev declared the boundary of Europe to be the Ural Mountains in 1725, he committed ideologues and statesmen to the idea that the Russian metropole was coterminous with its European territory, while "Asiatic" Russia held the colonies. Appealing in its simplicity, this definition proved problematic. Was the Caucasus part of Asiatic Russia? It would seem so. Siberia surely was, insofar as it lay east of the Urals, and yet by the early nineteenth century a growing consensus held that while remote, it was nevertheless Russian. In 1865, A. V. Golovnin made a telling revision to Tatishchev's proposal. According to him, "Siberia, the Caucasus, the Crimea, and the Baltic provinces . . . were constituent parts of the Russian empire," while Poland, Finland and, in time, Central Asia, held some other distinguishing status. Siberia, the Caucasus,

Crimea, and the Baltics might be constituent parts of the empire, but were they part of the imperial core? If so, that core was not purely European. If not, Russia's colonial holdings spread well west of the Urals. Either way, Russia's regional geography seemed to challenge the sort of easy core-periphery bifurcation supposedly characteristic of other European empires.[13]

The late Anatolii Remnev, another historian of Siberia, argued that the regional approach inevitably leads us to acknowledge the crucial importance of the center-periphery relationship while at the same time exposing its limits. "The center represented a special symbolic and organizational formation," Remnev explains, "which not only sought to extract resources from the periphery, but also to penetrate into the periphery and to transfer its own spiritual-symbolic principles to these areas and, organizationally, to mobilize the periphery for its own goals." Remnev details the complex and often contradictory ways in which the region mediated between core and periphery, serving as a space where particularity was in some cases celebrated and in others expunged from the record and where local, regional, and imperial interests collided.[14]

Here we begin to get a sense of both what region meant in the imperial context, and how the imperial topology functioned. We can see it in the interplay of administrative institutions, geographical imaginings, economic activity, and demographic transformations that created a landscape in which all of these forces could coexist and interact. Evtuhov's innovative study of Nizhnii Novgorod province works in a similar vein. Building from the premise that provincial space (rather than regional space) was a meaningful category, and mining every nuance of its material and immaterial manifestations, she shows that the province was far more than an administrative unit or constricting force; it was the site of a range of economic, scientific, and cultural activities that moved effortlessly back and forth from the intensely local to the grand imperial scale.[15]

The province then, like the region, fits neatly with Nick Baron's proposal that we conceive of space "as an historically-contingent and place-bound project or process." While I would argue that space is place-*based* rather than place-*bound*, the combination of place and process is crucial. This is what makes space a productive tool for studying history. It is why a region—a quintessential space—can be defined as something far more complex than simply an administrative-territorial unit. It becomes, instead, an assemblage of places related to one another through a common set of social, economic, political, or cultural characteristics, as well as a discernible infrastructure or a set of institutions or practices that links them in meaningful (sometimes even quantifiable) ways. At its best then, place-based history is more than local history; it becomes the history of a system of sites, relationships, and their meanings, and a productive way to uncover the spatial logic of the empire.[16]

This book is interested both in the material reality of place, and in the ways in which people imagined and conceptualized it. My approach bears resemblance to that of Remnev, who advocates approaching the region as "not only a historical-geographic or political-administrative reality, but also a mental construct with dynamic borders that are difficult to define." In this context "ideologically and politically colored toponymies and symbolic figures of regional historical actors" were essential, for they helped create the immaterial, portable, and often dominant version of any given place.[17] In order to understand the spatial logic of empire however, we need to pay attention to the processes that wrought continual, tangible change as well. These include the construction of communications infrastructures (railroads, canal systems, et cetera) and ceremonial spaces (governors' mansions, Orthodox cathedrals), but also the more prosaic sites of kitchen gardens, post stations, and storage depots. Sites and networks such as these existed throughout the empire. But in every village or stretch of pine tree-studded terrain they took on a different form and character. Roads, urban layouts, dwellings: all were embedded in particular topographical, biological, climatological spaces. As a result, the urban plan of Feodosiia might bear strong resemblance to that of Tambov, and yet the flows of people and goods in and out of each city, up from the wharves and down to the market squares, functioned very differently, creating diverse experiences and a multitude of spatial relationships.

PLACING CRIMEA

This book does not offer an exhaustive chorography of the southern empire or even of Crimea itself, but it embraces the perspective of the local in order to push in that direction as well as to unearth connections to vastly bigger spaces. The tradition of narrating Crimea as a place both within and beyond empire goes back to Herodotus, but it took on new life as men with the requisite skills and spirit began congregating in Kerch, Sevastopol, Simferopol, and Odessa over the course of the nineteenth century. On the evening of January 24, 1887, more than one hundred men gathered at the governor's residence for the ceremonial opening of the Tavrida Scholarly Archival Commission and Historical Archives. In his remarks, Governor Vsevolozhskii reminded the assembled guests of the appalling treatment of documents in the provincial chancelleries, from their haphazard binding and indexing, to the unfortunate habit of certain organs (such as the police) of selling old documents by the carton to bookbinders and upholsterers who in turn pasted the shredded record of the past onto the walls of homes throughout the peninsula. Unable to stomach this state of affairs, Vsevolozhskii—by his own account—seized the opportunity to create a provincial archival commission. Crimea, he explained to his audience, had been under Russian rule for only a century "but had a history extending back several epochs, not only to the time of the khans, but to the most ancient times. The monuments and ruins found in many places attest to this and I believe that in addition to the very visible [physical] monuments our archives contain as many written monuments to the epochs of the Crimean past." These, urged the governor, must be treated with unflagging dedication and no less reverence than was directed toward the limestone slabs unearthed at Chersonesos.[18]

When the dust settled from this rousing speech, sixty men had affixed their signatures to the membership register of the Tavrida Archival Commission.[19] The commission began its fevered publication of scholarly articles and edited documents in 1887 and by 1920, when it ceased to exist, had published fifty-seven hefty volumes documenting the establishment of ports and towns, the construction of Orthodox cathedrals and monasteries, military engagements, Potemkin's orders and correspondence, reports on archaeological sites, Ottoman *firmans* (imperial decrees), Crimean *iarlyks* (charters issued by the khans), and thick descriptions of gardens, caves, and monuments. In 1894 Arsenii Markevich published the first of three bibliographies of scholarly works on Crimea and Tavrida Province. The list ran to 7,298 items and included print and manuscript material from the libraries of local luminaries such as A. L. Berte-Delagard in Sevastopol, Aleksandr Steven (chairman of the archival commission), and N. A. Sultan-Krym-Giray, as well as the zemstvo libraries in Simferopol and Feodosiia.[20] This was a rich body of work. It covered a chronology extending back millennia, defined Tavrida as a temporal palimpsest, rich in material and documentary layers, and claimed the right to know, to explain, and to preserve, for a finite set of ambitious scholars arrayed along the Black Sea littoral.

Just what kind of a place was Crimea? To begin with, Crimea and its hinterland belonged to the worlds of Turkic culture, steppe politics, and Greco-Roman civilization. It belonged to the worlds of the Pontic steppe and the Black Sea, the worlds of Islam and Orthodox Christianity. It was a portal to the spaces of Muscovy, the Polish-Lithuanian Common-wealth, the Cossack hordes, and the Ottoman Empire. Its centers of gravity were Bahçesaray, the seat of the Giray khans, and Caffa, the fa-mous trading emporium on the southeast coast of the peninsula. It was connected to the Slavic lands of the north by a series of slave-raiding trails, to the clans of the northern Caucasus by a series of bloodlines and kinship links, and to the entire littoral by a network of trade routes distributing precious cargoes of slaves, grain, and wine.

This sweeping geographical profile found expression in maps, particu-larly from the sixteenth century onward. European cartographers lo-cated Crimea within what they called Tartaria—a region that stretched from the northern frontier of China to the borders of Hungary—and specifically within Little Tartary, an entity roughly coterminous with the Golden Horde (Kipchak Khanate) that dominated much of western Eurasia in the thirteenth and fourteenth centuries. Mapmakers were consistent in their depiction of Little Tartary as wild, uncultivated, and empty, staying true to a tradition with roots in antiquity but revived by Abraham Ortelius, the famous Flemish mapmaker, in his remarkable *Teatrum Orbis Terrarum* (*Theater of the World*)—the first atlas of the world—published in 1570. Tucked into the end of the atlas is a map titled *Russiae, Moscoviae et Tartariae* (figure I.1). The title cartouche covers most of the Black Sea; Crimea is represented by a fierce rider on horseback, arrow drawn taut and shield flung across his back, gallop-ing across the southern steppe toward Azov. The area surrounding him is blank, save for a scattering of trees and the sinuous lines of the Dnieper and Don rivers. Gerard Mercator visualized the region in similar carto-graphic terms in his *Taurica Chersonesus* map (figure I.2), published as part of his famous *Atlas minor* in 1607. There "Crimea seu Tartaria Przecopensis" (Crimea or Perekop Tartary) lies south of the bountiful

Figure I.1. Ortelius, *Russiae, Moscoviae et Tartariae* (David Rumsey Historical Map Collection)

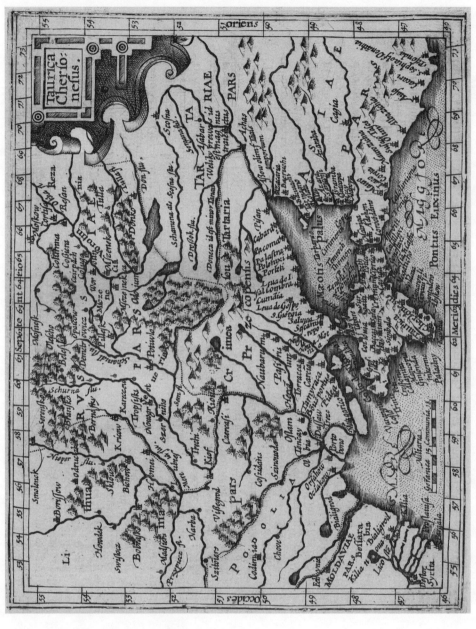

Figure I.2. Mercator, *Taurica Chersonesus* (David Rumsey Historical Map Collection)

Muscovite forests, with little to recommend it but an elaborate symbology meant to draw the viewer's eye to the coastal ports and towns. Over a century later the Russian Academy of Sciences in St. Petersburg published a map of Little Tartary by Joseph de L'Isle, titled *Malaia Tatariia,* which banished any lingering doubt that the Crimean Khanate was a barren, uninhabited, and perhaps even undesirable space by simply leaving it unmarked—save for the comfortingly thick line of the Dnepr and a careless depiction of the Crimean mountains. The motif was set. No one would mistake the wild field for the lands of the Muscovite tsar.[21]

The khanate was a maritime space as well. Mercator's map acknowledges this. Here the peninsula juts out into the churning waters of the Black Sea. Faint traces of the routes followed by Tatar and Nogay raiding parties reach northward from Perekop toward Riazan and Smolensk, but the peninsula occupies prime real estate on the map. It is rimmed with harbors and ports, their names arranged on the familiar diagonals of a portolan chart. Crimea, the map tells us, is the hinge of the Black Sea and its northern littoral, as well as the anchor to a north-south corridor that had connected the Baltic to the Black Sea since the ninth century. On the other hand, it is nothing but an extended piece of coastline at the edge of a vast expanse of water (only part of which is visible on the map). The Black Sea moves according to its own rhythms, regardless of who claims sovereignty over the land. Its distinguishing feature (other than the fact that the sea is almost entirely dead) is its current. Known from the late seventeenth century as the *corrente sottano,* this mysterious "lower current" of heavy, salt-rich water from the Mediterranean rushes in through the Bosporus and then flows in a counterclockwise direction, following the northern coast of Anatolia to the Caucasus, Crimea, and finally past Romania and Bulgaria to Constantinople, pushing lighter river-fed water to the surface and southward, back through the Bosporus. This is the dominant current of the Black Sea. This is the unceasing circularity to which the southern empire was exposed.[22]

Until 1774 the Ottoman sultan claimed the southern slopes of the Tauric mountains down to the sea, while the Giray khan claimed the northern slopes as they descended through lush, thickly wooded valleys to Bahçesaray. From there the khanate stretched past the hills outside Akmechet (Simferopol) into open plains running westward to the salt lakes and bustling port of Gözleve (Evpatoriia), eastward to the lagoons of the Putrid Sea, and northward to the narrow isthmus opening onto the Pontic steppe. Beyond Perekop the Crimean khans claimed (but did not always enjoy) the allegiance of the Nogay tribes and by extension the land on which they pastured their livestock (figure I.3). According to this understanding of the geography of the khanate, the Girays ruled over territory extending from the Dnestr River to the Kuban and even into Circassia, where clan leaders paid tribute in fur, honey, and slaves. Their domain ran to the sea in the south, and across the sea of grass in the north, to the vague line where the steppe met the forest.[23]

And contrary to what the maps might have suggested, the khanate was neither isolated nor unknown to its neighbors. Martin Broniowski, Polish noble and ambassador of Stefan Batory to Khan Mehmed Giray, left a famous account of his time in the khanate, and he was not the only one. Moscow's diplomatic relations with Crimea extended back to the late-fifteenth-century reigns of Tsar Ivan III and Khan Mengli Giray, and since that time subjects of the grand princes and tsars—merchants and diplomats as well as slaves—had filled the foreign affairs chancellery archives with diplomatic correspondence, ambassadorial accounts, unofficial reports on Giray affairs, and other forms of seventeenth-century intelligence. Unlike the Ottomans however, who exercised some measure of political, economic, and cultural control over the khanate, Muscovite officials did not develop a systematic understanding of its inner workings. It was not until the tsars set their sights on subduing the southern frontier that Little Tartary took distinct shape in the contemporary European geographic imagination.[24]

For centuries, power radiated outward from Crimea. Though a vassal of the Porte, the Crimean khan enjoyed a great deal of autonomy, sending tens of thousands of horsemen into the steppe at will, striking up alliances with kings and hetmen, and collecting tribute from Moscow. By the middle of the seventeenth century securing the frontier was of deep concern to Russian officials who were determined to put an end to the frequent raids that carried thousands, and sometimes tens of thousands, of Slavic captives away from their fields to an entirely different set of productive spaces—the slave markets of Caffa and Constantinople and the galley ships of the Ottoman fleet.[25]

Peter I's decision to shed the burden of paying tribute to the khan and in particular to capture the Ottoman fortress at Azov proved a watershed. The Don River held great strategic significance: controlling

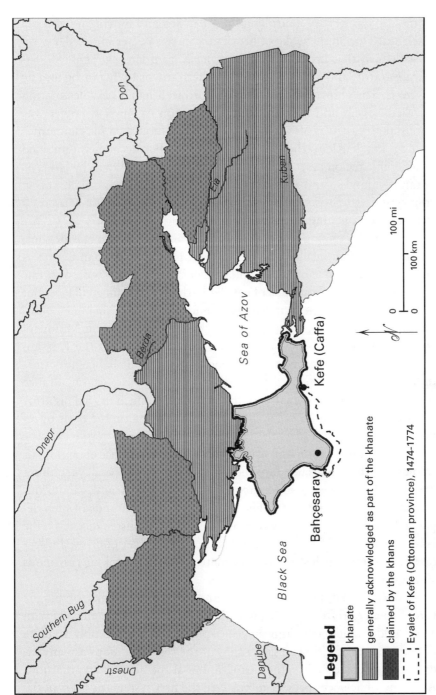

Figure I.3. The Crimean Khanate

its mouth was key to controlling the Azov Sea and moving toward the Black Sea. Thus in the wake of his victory in 1696 Peter initiated a wave of settlement that brought peasants from Kazan, Iarensk, Simbirsk, Samara, Saratov, and a host of lesser southern towns to Taganrog and its environs. The shipyards upstream at Voronezh had a new destination for their vessels and the southward projection of Russian power was unmistakable. It was also temporary: Peter relinquished his claim after losing a key battle to the Ottomans in 1711. For decades it remained a vulnerable region beset by fires, floods, contagion, and raids by Nogays, Tatars, Kalmyks, and Cossacks, its intrepid inhabitants cultivating connections to Moscow by exchanging Azov's grapes for Moscow's strawberries, opening markets and building fortifications.[26]

Azov was a stepping stone. The Kerch straits served as a marine thoroughfare from an insular and shallow sea to one more than ten times larger, more than one hundred times deeper, and rimmed with over one hundred ports and thousands of smaller harbors and fishing villages. But it was not until 1736 that Russia would again push that far southward, this time helmed by Baron Burchard Christoph von Münnich, count of the Holy Roman Empire and field marshal of the Russian army. His forces managed to sack the Giray palace at Bahçesaray (neither library nor wine cellar survived), but their geographical ignorance proved disastrous. At the onset of the invasion Münnich moved his army toward Perekop with meager supply lines, believing on the basis of reports from Cossack traders that, "as it was an extremely fertile country, the army would, as soon as it arrived there, find subsistence enough." His soldiers dutifully marched into the peninsula after twelve days without bread, only to meet a landscape of scorched earth and calamitous shortages of food and water. The lives of tens of thousands of men depended on the army's ability to navigate and draw sustenance from the land. The quality of roads, the location of wells, river courses, and extent of pasture—such stores of information suddenly took on enormous strategic value.[27]

Debilitating supply line failures and severe outbreaks of plague forced them to retreat, but Münnich's men departed the peninsula with a new understanding of Crimean geography. It was not a terribly accurate understanding of Crimean geography, if the resulting maps are any indication. Joseph de L'Isle, the cartographer at the helm of an ambitious Academy of Sciences project to produce the first systematic atlas of the

Russian Empire, is credited with both. The first provides a careful articulation of the invasion route, with the sites of maritime and land battles marked with crossed swords and sailing ships (figure I.4). Tatar villages appear as small rectangular towers topped with crescents; the salt lakes of Gözleve are in place, and the map even names the Bulganak, Alma, and Salgir rivers. However, all of the topographical and toponymical detail is crowded into the western third of the peninsula. The rest is a blank slate, and a misshapen one at that: the narrow Arbat spit and jutting protrusion of the Kerch peninsula are missing, lost in the amorphous blob that stands in for the peninsula, and farther east, Taman appears as an island.

The 1736 invasion route is the signature element of the second map as well, though here the peninsula takes a more recognizable form (figure I.5). The map shows Arbat and Kerch clearly, restores Taman's rightful status as a peninsula, and even manages to articulate the small cape of "Koslow" (Gözleve). Differences notwithstanding, together the maps make two crucial points. First, geographic knowledge of the Crimean Khanate extended only as far as the footfalls of the Russian soldier. Second, the khanate remained an unmastered space at Russia's peril. In fact, the campaigns forced a shift in the way Russia's ruling elite viewed the khanate. Between the conclusion of the Russian-Ottoman war of 1735–1739 and the outbreak of the Russian-Ottoman war of 1768–1774, cartographers and statesmen alike began to conceptualize the steppe as an object of imperial desire. Russia's wars against the Bashkirs, Crimeans, Persians, and Ottomans were shifting the political calculus along the Eurasian steppe in Russia's favor and inspiring an outpouring of expansionist schemes. Thus when the Academy of Sciences published the *Atlas Russicus,* the first comprehensive atlas of the empire, in 1745 it included, appended to the series of maps depicting long-established provinces such as Arkhangel'sk and Moscow, both maps of the Crimean Khanate. The decision to include a piece of territory located outside the boundaries of the empire was a less than subtle articulation of the idea that that territory, though not yet within the tsar's domain, was in some meaningful way part of the Russian world.

While de L'Isle was busy mapping, a powerful court contingent began campaigning for the subjugation of the khanate. Just days after her coronation Catherine II received a report outlining the "dangers" posed by the Crimean Tatars and the other inhabitants of Little Tartary, which

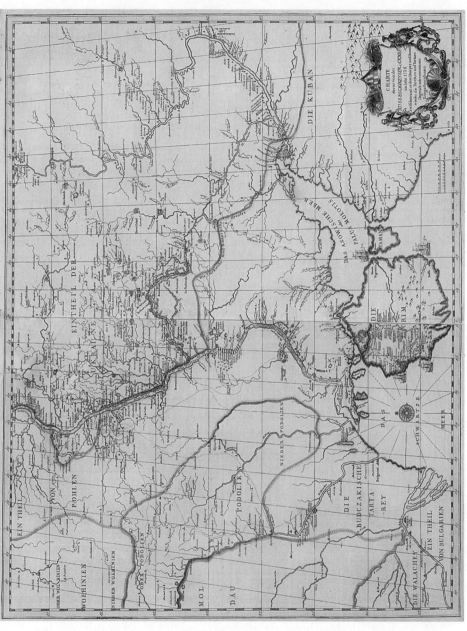

Figure I.4. De L'Isle, *Charte derer von der Russisch-Keyser Armee im Jahr 1736* (David Rumsey Historical Map Collection)

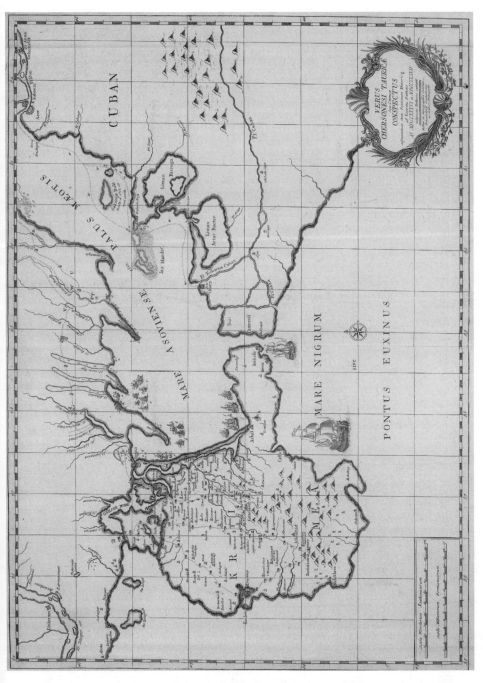

Figure I.5. De L'Isle, *Verus Chersonesi Tauricae Seu Crimeae Conspectus* (David Rumsey Historical Map Collection)

it described as a region rife with "thievery and villainy." In 1767 the Russian and Ottoman empires went to war yet again, and this time the outcome radically altered the political landscape. The Treaty of Kuchuk Kainardzhii (Küçük Kaynarca) in 1774 declared the Crimean Khanate and Kuban region formally independent of the sultan's authority. Catherine installed the mercurial but compliant Şahin Giray as khan and sent Russian forces to keep him on the throne. By 1777 they had ousted Şahin's rivals from their stronghold at Caffa and arrived, for all intents and purposes, on the prized southern coast. Many members of the Russian ruling elite who had remained indifferent to the notion of conquering the steppe found themselves persuaded (or intrigued) by the ideologues and poets who set out in coming years to dissociate the peninsula from the Pontic steppe and reinvent the land of barbaric Tatar horsemen as nothing less than the "garden of the empire."[28]

Thirst for information about the southern empire had grown during the war. In 1768, Johann Anton Güldenstädt, a Baltic German naturalist and member of the Academy of Sciences, set out on an expedition to study the geography and natural history of Astrakhan, the Caucasus, and Novorossiia. Though he intended to include Crimea in his study, he was recalled to Petersburg before he could travel to Perekop. In 1781 the expedition of Adjutant V. F. Zuev was cut short by a revolt, leaving the door open for surveyor Fedor Chernoi to execute the first successful academy expedition to Crimea in 1785. Catherine tasked Chernoi's expedition with taking the necessary astronomical observations to make accurate measurements of Perekop, Feodosiia, Enikale, Inkerman, and Evpatoriia, as well as several sites in the Caucasus. However, there was a lot more to know about the former khanate than simply the latitude and longitude of its major towns. The diary kept by Prince V. M. Dolgorukov, commander of the Russian army during the war of 1768–1774, offered only tantalizing glimpses—homes in Gözleve abandoned during the siege of 1771, the ancient walls of Chersonesos outside Aktiar, the fortress at Perekop—but the floodgates had opened. The men charged with conquering the south generated a wealth of decrees, reports, and correspondence. A 1774 topographical description of the lands running westward from Kinburn to Hadji-bey included a rich narration of the border, its line based on triangulated locations of kurgans (burial mounds) and the idiosyncratic features of local rivers. The memoirs of Baron de Tott (who, among other things, served as French consul to the khan in

1767–1770) were published in 1784, followed swiftly by the letters of Lady Craven, whose travels from Kiev to Constantinople caused a sensation throughout Europe.[29]

The opening of a new metaphorical space was as widely celebrated as the political fact of annexation. Before and after Catherine issued the annexation manifesto in April 1783, odes and honorifics spilled out from the imperial palace, along with a contagious confidence that she would remake Crimea into something splendid. "No friend of humanity can do otherwise than rejoice," explained Sir William Eton, a close friend of Potemkin, that Russia had set out "to revive a decayed commerce, to polish barbarian ferocity, and to render a portion of the globe, which had been almost a desert, again fertile and productive." As writing about Crimea expanded beyond the ranks of adjutants and admirals to include intrepid naturalists, mineralogists, surveyors, and archaeologists, appointed and elected officials serving in the provincial government, Orthodox clergy struggling to establish (or reestablish, as they saw it) Christianity's hold on the region, landowners, poets, memoirists, statisticians, scholars, and publicists, their texts not only communicated the innumerable ways in which Russian rule would renovate life throughout the south, but also shaped the integration process.[30]

Among other things, they reestablished the region's maritime character. Along with the Mediterranean, the Black Sea had been the subject of a flurry of mapmaking activity in the fourteenth to sixteenth centuries, as portolan charts rushed to describe the harbors and trade routes essential to navigation in closed seas (and usually within sight of land). The famous portolan atlas produced by Battista Agnese in 1544 included among its nine gorgeously illuminated vellum charts one depicting the Black Sea as a ring of evenly spaced, meticulously labeled harbors. The next major maritime mapping of the Black Sea followed a full two centuries later. In 1764, Jacques Nicolas Bellin, the French master hydrographer and cartographer, published his *Petit atlas maritime*. Among the 580 charts covering four continents were maps of the Black Sea and of Crimea itself. The latter clearly drew on de L'Isle's work in the *Atlas Russicus* and added little to what was already known about Crimean geography. By contrast, the Black Sea map offered a groundbreaking remapping of the Crimean coast, with attention lavished on the harbor topography as well as on coastal relief and even a few soundings (figure I.6). Just a few years later, a facsimile of the Agnese portolan

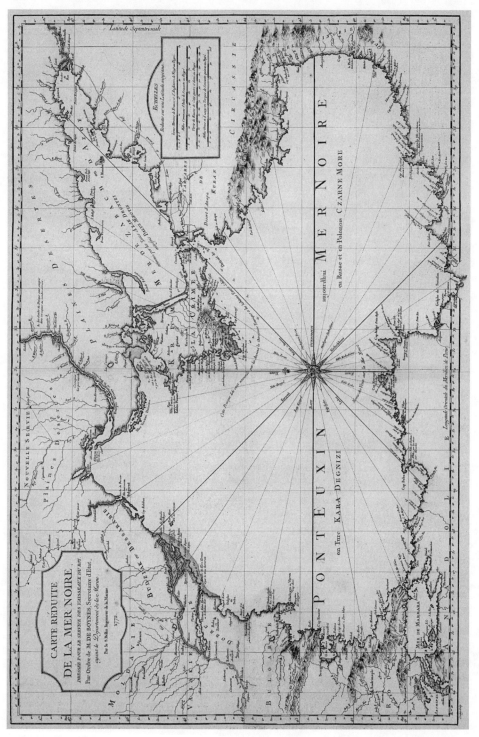

Figure I.6. Bellin, *Carte réduite de la Mer Noire* (David Rumsey Historical Map Collection)

chart of the Black Sea was published as well (figure I.7). This time the printer stripped away the rhumb lines, compass rose, and cartouches depicting the primary winds that had enhanced the nautical utility and aesthetic qualities of the original, though the articulation of shoals, reefs, and islands remained intact. Together, these maps announced Crimea's emergence from a relatively insular existence as an Ottoman lake and its reintegration into European maritime space.[31]

Crimea was not the first coastal territory Russia had acquired, nor was maritime activity completely foreign to its statesmen, merchants, or military. Yet nowhere else—not along the White Sea or the Baltic, let alone the Pacific Ocean—was there such a pronounced littoral identity. Elena Druzhinina gave her authoritative study of the region the title *Severnoe Prichernomor'e* (*The Northern Black Sea Littoral*)—a title designed to emphasize the multidirectionality of "the economic and strategic connections" that extended across the Black Sea watershed. But inhabitants of (and visitors to) the southern empire hardly needed anyone to tell them they had entered an area in which the significance of water was inescapable. One of the first modern guidebooks published in the Russian Empire elaborated on the intimate, inescapable connection between Crimea and the sea. The peninsula was, according to the text, "washed, from the west and south by the Black Sea, from the east by the Kerch strait and Azov Sea" and linked only "by way of the Perekop isthmus, which is never more than 7 versts wide, to the mainland steppes of southern Russia." The authors underscored the flimsy nature of the tissue connecting Crimea to the rest of the empire by noting the popular belief in a prehistoric water route that had once linked the Black and Azov seas and made Crimea an island. Even the mainland districts (Berdiansk, Dneprovsk, and Melitopol) followed the maritime-riverine lines of the Berda, Konka, Takmachkaia, and Dnepr rivers. Places like Aleshki (on the lower Dnepr) were known to enjoy "an abundance of waters," and travelers often celebrated the fountains and elaborate irrigation systems Tatars maintained for ablutions, household use, and cultivation. Sailing vessels and oared boats, naval battles and contraband trade, ports and wharves, fisheries and beaches—all of the elements of maritime culture were present in daily life and prized by officials and members of Russian society, many of whom believed such elements would invigorate not just the south but the empire as a whole.[32]

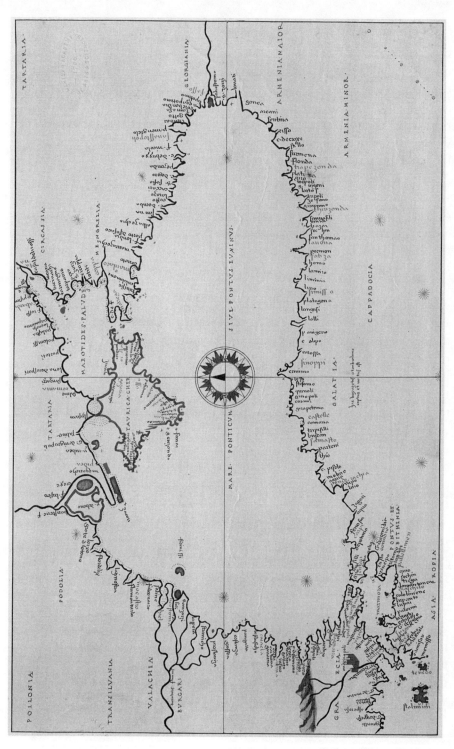

Figure I.7. *Mare Ponticum sive Pontus Euxinus*, an undated facsimile of a portolan chart originally produced by Battista Agnese for an atlas published in 1544 (Harvard Map Collection, Harvard Library)

Water had a dark side as well. The dangers and devastation wrought by the Black Sea famously included shipwrecks and punishing storms, but also treacherous anchorages, shallow estuaries, and unnavigable marshes stretching from the Danube to the Dnepr. In ancient times, unnerved by the "marine desert" that stretched out before them, Greeks sailing north out of the Bosporus christened it the Inhospitable Sea. Two millennia later, one could still call its hospitality into question. In this hybrid riverine/maritime environment illness was an all too common theme, with travelers complaining incessantly of incapacitating fevers and epidemic disease well into the nineteenth century.[33]

Careful observers also noted the treacherous nature of the water coursing through the Crimean landscape. The noted naturalist Peter Simon Pallas described a particularly disturbing event at the coastal village of Küçük-Koi—a well-watered place, with four freshwater springs nearby flowing together down to the sea only half a mile away. The village was located at the foot of steep mountains and on the side of a deep glen. Elders remembered an earthquake that had occurred some fifty years earlier, but none expected the quake of February 10, 1786, which was felt as far away as Silesia. At Küçük-Koi the glen split open and the freshwater stream disappeared. Frightened villagers collected their belongings and their cattle and sought sanctuary elsewhere. Over the next two weeks the ground between the glens sloping down to the sea collapsed, forming a "terrific abyss from ten to twenty fathoms deep." Strangely enough, the stream reappeared, flowing in a different direction altogether, past the ruins of orchards, corn fields, gardens, and dwellings. According to Pallas, this and the many similar "devastations" along the southern coast were caused by the massing of water in subterranean springs that eventually caused the claylike soil to collapse. While most wreaked havoc on fields and pathways, there were other deadly episodes such as the 1897 flood that claimed more than a hundred lives in Kerch.[34]

Meanwhile, settlers complained that much of the southern empire was astonishingly dry. This "disease of the steppe" only grew acute in the middle of the nineteenth century, when the Tatar and Nogay population, which had long since mastered the art of managing the water sources of their homeland, took their intimate knowledge with them during mass emigrations to Anatolia and Rumelia. They were replaced with Russian and Bulgarian peasants unaccustomed to the rigors of cultivating the steppe and ignorant of its secrets: it was their vociferous complaints that eventually pushed the Ministry of State Domains to establish an Office for the Irrigation of the Steppe in 1861. While studying the geology of the route across the mainland steppe to Feodosiia one of the engineers made a tantalizing discovery: beneath layers of soil and clay was a stratum of quartz sand through which flowed fresh water from the Dnepr. If he was right, "there was no reason to fear for the future of the Tavridan steppe." But until its fate could be determined, engineers set about digging wells, building and repairing dams and reservoirs for rainwater.[35]

The southern empire was a place where officials and ideologues sought to inscribe empire not just in political boundaries and social structures but in the built environment and natural landscape. I develop this idea in subsequent chapters; here perhaps the (possibly apocryphal) story of a lone apricot tree will suffice to communicate the significance of the tangible, material, even visceral quality of empire building in the south. During her grand ceremonial tour in 1787, Catherine II stopped in the newly founded town of Kherson. There, in the garden adjacent to her lodgings, she planted an apricot pit. In time, the pit grew into "the most magnificent of trees," standing thirty-six feet high with a trunk seven feet thick and endowed with innumerable branches. In summer, "when dressed in its finery of leaves and fruit, its aspect [was] astoundingly majestic," reported a rapturous member of the Odessa Society of History and Antiquities. The only apricot tree in all of Kherson, it was said to have no equal along the southern coast of Crimea. In the 1840s, after nearly sixty years, it was known to bear ten to twelve puds (360 to 433 pounds) of apricots each year. It was watered by a machine that drew from a well dug solely for that purpose, and gardeners found it necessary to support the branches with ropes, so heavy was the fruit. Given the extraordinary productivity and provenance of the tree, as well as the reverence and love inhabitants felt for the empress, city officials erected protective iron fencing with a succinct inscription: "All that You planted / is for us a sacred duty to preserve."[36]

This report is wedged in among dozens of others in the "Correspondence" section of the very first issue of the *Proceedings of the Odessa Society for History and Antiquities,* published in 1844. Amateurish as it may be, the report offers an exquisite metaphor for empire building. The physical presence of the tsar, the humble seed, the judicious choice of location, the productive soil, the deep roots and wide reach of the branches, the abundant yield, the magnificent (and slightly exotic) aesthetics, the application of technology to protect and improve the natural endowments, the permanence, the connection with the broader littoral landscape, the sacred quality of the site and its power to evoke love of country and reverence for the sovereign—all of the elements are here, united in an expression of what is, in the end, the crucial binary of empire: preservation and transformation.

Metaphors aside, the elements that Catherine and her successors would need to preserve or transform included not just soil and sea, but the social, cultural, and economic infrastructures that had shaped the south for millennia. These infrastructures had evolved in the hands of the Greeks, Romans, Genoese, Ottomans, and Tatars who preceded the Romanovs in asserting their authority over the region. Striking the right balance between preservation and transformation in the space of the former khanate was therefore a project that would require a great deal of patience, knowledge, and energy. In the immediate aftermath of annexation officials couldn't help but speculate about how the region might look once Russian rule was firmly established. Potemkin argued that it would provide the empire with a thriving southern capital and a necessary balance to Petersburg and Moscow. General Mikhail Kakhovskii, who briefly held the post of military governor of Novorossiia, described it as a land of untapped potential, a blank slate waiting to be inscribed with meaning. "If you can," he wrote, "paint yourself a picture of the open space from Perekop to the Salgir river, spreading out over 100 versts, surrounded on the western side by the Black Sea and to the northeast by the Sivash and Azov seas. Sometime in the future," Kakhovskii assured his readers, "this vast plain will be filled with villages, embellished with churches, palaces, and other buildings, and around them will be gardens." A great many governors, vice governors, landowners, and travelers cherished similar hopes that in short order the province would, in the words of Crimean landowner Count N. S. Mordvinov, provide "abundant grapes, olives, pomegranates, and other rich produce for the empire" rather than remain "poor, wild, doleful, and rushing toward its own destruction."[37]

Most believed that this transformation would only be possible once sufficiently large numbers of Slavic and German-speaking peasants had settled the region. Settlement had, of course, been the signature policy in Novorossiia since its establishment in 1764, but its pace did not always and everywhere keep up with the grand plans of visionaries like

Potemkin and the Duke of Richelieu, the governor-general of Novorossiia from 1805 to 1814. This was particularly so in Tavrida, where by
the end of Catherine's reign in 1796 less than 13,000 members of the
clerical estate, Old Believers, and foreign settlers had arrived in small
clusters to settle the mainland districts of Melitopol and Dneprovsk. In
the early nineteenth century, Mennonite and Lutheran immigrants as
well as Dukhobors and Old Believers from central Russian provinces
settled in larger numbers (47,000 arrived between 1804 and 1827) north
of Perekop. By contrast, the peninsula itself was home to a handful of
Armenian, Bulgarian, and German settlements; only 15,000 Russians
had settled there by the outbreak of war in 1853 (table I.1).[38]

Unlike much of Novorossiia then, Crimea was viewed by Russia neither primarily as a colonization project nor as an internal resettlement
project. Instead it was one that involved reconfiguring the allegiance
and interests of the Tatar population (and the Greeks and Karaites as
well) that had resided there for centuries. This struck many contemporaries
as a unique and daunting challenge. It meant that a quarter million
people would have to be trained "imperceptibly in our customs, our
amusements, the pleasure we take in our lives and even in our work,"

Table I.1. Population of the Crimean Peninsula
(All figures are percentages of the total)

	1785	1795	1816	1835	1850	1864
Tatars	84.1	87.6	85.9	83.5	77.8	50.3
Russians	2.2	4.3	4.8	4.4	6.6	28.5
Ukrainians[a]		1.3	3.6	3.1	7.0	
Greeks	2.3	1.9	0.8	2.0	2.0	6.5
Armenians		0.6	1.3	1.5	1.0	2.9
Karaites		1.5	1.4	1.1	1.3	1.7
Rabbinical Jews		0.8	0.9	0.9	0.9	5.3
Roma		1.5		2.4	1.9	
Bulgarians		0.1	0.4	0.4	0.5	1.6
Germans		0.1	0.7	0.7	1.0	2.7

Source: Bodarskii, *Naselenie Kryma*, 88, 121–125, 128. See the accompanying interactive
visualization on the *Beautiful Spaces* site.

[a] In the 1864 data, Ukrainians were counted in with Russians.

wrote one nobleman. It might well be worth it, he mused, for among the *mirzas* (clan leaders and members of the Crimean Tatar elite) "there are those who descended from Chingis Khan, and Your Excellency well knows in what high regard and with what level of respect they are therefore held by the Muslim people. Whether they are indigent or legitimate heirs is immaterial—it is enough that the crowds believe them. . . . Their devotion to Russia, their acclimation to our way of life secured, they might in the future prove very useful in political, military, and trade relations with Turkey."[39]

They might, or they might not. Only time would tell. The true challenge for empire builders would be to find a way to reconfigure space and society; to redirect, rather than destroy, the forces that made the southern empire so alluring, so valuable, and so difficult to possess.

STRUCTURE OF THE BOOK

In the pages that follow I do not set out to define the former khanate as an inherently Muslim or Christian space, a colonial possession, or an intrinsic part of a unitary Russia. My goal is to seek a means of transcending the language of core and periphery, and perhaps even to propose an alternate vocabulary for the configuration of imperial rule. Crimea is fertile ground for this sort of inquiry, having endured countless political and social reconfigurations over the centuries. Catherine II famously staked her claim to this terrain through its toponymy, replacing Kırım with Tavrida, Caffa with Feodosiia, Aktiar with Sevastopol. In so doing she sent a clear message to Constantinople, London, Vienna, and Petersburg. The khanate that posed so grave a threat to the stability of her southern frontier had ceased to exist. Where it had been, now there was only Russia.

But renovating the region's toponymy was one thing; mastering its topography—let alone its population and economy—proved quite another. This book describes that process. It argues that the integration of the khanate, a process that began in 1783 and effectively ended with the outbreak of the Crimean War in 1853, constitutes the core narrative in the history of Russia's southern empire. In part this is because Crimea was never an end in itself. Russian policy toward it (and its inhabitants) was always subsumed within broader geopolitical, social, and cultural projects, just as the annexation of the khanate was a strategic move within the larger Russian-Ottoman struggle for dominance in the Black Sea. This is how many scholars have contextualized it, and how Potemkin himself (however disingenuously) defined its utility. "The acquisition of Crimea can not strengthen or enrich You," he told Catherine in autumn 1782, "but only provide you with peace."[40] Peace proved elusive, but the Russian south gained new status in 1783. Maritime and terrestrial, nomadic and settled, Muslim and Christian, commercial and agricultural, what I call the southern empire operated according to its own logic. The goal here is to understand that logic, and through it the dynamics and topology of imperial rule as a whole.

Despite the fertile ground it offers to those interested in empire, in the importance of Islam in Russian history, and in the persistent relevance of the contest for dominance in the Black Sea, the story of how the khanate became a province of the Russian Empire has been largely neglected. Those historians who worked on Crimea even tangentially have supplied tantalizing glimpses of a process rife with ambiguities and complexities. In *La formation de l'Empire russe,* Boris Nolde suggested that "the difficulties of assimilating this country [were] far greater than those met during the annexation of the Volga states," and Elena Druzhinina likewise alluded to the fact that "the Russian administration had to come to terms with extremely complex social relationships and with the national and religious peculiarities of the Crimean population" (though her analysis largely sidesteps such issues). In his classic work on the annexation, Alan Fisher confined his treatment of the post-1783 period to a mere twelve pages. He returned to it several years later, but like most other historians of the Ottoman Empire, never made the mechanics of what he described as "colonial rule" the main focus of his research. Scholars such as Edward Lazzerini, Brian Glyn Williams, and Robert Paul Magosci have worked both to reestablish the Crimean Tatars as agents in Crimean history and to expand the conceptual framework of Crimean history by engaging with questions of colonialism, nationalism, and ethnic identity. They have done so without tapping into archival materials, however, and Russian history tends to look quite different when viewed through the lens of the archive—particularly that of the local archive. Mara Kozelsky has demonstrated this beautifully, producing a rich study of the role of Russian Orthodoxy in the evolution of identities and politics across the nineteenth century. A handful of young scholars trained in Simferopol have, in recent years, also set about combing through the documents in the humble building on Kechkemetskaia Street. They are publishing histories of everything from Romanov estates and foreign colonies to the Tavrida Muslim Spiritual Board.[41]

The new generation of *krymovedy* owes an enormous debt to Arsenii Markevich, Fedor Fedorovich Lashkov, Apollon Aleksandrovich Skal'kovskii—the "Herodotus of Novorossiia"—and other similarly devoted men of letters who dug deeply into the question of what empire meant in Crimea, probing the subtleties of land ownership, demographics, and economic activity from the vantage point of the late nineteenth century. They did this not only by producing their own analyses but by preserving huge chunks of the historical record. This was no small task considering the appalling conditions in which most government archives were kept. In 1905 for example, a fire destroyed most of the documentary record of the Feodosiia city administration (*gradonachal'stvo*). The extant portion survived only because it had been stowed away in the city bank and forgotten. Eventually, in the aftermath of the catastrophic blaze, local officials realized their oversight and transferred the material to the new customs building, where it promptly suffered extensive damage from wind and rain. Finally, in 1909 officials pushed the remaining three cartloads of documents out on to the quarantine dock and burned them in an effort to increase storage space.[42]

Given such routine episodes of neglect, the destructive impact of the Russian Civil War and German occupation during World War II, and the reorganization of archives during the Soviet period, it is astonishing that so much remained intact. Despite all odds, the State Archive of the Autonomous Republic of Crimea was a researcher's delight, filled with stashes of policy drafts, petitions, court records, maps of long-forgotten properties, and the endless marginalia of imperial governance. There is ample room then—and perhaps even a particular need—for a study such as this one. In the chapters that follow I explore the constant triangulation between institutions, people, and places that shaped daily life in Tavrida. I begin in chapter 1 with an exploration of the administrative reorganization of the khanate and the development of new structures of authority. The chapter describes the implementation of Catherine's provincial reform and charter to the nobility, as well as the creation of the Tavrida Muslim Spiritual Board, as events that demonstrate the empire's capacity to preserve and control difference. While previous scholarship has suggested that Tavrida became a regular province of the empire in a matter of months, and certainly by 1802, I argue that the end of local particularity came much later, the result of nearly half a century of wrangling over the shape of administrative, social, and cultural institutions. In this chapter the noble assembly emerges as a crucial site of debate and struggle over access to authority, for it was this body that served as gatekeeper of noble status.

In chapter 2 I focus on one of the crucial mechanisms of empire building: the integration of elites. Previous scholars have presumed that the Crimean elite followed a path similar to that of their Georgian and Ukrainian peers. According to the accepted narrative, officials offered the mirzas a role in facilitating the establishment of Russian rule, and they accepted. By the early nineteenth century mirzas relinquished the reins of authority to Russian officials and landowners, thus removing any vestiges of local particularity in the Tavrida administration. Those who remained in positions of power did so only by forsaking their previous allegiances and becoming part of the Russian social and cultural fabric. In so doing, they left the Crimean Tatar population vulnerable to integrationist policies.

In truth, elite integration—and the creation of imperial communities more generally—was a far more complex affair. Ascribing noble status to non-Russians, and in this case non-Christians, involved reconciling the political implications of accepting the nobility of men (and women) who derived their prestige and power from sources outside the empire and its cultural sphere. This posed a momentous challenge in the tsarist system, where there could be no contractual relationship with indigenous elites: any privileges they enjoyed had to be construed as gifts from the sovereign rather than concessions to her monopoly on authority. By mining service records, landownership records, and petitions for noble status I assess the impact of Russian administrative institutions on the structure of elite society. Did the Crimean Tatar elite—the beys and mirzas—submit to or subvert Russian policies? To what extent did they participate in, and possibly shape, the architecture of administrative or cultural authority? Did Russian concepts of nobility—grounded in lineage and service—replace Crimea's clan hierarchy? Did service (civil or military) foster stronger linkages between Crimean Tatars and the regime? What were the terms of inclusion in Russian society?

Service—whether elected or appointed—had great potential as an integrative tool, but chapters 2 and 3 also show how it could be used as a mechanism for preserving local social hierarchies. I argue that the provincial government itself was part of an imperial system that cultivated multiple jurisdictions and multiple centers of power—a kind of flexibility essential to the function of a composite multiethnic empire. This flexibility or layered structure had a resonance even in the army, which had long served as a mechanism for integrating non-Russian elites. This was a form of interaction with the tsarist regime that the Crimeans found palatable, and chapter 3 examines both the record of their service and the ways in which Russians and Tatars used stints in a series of light horse regiments to their own ends: as a tool for maintaining the stability of the borderland during wars with the Ottomans, and as a vehicle for the acquisition (or maintenance) of rank and power.

Chapter 4 examines changes to the regime of landownership and land use in the decades following annexation. In the second half of the eighteenth century officials and scholars alike were developing new methods of quantifying Russian terrain. In their deployment of the cadastral survey and estate mapping and the compilation of statistics they helped standardize the management and definition of imperial space. But their efforts also cultivated an increasing awareness of the value and idiosyncrasies of micro-landscapes and shed light on differences in the cultural understanding of landownership in Russia and the former khanate. The chapter shows how imperial officials, Russian *pomeshchiki* (landowners), and Crimean Tatars used landownership practices—the distribution of dachas, appropriation, inheritance, and contestation of ownership claims—to shore up social and political hierarchies. Perhaps most important, although by the middle of the nineteenth century pomeshchiki succeeded in wresting control of many of Tavrida's most productive spaces from their former owners, Russian notions of the value of land shifted dramatically to accommodate local conditions.

Chapter 5 examines the flow of goods across and through Crimea in an attempt to understand the impact of Russian rule on the economic landscape. I pay attention here to patterns of exchange and consumption, and argue for the significance of small-scale transactions for understanding the economic geography of the region. To that end this chapter explores the evolution of the coasting trade—a genre of maritime shipping that played a crucial role in maintaining the commercial integration of Crimea, the Caucasus, and the Anatolian coast. Skippers tucked all sorts of commodities into the holds of their one- and two-masted vessels, from pearls and books to diamond-studded saddles and girdles, bags full of tin buttons and stacks of copper saucers, some of it legal, much of it contraband. They sailed into Crimean and Azov ports and sailed out again with salt, grain, leather goods, and honey, much as they had for centuries. While Russian officials were eager to facilitate and control Black Sea trade, farmers and gardeners and craftsmen began participating in the system of overland markets and fairs that connected the southern provinces to merchants and consumers everywhere from Kharkov and Moscow to Nizhnii Novgorod and Kazan. The Crimean economy thus moved southward toward Constantinople and northward toward Moscow, yet the towns of the peninsula remained key nodes of consumption and production, the orchards and vineyards key sites of prosperity.

Finally, I argue here that the empire-building process cannot be understood apart from its spatial context. On one hand, the exercise and experience of authority were shaped in important ways by the built and natural environments. Russian officials paid an inordinate amount of attention to sites—mosques, towns, and country homes, but also mountains, rivers, and gardens—and attempted to infuse many of them with particular symbolic significance. They had their work cut out for them. When the Crimean War broke out in 1853, a full seventy years after annexation, the Orthodox Archbishop Innokentii Borisov found it necessary to remind the faithful gathered in Sevastopol that they inhabited not "Muslim Akhtiar," but "Orthodox Chersonesos." The bishop felt members of his Crimean flock were confused by their easy passage from Russian ports to Tatar towns, from broad, straight boulevards to narrow, walled streets. In a landscape where minarets and Greek-columned mansions vied for attention, could one possibly feel as much a part of the Russian—that is, Orthodox—space as residents of Vladimir or Riazan? Innokentii lobbied incessantly for the Holy Synod to invest in the renovation of the (Greek) Christian churches and monasteries of the region because he believed this to be critical to the renovation of the spiritual identity of Tavrida's inhabitants as well as their political loyalty. "If they enter Christianity through these doors it can only be to the good of the state," he wrote, for "until a Muslim enters a church, he will always turn his gaze and his heart toward Mecca and honor the foreign padi-shah as the leader of his faith and that of all faithful Muslims."[43]

In another sense, the cultural and economic connections that integrated Crimeans into non-Russian, and usually trans-imperial, spaces were themselves valuable to the empire-building process. Commercial net-works, family estates, and pilgrimage routes continually took Crimeans across the border of the empire. There was risk involved in allowing these forms of mobility to continue. Provincial governors constantly fretted over rumors of Ottoman agents arriving to incite rebellion among their co-religionists, though officials rarely had access to sufficient resources to control the borders. Nevertheless, cross-border transactions pro-vided the empire with channels for expanding its own sphere of influ-ence. The massive quantities of high-quality salt harvested from the peninsula's salt lakes each year provided entrepreneurs with the perfect commodity for trade with Caucasian mountaineers, while Greek mer-chants sailing from Evpatoriia to Trabzon under the Russian flag served as conduits of information about conditions in the Ottoman Empire. Thus this book argues that understanding the place of Crimea requires thinking carefully about a range of spatial categories, such as distance and proximity, insularity and externality, intersection, directionality, and boundedness. It is impossible to reconstruct the daily experiences, let along the thought processes, of most Muslims of Tavrida or of other inhabitants of the southern empire. But by aggregating documentary rec-ords, identifying patterns of exchange, and uncovering the material and immaterial relationships that structure and transcend communities, my hope is that this book captures some of the rich texture of the experi-ence of empire.

PRELUDE

An empire is nothing without its subjects. When Catherine II annexed the Crimean Khanate she introduced a large Muslim population (of roughly 300,000) into Russian society for the first time in over two hun-dred years. In so doing Catherine gave herself the perfect opportunity to see whether the suite of reforms she had been elaborating for well over a decade—reforms designed to introduce an Enlightened rational-ity and uniformity to governance—could work in tandem with a mode of empire building that relied on the preservation of local particularities, the co-optation of elites, and the notion that allegiance to the tsar defined Russian subjecthood.

Allegiance was the foundation of the tsarist order, and in a newly acquired province like Tavrida establishing and maintaining it was an essential task of the newly established government, and the necessary first step toward integration. Catherine had harbored suspicions about the reliability of Tatar loyalty ever since approving the treaty of Küçük Kaynarca in 1774. At that point she informed one of her most senior advisors: "As a result of conditions in Crimea and those other places the Tatars inhabit, and no less because of their own qualities, they will never be useful subjects of Our Empire." The primary reason for her skepticism—and a major theme in this book—was the Muslim identity of the Tavridan population.[44]

It fell to Grigorii Potemkin to secure their allegiance, and he threw himself into the task with characteristic gusto. "We must ascertain who among the residents of the peninsula harbors ill intentions toward Russia and who receives us favorably," Potemkin wrote in May 1783. "We must examine each individual, especially those who wield power and influence over the masses, rather than simply taking the sum of their opinions." Potemkin set his officers to work evaluating the sympathies of the bey and mirza clans, but before they had a chance to complete their research the order came to administer a formal oath of allegiance and to do so immediately. Catherine informed the viceroy that he should compose the oath such that it struck an appropriately "triumphal" chord but remained "in accordance with [Crimean] law." Potemkin agreed that the oath—the political institution that would transform Crimeans into Russian subjects—must integrate "the customs of the Muslims." In fact, he was adamant in his belief that invoking the rituals of kissing the Koran and affixing seals in the Crimean manner would imbue the oaths of the mirzas and *ulema* (Muslim scholarly elite) in particular with legitimacy.[45]

This was no innovation. For centuries, oaths had functioned as quasi-legal agreements through which Russian authorities secured the loyalty of indigenous elites—and presumably their political and social networks—in exchange for the confirmation of various social and economic privileges. In the late eighteenth century, oath-taking transformed inhabitants of the steppe or of rival states into subjects of the empire, and for this reason the form of the oath was a matter of no small concern. Potemkin's decision to incorporate Islamic elements reflected his belief that invoking Allah would lend legitimacy to the bond forged between sovereign and subject. It also signaled that the empress did not, in the end, consider "Muslim" and "loyal subject of the Russian Empire" mutually exclusive terms. Whether the Crimean Tatars defined themselves first and foremost as members of the *umma* (community of Muslims) or not, Russian authorities saw their faith as the most important factor in calibrating their relationship to sovereign authority. Potemkin described members of the Giray house as "Muslim princes (*magometanskie kniazia*)" rather than Chingissids (as they would likely have preferred), and threatened severe punishments for any soldiers who showed disrespect toward members of the ulema, disrupted prayer services, or desecrated mosques. He instructed the military governor to encourage Russian soldiers to treat the Tatars gently, "as they would their own brothers and any other of Her Majesty's loyal subjects." There was no doubt in Potemkin's mind that the situation was delicate, and that any insult to Islamic institutions would come at the expense of order and possibly another Russian-Ottoman war.[46]

This strategic consideration of cultural difference had important long-term consequences. In fact, it established the official framework that defined Crimean Tatars within imperial society and shaped Russian policy toward them for over a century. When Governor Igel'strom administered the oath of allegiance at Ak Kaya ("White Rock") in early July 1783, each of the assembled members of the secular and religious elite swore before God to "submit [him]self in eternal subjecthood and accept the blessing of being as one people before the empress." "I therefore swear in the name of the One Lord and All-powerful God, and the prophet [Mohammad]," read the oath, "to try not only to fulfill [the empress's] sublime will, but also to sacrifice my soul and life for Her Majesty. . . . In pledging this oath, I kiss the Koran. And in so doing I [agree to] submit to the cruelest of punishments as an example to all people, should I commit any crime or disobedience."[47]

Potemkin wasted no time announcing the oath to Field Marshal Rumiantsev and to Catherine. However, the issue of Tatar loyalty to the Russian monarch had by no means been resolved. In time, it became apparent that many mirzas had chosen not to appear at Ak Kaya. Some, like Kutlu Giray Mirza Şirin and Mehmet Giray Mirza Şirin, the son-in-law of Selim Giray Khan, excused their absence by citing outbreaks of plague in their villages, which prevented them from traveling. Others were less diplomatic. In late July, Igel'strom reported that members of the Mansur clan refused to take the oath because "it was against their law to succumb to [a Christian ruler] without an outpouring of blood." Whole villages followed suit, preferring to wait and see whether the Russians would force them to pledge allegiance to the empress. They soon had their answer. By midsummer Igel'strom issued an ultimatum to all hesitant Tatars: swear the oath within a month's time, or leave Crimea.[48]

Empire building had begun.

1   Geographies of Authority

Big with the Fates of Oriental Pow'rs,
See where, sublime, Her eagle Genius soars!
Her Eyry builds on Theodosia's Tow'rs,
And flies in Triumph round her Euxine Shores.
　　　　　—Peter Cunningham, *The Russian Prophecy: A Poem,*
　　　　　Occasioned by a Remarkable Phenomenon in the Heavens,
　　　　　Observed in Russia, February 19, 1785

IN 1834 C. H. Montandon published the first European travel guide to Crimea. His collection of distance tables and suggested itineraries obsessively documents the pathways linking one corner of the peninsula to another, organizing its space into coastal journeys and interior passages. They locate Crimea in a broader world as well, describing overland connections with the imperial capitals and the hot springs of Taman, and maritime connections with the bustling port of Odessa. Not surprisingly, Montandon embellished the guide with a fold-out map. The map, "drawn from the best available sources," includes well-defined coasts, rough hachures and bathymetric lines, and a clear network of roads radiating out from postal stations and towns. The most distinctive feature of its design, however, is the absence of villages. In his effort to emphasize the infrastructure of mobility, Montandon deliberately omitted the villages north of the mountains because, as he put it, they "offer[ed] little of interest to travelers." Travelers—at least those cut from the same cloth as Montandon—required certain kinds of information in order to navigate from one destination to another; no more, no less. The transmission of that information is the simple logic that structures his work.[1]

Montandon's guidebook is an effective mapping of Crimea. It splashed onto the scene at a moment when Russian officials from an astonishing array of departments and ministries were attempting to pull off just such a feat. Governors, naval officers, clan leaders, bureaucrats, district police, noble marshals, ecclesiastical leaders, customs officials, and countless others were engrossed in the work of defining the scope and scale of their authority. This chapter attempts to make sense of that process by plotting jurisdictions and exploring the ways in which institutions and individuals wielded power, paying attention to its attenuation, its concentration, and its consequences. After all, while there is no avoiding the fact that the Russian system was hierarchical, that does not mean it was static. Power was constantly flowing through various channels, its itineraries changing mid-voyage, so to speak.

What did imperial governance look like? Did it change the way new subjects related to one another, or what role they played in society? Did it change the way they defined allegiance or belonging, to one community or another? Did it impact the way they navigated to meet the demands of private and public life? The core argument of this chapter is that reconfiguring the pathways of power after 1783 was no easy task. Governing a province like Tavrida required establishing Tavrida's location in layered geographies of authority that manipulated the distance between tsar and subject and defined the province as local or regional, secular or spiritual, familiar or foreign, proximate or distant, depending on one's vantage point. It required nearly half a century of wrangling with administrative, social, and cultural institutions. The tipping point came in 1831. In Simferopol the noble assembly had emerged as a crucial site for defining relations between various strata of provincial society. That year inaugurated an empire-wide push to bar non-Russians from participating in noble assemblies, as well as the establishment of new criteria for inclusion in the ranks of Muslim clerics. Tavrida felt the reverberations of such Nicholaevan policies in its own way, but the region was undeniably part of a process unfolding across the near and far reaches of the empire. As the nineteenth century wore on it seemed that the government in St. Petersburg was losing patience with the decaying structures of what Andreas Kappeler calls the "pre-modern" mode of empire building. As the bureaucratic capacity of the state grew and its ideology increasingly embraced the idea of *russkii* (ethnic Russian) over *rossiiskii* (Russian by subjecthood), the need to tolerate regional idiosyncrasies in policy or practice diminished.

With that in mind, this chapter examines the ways in which Tavrida's inhabitants used the tools of rank, status, and office. They wielded these tools for one and sometimes two reasons: to engage in the practices of governance, and to define themselves as sources of authority. In order to understand their successes and failures, we need to remember that when Catherine annexed the khanate, a great many men of power and of the pen remained firm in the belief that true possession of a new territory required military strength, administrative capacity, and skill in the art of ritual. Mircea Eliade described ritual as a process of giving form to unknown, unmapped space, and consecration as a process of recreating space in the image of the known and possessed world. These ideas are taken up in the work of historians such as Patricia Seed, who includes "planting crosses, standards, banners, and coats of arms" along with "marching in processions, picking up dirt, measuring the stars, drawing maps, speaking certain words, or remaining silent" in her compelling discussion of the role of ceremony in the colonial possession of the Americas. Many of these practices crop up in this book if not this chapter, and they are augmented by others. Rituals of possession in this corner of the world included, among other things, writing odes, designing snuffboxes, planting cypress trees, climbing mountains, and restoring mosques. Each of these gestures contributed, in small ways and over time, to the narrative Catherine and Potemkin so desperately wanted to tell about Russia's imperial project: that it was a transformative, civilizing enterprise.[2]

In the south, empire building was an act of restoration as well as one of transformation. The reason for this is simple. As a long line of fascinated western observers insisted, the human experience here dates back to Paleolithic times. It is first mentioned in Greek mythology as a space occupied for millennia by a barbaric people; it is home to cave monasteries and artifacts that suggest a druidic presence much like that of the Celts in France and Ireland. According to legend, Jason and the Argonauts spotted Crimea a century before the siege of Troy, and by the sixth century BCE, Greeks from Mileta and Heraclea had established an isolated yet opulent fringe of the Greek world along the Crimean coast. This was the formative moment. Mikhail Rostovtzeff, in his influential study in 1922, *Iranians and Greeks in South Russia,* explained that despite being dominated by waves of Cimmerians, Scythians, Sarmatians,

Goths, Huns, and Avars, the steppe ocean had been "swept clean of her German, Iranian, and Mongolian rulers and inhabitants." All that remained for Russia to inherit was a Greek (or possibly Greco-Iranian) landscape that drew on the Bosporus, whence culture and wealth flowed north along a flourishing trade axis.[3]

Civilization—classical Greek civilization to boot—was imprinted on the land. Catherine and Potemkin need not start from scratch. They had only to decide how to reconcile the evidence of other civilizational legacies—legacies that might muddle the connection between Athens and Petersburg. This was the real work of claiming the Black Sea littoral. Potemkin's frenzied efforts to create the perfect prize for Catherine—lighting roadside bonfires, arranging fireworks, presenting Amazon princesses decked out in crimson skirts and feathers, slapping paint on shop fronts, and paving roads in advance of her ceremonial trip to Bahçesaray in 1787—gave rise to the infamous stories of Potemkin villages.[4] But in his calmer moments Potemkin began the work of introducing Russian institutions. His program involved implementing Catherine's framework for provincial governance, establishing offices, courts, and noble assemblies, but also performing rituals of possession, from stage-managing oaths to doling out ranks and medals. This work was carried on for decades by his successors. It produced the structures necessary for the empire to exercise authority, but it also produced a range of expressions of power—in the form of architecture, patronage, and Muslim clerics—that neither Potemkin nor Catherine had anticipated.

POLITICS OF PLACE

Throughout his tenure as governor-general of New Russia (from 1774 until his death in 1791), Grigorii Potemkin poured enormous resources into transforming the south into a showpiece of imperial power. The towns, ports, and fortifications he built on behalf of his sovereign were designed to project the coherence and permanence of Russia's possession of the steppe and Black Sea littoral.[5] Location, therefore, mattered to Potemkin. In fact, it mattered a great deal. An owner of vast properties in his own right, a field commander, and a statesman to boot, he was attuned to the economic, strategic, and political significance of land. He was, in many ways, a master of managing imperial space.

Proof of this came almost immediately, with Potemkin's decision to convene the oath-taking ceremony at Ak Kaya. He chose the location for this crucial ritual with great care, forgoing obvious choices such as Karasubazar (the capital of the last khan) and Bahçesaray (the traditional seat of Giray authority). Ak Kaya suited his purposes beautifully. For centuries, the Crimean elite had used this mountaintop site for *kurultays*—assemblies at which clan leaders determined whether and when to go to war, and whom to elect as khan. By extracting a promise of allegiance from members of the elite at Ak Kaya, Potemkin both acknowledged Crimean tradition and asserted Russian authority over the men and the sites that had served as sources of political authority in the past.[6]

The same awareness of the value of space informed Potemkin's approach to the khan-saray—the famous palace of the Girays at Bahçesaray. For centuries Bahçesaray had served as the religious and political capital of the khanate, and it retained those functions even after 1783, albeit in an informal way. Nestled in a valley and hemmed in by the cliffs sloping down from Chufut Kale (Çufut Qale, "Jewish Fortress"), Bahçesaray's terrain encompassed palaces, shops, homes, mosques, and medreses. Tombs and shrines marked its edges—liminal spaces defining the boundary between civilization and nature, present and past, sacred and secular. Tatars washed at its fountains and talked in its coffeehouses: in fact, by decree of the tsar only Tatars could reside within its limits. For many reasons, then, many Tatars continued to consider Bahçesaray their capital, looking to it rather than to distant St. Petersburg as the site of historical memory and cultural authority.

In symbolic terms the khan-saray represented a serious challenge to Russia's ritual possession of the former khanate. And in the wake of annexation most Tatars likely expected the palace complex to suffer the fate of Aşlama. According to nearly every traveler who wrote about it, the summer palace was the epitome of exotic splendor, replete with gardens and fountains, orchards and birds; that is, until the night when, during the invasion of the Russian army, an explosion and subsequent fire leveled it. "So utterly did the stranger's hand demolish [Aşlama]," wrote one Englishman, "that the site is not to be identified without a guide." This was not the fate of the khan-saray. The site had a history of leveling and reconstruction dating back to the building of the original structure circa 1519. Renovations, some minor, some significant, continued under a long line of khans until it had become, according to one of the most detailed eighteenth-century accounts of its appearance, a sprawling complex laced with bridges, gardens, and galleries, with pools and fountains carved of white marble, and chambers decorated in blue and gold mosaic. The author of the account, Cristof Hermann Manstein, was an adjutant of Field Marshal von Münnich, under whose command the Russian army invaded in 1736. Cossacks set fire to the palace, but much of the structure survived and was restored by Mengli Giray II and Seliamet Giray II.[7]

The integrity of the palace suffered another serious blow at the hands of the last khan himself. When Şahin Giray, the last khan (reigned 1777–1783), fled Crimea he took everything of value with him—gold and silver items, expensive rugs, furniture, and decorations—such that the apartments of the palace were left quite bare. In the process of establishing his own authority, Potemkin wasted little time rectifying the situation. In June 1784 he allocated 10,000 rubles and appointed an architect (first the Englishman William Hastie and later Major Joseph de Ribas, future admiral and founder of Odessa) to restore the complex. The work, carried out by a small army of carpenters, masons, painters, and joiners, went on almost to the day of Catherine's arrival in May 1787. By that time, through sheer force of will, the palace rooms had been furnished with pieces purchased in Moscow and Constantinople, and de Ribas had provided the finishing touch by replacing the crescent above the main palace gate with a two-headed eagle—the imperial symbol of the Romanovs. The site exuded the exotic eastern ambiance its illustrious visitors surely expected.[8]

When Catherine arrived with her retinue she was eager "to be crowned Queen of Tavrida in the old capital of the khans" and "show the [Ottoman] sultan that she could have a bath if she chose in the Black Sea." She took great pride in seating herself on the throne at Bahçesaray and must have been pleased by the gilt inscriptions proclaiming that "In defiance of Envy, the whole world is informed that there is nothing in Ispahan, Damascus, or Stamboul as rich as this."[9] Potemkin had successfully converted the most potent political monument of the khanate into a symbol of Tatar submission to Russian rule. Nearly every subsequent tsar took in the wonders of the khan-saray, their ceremonial visits reaffirming the dominance of the Romanov house over previous occupants.

Potemkin further reduced Bahçesaray's status by locating his administrative center elsewhere. After briefly considering Eski Kırım (Staryi Krym, formerly Solhat), the original capital of the Giray khans but more recently a hub of clan power, he chose Akmescit ("White Mosque"), the traditional residence of the *kalga sultan* (second-in-command to the khan and always a member of the Giray dynasty). The kalga sultan's palace had sat on the left bank of the Salgir River, but at some point either in the turbulent years leading up to Şahin Giray's abdication or in the months following annexation it was razed to the ground (possibly by Şahin Giray himself). Well into the nineteenth century the careful observer could still make out the subtle footprint of its ruins. Perhaps aware of the potency of its legacy as well as the convenience of its geography, Potemkin determined that Akmescit was perfectly positioned to become the provincial capital of the new Russian province.[10]

The official plan for Simferopol, as Akmescit was officially called after May 1785, plotted an ideal neoclassical town very much akin to the famous naval port of Sevastopol just to the south. But whereas the small cluster of fishermen's homes at Aktiar had posed no challenge to the construction of Sevastopol, Simferopol rose in the midst of a substantial built environment. There were both logistical and ideological implications to this. In the opinion of Russian officials and European observers alike, the structure—indeed, the very essence—of Tatar towns was inimical to the enlightened ideals inherent in urban planning. They had a certain charm, of course. From a distance, the view of Evpatoriia (Gözleve) with its "lovely houses on the seashore, the Greco-Russian church, the vast and wondrous mosque and a riot of slender, straight minarets" was quite pleasing, one scholar reminded officials. However, the charm fell swiftly away as one approached. The labyrinth of narrow, crooked streets lined with windowless high walls through which the curious eye could not penetrate created a uniquely "gloomy appearance." Russian officials and foreign visitors fretted that disease and moral depravity might be lurking in those inaccessible dark spaces.[11]

The solution was to rearrange Crimea's urban spaces in such a way that they represented the new political authority. In Akmescit, Caffa, and Gözleve, this involved shifting city centers away from the mosques and markets of the old towns toward new cathedrals and government buildings. This was a slow process. When Emperor Paul I abolished Tavrida's provincial status in 1797, Simferopol consisted of little more than a barracks (the former governor's mansion), a Russian school, several buildings for administrative offices and courts, one "very indifferent Greco-Russian church," an Armenian chapel, three mosques, a Tatar bath-cum-prison, and a handful of stone houses. Residents abandoned the demoted town, taking what building materials they could with them, and returning only when Simferopol regained its status with the restoration of Tavrida as a province in 1802. The number of houses began to grow steadily in subsequent decades, from 445 in 1816 to 1,014 in 1836, and eventually 2,300 in 1851. Lovely garden-rimmed estates sprang up along the Salgir River, and in 1820 Governor A. N. Baranov built a public garden immediately across from his residence. By the mid-1830s four Orthodox churches, one Armenian Catholic church, and a synagogue graced the "European quarter" of town, and by 1845 the number of Christian churches (including Orthodox, Lutheran and Catholic) equaled that of mosques.[12]

But the Tatar identity of Simferopol persisted. The official town plan approved in 1794 had located the main cathedral square precisely on the border between the Russian and Tatar quarters, as if to draw the two into dialogue with one another. The preservation of four large mosques, including the sixteenth-century Kebir Cami, and constant construction of houses and shops in "the Asiatic manner," suggested that Akmeçet would serve a different purpose than Sevastopol or Bahçesaray. Here Catherine and her successors contented themselves with a provincial capital that fused "Asiatic" and "European" elements not only because of the limits of treasury coffers and manpower, but because it was accepted imperial practice to build on the foundations—literal and figurative—of what had come before. It was a good thing they did. According to E. D. Clarke, who visited in 1800, "The Russians, since the Peninsula came into their hands, have endeavoured to give to this place the name of Sympheropol; but we never heard it called by any other appellation, in the country, than that which it received from the Tahtars."[13]

This approach informed many of the official ceremonies performed in Simferopol; none more so than the reopening of the province in 1802. That celebratory day began with Russian and Tatar elites processing to their respective places of worship, where each pledged "in his own language to be impartial in the upcoming elections" before sitting down together for a Russian-style breakfast, consuming what the eighty mirzas at table found to be "strange fare." The evening entertainment con-

sisted of a ball hosted by the mirzas, "the likes of which," explained Pavel
Sumarokov, "no one in [St. Petersburg] will ever see. A Greek man
leapt about with an Armenian woman, a Tatar danced with a very proper
Russian lady, and the differences in costume [among the mirzas]—the
filleted turbans, the various beards and faces—would have attracted anyone's curiosity." The presence of the mirzas, like the presence of the
mosques, was crucial to the symbolism of the day: it lent legitimacy to
the proceedings and confirmed that Russian authority drew strength
from its imperial character.[14]

LAYERED JURISDICTIONS

If Simferopol was the hub of Russian authority in the former khanate, how far did that authority extend? In terms of administrative geography the answer is straightforward. The boundaries of the province
were fixed by the Black Sea in the south (a provincial boundary that
doubled as the border of the empire itself), the Dnepr River in the west
and north, and the Berda River in the east (figure 1.1). But that is only
the beginning. As part of Novorossiia (New Russia), Tavrida fell under
the jurisdiction of the viceroy (*namestnik*) in Ekaterinoslav along
with the provinces of Kherson, Ekaterinoslav, and the lands of the Don
Cossacks. To put it another way, Novorossiia extended from the Dnestr
River just west of Odessa across the northern coast of the Black Sea
and the Sea of Azov to the Kuban River, and northward to the provinces of Kherson, Voronezh, and Tambov. Until 1795, civil and military
authority over the region were combined in the person of the namestnik, and Catherine vested the extraordinary power of this position in
men whose loyalty was beyond suspicion: first Potemkin, and later
Zubov. At the end of her reign she gave General Alexander Suvorov
military command of New Russia, but when Alexander I reconfigured
the governor-generalship of Novorossiia in 1802, civil and military
powers were again combined. The capital moved from Ekaterinoslav
to Nikolaev (1803), and finally to Odessa in 1805. From that point
forward, until the dissolution of the governor-generalship in 1873, this
was the basic administrative geography of Crimea and with it, the southern empire.[15]

If we think in topological rather than administrative terms, we can
get a much better sense of Tavrida's place in the empire. For most of its

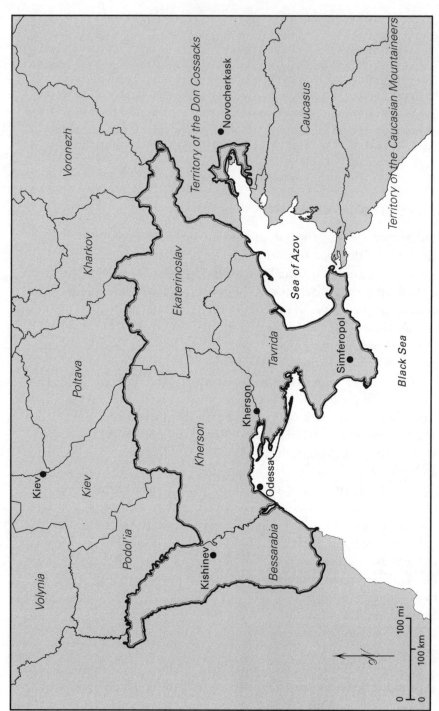

Figure 1.1. Tavrida Province and the Governor-Generalship of Novorossiia, 1802–1873

history the khanate had a place in the Ottoman administrative geography. In addition to the khanate having vassal status, which gave the Ottoman sultan the power to confirm the election of each khan and invest him with the appropriate regalia, a *beylerbey* (vizier) appointed in Constantinople ruled the *eyalet* (province) of Kefe directly, sending a portion of the tariff revenues to Bahçesaray. Within the khanate itself, secular power mapped onto four territories. First, the khan owned vast lands in his own right and exercised sovereign authority over them. The sultans (lesser members of the Giray clan)—particularly the kalga and nureddin sultans who stood next in line for the throne—maintained their own courts, commanded their own armies (as well as that of the khan when he chose not to go on campaign), and collected tribute from the Danubian principalities as well as taxes from certain Crimean towns. The beys (chiefs of the most influential clans) also maintained their own courts, chose and deposed khans, and often engaged in raiding or other military activity without the khan's approval. The khan could not tax the beys or those who paid taxes or rents to them, nor could he appoint kadıs (judges) within a *beylik* (the lands of a bey clan). Finally, the Nogay hordes were more or less autonomous entities led by *seraskers* (commanders-in-chief) appointed from among the Giray princes. Their territory varied, along with their allegiance to the khan.[16]

When Şahin Giray became khan he sought to eliminate these instances of territorialized autonomy. Intent on transforming the khanate into a hereditary autocracy, he converted the *divan* (governing council)[17] into an advisory council and restricted participation to members he appointed himself. Even more important, he stripped the clans of the landed basis of their power by converting the beyliks into administrative units controlled by centrally appointed officials. In one fell swoop, Crimea's irregular clan-based geography thus gave way to six *kaymakamlıks* (Bahçesaray, Akmeçit, Karasubazar, Gözleve, Kefe, and Perekop), with *kaymakams*—governors dependent on the khan for authority and prestige—theoretically replacing the beys. Şahin Giray further subdivided each kaymakamlık into *kadılıks*—territorial units under the jurisdiction of a kadı, or Muslim judge.

This was the political landscape Potemkin inherited in 1783, a territory destabilized by a decade of occupation and civil war and by the radical reforms of the khan. His response was to move boundary lines and men until he had found a satisfactory new alignment.

Potemkin's first priority was to remove the rebellious (or at best un-cooperative) Giray sultans from the khanate. Like the Bagration dynasty in eastern Georgia, the Girays posed too much of a threat to the perceived legitimacy of Russian rule to be allowed to remain in Crimea. While the exiled heirs to the Chingissid legacy took up residence in the Caucasus, Rumelia, and Constantinople, Potemkin recruited other factions into a collaborative relationship. A significant portion of the administrative and military elite had fled in the years leading up to 1783—some to avoid Şahin's westernizing reforms, others to avoid Russian rule—and between 1783 and 1787 another eight thousand inhabitants abandoned Crimea, many mirzas among them. But Potemkin was able to forge a working relationship with remaining members of the Şirin clan, whose beys had dominated the clan structure since the establishment of the khanate. According to the agreement between Potemkin and Mehmetşa Bey, the Şirins would serve as loyal subjects of the tsarist empire "so long as it would not violate their laws or ancient customs" or bar them from serving as military officers.[18]

The cooperation of members of the hereditary elite—the Czartoryskis and Potockis in Poland, the Bagratids and Chavchavadzes in Georgia—was central to the Russian empire-building project. As in Bessarabia two decades later, where Alexandre Scarlat Sturdza took the reins of civilian administration, Potemkin appointed Mehmetşa Bey head of the new Crimean government (*krymskoe zemskoe pravlenie*). As *Krym valısı*, or governor of Crimea, the Şirin bey presided over a governing board composed of Haji Gazy Aga, a close advisor of the Şirin bey under the khans, kadıasker Musledin Efendi, and the six kaymakams. The Krym valısı was responsible for civil and administrative affairs, leaving taxation and security to a military governor appointed by the viceroy.[19]

Even with this circumscribed portfolio, empowering the Crimean elite was a gamble on Potemkin's part. In January 1784 he received reports of "audacious actions" on the part of Mehmetşa Bey, who among other things continued to collect taxes and tribute from residents of Şirin-owned lands. But Mehmetşa Bey, Haji Gazy Aga, and their peers lent the trappings of legitimacy and continuity to the new government. They also represented a key source of valuable information. Officials stationed throughout the expanding south, from Crimea to eastern Georgia, quickly realized the extent of their ignorance about the territories in their charge and became dependent on locals to facilitate basic tasks of governance, from oaths of allegiance to tax collection.

For starters, officials had little idea of the size of the remaining population, let alone the scope of economic resources or the condition of the infrastructure. Baron Igel'strom, the first military governor of Crimea, therefore worked closely with Mehmetşa Bey and relied heavily on former treasury chief Kutluşa Aga Kiiatov and chief of the mint Abdul Hamid Aga, who together provided him with a detailed account of Şahin Giray's annual income and compiled the "administrative description" (*kameral'noe opisanie*) Potemkin commissioned in August 1783. Completed in 1787, this was a set of thirty-three detailed reports addressing, among other things, the names and populations of the villages in each kadılık, the responsibilities and salaries of Muslim clerics, the size of various confessional groups, the number of ruined and working churches and mosques, the number of pastoral nomads living on the steppe, tariff rates, and the frequency with which ships called at the ports of Evpatoriia and Caffa.[20]

Potemkin's obvious interest in the particularities of the Crimean population and economy seems hard to square with the decision to apply the famous provincial statute to Tavrida in February 1784—less than a year after annexation and well before the completion of the administrative description. Catherine's statute—the Fundamental Law for the Administration of the Provinces of the All-Russian Empire, issued in November 1775—introduced a new geography of administrative jurisdiction and was in many ways the cornerstone of her domestic policies. The reform introduced new posts, sending authorities in provinces throughout the empire scrambling to staff treasury chambers, provincial procuracies, district courts, appellate courts, and magistrates, all with their respective chairmen, deputies, advisors, assessors, jurists, and clerks. It also redefined the structure and size of the two fundamental units of governance, requiring provinces (*guberniia*) to contain 300,000–400,000 revision souls (adult males) and districts (*uezdy*) to contain 20,000–30,000.

In its earliest incarnation, the resulting province consisted of six districts: four on the peninsula (Simferopol, Feodosiia, Evpatoriia, and Perekop), and two on the mainland (Dneprovsk and Melitopol; figure 1.2). Most of the district boundaries followed natural lines: the Belbek and Salgir rivers formed the northern boundary of Simferopol,

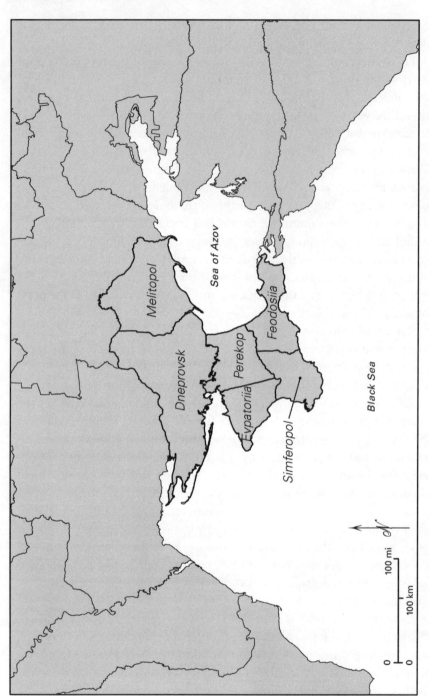

Figure 1.2. Districts of Tavrida Province, 1784–1837

and the Dnepr and Berda did the same for Dneprovsk and Melitopol. The Black Sea hems in Dneprovsk, Perekop, Evpatoriia, Simferopol, and Feodosiia, and the Sea of Azov shapes Dneprovsk, Melitopol, Perekop, and Feodosiia. In fact, the north-south lines splitting the mainland districts from one another, Evpatoriia from Perekop, and Simferopol from Feodosiia, appear to be the only "unnatural" boundaries imposed by Potemkin and his staff. In his excellent study of the annexation, Alan Fisher interprets the definition of district boundaries as evidence that the empress entertained "a certain lack of interest in the Crimea as a special region different from the rest of the Russian southern frontier." While it took several years to build and populate the requisite offices, the official opening of the new provincial government in February 1787 seemed to signal the end of Crimea particularity. Governor Kakhovskii's dissolution of the temporary government headed by Mehmetşa Bey effectively added Tavrida to the list of "regular" provinces, that is, those fully integrated into a centrally defined framework of governance.[21]

On the ground though, whatever measure of regularity the district boundaries might have generated was diminished by alternate channels of authority. First, the boundaries of the kaymakamlıks and kadılıks effectively remained in place, mapping traditional clan and juridical power onto the terrain. The steppe north of Perekop was inhabited by Nogay Tatars and a growing number of foreign colonists, both of whom enjoyed varying degrees of autonomy. The Nogay chief answered not to the provincial governor in Simferopol, but directly to the governor-general of Novorossiia. The latter was administered by a special office for foreign colonists in St. Petersburg. On the peninsula, the "Albantsy" (archipelago Greeks) at Balaklava and a handful of small foreign colonies stood outside the jurisdiction of the provincial government, and thousands of soldiers and sailors stationed in the province remained under military command. In 1804, Feodosiia became a self-governing town (*gradonachal'stvo*). Henceforth its governor reported to the governor-general rather than the civil governor, forging yet another tie between Crimea and Odessa. Kerch followed suit in 1821.[22]

The picture becomes even more complicated. By the early nineteenth century, Tavrida's educational institutions fell under the jurisdiction of Kharkov University (along with Sloboda Ukraine, Voronezh, Kursk, Chernigov, Kiev, Poltava, Podol'ia, Volynia, Ekaterinoslav, Kherson, the lands of the Don and Black Sea Cossacks, and Kavkaz oblast').

Meanwhile, its Orthodox churches belonged to the ecclesiastical space of the empire. In the early days after annexation the lands of the former khanate were located in the Slaviansk and Kherson eparchy based in Poltava. In 1799, they were placed in the Ekaterinoslav eparchy. By 1837 they belonged to the Kherson eparchy, where they remained until the establishment of the eparchy of Tavrida and Simferopol in 1859. Tavrida belonged to the fourth district of the Ministry of Water Transport, which included the provinces watered by the Don, Donets, Terek, and Kuban—effectively linking Tavrida to the Don Cossack lands, the Caucasus, Saratov, and even Tula, while drawing a line between it and Kherson and the other Dnepr provinces. By contrast, all of Novorossiia fell into the second division of the Admiralty's forestry department, which followed the Dnepr northward and extended as far as the Baltic provinces.[23]

The death of a tsar, the outbreak of a war, the charisma of a bey, the whim of a governor, a proliferation of oak trees—any of these could, and did, redirect the official channels through which power flowed across imperial space. When it comes down to it, though, what does the work of disaggregating layer after layer reveal? First, it challenges the idea that any one administrative unit—even one as crucial as a province—encompasses the space of political activity or the system of connections linking one parcel of the empire to the whole. Second, it emphasizes that the Russian system thrived by maintaining multiple jurisdictions and multiple centers of power. As important a role as Petersburg played in determining the fate of the south, that fate was the result of conversations, exchanges, and relationships cultivated in a constellation of sites and in a variety of jurisdictional contexts. Empire building was a complex spatial process, not a zero-sum game.

THE WEALTH (AND DEARTH) OF SEATS AT THE TABLE

Governing Russia was a social process as well. In fact, if there was a single logic animating the entire system it was not the logic of administrative institutions. In Russia, until the middle of the nineteenth century, power derived from social status; government offices and ranks were mechanisms for preserving or managing status, rather than generating it.

Service and status had been intimately linked for centuries, and they remained so after Peter I introduced his famous Table of Ranks in 1722.

The table established, once and for all, the ostensible framework for a regime shaped by merit *and* lineage.[24] Even after Peter III emancipated the nobility from the obligation to serve, service remained the foundation of noble identity, in no small part because it was the most effective mechanism for acquiring (or improving) one's status. Catherine's provincial reform and her charters to the urban and noble populations attempted to draw a broader swath of society into the daily practice of governance by extending the authority of central institutions into the countryside. Together with the expansion of the empire westward and southward, this caused a significant spike in the number of officials needed to govern the provinces. Between 1774 and 1796 the number of posts rose from 12,712 to 27,000, but many failed to offer the material or social capital necessary to make them appealing to Russian noblemen. Eventually, the sons of priests and merchants, and even free peasants, began to fill the vacancies. In central provinces this famously led to the divergence of the bureaucracy from the nobility. In borderland provinces, where Russian nobles were both scarce and unwilling, the ranks of state service opened up to non-Russian elites, causing convergences and divergences of a different kind.[25]

Civil service had great potential as an integrative tool. But it also had the potential to serve as a mechanism for preserving local social hierarchies and, through them, structures of authority. Generally speaking, there were two ways to acquire a position in the provincial government: appointment and election. Throughout New Russia appointments originated with either the civil governor or the governor-general, and none went before the Senate without the latter's approval. In the period between the application of the provincial reform in 1784 and the opening of the new government in 1787, Potemkin and Governor Vasilii Kakhovskii worked to assemble a crack team of qualified servitors. Members of the Şirin clan grumbled at the viceroy's willingness to award positions "according to personal qualifications rather than clan [affiliations]," but Potemkin, mindful of Catherine's order to appoint "worthy elders" to serve on the governing board and civil, criminal, and treasury chambers, was in fact careful to appoint Tatars from lesser clans to influential positions (table 1.1).[26]

Over the next decade, Tatars maintained a similar presence in every bureau of the administration, including the conscience court, upper land court (where many mirzas from non-elite clans served as deputies), and

Table 1.1. Crimean Tatars with Positions in Provincial Government, 1784–1786

Name	Office prior to 1783	Office
Mehmetşa Mirza Şirin[a]	Şirin bey	governing board advisor
Kutluşa Aga Kiiatov	treasurer	criminal chamber advisor
Dzhaum Aga Cholbaş		criminal chamber assessor
Temir Aga Nogay	envoy to Russia	civil chamber advisor
Haji Gazy Aga	chief accountant	civil chamber assessor
Mehmet Aga Biiarslanov	chief accountant	treasury chamber advisor
Mehmetşa Mirza Argin		treasury chamber assessor

Source: *Mesiatseslov* (1785): 440–442; (1786): 371–372.

[a] The register lists Mehmetşa as governing board advisor; on the ground, he held the office of *Krym valısı*.

Table 1.2. Crimean Tatar Representation in Provincial Government, 1785–1796

Provincial level offices	18.9%
District-level offices	45.2%
Appointed offices	14.5%
Elected offices	81.7%
Total offices	29.7%

Source: *Mesiatseslov* (1785): 440–442; (1786): 371–372; (1787): 386–387; (1788): 357–361; (1789): 356–359; (1790): 367–371; (1791): 377–380; (1792): 359–362; (1793): 371–374; (1794): 180–184; (1795): 390–394; (1796): 409–414.

the provincial magistrate (table 1.2). They also served in positions which, according to the provincial statute, did not exist. This was particularly true in the years leading up to the official opening of the provincial government in 1787. Until that time, the province was administered by kadıs and kaymakams, and local particularity permeated the structure of the governing board as well, where Mehmetşa Bey Şirin, Mufti Musledin Efendi, and Kadıasker Seit Mehmet Efendi, as well as representatives from the Şirin and Sicivüt clans, all held office unbeknownst to the compilers of the official registers of service.[27]

The reorganization of government in 1787 converted kaymakams into land captains (*ispravniks*) and ended the participation of clan leaders on the governing board. According to the organization chart published in 1796, the only notable differences between the administrative structures of Tavrida and those of other provinces were the appointment of officials to handle customs, the salt expedition, and quarantines, and the inclusion of translators in the treasury, provincial chancellery, conscience court, higher land court, district courts, and city magistrates. The organization chart did not necessarily reflect reality on the ground, of course. In fact, Catherine advised Potemkin to establish the various courts and other offices only as the population of each district required. It was not until 1802, when the Senate decided to reduce the access of Crimean Tatars to provincial posts, that it seemed clear that the demographic profile of servitors would come into line with other Russian provinces.[28]

If institutional uniformity was the measure of successful empire building, Russia was indeed scoring high marks. But as Alan Fisher points out, the structure of governance in the former khanate made no provisions for what he calls "the Tatar problem"—the unique challenges of administering a predominantly Muslim population with a strong steppe tradition. In time, this would prove problematic. Institutional renovations were simply not, in and of themselves, sufficient to dissolve all vestiges of the khanate's legacy. Russian officials were aware of this. They fretted in particular over the influence the Crimeans' Muslim faith might have on order and security along the entire Black Sea littoral. They could not shake the suspicion that, given the chance, the Tatars would aid their co-religionists despite their sworn allegiance to the tsar, and this abiding lack of trust spurred authorities to seek an institutional structure through which they could exert some measure of control over manifestations of Crimea's Muslim identity. Thus when the mufti died in 1791, they recognized a golden opportunity to begin corralling the sources of "fanatic" behavior. Breaking with a decade-long practice according to which Tatar elders and members of the ulema selected candidates for religious office (they were confirmed, more or less via rubber stamp, by the Senate), Governor Semen Zhegulin appointed a new mufti himself. He chose the current kadıasker, whom he described as "a person filled with loyalty toward the Throne, faithful to his duty, intelligent and just," and in return Seit Mehmet Efendi dutifully supported Zhegulin's proposal to establish a six-member advisory board.[29]

Zhegulin's proposal drew on the model of the Orenburg Muslim Spiritual Board established in September 1788 by Baron Igel'strom, himself a former governor of Tavrida and then governor-general of Simbirsk and Ufa. Igel'strom's enthusiasm for incorporating Muslim clerics into a specially created administrative structure stemmed in part from his concern with the influence of itinerant mullas, whose influence over public opinion and close links to Ottoman officials struck the governor as potentially dangerous. In exchange for bringing the mufti, kadıasker, and other leaders into a close relationship with provincial authorities and providing them with generous salaries, Igel'strom expected the Orenburg board to monitor the activities and loyalties of itinerant mullas and local members of the ulema, as well as cultivating a comfortably "orthodox" variety of Islam.[30]

Figure 1.3. Tatars leaving a mosque in Bahçesaray; from Demidov, *Album* (John Hay Library, Brown University Library)

The board operated without a formal statute, and in Tavrida too Catherine initially went no further than to declare the existence of a Tavrida Muslim Spiritual Board composed of seven members. After years of prodding from Zhegulin, in 1794 she declared the body responsible for "overseeing Muslim spiritual life in Tavrida Province" and instructed the treasury to pay salaries of 2,000 rubles to the mufti, 500 rubles to the kadıasker, and 200 rubles to the five other members. The board otherwise remained a "rather amorphous structure" under the jurisdiction of the Interior Ministry one minute and the Ministry of Education the next. Zhegulin took pains though to present it in a favorable light. On June 23, 1794, he invited the provincial and district marshals (all Tatars), members of the ulema, and all manner of officials, to attend a reading of Catherine's decree at the noble assembly hall in Simferopol. "I cannot describe," Zhegulin wrote to Prince Zubov, "the delight of those who received this favor, nor the joyous participation and gratitude for the generosity of Her Imperial Highness on the part of the entire Tavrida nobility and clergy (*dukhovenstvo*)." According to the proud governor, the mufti and his deputies "shed tears" as they prayed for endless years of health for Catherine and swore a ceremonial oath on the Koran. The assembly then moved to the city mosque, where they prayed again for the empress and her family, before concluding the day-long ritual with a feast.[31]

Establishing control over the ulema, and through them the loyalty of the Muslim population, would require much more than simply endowing the Tavrida Muslim Spiritual Board with a nebulous set of powers and responsibilities. After all, the board was an innovation. While traditionally the Crimean mufti was quite powerful, he did not sit atop a religious or spiritual hierarchy such as existed in the Ottoman Empire. As an appointee of the Ottoman sultan, he was vested with the power to appoint Crimea's kadıs, though in practice each bey selected the kadı with jurisdiction over his lands; these selections were presented to kadıasker and khan as *faits accomplis*. In the new scenario, the mufti retained his authority over *waqf* (pious endowments) as well as the right to issue fetwas, but also sat in Simferopol as the spiritual leader of the Muslims of Tavrida and the western provinces. The kadıasker, formerly the highest-ranking judge in Crimea, shed his judicial portfolio and became the mufti's second-in-command. But the relationship between them and the 1,531 mosques, twenty-one *tekkes* (monasteries), twenty-five *medreses* (upper-level schools), and thirty-five *mektebs* (lower-level schools) in Crimea alone remained vague.[32]

Russian officials were far more concerned with exercising control over the selection of personnel than they were with articulating the powers associated with each office. Mufti Seit Mehmet Efendi's death in November 1806 provided a perfect opportunity for imperial officials to orchestrate a personnel shift. In September 1796 Catherine had decreed that the mufti be elected from among the members of the spiritual board, the prime candidate being the kadıasker. But Governor Mertvago found what he described as Kadıasker Abdurahim Efendi's "poor moral character" and blatant sympathy for the Ottomans unacceptable. He recommended that the governor-general of Novorossiia, Armand-Emmanuel du Plessis, duc de Richelieu, convene an assembly of the Muslim nobility as well as the ulema and peasant elders in hopes that they would nominate a more palatable candidate. Richelieu agreed, and the assembly met on December 20. To Mertvago's chagrin, the fifty mirzas, twenty-seven elders, and more than two hundred ulema voted overwhelmingly in favor of Abdurahim Efendi. Undaunted, Mertvago sought a way to engineer the election of his candidate, Murtaza Çelebi. He announced that out of respect for the mirzas he could not allow them to be outnumbered by "clergy." He was compelled to reduce the contingent of ulema to fifty delegates. When the result came back yet again in favor of Abdurahim Efendi, Mertvago called for yet another vote and reduced the number of delegates to eight mirzas, seven ulema, and five elders. Hand-selected for the task, these men proposed two candidates—Abdurahim Efendi and Murtaza Çelebi—and Mertvago and Minister of Internal Affairs Kochubei happily confirmed the latter. Tavrida had its new mufti.[33]

It was not until 1831 that Russian officials finally defined the institutional structure of Islam for Muslims of Tavrida and the western provinces of the empire. Like those prepared for other non-Orthodox confessions, the statute of December 23, 1831, "on the Tavrida Muslim spiritual leadership and matters subject to its authority" enumerated the various offices and described their responsibilities and privileges. Its primary task, though, was to ensure that no one with questionable loyalties rose to a position of spiritual leadership along the Russian-Ottoman border. The statute created a hierarchy encompassing all members of the ulema and dividing them into "higher" and "parish" clerics. The former category included kadıs, the kadıasker, and mufti; the latter included *kâtibs* (scribes), imams, mullas, muezzins, and other mosque functionaries. New rules for the election of muftis and kadıaskers required the assembly of representatives of "parish" rank, the provincial marshal, mirzas, and other Tatar elders who would elect three candidates from among the ulema or "other worthy men from among the Muslim Nobility and Mirzas." Ultimately, the appointment depended on the governor's recommendation and the decision of the chief of the Main Administration of Spiritual Affairs of Foreign Faiths.[34]

Officials in St. Petersburg were pleased with the assurance of order built into the 1831 statute. By contrast, provincial officials were frustrated to find that the authority vested in the Tavrida board reduced the scope of their own. According to a report compiled by the mufti for the Department of Foreign Confessions, in 1826 there were some three thousand "parish clergy": roughly one cleric for every eighty-five Muslims. These three thousand Muslim clerics were now exempt from military recruitment and from the payment of taxes. The constantly cash-strapped provincial government was as anxious about losing so many souls from the tax registers as it was about allowing clerics to shape the population's compliance with the regime. They therefore keyed into the statute's stipulation that the right to "Muslim clergy" status was heritable and belonged only to those who maintained their tax-exempt status. They argued that in 1833 some 864 men serving as mullas, naips, imams, and kadıs were enrolled in the taxpaying registers and therefore not qualified for ulema status. Even better, they set up a complicated bureaucratic procedure that anyone must complete in order to strike his name from the tax register and remain a recognized cleric. The move followed on the heels of a similar crackdown on unlicensed clerics under the jurisdiction of the Orenburg Muslim Spiritual Board in 1829, where officials counted 207 unofficial clerics. The Tavrida executive department tried to insist that every member of the ulema present original documentation of his appointment, but the mufti and his staff proved adept at fending off the provincial government's assault on their legitimacy. They pointed to the futility of this last proposal, given that prior to 1831 no such contracts were drawn up. Over the next year, 861 of the 864 accused ulema passed their examinations, obtained notarized contracts

Figure 1.4. Tatars praying at the Istrim Cami in Karasubazar; from Demidov, *Album* (John Hay Library, Brown University Library)

attesting to the fact that their "parishioners" supported them, swore the requisite oaths in district court, and received official confirmation as tax-exempt subjects.[35]

These clerics exercised broad authority in spiritual, administrative, social, and judicial matters, from all questions concerning "the order and conduct of religious services and rites," to the staffing of mosques and schools, the management of waqf, and the maintenance of records on births, deaths, and marriages. This confessional institution therefore eliminated much of the need for direct control over the Muslim population and provided the same measure of administrative autonomy allocated to other non-Orthodox populations. In other words, it was not just the Orthodox Church that provided an alternate jurisdictional geography. Tavrida's Roman Catholics belonged to the Tiraspol diocese centered in Saratov; its Armenian Gregorians belonged to the Nakhichevan-Bessarabian diocese based in Kishinev; and the Karaites had their confessional center in Evpatoriia. These institutions translated what began as Catherine II's 1773 pronouncement of "toleration of all faiths" into a policy that distributed power to religious leaders in return for guarantees of order as well as the otherwise hard-to-come-by documentation of confessional groups.

In fact, document production (*deloproizvodstvo*) was one of the essential functions of the mufti's staff in Simferopol. The sworn testimonials, affidavits, petitions, and other notarized documents they produced made important pieces of information about Muslim lives available to Russian authorities; they also produced evidence of membership in the Crimean Muslim community—a matter of no small importance. Being a Crimean Muslim meant being exempt from the poll tax and military recruitment, and having the right to educate one's children in Islamic schools and to seek justice in kadı courts. In other words, until the 1830s it had allowed Crimean Tatars to navigate most of their lives away from the penetrating gaze of the state. Metrical registers ended that era of invisibility, but offered something in return: they were, after all, the keys to social mobility and economic gain. They served as passports to civil and military rank, institutes of higher education, property acquisition, and legal privilege. It is not surprising then that as the nineteenth century wore on, requests for such documents arrived with greater frequency, submitted by Muslim men who sought a place in the officer corps or confirmation of their noble status.[36]

Some historians argue that this form of administrative integration and the written documentation it produced had the power to "link the individual subject with the regime" in new and meaningful ways. This is no doubt true. To a certain extent, the Tavrida Muslim Spiritual Board functioned as an integrative tool, weaving Crimean Muslims into the fabric of the administration through metrical registers and legal directives. But those same documents—the very institutional structure and bureaucratic tools that brought Crimean Muslims into the fold of the imperial administration—also preserved the social, cultural, and even legal properties that distinguished Crimeans from their Russian, Polish, Bashkir, and even Tatar counterparts.[37]

THE NOBLE ASSEMBLY

As important as administrative and confessional institutions were to governing, the most important venue for working out questions of social status and, ultimately, imperial authority, was the provincial noble assembly. As numerous scholars have pointed out, "Russia had a government of men, not of laws" and in these conditions the noble assemblies created by Catherine's Charter to the Nobility in 1785 functioned as vehicles through which traditional social hierarchies and patronage networks survived and contributed to the legitimacy of the empire. Until 1831, the Tavrida noble assembly was no exception.[38]

The concept of a provincial nobility with unified interests and a sense of autonomy vis-à-vis the larger imperial nobility (as well as the provincial administration) evolved over the 1770s and 1780s. After their emancipation from service Russian nobles could choose whether to serve or seek a qualitatively different life on their estates. Those who chose the latter path constituted the provincial elite Catherine sought to cultivate and co-opt. She believed that tapping into the initiative and talent of these nobles would yield an increase in the wealth and power of the state that offset the cost of surrendering provincial offices otherwise held by men appointed from the capitals.[39]

In Tavrida, applying the terms of the 1785 charter meant opening up a series of influential positions to a non-Russian, non-Orthodox elite. Catherine applied the charter to Tavrida almost immediately, and the first assembly took place in Simferopol in January 1787 with over one hundred mirzas in attendance. When the votes were tallied, Crimean

Table 1.3. Results of the Tavrida Noble Assembly Election,
January 1787

	Marshal	District Judge	Land Captain
Simferopol	Abduveli Aga Uzdemikov	Mehmet Aga Balatukov	Bulat Bey [Argin]
Feodosiia	Atay Mirza Şirin	Sultan Mambet Şirin	Temirşa Mirza Şirin
Perekop	Usein Bey Mansur	Merdimşa Mansur	Seit Ibrahim Aga Taşı-oğlu
Evpatoriia	Arslanşa Şirin	Batyr Aga Krımtay	Abduraman Aga Mamay

Source: *Mesiatseslov* (1788): 357–381.

Tatars occupied all but three of the elected positions (table 1.3). Governor Kakhovskii was apprehensive. In his eyes, the list of mirzas worthy to serve and acquire imperial rank was terribly short. "I must tell you," he wrote Potemkin in early February, "that there is no one to present as suitable for service to the crown." His successor, Semen Zhegulin, shared this sentiment. As he began preparations for the second noble assembly election in late September 1789, Zhegulin pondered ways to dilute mirza influence. He even asked Potemkin whether it would "not be advantageous to publish an invitation in *The News of St. Petersburg* (*Sankt-Peterburgskie Vedomosti*) to all Tavrida nobles who reside in other provinces and do not already serve Her Imperial Highness in some capacity to come to the provincial capital" and participate in the elections.[40]

Both Kakhovskii and Zhegulin were keenly aware that many of the offices elected by the assembly were conduits for a significant amount of power. Conscience court, higher land court, and district court judges adjudicated both criminal and civil cases, with the higher land court serving as an appellate court for the lower land and district courts. As a result, many cases found resolution without ever coming before the appointed officials of the civil and criminal chambers. The duties of the provincial marshal were particularly extensive. He was responsible for supervising and maintaining the noble register as well as the lists of nobles with the right to participate and vote in assembly elections. The marshal monitored (in theory, at least) the morality and loyalty of members of noble society, provided references for those entering service, oversaw wardships and the provision of military recruits, and represented noble interests to both the provincial government and the minister of internal affairs in between assemblies. He even controlled appointments to lower posts within the provincial administration. Meanwhile, no hierarchical relationship subordinated a district marshal to the provincial marshal, leaving the former "master of the district." He headed up many organs, participated on commissions, prepared lists of district nobles, represented the interests of the district before the provincial government, and even exercised a police function as overseer of the land court.[41]

Portfolio aside, the power and influence of any elected official was truly defined by "the authority he commanded as a person, his wealth, the support of the local nobility, and his knowledge of local conditions." In Tavrida, the Tatars enjoyed a near monopoly and thus laid claim to these attributes. Between 1787 and 1796 mirzas won over 70 percent of all elected posts (table 1.4). They occupied the key offices of district judge, marshal, and land captain in each of the four peninsular districts, excepting only the district judgeships in Evpatoriia 1790–1792 and Feodosiia 1788–1795. But it is the overwhelming presence of members of the most prestigious clans among marshals in particular that suggests that social status determined election to office, rather than the other way around.[42]

Table 1.4. Provincial and District Marshals, 1787–1796

Position	1787–1790	1790–1793	1793–1796
Provincial Marshal	Mehmetşa Bey Şirin	Kalga Selimşa Şirin	Mehmetşa Bey Şirin
Simferopol	Abdul Veli Aga	Mehmetşa Zuisk	Mehmetşa Bey Kantakuzin
Feodosiia	Atay Şirin	Atay Şirin	Katyrşa Şirin
Evpatoriia	Arslanşa Şirin	Derviş Aga	Merdimşa Mansur
Perekop	Gusein Bey Mansur	Gusein Bey Mansur	Osman Aga

Source: *Mesiatseslov* (1788): 357–361; (1789): 356–359; (1790): 367–371; (1791): 377–380; (1792): 359–362; (1793): 371–374; (1794): 180–184; (1795): 390–394; (1796): 409–414.

In terms of sheer numbers, mirzas dominated the provincial nobility and its assembly into the early 1830s. At that point, of the 1,010 nobles in Tavrida, 551 (54.5 percent) were mirzas, 259 (25.6 percent) were Greek, and 200 (19.8 percent) were of Russian origin. But a discrepancy between the percentage of mirzas among all nobles and the percentage of mirzas serving in elected office had already emerged (table 1.5). There are all sorts of possible explanations for the precipitous drop. Some mirzas may have preferred not to serve the Russian sovereign because they felt doing so contradicted their faith or their allegiance to the caliph, or out of lack of interest in participating in the regime that deposed the Girays. Lack of enthusiasm for elected office was pandemic: throughout the empire participation rates plummeted after the first series of elections such that few subsequent provincial assemblies commanded the presence of more than one-third of the resident nobility. Once elected, many tried to shirk their duties. Almost overnight elected service had become "a new form of compulsory service for noblemen," according to Baron S. A. Korf, author of a classic study of the Russian nobility, and "one so unpalatable that those who were selected entered fraudulent claims to escape it." As proof of this, the number of participants in Tavrida assembly elections exceeded 100 only once between 1809 and 1830, although the number of resident nobles ranged from 329 to over 1,000. The assembly archive contains innumerable requests for release

Table 1.5. Mirzas Among Officials Elected by Noble Assembly, 1804–1852 (All figures are percentages of the total)

	Simferopol		Perekop		Evpatoriia		Feodosiia	
	1804–1827	1828–1852	1804–1827	1828–1852	1804–1827	1828–1852	1804–1827	1828–1852
Marshals	71.4	0.0	85.7	20.0	57.1	8.0	38.1	8.0
Land captains[a]	9.5	0.0	52.4	12.0	61.9	24.0	19.0	20.0
Land court deputies	54.8	2.0	61.9	0.0	92.9	0.0	57.1	10.0

Source: Data drawn from the annual service records for Tavrida province, published along with the records for all provinces of the empire. See the relevant entries in *Mesiatseslov* (1804–1829); *Adres-kalendar'* (1831–1853).

[a] Land captains were appointed; I have included the office as a point of comparison.

from service submitted by Russians, Greeks, and mirzas alike who claimed to be suffering from an array of ailments often compounded—according to their own descriptions—by old age.[43]

Imperial officials and provincial Russian nobles—the *dvoriane*—also had a hand in transforming the assembly from a site of Muslim clan authority to one dominated by a Christian elite with decidedly different economic and political interests. The Senate's decree in October 1802 restoring Tavrida's status as a province initiated the dilution of mirza power by reducing the number of offices the assembly elected. It required the governor to appoint district court judges rather than allowing them to be elected in accordance with the 1785 charter. And it required that the governor appoint two Russian nobles or, in the event that none were available, two other "worthy"—but presumably non-Tatar—people to serve as deputies on each district land court. The adjustment was necessary, explained the Senate, since the predominantly Tatar nobility elected the land captains and "there [were] few among the Tatar nobles who [knew] the Russian language and would be able to carry out their duties according to regulation."[44]

In an 1803 memorandum to Alexander, Senator I. V. Lopukhin expressed concern with even a minimal Tatar presence in government. The land captain was, after all, a key position. The provincial statute of 1775 charged the lower land court, which functioned as the local police, with maintaining "decorum, good-behavior and order," executing the orders and verdicts of the provincial government and courts, and enforcing imperial legislation. The land captain himself was part of a powerful triumvirate, along with the district marshal and judge, which for all intents and purposes ruled the district. As a result of this close collaboration, the land captain often acted in accordance with the interests of his peers and "social superiors," rather than with the legal provisions attached to his office. Lopukhin found to his dismay that in Crimea those peers and social superiors consisted "either of Tatars, who do not follow our law and custom and are not reliable either in and of themselves, because of their family and other connections, or of the so-called new landowners" driven by poverty and greed. According to the senator, the only chance at achieving responsible district-level administration was to allow governors to appoint land captains.[45]

The fact that Russians and other settlers in the region did not present a more palatable option frustrated officials to no end. In 1805,

Governor-General Richelieu dismissed three Russians, one Prussian, and a fifth noble of "foreign origins" from the criminal and civil chambers on the grounds that they had "neither the knowledge nor the competence required of men in their posts." Alexander Ivanovich Mikhailovskii-Danilevskii—a senator and historian—made a point of mentioning the "barbarity of the *chinovniki*" (clerks) in his memoirs of a trip to southern Russia with Alexander I in 1818. The man at the helm in Simferopol during the tsar's trip, Governor A. S. Lavinskii, was aware of the problem and proposed measures intended to further "improve order and organization." Among them was a recommendation that all members of district courts—not just judges—be appointed, "since on account of the insufficiency of the Tavrida nobility, elections are for the most part useless. The people [elected to] these offices," Lavinskii explained, "neither know the rules nor possess the competence" to abide by them. Although he admitted that many of the *pomeshchiks* were "of the same quality as [the mirzas] . . . and in more established provinces would not be tolerated," the governor insisted that the problem in Tavrida was that natives still made up the majority of the "Russian (*rossiiskoe*) nobility."[46]

That is precisely what governors did from that point forward. Tavrida's nobles elected land captains only once after 1804, and just six months after that singular election in December 1820, the imperial government decreed that henceforth the governor would appoint all members of the lower land court. To the chagrin of men like Lopukhin, placing appointments in the hands of the governor did not guarantee that they went to Christian nobles. Despite the stipulations and regulations, until 1821 the land courts almost without exception included two mirza deputies each, and after that date the Evpatoriia and Perekop courts each included one. Moreover, Tatars held the post of land captain in every county at least once. They were, after all, better connected than their Russian and Greek colleagues to the networks through which many local issues were resolved.[47]

A few officials recognized that eliminating mirza authority had a significant and unintended drawback: it diminished the power of noble society as a whole. In 1829, Provincial Marshal S. E. Notara convinced the assembly to submit a formal request to Governor D. V. Naryshkin to overturn the 1821 decree and allow the assembly to elect deputies to the district and lower land courts from among either Russian or Tatar nobles. Remarkably, they justified the request by explaining that "currently, those offices are occupied by *chinovniki* who hail from various regions and, not being familiar with Tatar customs or language, fulfill their duties according to the direction of translators and scribes." As a result, the common people were suffering at the hands of culturally insensitive nobles who were fast reducing the province to a "half-wild condition." Both the governor-general and the minister of justice rejected Notara's appeal. Interior Minister Dmitrii Bludov, however, proposed that mirzas might serve on the lower land court so long as they met the minimum requirement of knowing Russian.[48]

Despite the fact that Bludov's opinion prevailed in that instance, anti-mirza momentum was gathering. The 1830s witnessed an intensification of the dvoriane's efforts to limit mirza access to the assembly. They had no lack of motivation. Though only eight of the 594 men who had petitioned for noble status by 1830 had been officially inscribed in the noble register (the rest still awaited approval from the Heraldry), at any moment the Senate might, on a whim, confirm hundreds of mirzas—an act that would cause a sea change in the social and political landscape of the province. For while the nobility as a whole gathered for only a few days every three years, the marshals and deputies they elected exercised a great deal of power in the interim, providing the documentation of noble status required of any noble seeking to enter civil or military service or gain access to the economic and legal protections associated with nobility.[49]

The ongoing effort to bar mirzas from the assembly dovetailed with an empire-wide reexamination of the election process and the watershed regulation of 1831 "on the order of Noble Assemblies, elections, and service." Nicholas signed the decree in an effort to reduce the "difficulties and misunderstandings" in procedure and culture occurring with alarming frequency as the number of propertied nobles rose across Russia. The problem was that these nobles held smaller and smaller amounts of land, due to the parceling of estates through sales and inheritance. They therefore looked to improve their own fortunes rather than "acting for the common good." In order to ensure the proper conduct of assemblies and their officials, the regulation reorganized attendees into three groups. The top tier consisted of those with the right to vote directly; the middle voted through plenipotentiaries; the third tier could participate in assembly affairs but could not vote. Assembly members were required to provide proof of "irreproachable behavior" and inscrip-

tion in the noble register, and to have attained both the age of majority
and the fourteenth class in the Table of Ranks. To cast his vote through
a plenipotentiary a noble had to prove the existence of five male peasants contracted to live on his land, or ownership of 150 desiatinas of
arable land. To qualify for the top tier, he had to prove possession of at
least 100 male souls or contracted peasants, or no less than 3,000 desiatinas of land in a single province.[50]

Almost immediately the mirzas objected that this decree replaced
local practice with universal standards. Even mirzas such as Mehmet Mirza
Krımtay and Batyr Bey Balatukov, who commanded more than enough
material wealth to qualify to vote directly, would be barred from participating in the assembly at all so long as the Heraldry lingered over
the confirmation of their noble status. So, before the convocation of the
1833 election, the mirzas sought validation of the privileges granted them
by Catherine II. During a preparatory district assembly in Feodosiia, the
mirzas, under the leadership of the Şirin clan, drafted a petition to
Marshal Notara asking him to safeguard their longstanding right to
participate in the elections despite their "unofficial" status.

Captain Ali Mirza Şirin, marshal of Feodosiia, wrote the petition. In it
he explained that "the mirzas of the Şirin, Edige, Mansur, Sicivüt, Argin,
Kipchat, Kekuvat, and Iaşlav clans came from ancient noble lineages,
whose ancestors always distinguished themselves through their loyalty
to their sovereign," whether khan or tsar. They "were always prepared to
render civil and military service and sacrifice their lives, to the last drop
of blood." As a result, many among them had received chivalric orders
and imperial rank. Moreover, in 1820 the Tavrida noble assembly recognized them as nobles of ancient lineage and presented their documents to the Heraldry.[51]

Notara turned to the military governor. "There is no doubt," he
wrote, "that the upcoming elections should be governed by the 1831
regulation." However, "In order to put an end to any incorrect interpretations" of imperial policy and avoid the unpleasantness sure to develop should the dvoriane succeed in barring the mirzas, Notara asked
Pahlen to confirm that "alone, the fact that the Heraldry had not yet
confirmed the Tatar mirzas' and Greek nobles' status was not sufficient
grounds to deny them the right to participate in the election." Pahlen
agreed, and when Prince Vorontsov returned to his post he weighed in,
emphasizing that the mirzas' status was not simply a local tradition—it

had been publicly and officially acknowledged by the Sovereign of All Russia long ago. Most important, "Tatar mirzas and beys represented not only the majority, but the sole foundation of the noble assembly. They never lost the right to serve" and it could not be otherwise, "for in Tavrida as in other newly acquired provinces the indigenous elite constituted the nobility in its entirety." Should they be barred, the quality of future officials would suffer. An exception had been made in Bessarabia, Vorontsov noted, and there was no reason the same couldn't be done here. On December 17, 1835, the Committee of Ministers concurred.[52]

With the approval of St. Petersburg, the mirzas retained the right, on paper, to participate in elections. But dominance in the assembly had slipped through their fingers. From 1836 onward elections placed mirzas only as deputies to the conscience court and to the lower land courts of Perekop and Feodosiia. Others periodically won election but were removed from office once the provincial government determined that they did not speak Russian. By the late 1830s, Tavrida's elected officials included an assemblage of landless chinovniki, a handful of former officers of Greek and Ukrainian stock, and a smattering of Russian landowners who had retired to estates on the southern coast.[53]

PATRONAGE AND PERSUASION

As the struggle for control of the noble assembly shows, informal channels of influence were crucial elements of the political landscape. At times they manifested in correspondence between men whose authority had a local basis—such as Notara—and those whose authority derived from their status and standing at court, such as Richelieu and Vorontsov. And at times they manifested as patronage networks. Tenure even in district-level office could provide the sort of connections in Simferopol, Odessa, and even St. Petersburg that enabled one to appoint relatives and friends to important or lucrative positions. Colonel Mehmetşa Bey Kantakuzin, for example, positioned himself at the head of a patronage network that hinged on both his connections to Russian authorities and his status as the leader of a princely clan. Kantakuzin commanded a Tatar light horse (beşli) regiment that returned to Tavrida in 1792 after several years of duty along the Polish border. At that time, Catherine dissolved four of the six squadrons, and the horsemen who remained in service quickly found that their new duties offered little in the way of glory or adventure. Two dozen were reassigned to guard state forests. Twenty-seven more spent their days patrolling the salt lakes of Feodosiia, Perekop, Evpatoriia, and Kerch. Dozens busied themselves with the somewhat more exciting tasks of transporting criminals, rounding up troublemakers, and guarding the province's coasts and postal routes.[54]

This group of disgruntled soldiers, now little more than an indigenous security detail, remained squarely under Kantakuzin's command. They had him to thank for their salaries. Kantakuzin had sole authority over such appointments, and those who rendered satisfactory service or were connected to the colonel received more frequent and more lucrative assignments. Indeed, monetary compensation was one of the few inducements that motivated men who were otherwise reluctant to serve. According to a report from the treasury chamber in September 1794, privates serving in various posts throughout the province received a salary of thirty-five rubles; noncommissioned officers received forty rubles annually. Whenever the treasury chamber fell behind in payment, the soldiers-for-hire showed their displeasure by absenting themselves from their posts. This of course caused no end of frustration to district officials who were suddenly unable to guard the prisoners, salt lakes, and other resources for which they were responsible. The vice governor, K. I. Gablits, the overseer of state forests, Nikolai Metaksa, and the overseer of salt lakes, Alexander Taranov, all relied on Mehmetşa Bey's singular authority. When his men failed to perform their duties, Metaksa and Taranov had no choice but to ask the colonel to command their presence, as their own exhortations fell on deaf ears. Exasperated as he was by their petulant behavior, Kantakuzin was well acquainted with the Tatar and Russian landowners who often gave asylum to the beşlis. Extracting them from their hideaways in sheds and orchards was the price he paid for power.[55]

Members of the Crimean elite who served in civil office also used their positions to advance the interests of their clans. Mehmet Aga Balatukov, for example, initiated a clan tradition of service that extended well into the nineteenth century. Born in 1734, he was one of only four mirzas who reached class five in the Table of Ranks in the eighteenth century. Mehmet was descended from a Cherkess princely clan, and his grandfather, Haji Bekir Aga, served Kaplan Giray Khan (1707 and

1730–1736) as *baş kaznadar*, or chief accountant. Bekir Aga's son occupied the same office under Selim Giray Khan (1743–1748) and passed the position on to his own son. Şahin Giray appointed Mehmet kaymakam of Bahçesaray, and in that capacity he came to Potemkin's attention. His peers elected him Simferopol district judge in 1787 and again in 1793.[56]

Balatukov's success paved the way for his son, Ismail Bey. Born in 1766, Ismail volunteered for the Black Sea fleet in 1785, where he caught the attention of Brigadier (future Admiral) Ushakov. He joined other young mirzas in the beşli regiment two years later, and in April 1789, Governor Zhegulin informed Potemkin that "as a result of his blood relation to Collegiate Councilor [Mehmet] Aga as much as his abilities and devotion to service and to fulfilling Your Grace's will," the senior Balatukov had recommended Ismail Bey to oversee the provisioning of lumber for the port of Sevastopol—a plum post if ever there was one. Zhegulin also passed along Ushakov's glowing review of Ismail's "vigilance and diligence in the careful and exact execution of any duties assigned to him." Within a year, Catherine assigned him the rank of captain, and his peers elected him lower land court deputy and then land captain of Simferopol. By 1802 he was a collegiate assessor. Armed with an exemplary service record and elite lineage, Ismail Bey petitioned for noble status in 1804. The assembly approved his petition and subsequently elected him Simferopol marshal (1812; he was reelected consecutively until 1820). By virtue of a felicitous combination of prestige, patronage, and service, the Balatukovs thus became one of the first Crimean clans accepted into the ranks of imperial nobility.[57]

Knowledge—of the land, kinship relations, the nuances of clan politics, the predilections of Russian bureaucrats, and the contours of Russian law—was a currency one could easily convert into power. Kantakuzin and Balatukov enjoyed success because of their lineage and their competence, to be sure. But they enjoyed success also because they knew how to navigate the landscape of authority—an art that required knowing when to abide by the rules and when to skirt them through appeal to the vanity or discretion of a superior official. There is nothing terribly unique about the exercise of informal, or personal, authority persisting alongside an expanding bureaucratic structure: this is the stuff of imperial narratives all over the world. The blurring of formal and informal authority in the pursuit of social or economic interests and administration of justice was an attractive solution to the problems of weak state capacity (in the form of insufficient staff, incompetence, or insufficient information). But it was not just a stopgap measure; it was one of the core tensions animating and perpetuating the tsarist system itself.

Some contemporaries complained that the signature feature of the Russian bureaucracy, and particularly its court system, was its inefficiency. Marie Guthrie, a French woman who toured the Black Sea region in 1795–1796 and documented her observations in a series of letters, suggested that justice in Tavrida took so long to be administered that "the accused may grow *light* in the scale before his merits are weighed." Russia certainly had an ambiguous relationship with the rule of law. There was no shortage of decrees and legislation, but at no time did they or the institutions that in theory guarded their integrity proscribe the power of the tsar. Richard Wortman has argued that law remained an "ornament in Russian political culture" and "an attribute of power that identified the ruler with exalted foreign images of sovereignty just as it served as a means to control and civilize the Russian administration." The key point in the context of this book is that the tsar's refusal to acknowledge any one judicial institution as independently legitimate made it possible for multiple sources of legal authority and a multiplicity of jurisdictions to coexist. Catherine's provincial reform pushed in this direction. The statute called for a wide array of courts, including all-estate courts (the criminal and civil chambers), specialized courts (such as the conscience courts, or courts of equity), and courts designed for each estate, such as the higher land court and district court for the nobility, provincial and town magistrate for townspeople, and upper and lower summary courts (*rasprava*) for *odnodvortsy* ("homesteaders," or state peasants with the right to own single estates) and other free peasants. This profusion of venues did not lead to judicial efficiency. A case originating in district court might be appealed to the civil or criminal chamber and then to the Senate whence, should the senators of the appropriate department fail to come to an agreement, it would proceed to the general assembly, the Ministry of Justice, State Council, and eventually, the emperor. As a result of such complex and often arbitrary procedures, the number of undecided cases generally far outnumbered those resolved in the course of each year.[58]

These were not the only courts in operation. For non-Russian, non-Orthodox populations, justice was administered in an array of other venues. Virginia Martin has shown that over the course of the nineteenth century the government often attempted to "effect social and cultural change, as well as to legitimize imperial claims to rule" by constructing legal-administrative systems that incorporated, rather than abolished, local forms of legality such as customary law (*adat*). This is not to say that the tsarist system wholeheartedly embraced the idea of multiple legalities. Nicholas I, for example, was not at all enamored of the idea. Though he confirmed the judicial autonomy of the Grand Duchy of Finland and of Bessarabia, he revoked the Lithuanian Statute from the Belorussian and Lithuanian provinces between 1831 and 1843, abrogated Magdeburg law in Ukrainian towns in 1831 and Swedish church law in the Baltic provinces in 1832, and abolished the judicial function of the *kahal* (the autonomous organization of Jewish communities) in the Pale of Settlement, which included the provinces of New Russia, in 1844.[59]

Tavrida, however, retained its legal pluralism. Its judicial landscape included Karaite, Roman Catholic, and Islamic law courts, in addition to the full panoply of Russian courts. This multiplicity of jurisdictions was not new to the khanate, where non-Muslims maintained courts according to their own laws, Muslims had access to Islamic law courts, and all had access to the divan (which functioned as the highest appellate court in accordance with steppe tradition) and arbitration by the beys and mirzas. The problem was that many Russian officials viewed the practice of Islamic law as a form of disloyalty. According to this view, whereas customary law, or adat, was native, genuine, and therefore worthy of codification, Islamic law represented "a viable expression of legal resistance"—and therefore a significant threat—to Russian authority. In the north Caucasus, Russian administrators "emphasized the cultural authenticity of the adat" and set up customary law courts for Kabarda, Ossetia, and parts of Chechnia, while restricting the application of Islamic law to cases involving marriage and inheritance. It was no easy thing to simply eliminate the kadı courts, however. In Crimea, Catherine II had explicitly tied the legitimacy of Russian rule at least in part to her guarantee to protect Islamic institutions and practices as well as the rights and privileges of members of the ulema. Thus, eager as they were to limit the authority of Islam, its judges, and jurisconsults, to the sphere of "spiritual affairs," the bureaucrats and officials found they had to tread carefully on this sensitive legal ground.[60]

In the late 1820s the State Council and Senate began issuing opinions and decrees in an effort to legislate the boundaries between Islamic, customary, and Russian law. Rather than act unilaterally, they solicited the opinions of the Tavrida and Orenburg Muslim Spiritual Boards. Tavrida's muftis, Haji Abdurahim Efendi (1816–1829) and Seit Abdul Dzhemil Efendi (1829–1849), were particularly adept at claiming as expansive a terrain of authority as possible by grounding their opinions in sacred texts. For example, in his objection to the Russian common law stipulating that the dead be buried only after three days, Haji Abdurahim explained to the Senate that not only the assembly of mullas, but also "various legal books read by learned men of faith," confirmed that Muslims must be buried on the day of their death. The mufti's reliance on the authority of the written word fit beautifully with what Robert Crews describes as Russian authorities' desire to establish the contours of Islamic orthodoxy. To that end, they sought opportunities to redefine Islamic law, understood as "localized readings of diverse texts, read for a multiplicity of outcomes and interpretations" as "a limited collection of texts" that functioned as "both a fixed code of law and a statement of orthodoxy."[61]

This was clearly a push toward bureaucratization and formalization of authority. But it was awfully hard to achieve, for any number of reasons. Whether in Tavrida or in Tula, the quality of court officials was problematic. Corruption was rampant at all levels. Judges tended to be illiterate and to bring neither experience nor training to the bench. Those who did faced the daunting task of navigating the vagaries of the inquisitorial system. Many relied on their subordinates, particularly the low-ranking court officers known as *striapchie,* whom William Pomeranz describes as "an amorphous group of legal practitioners" roughly divisible into three main categories: "judicial chinovniki" (secretaries, clerks, and registrars), "professional advocates" (usually retired bureaucrats who argued cases before the courts), and *iudebniki* (retired servitors or ruined landowners who wrote up petitions or complaints for a fee). Corrupt or honest, most were far better versed in legal procedure than the presiding judges. Few, if any, had recourse to the wells of knowledge or experience that might equip them to make sense of the cases brought before them, and none could pretend to operate in an environment impervious to the interventions of governors, princes, or tsars.[62]

The statute of 1831 continued the painstaking work of defining the authority of Islamic courts; meanwhile the intersection of customary and imperial law was just as difficult to manage. In practice, the pursuit of justice (or satisfaction), no matter the venue, remained a complex endeavor, reliant on informal channels of authority and riddled with procedural imperfection. However, not everyone chafed at the imprecision, ponderous space, and negotiability of the system. In fact, some found these features useful tools.

Such was the case in a particularly colorful dispute between members of two powerful clans. In 1840 a Şirin mirza lodged a complaint with the provincial governor against a twenty-year-old member of the Krımtay clan. According to the complaint, under cover of darkness Krımtay had forced his way onto Şirin's property accompanied by several dozen accomplices. Leaving his entourage outside the courtyard, Krımtay allegedly climbed to the window of Şirin's stepdaughter, Kaya Sultan, and was about to climb in when a group of Şirin's relatives and peasants appeared. In the ensuing chaos, Krımtay's men fired several shots and the entire company ran off. According to the plaintiff, Krımtay's intention was not to steal anything from the house, but rather "to sneak a look at his betrothed and perhaps take advantage of the defenseless girl." Şirin's relatives confirmed the story, and investigators found the gate of his house, as well as the window in question, damaged.[63]

The legal wrangling that ensued allows us to map the sophisticated navigation of jurisdictional boundaries, official hierarchies, patronage networks, and cultural norms that defined the relationship between ruler and ruled in the former khanate. The defendant, Krımtay, naturally disputed the plaintiff's narrative. According to his testimony, he arrived with six unarmed men in order to carry out what he described as "the Muslim ritual of looking in the window of his betrothed." When he noticed Şirin's men, he left. Under interrogation, the accused men acknowledged that they had accompanied Krımtay to the house, but insisted that nothing else occurred. It was Mehmet Mirza Krımtay, the father of the accused, who pulled the trump card. Şirin, he alleged, "manufactured the charges against [Krımtay's] son in order to dissolve the contract between him and Kaya Sultan and marry her instead to [Şirin's] own cousin." He had more than enough motivation to do so: Şirin had mishandled his stepdaughter's estate and was desperate to avoid being held responsible for bringing his ward to ruin. Had the marriage become official, the entire community would have known of his misdeeds.

Henceforth, the main point of contention revolved around whether or not Krımtay and Şirin had in fact agreed to a wedding contract. Kaya Sultan testified that she did not know Krımtay, and that her uncle had not informed her of his intention to marry her off. However, neither of these points proved that the contract had not existed. In fact, four associates of the defendant testified that the marriage agreement had indeed been in place; two claimed to have secured Şirin's consent themselves. Krımtay then made a controversial move. He presented a letter from Kaya Sultan's grandmother inviting him to come see his bride "at night, taking all appropriate precautions." Conveniently (or inconveniently), the grandmother had died before the start of proceedings and authorities were at a loss as to how to establish the authenticity of the document. Several men testified to having heard of its existence prior to the fateful night, but the case was getting bogged down with inconclusive evidence and contradictory testimony. Neither side could get any traction.

While the notoriously slow bureaucratic engine chugged along, Kaya Sultan married her kinsman. Şirin might well have dropped the charges at that point, for they had served their purpose: they had effectively prevented Kaya from marrying into another clan and exposing him to the financial and social cost of mismanaging the estate. However, the Tavrida criminal chamber, the court of first instance in this case, continued its investigation. Unfamiliar with the nuances of Tatar marriage rituals, members of the court decided to do some old-fashioned research. They consulted a number of different sources including, surprisingly, the governor-general, Prince Vorontsov. Vorontsov, who in fact prided himself on his sympathy for the Tatar situation and familiarity with their culture, was among those who mentioned a custom according to which the relatives of an underaged girl, on promising her in marriage, might allow the prospective groom to secretly see her *before* completing the contract. The court found this compelling evidence and concluded that Krımtay's actions amounted to little more than "unruly conduct and disturbing the peace"—charges carrying no punishment, according to recent changes to the law code.[64]

But the provincial procurator disagreed. Mindful of his role as the local guardian of the integrity of Russian law, he determined that

Krımtay's actions amounted to robbery and therefore could not be pardoned according to the provisions of the 1841 manifesto referenced by the criminal chamber. Based on this finding, the case made its way to St. Petersburg. Upon review, the Senate confirmed that while Krımtay's actions constituted "unruly conduct and disturbing the peace" under the new criminal law code, the procurator was correct that they constituted robbery under the previous legislation. There the Senate parted company with the procurator. Surprisingly, the Senate ruled that the finding of the court should be based on the current legislation rather than on that in place at the time of the crime. Thus in 1847, seven years after the incident at Kaya Sultan's window, they found Krımtay guilty of the innocuous charge of unruly conduct, and innocent of the far more serious charge of robbery.

This case cannot by itself articulate the many idiosyncrasies of legal and bureaucratic practice. However, it makes four crucial points. First, Russian authorities were deeply concerned with local laws and customs: not with buttressing them, necessarily, but with documenting them. Second, their ignorance or uncertainty about local laws and customs made room for members of the local elite—Tatars as well as Russians—to intervene, acting as cultural translators and pushing authorities toward rulings that served their own interests. Third, Crimeans were generally willing to engage Russian institutions in their pursuit of office, status, or legal satisfaction. They used Russian courts in the first instance when doing so would serve their interests, or when they were dissatisfied with the decision of a kadı. But they were just as likely to reject the authority of a land court or criminal chamber. In fact, Crimean Tatars made a habit of renouncing the oaths they swore in Russian courts and declaring any decisions derived from their testimony invalid and nonbinding. The practice was widespread and serious enough that in 1831 Mufti Abdul Dzhemil found it necessary to remind the Muslim community that all oaths, including those sworn in legal proceedings involving Christians, were binding.[65]

Finally, the battle between Şirin and Krımtay confirms that social status was an important factor—perhaps the most important factor—in determining the outcome of any interaction with the administration. The involvement of Vorontsov is striking in this regard: as governor-general of Novorossiia and then viceroy of the Caucasus, he was without question the most influential agent of Russian authority from Odessa to

Tiflis. But it is the intervention of the elder Krımtay that drives the point home. Mehmet Mirza was one of the most remarkable men in all of Tavrida. Renowned as "the richest Tartar nobleman of the country," he had a documented income of 12,700 rubles from estates covering over 21,000 desiatinas. According to the German geographer Johann Georg Kohl, who visited Krımtay's residence in the early 1840s, the provincial secretary had built a "spacious house, and furnished it with every convenience; with divans and carpets, for Tartars, and tables and chairs, for Europeans." Krımtay played gracious host to many distinguished guests, allowing them the pleasure of touring the orchards that produced "the Krymtayeff apple, so celebrated in St. Petersburg," as well as the gardens and picturesque meadows of his estate. When Krımtay pointed to the nature of Şirin's motivations for hauling Krımtay's son before authorities, he changed the entire course of the investigation. From that point forward the efforts of the authorities focused on determining the legitimacy of the marriage contract. While "justice" was slow in coming, it came as a result of Krımtay's carefully calibrated testimony— testimony that demonstrated his knowledge of both Crimean culture and the culture of the imperial bureaucracy.[66]

In the end, Russian law would win the day. Though it would not curb the power of the tsar until 1905, it would trump Islamic law whenever a kadı's decision strayed beyond the confines of (what the empire determined to be) spiritual matters. Likewise, the formal particularities of the khanate's administrative structure sank into the sedimentary depths that held the evidence of Greek and Byzantine tradition as well. But as much as tsarist institutions strove to impose the same procedures and frameworks found in the "interior" spaces of the empire, the system truly thrived when its own hierarchies and jurisdictions overlapped, or when their boundaries grew indistinct. Negotiating this ambiguous terrain was a central part of the Crimean experience of empire, and a crucial characteristic of the dynamics of imperial rule.

2   Elusive Subjects and the Instability of Noble Society

THIS CHAPTER EXPLORES the process of elite integration. Elite integration was fundamental to the work of the tsarist empire: maintaining order, securing borders, controlling the flow of wealth, and accruing prestige both home and abroad. It was also iterative—part of the aftermath of conquest or annexation from the sixteenth century through the nineteenth, from the khanate of Kazan to the kingdoms of Poland and Georgia. There was a stock script and a portfolio of policies from which to draw inspiration, yet pulling non-Russian elites into the orbit of the court and nobility was always a challenge. It required the careful calibration of privilege and obligation, and determination of the correct balance between the preservation of local particularities and insistence on Russian norms. In a sense, imperial officials were doomed to reinvent the wheel with each territorial acquisition, for what worked with the Cossack *starshyna* would not necessarily work with the Baltic Germans. Thus there is good reason to characterize the history of elite integration in Russia as a narrative of separate deals. But as productive as that approach can be, it is even more accurate to approach elite integration as a form of networking: a process of defining and building a whole system of linkages among individuals and communities, across district, provincial, and regional boundaries. That is the core argument of this chapter: that the elite of the empire was a multidimensional network, and that the process of elite integration in Tavrida shaped that network in important and identifiable ways.

Three factors shaped this process above all others: the faith of the majority of local elites, the traditional clan structure of Crimean society, and the influence of Enlightenment-inspired ideals on the Russian state. Islam would have been a factor regardless, but it was Russian officials' insistence on perceiving the Crimean Tatars as Muslims first and foremost that infused the process of social and cultural integration with distinctly political overtones. The result was a series of ambiguous and contradictory policies that made it impossible to know whether a Crimean mirza would—or could ever—be a *dvorianin* (Russian nobleman). The secular elite—the beys and mirzas—at the center of this long navigation were potentially valuable assets in a resource-starved environment. Their fates within imperial society were, however, as varied as their backgrounds. In the end, some served as temporary proxies for Romanov authority; others became permanent fixtures in regional governance. Some were amenable to co-optation; others resisted assimilation in any guise.

The Crimean elite was a small but significant group within the dvorianstvo (Russian nobility). Baltic Germans generally outranked them and Polish szlachta surely outnumbered them, but the beys and mirzas exercised the minds of imperial officials for nearly six decades. There is good reason for this. The mirzas were a diminutive population—never more than five hundred at given time—but they were Muslims in an era of religious toleration, former vassals of the sultan in the age of Russian-Ottoman rivalry, and heirs to steppe traditions in the midst of Russia's attempt to reinvent itself as a European state. Determining whether and how a mirza might become a dvorianin therefore had wide-ranging logistical and ideological implications. Officials in St. Petersburg fretted over the ennoblement process unfolding in Simferopol because they knew that the boundaries separating elite entities—Russian and non-Russian, ranked and unranked—were porous, and that even seemingly localized policies had empire-wide implications. Thus as much as the integration of Crimean mirzas is rooted in its own time and place, it also suggests that we rethink the geography of social categories and the dynamics of the process through which officials and elites continually curated noble society.

LOYALTY AND MOBILITY

If there was a single silver thread binding the web of empire together it was the concept of loyalty. The thread snapped at times (Russia has a healthy history of peasant revolts as well as Polish rebellions); in Tavrida it remained perilously thin. Rather than rise together in armed rebellion, the Crimean Tatars tended to distance themselves from Russian authority, either by attenuating the connections binding them to the state, or by physically removing themselves from the empire. In the wake of annexation so many left Feodosiia, for example, that the town was nearly deserted by midsummer 1783. It was not uncommon for two to three dozen families from a single kadılık to request permission to go abroad on any given day. In his careful study of the Crimean emigrations, Arsenii Markevich concluded that approximately one thousand families—mainly inhabitants of the coastal areas of the peninsula—fled in the period immediately following annexation.[1]

The political ramifications of cross-border travel were clear from the start. Through their travels, Tatar émigrés, pilgrims, and merchants maintained channels of communication with friends and family in Ottoman lands. They also facilitated influential scholarly, religious, and political networks forged in Constantinople, where the émigré community played a vital role in shaping policy toward Russia: many members of powerful Crimean clans who settled in the Ottoman Empire received monthly salaries and other payments from the Porte well into the nineteenth century. By 1784 Governor Kakhovskii recognized the threat the exodus posed to the economic viability of the empire's new territory as well, but neither he nor Potemkin closed the border. The southern frontier was a delicate political landscape, after all. Catherine's annexation manifesto did not contradict the sultan's claim (asserted in the 1774 treaty of Küçük Kaynarcı) to spiritual authority over Crimean Muslims. Instead, it guaranteed Tatars the privilege of practicing their faith and maintaining their mosques, and preserved the social and economic privileges of the ulema. Catherine sought to create an environment in which simultaneous loyalty to the Orthodox sovereign and to Islam was not a contradiction in terms. But she knew, as did Potemkin, that even the empress of all Russia could not make confessional and political borders coterminous through sheer force of will.[2]

Thus while initially Potemkin was content to let Crimean inhabitants flee to Rumelia, the Caucasus, and Anatolia, he instructed the military and civil governors to keep detailed records of the identities of those who crossed the border, whether their intention was to conduct trade, make a pilgrimage, or emigrate. By June 1786, Potemkin had had enough. He decreed that no Tatar who fled Crimea rather than become a subject of the Russian Empire would be allowed to return.[3]

When Catherine II visited Tavrida province one year later, a steady stream of Tatars seized the opportunity of her proximity to petition the empress for permission to resettle in the Ottoman Empire. Instead, she declared emigration an unambiguous act of treason. On May 31, 1787, Governor Kakhovskii told the governing board to identify every Tatar who submitted such a petition without delay and exile them to an interior province of the Russian Empire. These "unworthy subjects," Kakhovskii explained, had enjoyed the choice between emigrating and taking the oath of allegiance in the months after annexation. Because they had elected to stay and had, at least in theory, "pledged their loyalty to Her Imperial Highness," their decision to leave now was clearly a violation of their oaths to the "generous and gracious sovereign."[4]

The sentiment may have been sincere, but this is a classic case of the divergence between policy and practice. Throughout his tenure in Novorossiia (he died in 1791), Potemkin approved the requests of Crimean Muslims to travel to Mecca despite the fact that it was rarely clear whether crossing the border meant fulfilling a pillar of Islam or fleeing Russian rule. Catherine herself threw open the arms of empire to those who sought reentry. As early as February 1784 mirzas who had resettled in Anatolia began writing their relatives to complain of the high cost of living in Ottoman cities. In some cases correspondents followed on the heels of their missives, arriving in Crimea from Constantinople, Amasya, and Trabzon. Immigrants who could prove their value to the government received particular support from local officials. In July 1788 Çoban Haji Sali, a merchant and former resident of Feodosiia, returned from abroad. Kakhovskii found that as a result of Haji Sali's intellect, wealth, and the respect he had garnered in Constantinople, "he [was] quite capable of convincing the muddle-headed and haughty (*beztolkovye i nadutye*) Şirins to sign any kind of petition." He would keep an eye on him, but Kakhovskii allowed the Feodosiia native to return.[5]

Tayar Bey, a highly decorated Ottoman military officer, received a particularly warm welcome—and a generous monthly pension of 500 rubles—in exchange for ongoing reports on his communications with Turkish contacts in Anatolia and the Caucasus. Tayar had grand ideas about leading Russian armies in the conquest of Anatolia and Persia. He settled for fighting in the Russian army against the French and returning in 1807 to Constantinople to participate in the overthrow of Selim III. Most would-be subjects, however, such as Kutluşa Mirza Şirin, who arrived in Feodosiia from Anatolia in 1805, simply found that they could live more comfortably in Russia and sought permission to rejoin their families. Governor Mertvago approved Kutluşa's petition to take the oath of allegiance and enter noble society based on his Şirin connections, but he was only one out of hundreds of Tatars and other Ottoman subjects who petitioned for permission to become Russian subjects. Some lived several years in Tavrida before petitioning, others approached authorities upon crossing the border or arriving at port.[6]

Regardless of a petitioner's connections, wealth, or military skills, approval was contingent on swearing the oath of allegiance to the Sovereign of All Russia as well as to the laws of Islam. Well into the nineteenth century, Muslims would seal that oath by kissing the Koran: a symbolic nod to the feasibility of simultaneous allegiance to tsar and Allah. The precarious nature of this formulation of loyalty, which theoretically allowed Crimean Muslims to look to Petersburg for the source of political authority and to Constantinople for religious guidance, was clear enough, but war between the rival Black Sea powers brought the shifting, unstable nature of Crimean loyalties into stark relief. During the Russian-Ottoman wars of 1787–1791, 1806–1812, and 1828–1829, the boundaries between religious and political identity became as saturated with symbolic meaning as the physical borders contested by soldiers and sailors.

In the spring of 1787, as relations between the two powers deteriorated, rumors began to circulate in Crimea about—in the words of Governor Kakhovskii—the imminent arrival of "the false prophet Mansur," who was coming to deliver Crimea from Christian rule. This "false prophet," known as Ušurma or Sheikh Mansur, had styled himself a holy warrior and the leader of a rebellion against the expansion of Russia into the Caucasus since 1785. Rumors of his feats, let alone of his impending arrival, were quite enough to set local Russian officials on edge, particularly after the Porte declared war in August. Throughout the autumn the governor's staff nursed fears of a revolt. "The local Tatars have begun to whisper among themselves," Kakhovskii wrote to the Russian envoy in Constantinople. "They are deriving prophesies from their books, giving credence to the rumors and turning their hopes to [Mansur]."[7]

In January 1788, matters came to a head. The governor received reports that the inhabitants of several villages in Perekop and Evpatoriia districts had been praying, fasting, and sacrificing black horses, oxen, and rams. Alarmed by what he saw as a display of Muslim fanaticism, Kakhovskii promptly announced that the Tatars had "disobeyed Mohammad's law." Moreover, in their "deviation from the prescribed terms of prayer, fasting, and sacrifice," Kakhovskii discerned a betrayal of the Russian state and a "violation of their oath of allegiance." The "mullas" (a term Kakhovskii and many other officials used as a catch-all reference to Muslim clerics), he concluded, were encouraging the people to follow Sheikh Mansur's example.[8]

Kakhovskii summoned the mufti and kadıasker, the highest-ranking Muslim officials in the province, to provide an explanation. Seit Muslar Effendi and Seit Mehmet Effendi tried to assure Kakhovskii that the rituals were in accordance with Islamic practice, and that they were in fact necessary in order to gain the favor of Allah and protect the faithful and their crops against hail, rain, and all manner of plagues. Unconvinced, Kakhovskii dispatched two trusted members of the provincial government, Mehmet Aga Balatukov and Batyr Aga Krımtay, to investigate. Within days, Kakhovskii had tracked the rumors of Sheikh Mansur's imminent arrival to a Turk named Vaap, whom the governor accused of having posed as a merchant from Anapa. According to Vaap's testimony, the whole matter arose because he had brought a letter he received from Mansur with him, quite by chance and certainly with no intentions to sow rebellion, when he traveled from Anapa to Feodosiia. He conducted his business, selling his wares and staying with friends. Vaap claimed to have mentioned Mansur to no one, and to have heard nothing of the sheikh from the Crimean Tatars. Trouble started when he unwittingly dropped the letter in a shop in Karasubazar. The shopkeeper found it and brought it to a local mulla, who deciphered the prophecy of Mansur and his immanent victory over the infidels.[9]

Regardless of how the letter fell into other hands (for his part the mulla claimed that Vaap had actually handed out manuscript copies of the letter), Kakhovskii concluded that Vaap was a troublemaker who came to Crimea with the intention of "seducing the people, perhaps even instigating a revolt." He cited the fact that Vaap had goods worth only 300 rubles as proof that he was not a legitimate merchant. But to be sure, he ordered that all artisans, merchants, and visitors, especially those who were subjects of the sultan, be rounded up and questioned. Mehmet Aga and Batyr Aga quickly apprehended Vaap, together with every "mulla" involved in the spread of the Mansur rumors or the worrisome rites. Kakhovskii interrogated them all and kept them in custody to await sentencing.[10]

Meanwhile Mehmetşa Bey Şirin carried out his own investigation. The prayers, fasting, and sacrificial rites, Mehmetşa explained to Kakhovskii, had been carried out according to the instruction of Haji Mustafa, an influential Perekop mulla, and were meant to mark "the birth of the new year." New Year was celebrated throughout the Islamic world on the first day of the first month of the Islamic calendar. In fact in 1787 this fell in early October; not in January 1788. Moreover the traditional Crimean celebration of Navrez, the agricultural New Year, would not be held until the vernal equinox. Of course, there is no evidence that Kakhovskii was aware of the discrepancy. The Şirin bey's testimony would likely have been accepted had it not been contradicted by several more persuasive sources. First, under interrogation several mullas admitted that they led the prayers at the bidding of a "strange dervish" who had shared the prophecy about Sheikh Mansur. Mehmet Bey Balatukov's report described a foreign sheikh who had attended the funeral of a wealthy local Tatar and there proclaimed that "the conquering sword of Islam had been taken by the infidels, but from this point forward he will triumph over them. For this, we must pray and give thanks to God." Word spread quickly, Balatukov informed the governor, and Muslims were carrying out similar ceremonies from the Caucasus to the Arabian peninsula in hopes that Allah would grant victory over Russia to Sultan Abdulhamid.[11]

Convinced of the connection between Mansur and the prayer services, Kakhovskii declared all who were in any way involved with recent events guilty of demonstrating pro-Ottoman sympathies. He accused them of two distinct but related crimes: first, spreading the seeds of revolt, and second, leading the people in the practice of a fanatic, deviant form of Islam. In the presence of the mufti and kadıasker, as well as Tatar and Russian elites, Kakhovskii pronounced individual sentences on seventy-one mullas, sheikhs, and kadıs of Perekop, Evpatoriia, and the steppe districts. He sent some to do hard labor in internal provinces for two years before permanent exile from Tavrida. He exiled others (particularly those who interpreted the prophecy for the people or otherwise spread news of it) immediately.[12]

In his report to Potemkin, Kakhovskii admitted that he found the "mullas"—a term Kakhovskii used in a decidedly derogatory manner to describe any member of the ulema suspected of harboring ill will against the empress—worthy of a certain kind of respect. "The strong impression that the words of the Koran make on them," he explained, "compels them to consider dying to protect their faith, and the hatred and loathing they harbor toward us is similar to that of our own *raskol'niki* (heretics)." The influence they wielded was troublesome: the "mullas" might even be more powerful, Kakhovskii speculated, than the "fanatical" Catholic priests his colleagues were encountering in the Polish provinces. Certainly they were creating "bad" Muslims—the kind that betrayed oaths and caused disorder—at an alarming rate.[13] The bonds of allegiance were wearing thin.

MISSIONARY WORK AND THE PERSISTENCE OF CONFESSIONAL BOUNDARIES

Had Crimea come within the boundaries of the Russian state earlier in the eighteenth century authorities might well have pursued a much different confessional policy. But in 1764 Catherine had declared that henceforth conversion of the empire's non-Christians would be the result of education rather than coercion. And at the very moment when she brought the Crimean Tatars into the imperial fold she guaranteed their right to practice their faith despite having justified the act of annexation in part by explaining that the Tatars "on account of their ignorance and wildness (*nevezhestvo i dikost'*) [were] not capable" of maintaining a free and independent state. In addition to rendering them susceptible to Ottoman and Caucasian propaganda, officials worried, the Tatars' ignorance made them a public health threat. Because of their faith, Tatars refused to follow the prescriptions of western medical and hygienic standards, preferring to ward off plague and other ailments by procuring small bits of sacred paper and either sewing them into silk purses and wearing them like amulets, or burning them and inhaling the smoke. But they weren't the only ones whose disregard for western medicine appalled observers. According to Mary Holderness, after one Bulgarian village escaped the plague, a tale spread that evil personified had visited the village and was treated with the customary hospitality, in return for which he passed them over. Holderness decried the credulity of the people who subscribed to this theory. "But until education dispels the native darkness of the mind, we cannot hope to see this universal power of superstition subdued, any more than we can expect the light and genial warmth of the sun, before he has risen in our horizon."[14]

For many reasons then, Potemkin saw no reason to put obstacles in the way of those who sought baptism. In April 1785 he instructed Kakhovskii to approve the applications of any Tatars seeking conversion and to keep him apprised of their numbers. Careful to avoid the appearance of sponsoring a Christianization project, Potemkin meanwhile arranged for the Orthodox Church to appoint a bishop for the Greeks of Feodosiia and Mariupol; in September 1787 Kakhovskii invited Archimandrite Dorofei, bishop of Feodosiia, to come to Simferopol and illustrate to an assembly of mirzas "the difference between our pastor and their mufti."[15] Kakhovskii hoped such an encounter might inspire the mirzas to seek baptism, but the meeting does not appear to have had the desired effect. Nor did the Feodosiia consistory flourish. When it was folded into the diocese of Kherson in January 1800 its six Crimean parishes catered to 2,646 male and female Christians, or 1.3 percent of the peninsula's population. By 1803, the percentage of Christians had increased to close to 10 percent—an increase tied almost exclusively to the immigration of Orthodox, Catholic, and Protestant settlers, rather than the conversion of the local population.[16]

That is not to say there were no converts. Many of the earliest were individuals who claimed to have been born Christian, sold into slavery, and forced to convert to Islam; or to have descended from Greek families that converted long ago. Between 1783 and 1785, twenty-seven Greek Muslims "whole-heartedly decided to return to the Christian faith," along with twenty-one Tatars. In 1786, another twenty-nine individuals converted, including both Tatars and those who claimed to have been born Christian. But in subsequent years, the number of converts of both kinds fell. According to Governor Naryshkin's report to the Ministry of Education in June 1824, Orthodoxy won nine converts in 1819, and an average of three each of the next six years. After 1825, they were few and far between.[17]

There was, after all, no economic incentive to convert. Crimean Muslims paid no taxes or duties except those owed their landlords through contracts. They were responsible for maintaining and provisioning the beşli regiments, supplying Sevastopol with firewood, providing grain and horses for the army during wartime and, in time, those who lived along the postal roads were expected to provide shelter and horses. As heavy as this burden was, the tax burden of converts was oppressive enough to force them into lives of crime and decidedly un-Christian behavior that in turn discouraged others from seeking baptism.[18] In 1825, Minister of Education Alexander Semenovich Shishkov and Over-Procurator of the Holy Synod Peter Sergeevich Mesherskii agreed with Prince Golitsyn that Tatar converts ought to be removed from Tatar society, "resettled among Christians and bear taxes no greater than what they paid as Muslims." This was the only way, Mesherskii felt, to wean former Muslims away from "the way of thinking, morals, and customs" engrained in them from their youth, and in June 1826 the State Council concluded that baptized *inovertsy* must be fully integrated into Christian society, relieved of taxes for three years, and permanently exempted from military recruitment.[19]

If conversion promised no direct material benefit there were other practical reasons for Crimean Muslims to seek baptism. For some, conversion was a critical step on the path to a successful career in Russian service. Mehmet Çelebi from the village of Karaş in Akmescit district was baptized in May 1786 in Balaklava. With a new name—Petr (Peter)— and his ability to speak and write in Russian, he easily found work in the provincial government as a translator.[20] For others, conversion offered legal protection. Mehmet Bek, a down-on-his-luck craftsman who had fallen into poverty, renounced his second wife, sold his daughter to a local mirza, lost his passport en route to Mariupol, landed in jail in Feodosiia, and proceeded to escape from jail and head straight for the Orthodox bishop's residence at Staryi Krym. There he pleaded for baptism and, with the approval of the viceroy, Mehmet received Christianity and absolution from the debt he incurred in his former life as a Muslim.[21]

The quality and quantity of Crimean Tatar converts was a concern for Orthodox officials, but also for members of the Scottish and Russian Bible Societies. In January 1819, a prominent member of the Russian Bible Society wrote to Prince Alexander Nikolaevich Golitsyn,

minister of education and spiritual affairs, decrying the paucity of resources directed at Crimea, where many Tatars "had already begun to
read the holy scriptures" and were in need of further guidance. According to the Baron de Bode, resident pomeshchiki felt "little need to fulfill
their obligations to the Christian faith." They did not bother to build
village churches, and their inactivity did little to inspire Tatars to draw
"spiritual sustenance" from Christian practice. Crimea was sorely in
need of church buildings but also priests well versed in scripture, since
Crimean Muslims currently adhered closely to the intricate customs of
their law and would not likely be persuaded to convert to a faith bereft
of such traditions. Moreover, they needed to hear the word of God in
their own language, as learning Russian (or English) in order to understand Christian scripture and ritual presented a formidable obstacle to
conversion.[22]

Some tried their hand at converting the Tatars. Scottish missionaries
settled among the Nogays in the Beştev (Piatigorsk) region of the north
Caucasus in 1802, when members of the Edinburgh Missionary Society
gained permission from Alexander I to "turn various barbarian peoples
to an enlightened position." Reverend Henry Brunton and his fellow
missionaries found precious few followers, eventually pinning their hopes
on one man. Katti Giray, son of the serasker of the Kuban and brother
of Şahin Giray Khan, first came into contact with the missionaries in
1803. He decided to study Arabic with Brunton and within two years
had learned to read English as well as Russian and Turkish. He was baptized in 1807 with the name Aleksandr Ivanovich Sultan-Kırım-Giray
and spent the next nine years in Russian service, first as a court scribe
and later in the military, retiring with the rank of lieutenant. During
these years, the Beşlev mission struggled, and it was not difficult for Katti
to convince his mentors to establish a mission in Crimea, where the
Russian Bible Society was already translating the Gospels into Tatar and
distributing hundreds of copies of the Turkish-language New Testament
and Psalms sent from Scottish missions in Karaş and Astrakhan. The
Scottish Missionary Society set up a station in Bahçesaray in 1821.[23]

In the intervening years, Katti developed a plan for establishing a seminary for "native school-masters and teachers of the word of God," where
he hoped his status as a member of the former ruling house would prove
useful. His friendship with Tsar Alexander I certainly did. Katti struck

up a friendship with Alexander in St. Petersburg: the two went riding whenever the tsar visited Crimea, and Kattı's daughter was a lady-in-waiting at the imperial court. It was his complaints about the "lamentable position of the converted Tatars" that coaxed 5,000 rubles from Alexander. He argued that "the broader enlightenment" of Tatar youths was not necessary. All one had to do to bring about their conversion, Kattı explained, was "to teach them to read the Gospels and other spiritual texts, as well as some of the grammar of their own language so that they will be able to translate the holy scriptures and other important books." Meanwhile, the missionaries convinced local mullas to support (or at least not oppose) the seminary, which they presented as a school for the study of Russian and Turkish languages and natural and social sciences.[24]

Kattı himself arrived in Crimea in November 1821 only to find that the necessary funds had not materialized and that the seminary would not be opened. Undaunted, he used the generous stipend he received from Alexander (some 6,000 rubles annually) to hire a cleric to teach the Russian language and Bible study in Crimean Tatar. Two of the six students at Kattı's school were sons of Sultan Selim Giray of Kerch, who wanted his children "to have a European education and study the Bible," while curiously two others were, in Kattı's words, "studying for the priesthood of the Mohammedan faith." Even this modest and eclectic arrangement proved temporary: Golitsyn closed the school in 1823, and Alexander's death two years later brought the end of official support for the Scottish missions.[25]

Mary Holderness, an Englishwoman living at Karagoz, had high hopes for Kattı Giray's missionary work, which began just after her own departure in 1820. "The residence of the Sultan (the acknowledged descendant of their Khans), may be expected to have great weight and influence in favour of the cause he has engaged in," she wrote, "and I am induced to think, no missionaries will have fewer hardships and privations, or fewer impediments to contend Against, than those of Crim Tatary."[26] Holderness proved wrong on both counts. While the activities of foreign and native missionaries connected Crimea to the broader religious trends sweeping across Russia and Europe in the early nineteenth-century Europe, they did not succeed in integrating the Crimean Tatars into the Christian population of the empire.

KINSHIP, COMMUNITY, THE NOBLE SELF-IDENTIFICATION

Ranks, offices, commendations, and gifts were a much more effective way to forge the desired connections with Crimean society. Rank and office were valuable in and of themselves, but nobles and would-be nobles all over the empire attached enormous importance to the physical manifestations of prestige as well, such as medals, ribbons, jewels, watches, and sabers. Until the late eighteenth century, the tsars made gifts of precious gems and gold drinking vessels to Don Cossack delegations, for example, knowing that they would enhance the prestige of the ataman by highlighting, in an impressively tangible way, his close relationship with the tsar. Members of the Crimean elite received similar gifts. Catherine presented monetary awards to the Şirin bey, Şahin Giray, and various members of the khan's family. Mehmetşa Bey Şirin and several others received timepieces encrusted with diamonds from Prince Zubov, and in 1801 Mufti Seit Mehmed received a gold medal with a portrait of Catherine on one side and an inscription "to Mufti Seit Mehmed for loyal and steadfast service" on the other, worth 172 rubles. In 1808, as some of the exceptional mirzas of Crimea were being sent off to patrol the western border and later fight Napoleon, Governor-General Richelieu distributed gifts to them: for Mufti Murtaza Çelebi a gold medal encrusted with diamonds set on a blue ribbon, for Collegiate Councilors Batyr Aga Krımtay and Ismail Bey Balatukov, Majors Merdimşa Mansur, Atay Şirin, Seit Ibrahim Aga Taşı-oğlu, and Captain Katyrşa Şirin gold watches set with diamonds. Even Nicholas I continued the tradition, granting Major Khan Megmet Bulgakov, for example, 1,000 rubles and a diamond signet ring in 1838.[27]

Nothing was so palpable a connection with the emperor as the award of chivalric orders. It is true that during the Napoleonic wars some orders became so commonplace that their value plummeted, but that was not the case with the Orders of Saints Andrew and Alexander or of the first class of the lesser orders, which were (in principle) made at the discretion of the tsar himself. In a study of the various ranks and orders, Helja Bennett suggests that their distribution was a mechanism for making "real and believable the very assumptions upon which the political culture and autocratic state rested . . . that [the tsar] was personally the source of benefits and advantages, as well as of formal law." While most of the nearly thirty Crimean Tatar officers who returned from the Napoleonic wars as cavaliers did so as members of lesser orders, the effect was much the same. Each award, in the form of a silver medal on a blue ribbon with the inscription "not for ourselves, but for You," signaled the recipient's service to, and therefore bond with, the tsar, as well as his fellow recipients.[28]

These were but a few dozen filaments in what would need to be a dense web of connectivity. The performance of service—civil and military—and distribution of rank provided hundreds of those threads: 217 mirzas acquired civil or military rank between 1783 and 1850, 83 percent of whom earned ranks commensurate with hereditary noble status. Mirzas served in elected office, participated in land survey committees, and even hosted balls for the noble assembly. From the beginning, the participation of men like Iakub Rudzevich, Mehmetşa Bey Şirin, and Mehmetşa Bey Kantakuzin facilitated the administrative integration of the former khanate, and their performance suggested that stock integration techniques might well be enough to transform what Russian officials considered to be an icon of backwardness, such as a Crimean chieftain, into a paragon of enlightenment and civilization. "As far as I am concerned," an elated Governor Kakhovskii wrote to Potemkin in 1787, "[Kantakuzin] is quite necessary and useful to me here . . . as from his person all Muslim learning has been extirpated. *He is truly ours (on sovershenno nash).*"[29]

But over the next seven decades officials would say that about very few Crimeans. Even when articulated on a personal level, the bond between Crimea and the empire proved tenuous; it was one that had to be forged again and again, through a variety of different channels. The particularities of the Crimean context explain some of this. But the particularities of the temporal context explain just as much. Over the course of the eighteenth century, the meaning of nobility—and of belonging to the nobility—changed significantly. The introduction of the Table of Ranks in 1722 lent an air of credibility to the notion of a merit-based rank system, and seemed to signal a shift away from traditional honor- and kinship-based hierarchies toward principles of rationalization and bureaucratization. With Tsar Peter III's emancipation decree in 1762 the figure of the retired gentleman whiling away his hours in quiet contemplation or self-motivated industry on his estate was no longer confined to the realm of fiction. But it was Catherine II who invested heavily in the idea of the enlightened nobleman acting as agent of order and virtue everywhere from her own private theater—where she famously punished immoderate behavior with the consumption of a cold glass of water—to remote governmental posts in Siberia. She convened the legislative assembly of 1767 as a venue for airing grievances and floating ideas about the regulation and function of social status; she issued a series of decrees in 1775, 1778, and 1785 that created the noble assembly as a semi-autonomous entity endowed with specific privileges, powers, and obligations. This process was still unfolding when Catherine annexed the khanate, but already "manners and excellence in foreign languages," a certain refinement of mind and fluency in a particular cultural idiom, were fast becoming indelible marks of social status in Russia.[30]

Catherine's goals were to ensure the sovereign's monopoly on prestige, standardize the curation of noble status, and cultivate an organic link between estate ownership and state service in the provinces. Hierarchy still played an important role. In fact, her policy built distinctions into the foundations and even the documentary regime of noble society, which inscribed individuals in a six-tiered system that made a distinction between noble status based on service record and noble status based on lineage. But the empress balanced this stratification by fostering the development of provincial noble societies which would, in theory, promote a cohesive noble culture and shared sense of identity. Most important, henceforth nobility would be managed locally, according to rules and procedures implemented uniformly across the empire. Noble status would be defined and managed in the provinces, where marshals and assembly deputies vetted each case, compiled the noble register (*rodoslovnaia kniga*) and submitted it to the Heraldry for confirmation. According to this reasoning, the precious patents that flowed out of the Heraldry assuring nobles of their status confirmed the contours of noble society determined in the provinces.[31]

Of course, it did not always work quite that way. The process of defining membership in noble society was particularly fraught in areas dominated by non-Russian elites. Over the years, tsarist officials accrued substantial experience in the art of incorporating Volga Tatars, Baltic Germans, and Polish magnates into imperial society, but the 1785 charter changed everything. The charter, with its insistence on standardizing the definition and ascription of noble status, ran against the grain of general policy in regions like Crimea, where Catherine assured her new subjects that Russian rule would not entail a radical revision of the social hierarchy. The annexation manifesto thus promised, in return for the Tatars' loyalty, "to allow each [subject] all the rights and privileges enjoyed by a Russian of his status (*sostoianie*)" and to protect the faith and laws of the Crimean population. Catherine exempted the Crimeans from the poll tax and military recruitment as well—two of the most onerous burdens imposed on the Russian population—and later announced that the "worthy" among them had the right to acquire officer rank and serve in the provincial government. While it might have seemed obvious that those worthy men—the beys and mirzas—were the natural counterparts of the dvoriane, Catherine said nothing about ennoblement; nor did she ascribe status to any element of the population.[32]

After decades of military and diplomatic encounters, officials were roughly acquainted with the political and social hierarchy of the khanate. They were aware of its clan structure and the power of the karaçi beys, whose influence predated the establishment of the Giray dynasty. Membership in a bey clan had its privileges. Only a karaçi clan had the right to call its chief (often, but not always, the eldest) "bey," a title of social distinction and inherent political power. The beys maintained their own courts, and their rank was inferior only to that of the members of the ruling dynasty. The Şirins, first among equals in many ways, alone had the right to marry daughters of the khans. The turbulent decade between 1774 and 1783 brought scores of lesser mirza power-brokers into the Russian field of vision, but the successful implementation of imperial rule would require a much more systematic familiarity with the identity and position of the indigenous elite.[33]

Catherine's February 1784 decree allowing "Tatar princes and mirzas to enjoy all the privileges of the Russian nobility" is often cited as evidence of the integrative capacity of the nobility and of the ennoblement of mirzas from Bahçesaray to Kazan. It certainly opened a formal space for Muslims within the Russian elite. Nearly five thousand mirzas from 177 clans inscribed their names in the noble registers of Kazan, Saratov, Penza, Riazan, Simbirsk, Orenburg, and Nizhegorod by the time Catherine died, and by 1834 the registers of fifteen different provinces included mirzas. However, the 1784 decree did not actually ascribe noble status. It allowed some mirzas—those whose ancestors had received *pomest'e* from the tsars but who had effectively been removed from the nobility by the 1713 decree barring Muslims from owning serfs—to petition for it, and instructed officials to compile special lists of those "worthy of the privileges granted to the Russian nobility." In other words, technically speaking, it drew an equivalency between dvoriane (Russian nobles) and Tatar elites; a nuance lost on most noble assemblies, who went ahead and inscribed mirza names in the registers.[34]

This ruling was applied to Crimean mirzas in June 1784, in effect linking them to the broader geography of Tatar elites within the empire. Elsewhere, Russian officials had used such equivalencies to the empire's advantage. In the provinces of Left Bank Ukraine (the Hetmanate's autonomy was abolished in 1764) Catherine initially allowed the acceptance of patents from Russian and Polish rulers, evidence of ownership of settled land, or Cossack starshyna status as acceptable proofs of elite position. When written documentation of any kind proved scant, officials accepted the sworn testimony of peers to attest to the lineage of each applicant in accordance with the requirements of the 1785 charter. By 1790, over twenty thousand petitions for noble status from this region alone won approval, and although this number represented less than 2 percent of the provincial population, it was over 20 percent of the (male) noble population of the empire. Even more important than the ethnic and regional imbalance was Catherine's sense that her ennoblement procedures had been manipulated to corroborate claims based on foreign criteria of noble status. The Senate demanded a review and by 1795 removed over ten thousand individuals from the noble registers.[35]

In Crimea, Potemkin instructed Count de Balmen to prepare a complete list of all members of what he called the "Tavrida nobility." When the kaymakams proved reluctant to provide information, Potemkin sent Iakub Rudzevich, a native of Karasubazar and member of the prince's chancellery, to facilitate the production of the reports. Within two months, Rudzevich submitted the first known list of Crimean mirzas. The list named 202 individuals (less than 1 percent of the male Tatar population still resident in the former khanate), 26 percent of whom came from four karaçi clans: the Şirin (15 percent), Argin (5 percent), Mansur (4 percent), and Sicivüt (1 percent). The rest were *kapıhalkı*, or members of the service elite from lesser clans. A year later, Governor Igel'strom convened a commission of mirzas to collect and evaluate the documentary proof of each mirza's status in preparation for compiling the provincial noble register itself. This proved to be a formidable task for noble assemblies across the empire, and one which the Tavrida commission failed to complete: in 1796 Governor-General Zubov reprimanded the man ultimately responsible for compiling the record—provincial marshal Mehmetşa Bey Şirin—for not having discharged his task.[36]

Despite the fact that no register existed, and that neither the empress nor the Heraldry had confirmed that Tatar mirzas were in fact Russian nobles, from the first provincial elections in 1788 they participated in the assembly, dominating its ranks and serving as district and provincial marshals, judges, deputies, and land captains. Thus two important precedents were set: the reliance of Russian officials on the mirzas themselves to define the terms of inclusion in their community, and the ability of the mirzas to carry out the functions of nobility while their formal status in Russian society remained ambiguous.

Over the next few years the government repeatedly reminded noble assemblies throughout the empire that their job was to recognize and document noble status; the tsar alone had the authority to confer it. In order to drive this point home, in February 1803 Alexander I decreed that the sworn testimony of peers was insufficient proof of noble status. The impact of this decision was broad and immediate. French émigré families, for example, had no access to personal or official archives in France, and even wealthy, entrenched Russian nobles were often plagued by problems of insufficient documentation. In a province like Tavrida, where the vast majority of would-be nobles offered only the testimony of peers as proof of their descent from elite clans, this was potentially catastrophic.[37]

Then again, for years the Crimean elite had been lobbying for confirmation of the privileges outlined in the annexation manifesto rather than for official noble status. Among those privileges, which provincial marshal Mehmetşa Bey Şirin outlined in a petition to Zubov, were exemption from taxation, recruitment, and the obligation to provide quarter for Russian soldiers; recognition of the heritability of noble and ulema status as determined by Muslim law; and preservation of property rights as practiced under the khans. Mehmetşa followed this petition with an eloquent but insistent letter (in French) to Catherine herself. "We prostrate ourselves at Your Imperial Majesty's feet," he wrote, "and humbly entreat you, in the name of the clergy, the nobility, and the Tatar people of Tauride, to cast a favorable gaze on our nation and provide us with happiness from this day forward by deigning to grant us what You, in Your mercy, promise us."[38]

Zubov's response, the rescript of 1796, shaped a debate that ensued over the next fifty years. The rescript confirmed the "rights" enumerated in Mehmetşa Bey's petition. As a result, the Tatar population as a whole secured a series of privileges that rendered noble status, like conversion to Orthodoxy, redundant—at least in economic terms. In that moment "Crimean Tatar" emerged as a social category of its own: economic, legal, and social rights could henceforth be determined not by whether one was noble or common, but by whether one was a Crimean Tatar or not.[39]

In an effort to sort out what all of this implied for the provincial nobility, Governor G. P. Miloradovich convinced the tsar to convene a special commission to determine once and for all the status and composition of the Crimean elite. The Commission on the Noble Status of Muslim and Greek Clans opened in August 1803, staffed with both Russians and Tatars. Provincial marshal E. S. Notara, though hardly a blind supporter of mirza interests, expressed his approval of the commission's agenda. "The Tatar beys and mirzas of this province do not simply belong to noble society," he informed the minister of justice, "they constitute it." Notara did not anticipate any great difficulties in achieving this end, since their traditional elite status was clear to all. But as petitions from Greeks as well as mirzas poured into Simferopol it became clear that a definitive set of guidelines was needed to navigate the muddy waters of exceptional circumstance, cultural difference, and imperial standards.[40]

From the point of view of the mirzas, the matter was straightforward. The Crimean definition of nobility held that elite social status depended not on service or proximity to the khan, but rather on the prestige and power an individual or his clan accrued independently. The number and alignment of clans that composed the ruling elite of the khanate varied over time, but the main contours remained constant. The khan, his sons, and other members of the Giray dynasty occupied the top level of the hierarchy, followed by other descendants of the Chingissid house. The most powerful clans, known as the karaçi, included a varying combination of the Şirin, Mansur, Sicivüt, Argin, Kipchat, and Iaşlav clans. Next came the "princely" clans—the Kipchat, Kekuvat, Balatuk, Salgir, and Dair clans—who traced their origins to the Adyge (Cherkess) of the north Caucasus, followed by the lesser clans headed by mirzas, and finally the kapıhalkı—vassals or dependents who did not originally enjoy the hereditary title of mirza. This was the description mirza delegates provided to Governor Mertvago in response to his 1807 request for a report on "who among the mirza clans ought to be considered beys." This, they assured him, was the architecture of what they referred to in various documents as the "Tatar nobility," "Muslim nobility," or, on occasion, the "Muslim estate" (*magometanskoe soslovie*).[41]

The mirzas' primary goal was to preserve the integrity of the Crimean elite and the prestige of mirza status: a status that patents of Russian nobility could confirm but only lineage could confer. Members of the most powerful clans thus had a stake in the process of identifying legitimate members of the "Muslim nobility." In fact, well over half of those who affixed their seals or signatures to documents attesting to noble "worthiness" were members of the karaçi clans. Haji Ibrahim Aga Emirov's 1797 petition is an excellent example. It included five *firmans* from Crimean khans, three Russian *attestats* describing the petitioner's military service, and the testimony of thirteen peers. "We the native (*prirodnye*) nobles of Tavrida who have affixed our signatures below," began the testimony, "in accordance with the terms of the charter to the Russian nobility . . . do testify in regard to Ensign Emir Haji Ibrahim Aga and his brothers Abdul-Kerim and Samadin, that before the annexation of the Crimean peninsula to the rule of the most glorious Russian state, their fathers and grandfathers served the sovereign khans. They descended from the knee of the Emirs, have not deviated from the standards expected of them by virtue of their birth, and conduct themselves in the manner of noblemen." The list of witnesses included Captain Arslanşa Mirza Şirin, Prince Mehmetşa Bey Kantakuzin, State Councilor Mehmet Aga Biiarslan, and senior members of the Argin, Iaşlav, and Mansur clans, all of whom had either achieved noble rank or been elected to a position of authority in the provincial administration. Their testimony served as a social currency within Crimea, shoring up the role of a small cluster of mirzas as custodians of both the traditional and imperial social orders.[42]

This definition of elite origins presented a fundamental contradiction to the formal insistence that all prestige and power derived from the tsar. At the same time, throughout most of Russian history lineage was a far more accurate measure of prestige and power than anything else.

Genealogies were therefore useful tools for maintaining kinship bonds as well as the host of other interests bound up with them. They were, in the words of an historian of *nobiliários* in early modern Portugal, "social accreditation mechanism[s], with [their] field of action and influence expanding according to people's expectations and needs." The efficacy of such mechanisms improved dramatically when paired with antiquity of lineage and, as it did throughout the early modern world, the attraction of antiquity encouraged subjects of the tsars to indulge in occasional manipulations of the historical record. Fabrication was tolerated within certain limits, but there were narrative conventions to follow and hierarchies to respect. This was particularly so in the wake of regime change, as local practices came under the scrutiny of new authority.[43]

The genealogies of Crimea's elite clans dated back generations, if not centuries, and many boasted roots going back to the Kipchak Khanate (Golden Horde). The Giray dynasty descended from the "white bone"— the Chingissid line that had once dominated the Eurasian steppe. The Şirin clan looked back to the Volga region and a progenitor whose son, Ruktemir, was a constant companion and brother-in-law of Khan Tokhtamysh (d. 1395). The Mansurs identified their clan founder as Davii Bey: a great chieftain in his own right, an adversary of Tokhtamysh, and the great-great-grandson of Edige (from whom Russia's Iusupov princes claimed descent as well).[44]

Mirzas from lesser clans were under added pressure to compose pitch-perfect genealogies. In 1804, Abduraman Ulan-oğlu submitted a genealogy that traced the clan to no less a personage than Oğuz Khan, the founder of the Hun and (through descendants) Seljuk dynasties. According to his testimony, the family descended from the fifth son of Tiag Khan, "who ruled one of the successor states of the Mogul realm when it was divided among the six sons of Oğuz." Abduraman explained that Tiag Khan's sons ruled as a result of their "superior descent—unsurpassed among eastern rulers—their excellent physical strength and penetrating intellect." Eventually, Abduraman's direct ancestor moved westward to the Kipchak lands and from there to Crimea, where he received hereditary land grants from Sahib Giray Khan (reigned 1532–1551). These lands passed from generation to generation until they came into the possession of Abduraman himself.[45]

Russian authorities did not challenge the authenticity of such claims. Because mirza genealogies had to be approved by peers, there was little point claiming a lineage that either had no legitimacy or that explicitly challenged the primacy of the elite clans. This is at least part of the reason why so few mirzas claimed anything more than to have descended "from an ancient noble clan." It explains why Abduraman took care to describe his ancestor as the fifth son of Tiag Khan, for he was well aware of the importance of birth order, one of the three distinguishing characteristics of the typical lineage structure of Central Asian clans (along with genealogical distance and generational distance). Abduraman mitigated any potential resistance to his claim by admitting the existence of lineages superior to his own, as well as by locating the source of his status beyond the borders of the Crimean-Volga tradition yet still within the prestigious geography of Turkic empires.

Others were less discerning. When the Perekop lower land court inquired in 1822 about the status of the mysterious Mengli Mirza Adyloğlu, the assembly replied that despite his claim to be a kinsman of the Krımtay clan he was merely a poor bachelor from the village of Dair whose link to the Krımtays was tenuous at best. The mirzas showed a similarly cool response to the claims of Ignatii Vasilevich Tatarinov, formerly known as Ali Dzhangiz Giray Sultan. Tatarinov had enlisted in the Russian army in 1775, retired, entered civil service, and earned the rank of titular councilor. His saga, recounted in a lengthy petition submitted to the Ministry of Internal Affairs, began with his return to Crimea from Moscow in 1794. There he found his deceased brother's wife and children "poverty stricken, the lands, gardens and other properties belonging to the clan having been both wrongly distributed to various people by the local government, and despotically appropriated by the state."[46]

Tatarinov's subsequent petitions reflect the intimate knowledge of the Russian system he gained working as a *striapchii* in the provincial courts. He grounded his arguments, however, in principles of kinship familiar to any Crimean. Upon the death of one of Tatarinov's uncles and the emigration of another, he explained, "the Giray clan's hereditary estates, which from antiquity were held as one and included villages, lands, and other properties in various locations throughout Crimea and Taman, passed by the right of inheritance into the possession of the third brother." This brother swore an oath of loyalty to the Russian sovereign before passing away and leaving his property to his wife, three young sons, and five daughters. Although Tatarinov declared that he wanted to restore the lands to his nephews, his claim to be their uncle implied that he, the eldest surviving male, was the rightful heir.[47]

He would get nowhere without an accepted genealogy. But Tatarinov's incessant petitions made enemies of many of the men who had acquired the Giray lands, some of whom exercised a great deal of authority in the province. When the governor began making inquiries into the matter and found that Tatarinov could not produce a shred of evidence to back up his claims, he countered that Chingissids had never required documents to prove their descent. He was a Giray sultan, he argued, if the general public recognized him as such. By calling himself a Giray and playing the part with some skill, he was able to convince at least a portion of the population to treat him with honor. But he had trouble winning over the elite. When officials consulted the mufti in 1808, he claimed that he had never heard of Tatarinov or Ali Dzhangiz Giray for that matter. The beys agreed. Tatarinov was no Giray prince and had no claim to the family's estates. Nevertheless, despite the fact that Tatarinov's nephews submitted a single piece of evidence—a genealogy composed by none other than Tatarinov—the assembly recognized them as legitimate sultans and "foreign" nobles. The social status of Crimeans, everyone concurred, relied not on documentation but on custom and the collective memory of peers and kin. That collective memory could be tweaked on occasion, especially when it meant reclaiming land from voracious settlers on behalf of the Tatar people—even Tatars of such dubious claim to honor and status.[48]

In early 1815 the Senate solicited the advice of the former governor-general of New Russia, the duc de Richelieu. The situation in Tavrida, Richelieu explained, was unique. While a smattering of Greeks were able to produce documents attesting to their noble worthiness—either from the patriarch of Constantinople or from officers of the Black Sea fleet—most Tatars offered nothing but peer testimony regarding the legitimacy of their noble lineage. Richelieu felt the government was obliged to give greater latitude to the Tatars and consider the historical and cultural differences between Russia and the "Asiatic" states, wherein members of the elite were recognized by virtue of clan affiliation rather than an accumulation of written documents. The descendants of the bey clans, high-ranking servants of the khans, and Nogay chiefs, Richelieu suggested, should be required to submit a combination of genealogies and peer testimonies—nothing more. When the Senate and State Council accepted Richelieu's proposals it seemed the Crimean and Chingissid land-scapes had been successfully integrated into the geography of imperial nobility.[49]

In order to implement this vision, in August 1816 Alexander estab-lished a new commission chaired by the mufti and staffed by represen-tatives from the bey clans, kapıhalkı, and Greeks. The commission, like its counterparts in Bessarabia and the Caucasus, worked intermittently for over a decade. During that time it recommended everyone, from Cherkess princes to low-ranking service mirzas, for inscription in the fourth part of the noble register—that reserved for foreign elites. Even men with exemplary military and civil service records, such as Captain Kasim Argin and his brother, Court Councilor Mehmetşa Argin, regis-tered as foreign nobles because of the fame, antiquity, and honor of their clan. Ismail Bey Balatukov, who petitioned for noble status on the basis of descent from a line of Cherkess princes, chafed when the Heraldry defined him as noble by virtue of his civil rank. Several years later, the commission received a petition from Ismail's son, Lieutenant Kazy Bey. "Although the Heraldry ordered that my clan, along with others, be entered in the third part of the noble register," wrote Kazy, "because our ancestors descended from Cherkess princes I request examination of the distinguished evidence [to that effect] and inscription in the fourth part of the register." True to form, the commission recom-mended Kazy and his younger brother for confirmation as nobles of foreign origin.[50]

The commission was not as conservative as it might appear: in some cases it pushed the borders of Crimean elite society into uncharted ter-rain. Confronted with the petitions of a group of twenty-one "çelebis," or high-ranking clerics, who "under the rule of the khans constituted a distinct class from the beys and mirzas," the commission decided to in-novate. Its members found that "because of their prestigious backgrounds and the service of their ancestors they [nevertheless] exercised the rights of nobles as well." Mufti Seit Dzhelal Çelebi and his brothers in fact presented some of the most thoroughly documented cases, with firmans attesting to service on the khan's divan, pension grants to their forefathers from both sultans and khans, metrical documents confirm-ing the legitimacy of their births, sworn testimonies as to the prestige and honor of their clan, and proof of their possession of inherited estates.[51]

As the Çelebi case shows, documentation (and a bit of goodwill) could get you anywhere. Lack of documentation could be overcome, but no one received noble status without petitioning for it. For that reason it is difficult to know whether the petitions for noble status describe a Tatar community which, by 1820, had shifted dramatically, or had simply exposed itself to quantification for the first time. It is certainly true that petitions from mirzas of lesser clans vastly outnumbered those from the hereditary elite—the karaçi and princely clans (tables 2.1 and 2.2). Moreover, twenty-six of the forty Tatars inscribed in the noble registers and approved by the Senate (up to 1853) were members of clans that had no place among the elite of the former khanate. Defining—even creating—a clan identity clearly paid dividends.[52]

The continuities in mirza society are nevertheless striking. Despite being outnumbered, the hereditary elite clans remained powerful. Between 1783 and 1840, members of the bey clans accounted for nearly 20 percent of mirzas participating in noble assembly elections, and nearly 30 percent of those elected. Between 1783 and 1853, members of hereditary elite clans made up only 12 percent of the total mirza population (as I have

Table 2.1. Mirza Petitions Submitted to Governor-General Langeron, December 1820

	Karaçi clans	Princely clans	Major service clans	Minor clans/ unnamed	Total
Petitioners	5 (9.6%)	3 (5.8%)	14 (26.9%)	30 (57.7%)	52
Criteria for noble status cited in the petitions (percentage of status group)					
Lineage	40.0	100.0	50.0	50.0	51.9%
Own service	60.0	100.0	35.7	20.0	32.7%
Service of forefathers	40.0	66.7	71.4	83.3	75.0%
Noble rank	60.0	66.7	14.3	6.7	17.3%
Land ownership	0.0	0.0	35.7	63.3	46.2%
Noble lifestyle	0.0	0.0	21.4	33.3	25.0%
Oath of allegiance	20.0	0.0	0.0	10.0	7.7%

Source: Compiled from DAARK f. 49, op. 1, d. 607: 1–137. There are 124 individuals mentioned in these 52 petitions. The identities of the main applicants only are plotted here.

Table 2.2. Clan Types as Percentage of Mirza Population, 1783–1853

	All Mirzas (1,194)	With rank (217)	With noble rank (184)	Petitioners for noble status (622)	Inscribed in noble register (40)
Hereditary elite	12.4	28.6	27.7	9.6	35.0
Bey clans	9.8	20.3	17.9	6.1	20.0
Princely clans	2.6	8.3	9.8	3.5	15.0
Kapıhalkı	40.0	54.4	57.1	58.7	62.5
Major service clans	15.1	26.3	23.9	23.3	35.0
Other service clans	25.0	28.1	33.2	35.	27.5
No clan designation[a]	47.6	17.0	15.2	31.7	2.5

Sources: Data compiled from RGIA f. 1343, op. 51, dela 485–496 (Tavrida noble registers for the years 1804, 1830–1844); RGIA f. 1343, op. 51, d. 664 (nobles with provincial approval, 1815–1861); DAARK f. 49, op. 1, d. 6559 (mirza petitioners to the Tavrida commission on nobility in 1820); DAARK f. 49, op. 1, d. 1,026 (district-level noble registers for 1831).

[a] Many of those classified as without clan designation used a place name as an identifier ("Mehmet Mirza of Sarabuz").

been able to reconstruct it) and less than 10 percent of those who petitioned for noble status; yet they accounted for 28 percent of mirzas with noble rank and 35 *percent* of mirzas confirmed by the Senate as nobles. At the other end of the spectrum were the mirzas who did not identify themselves with any clan. They were by far the majority of petitioners (over 48 percent), but by far the least successful at convincing the Senate of the legitimacy of their status claims.

If this data is any indication, the structure of the Crimean elite remained more or less intact, with the hereditary elite enjoying more social and political power per capita than newly established clans or those who based their claim to elite status on the merits of their service, their status as landowners, or their "noble lifestyle." Thus while the tsar and Senate conceived the Commission on Muslim and Greek Clans as an instrument of integration and standardization, Crimeans used it to formalize the distinction between themselves and the rest of noble society, and to maintain the hierarchical structure that had defined them for centuries.

NARROWING THE TERMS OF INCLUSION

The viability of this system died with Alexander I. In February 1828 his successor, Nicholas I, moved to reestablish oversight over the ennoblement process throughout the empire. He instructed the Senate to investigate reports of rampant abuse, such as the submission of falsified documents and fabricated genealogies, and draft a set of corrective measures. Almost immediately the government turned its attention to Tavrida and its mirzas. In 1830 Dmitrii Bludov, then acting minister of justice, initiated an inquiry. "What are the rights and privileges of the mirzas and upon what are they based?" he asked provincial officials. What evidence were they required to present, and what rules had the Senate applied to such cases? Most tellingly, Bludov wanted to know whether the existing rules were "sufficient to diminish the number of petitioners, or must new ones be added to account for the poor education of the Tatars and their co-religionists, as well as their practice of polygamy, which without a doubt ought to complicate the confirmation of their noble status?"[53]

The government's concern with the education and morality of the mirzas reflected a growing unease with the previous willingness to tie social and economic privileges to ethnic and cultural differences. Nicholaevan officials saw increasingly negative implications in the persistence of separate elite cultures. The rise of nationalism in the Polish and Ukrainian provinces and the fierce resistance mounted by Muslim peoples in the north Caucasus certainly played a role, but the decision to redefine noble society was not directed against non-Russian elites per se. It was part of a concerted effort to centralize and enhance control over all of imperial society—an effort that was for Tsar Nicholas nothing less than a guiding principle of rule after the Decembrist revolt of 1825. Nicholas envisioned an Orthodox, Russian-speaking community protected by and devoted to the autocrat in St. Petersburg; the notion of "official nationality" announced by Minister of Education Count Sergei Uvarov in 1833 declared the principles of Orthodoxy, autocracy, and nationality to be the foundation of the Russian state and society. As Nicholas Riasanovsky points out, the proponents of this idea "put their faith in general in men rather than in institutions." It mattered now, more than ever before, that the men serving the tsar and preserving order throughout the empire meet specific criteria with regard to education, morality, and loyalty.[54]

As it had done before, the outbreak of yet another Russian-Ottoman war in 1828 reignited suspicions about the depth of Tatar loyalty. Russian authorities certainly did not have to look far to be reminded of the political implications of Islam on the Ottoman frontier: in December 1827, Sultan Mahmud II "exhorted all Muslims everywhere to wage a Holy War against Russia." According to the sultan, this would not be a war over territory, but "a struggle for the faith and for our national existence. Each of us, whether rich or poor, great or small, must look upon this struggle as a sacred duty."[55] The political implications of being Muslim in Tavrida were again at issue. The Tavrida provincial government refused to issue passports to pilgrims for fear that *hajis* would return from Mecca with a renewed sense of religious identity that was sure to foment revolt. Despite a litany of demonstrations of Crimean allegiance, from participation in the Napoleonic wars to the formation of the Crimean Tatar Life Guard regiment, officials constantly suspected that resentment against Russian rule was brewing.

The tendency to focus suspicions on one or two individuals says as much about continuities in Tatar social structures as it does about the Russian understanding of power relationships. For provincial governors and their lieutenants, the multitude of administrative jurisdictions— courts, assemblies, committees, boards—had their place, but real power was exercised through status, whether defined in imperial or local terms. Even a man as sympathetic to the Tatar position as Governor Naryshkin grew worried when he began fielding reports that Mehmet Krımtay might be inciting the population to revolt. Krımtay, who was born in 1785 and enjoyed a long career in civil service, serving at least three terms as district marshal of Perekop and Simferopol, was one of the wealthiest and most powerful mirzas in the province. But in 1828 he came under investigation for the 1822 murder of three men caught trespassing on his land. The influence he had accrued, complained Naryshkin, ought not be enjoyed by a man "whose moral standing was compromised by the crimes of which he was accused," particularly since Naryshkin now doubted Krımtay's allegiance.

Krımtay had obtained permission to travel to St. Petersburg, where his case was under review by the Senate. Naryshkin suggested that when he arrived in Odessa with his companion, Lieutenant Colonel Ahmet Bey Khunkalov, he should be detained and held until the conclusion of hostilities with the Porte. Vorontsov agreed. He solicited the opinions of Lieutenant Colonel Prince Adyl Bey Balatukov, another prominent

Crimean leader, and several officials in Odessa. "I am in agreement with the opinion of the governor regarding the temporary removal of Provincial Secretary Krımtay from Crimea," wrote one of the latter, "although at the present time I cannot imagine that Krımtay was conducting any business [in Crimea] that would be dangerous to the government." Vorontsov arranged for the military governor of St. Petersburg to keep Krımtay under surveillance.[56]

At some point after the ratification of the treaty of Adrianople (Edirne) in September 1829, Krımtay made his way home, a cloud of suspicion following him. For the next five years, Simferopol city police kept both him and Adyl Balatukov under constant surveillance. In fact, for most of that period they were the only two men under surveillance in Simferopol district. (Evpatoriia authorities, by contrast, had 146 men under surveillance: 122 Tatars accused of stealing horses and other livestock, and twenty-four non-Tatars under surveillance because of their "uncivilized appearance [nepis'mennyj vid].") Both were ordered to remain on their estates; both men refused. Instead, they made a point of traveling from town to town and "interfering in all sorts of matters that had nothing whatsoever to do with them." Worse still (from Naryshkin's point of view) Balatukov constantly gathered crowds of Tatars in his home in Simferopol district, which functioned as "the local divan." There they discussed many things—although what they were the local land captain could not say, because neither he nor his men understood Tatar, let alone Turkish.[57]

Vorontsov and Governor Kaznacheev (who replaced Naryshkin in 1829) both understood the amount of influence Balatukov and Krımtay wielded within the Tatar population. They also understood that that influence did not derive from their respective ranks as provincial secretary and lieutenant colonel, but rather from sources of authority rooted in networks and traditions that imperial institutions did not control. In this Crimea's elite was not unique. In fact, the government's awareness of the strength of such local networks spurred an 1833 statute forbidding the assignment of soldiers and noncommissioned officers to police and fire units in their native towns or districts, for fear that "the force of local ties and loyalties" would deter them from performing unpleasant and often repressive police duties. The growing aversion to local power networks also helps explain a 1831 Senate order that all noble titles—not just those claimed by non-Russians—be examined by special commissions. "Revision commissions" sprang up all over the empire, particularly in provinces where the Senate identified an abuse of power by the noble assembly and the confirmation of unworthy nobles. In some regions, the work of these commissions utterly transformed noble society. Some 72,000 names were struck from the registers of Podolia, Volhynia, and Kiev, while the Olonetsk commission determined that almost half the ennobled families in that province were registered incorrectly. Elsewhere, the effect was muted. The review of Georgian petitions carried out in 1844 declared twenty-five cases false and fifty-one "dubious" in nature, but the vast majority (424) authentic.[58]

Location and ethnicity alone do not explain the different outcomes. But together they explain what happened in Tavrida. The stakes were high in the Black Sea, and higher still among Muslims. And when the Tavrida noble assembly stepped up its scrutiny, changes came quickly. Almost immediately the provincial marshal began transferring mirzas and Greeks to the second and third parts of the noble register in an effort to diminish the perception that in the former khanate prestige might derive from anything but Romanov favor. Very few mirzas sensed (or reacted to) the changing tide. Captain Ali Mirza Şirin requested that the assembly revise its decision to define him as a foreign noble, insisting that his claim rested on the fact "that he received the rank of captain and possessed landed property" like any other dvorianin. But most waited for the revision commission to carry out its investigations. The commission opened in 1836 and began reviewing each and every case approved by the assembly since the compilation of the province's first noble register in 1804. The four-man commission reviewed approximately two hundred cases and, like commissions throughout the empire, transferred nearly every noble inscribed in the fourth to the first, second, and third parts of the register.[59]

Reshuffling entries in the noble registers was an essential component of the redefinition of nobility, but it was only the beginning. In March 1840 the State Council at long last announced the criteria by which the imperial government would officially judge Crimean Muslim (and Greek) claims to noble status. The council declared that petitioners could pursue any of three strategies. First, they had the option of proving that they or their predecessors had become Russian subjects and obtained rank through service to the tsar. Second, they could attempt to prove that they had come to Russia prior to 1805, been recognized as a noble at the provincial level, and obtained immovable property through purchase or inheritance. Muslims had the additional option of proving that they had owned their estates before 1783 and subsequently served as elected officials. Anyone who met these criteria had to prove authenticity of lineage by submitting birth and marriage documents drawn from metrical registers, and a genealogy verified by the provincial marshal and close relatives whose noble status had already been confirmed. Finally, the council required each petitioner to submit the sworn testimony of the provincial marshal and twelve nobles regarding his education and lifestyle.[60]

Only a handful of petitions contained this range of documentation. In fact, most applicants were born or married well before the government established metrical registers for Tavridan Muslims in 1831. The new guidelines thus stripped nearly every case of mirza nobility of its validity. The Heraldry sent hundreds of previously approved petitions back to Simferopol for supplementary documentation. It cited Seitşa Ahmetov, for example, for failing to include evidence of either inheriting land owned by his family prior to 1783 or having been educated "in the proper manner." Er Mambet Dzhamin suffered disqualification because his rank as *sotnik* in the Crimean Tatar cavalry regiment was not equivalent to that of a regular officer. Even members of the bey clans could not generate sufficient evidence to satisfy the Heraldry. In 1847 Nietşa Bey Iaşlav tried to convince officials of the legitimacy of his status, arguing that his was "one of the seven bey clans known by all to have descended from the ancient conquerors of Crimea and to still compose its elite." Successive khans had issued firmans confirming his forefathers' estates and testifying to their morality and prestige. Nietşa Bey even composed a detailed genealogy, but his efforts were in vain.[61]

For all but a few exceptional cases (forty out of 295), the 1840 State Council decision effectively ended the process of mirza ennoblement in Crimea. The impact of this watershed was anything but local. Sixty years earlier Catherine II's decision to apply the decree on Tatar princes and mirzas to Crimea had briefly reinvented the southern steppe and lower Volga as a continuous landscape of Muslim Tatar elites. In subsequent years neither the mirzas nor imperial officials embraced that strategy, and elite integration followed different trajectories in various parts of the empire. By the end of 1796 for example, Paul I had confirmed more than a dozen of Orenburg's Tatar clans, while it took forty years longer for the same number of Crimean clans to gain confirmation. Meanwhile the empire itself ceased to exist while Azerbaidzhani *begs* waited for the Senate to rule on their status. Special dispensations, procedural idiosyncrasies, gradations of all kinds—all of these created meaningful distinctions between regions and between the elite groups that inhabited them. While these distinctions never completely dissolved, the imperial government's ennoblement policies began forging linkages among non-Russian, and specifically Muslim, elites.[62] Beginning in 1841 the Senate adapted the terms of the State Council opinion on Tavrida's Muslim and Greek clans to conditions in Orenburg and Vilna, where noble assemblies faced similar challenges from Bashkirs, Mordvinians, and Lithuanian Tatars. The government also applied the model of the Commission on Muslim and Greek Clans to the Caucasus, where Viceroy M. S. Vorontsov and his successor, Grand Prince Mikhail Nikolaevich, were attempting to determine the complexion of the hereditary local elite. Would such cross-regional connections prove less troublesome than local networks? Would it be easier for Crimean Tatars to find common ground with co-religionists in Turkestan or the Kazakh steppe?[63]

NOBILITY AND THE BUILT ENVIRONMENT

The rapid progression from annexation in April 1783 to Catherine's decision to apply the terms of the provincial reform (February 1784) and the charter to the nobility (1785) pulled the new province and its Muslim elite into broadly conceived transformations of the administrative and social order. During the next fifty-five years the rules, the stakes, even the meaning of noble status, were in flux across time and space. Throughout this period the majority of Crimeans argued that they merited the privileges of Russian nobility by virtue of being mirzas, and they therefore sought confirmation of the equivalency Catherine herself had drawn between mirzas and dvoriane in the early days of Russian rule. By 1827, 295 mirza petitions had gained the approval of provincial officials, and most everyone had considered the matter resolved.[64]

Yet even those who acquired ranks, medals, orders, and estates tended to maintain their religious and cultural identity, confirming the relevance of non-Russian lifestyles and the persistence of alternate sources of prestige. With very few exceptions, they did not convert to Christianity, adopt Russian costume, or learn the Russian language. They were not blind to the correlation Russians drew between manners, morality, and noble worthiness (*dvorianskoe dostoinstvo*). In fact, they took care to include documents attesting to their "noble" behavior in petitions for noble status in an effort to preempt attacks on their integrity and morality. They were aware of the link that the Nicholaevan government was elaborating between cultural identity and belonging, between Russianness and nobility. But the government debated long and hard over whether, as an unnamed official suggested as early as 1809, "the most precious goal ought to be the creation of connections between Tatars, Karaims, and Armenians with Russians," or whether the empire was better off simply allowing the mirzas to withdraw into their courtyards, pastures, and mosques.[65]

Most officials would have dismissed out of hand the idea that the government could allow the mirzas to withdraw into their courtyards, pastures, and mosques and suffer no repercussions. The built environment in particular was nearly as crucial a site of noble culture and identity as the noble assembly, or even the noble register itself. For centuries, members of the Crimean elite had expressed power, wealth, and status in wood and stone, building mosques, fountains, caravansarays, mausoleums, and other structures. On one level these sites communicated personal messages of familial affection or spirituality. At the same time, they embedded Crimea in the vast cultural space of the Ottoman Empire and the steppe.

Wealthy patrons concentrated their building projects in urban areas, where mosques stood as prominent expressions of the munificence and cultural sophistication of the ruling elite. Both Karasubazar and Gözleve had a wealth of such monuments, as did Bahçesaray. Shrines were just as important, however, and many of them clustered around the khan's capital. The tomb of Hacı Giray Khan, founder of the dynasty, was located nearby, at Salachik (Salacıq, figure 2.1). Built by his son, Mengli Giray, the octagonal structure was richly decorated with arabesques and moldings, slender columns, and *muqarnas* (ornamental vaulting). The final resting place of two khans, the tomb was a significant site on its own. But in visual terms, its architectural elements linked it to the tomb of Nenkedzhan Hanim, the daughter of Tokhtamysh Khan, who was buried at nearby Chufut Kale; Tatars who visited these sites could not

Figure 2.1. Tomb of Mengli Giray near Bahçesaray; from Uvarov, *Sobranie* (General Research Division, The New York Public Library, Astor, Lenox, and Tilden Foundations)

miss the symbolic connection between the Giray dynasty, the Kipchak Khanate (Golden Horde), and the notion of Chingissid descent. Perhaps the most venerated shrine of all was at Eski Yurt, a village just west of Bahçesaray. The site contained a mosque and four *türbes* (tombs) from the fifteenth and sixteenth centuries, as well as the shrine of Malik Aşter, a seventh-century military leader. A trio of khans—Mehmed III, Mehmed IV, and Saadet II (father, son, and grandson)—were buried in one of the tombs, forging a direct link between the Giray dynasty and the golden age of Islamic expansion. Sites such as these demonstrated the wealth and status of the former ruling house and created a geography of religious and political authority that extended well beyond the administrative borders within which Russian authorities hoped to confine Tavrida.[66]

Russian invasion, civil war, and two Russian-Ottoman wars (1787–1791 and 1806–1812) took a heavy toll on the Crimean economy, and it was not until the 1820s that private construction began again in earnest. When it did, khans and mirzas had largely been replaced by Russian nobles. Beyond the gilt ballrooms and exclusive salons of St. Petersburg, much of Russian noble life took place in a landscape of hunting grounds, grain fields, and manor homes described in exquisite detail by writers such as Turgenev and Bunin. Architecture played an important role in shaping the noble presence in the countryside, particularly during what Priscilla Roosevelt describes as the "golden age of estate-building," from 1762 until 1830. Throughout those decades architects made the rounds of the provinces, where wealthy patrons wanted palaces and churches to decorate their estates. Imperial legislation did not regulate estate architecture, and noble landowners invested in varying degrees of stylistic imitation and innovation, either of which, when done well, signaled the property owner's membership in the privileged elite of the empire. In fact, the blurred boundary between private and public spheres in Russia meant that the provincial residence of a member of the nobility often embodied the presence and power of the central government. In the borderlands, building *usad'by* (noble manor houses) was a widely accepted and highly effective way of physically marking the terrain as part of imperial space.[67]

The first major usad'ba built on the Crimean coast belonged to the military governor of New Russia, the duc de Richelieu. Richelieu acquired a 140-desiatina property at Gurzuf in 1808 and within three years threw a five-day housewarming party for his new "Greek style" residence. Soon thereafter, Lieutenant General A. M. Borozdin, governor of Tavrida 1807–1816, completed a much-admired two-story house at Küçük Lampat. Other landowners followed suit, building country homes around Feodosiia and Simferopol as well as along the sought-after southern coast. Within decades, the constellation of imperial elites with residences in Crimea included Naryshkins, Golitsyns, Perovskiis, and Kochubeis, military brass and entrepreneurs such as General N. N. Raevskii, hero of the battle of Borodino, Admiral N. S. Mordvinov, and Nikolai N. Demidov.[68]

Rather than recreate the architecture of St. Petersburg on the Black Sea, many of those well-connected and well-to-do landowners made a conscious effort to accentuate the foreignness of Crimea in the architecture of their estates and palaces. For some, the distinctiveness of the landscape was rooted in its Greek legacy. Russians and foreigners alike pointed excitedly to the tangible residue of the classical legacy which suddenly restored Tavrida to the intellectual and cultural map of western civilization. The Belgian Prince de Ligne, who accompanied Catherine on her journey through the southern provinces, delighted in exploring sites associated with the writings of Herodotus and Strabo, setting eyes on "Eupatoria, founded by Mithridates" and picking through the fragments of alabaster columns strewn about the ruins of Khersones. Not surprisingly, Grecian elements dominated many nineteenth-century buildings, such as Richelieu's house at Gurzuf, which was surrounded on three sides by a colonnaded gallery and boasted symmetry and simplicity in its design.[69]

Other nobles incorporated a more "exotic" or "Asiatic" legacy into their domestic landscapes. To some this meant preserving the atmosphere experienced by Lady Elizabeth Craven who, traveling just ahead of Catherine II in 1786, was struck by the sense that here the natural and cultural landscapes were in agreement with one another. A long line of travelers, scholars, and writers echoed this sentiment, remarking on the organic relationship between the cypress trees and minarets of Bahçe-saray, between the date palms and marble columns scattered along the coast. This inspired the Perovskiis to feature a composite design at Mellas, where elements common in Islamic architecture, such as arches, niches, and arabesques, shaped the interior. At Simeiz and Miskhor the Mal'tsovs and Naryshkins pleased their guests with minaret-shaped chimneys and window casings "in the typical eastern style." And at Alupka, Governor-General Vorontsov created the most spectacular demonstration of what contemporaries described as "oriental" flair (figure 2.2). Perched atop a cliff running down to the sea, Alupka was "renowned far and wide," according to Kohl, "for its architectural

Figure 2.2. M. S. Vorontsov's residence at Alupka in 1837; from Demidov, *Album* (John Hay Library, Brown University Library)

and Hesperian splendours," the designs of which alone were rumored to have cost upwards of 60,000 rubles. The western side of the palace resembled a medieval castle wall with fortifications; the northern facade was done in the Tudor style; while the southern facade gained the nickname "Alhambra" because of its imposing arch, slender minarets, and a deeply recessed niche with an Arabic inscription reading "There is no God but Allah." It was here that in 1837 Vorontsov entertained the tsar and his entourage in grand style, with fireworks displays and lavish dinners.[70]

The link between estate building and empire building ran deep. Vorontsov, like his peers in British-ruled India, French-ruled Algeria, and Ottoman-ruled Syria, found it not just aesthetically pleasing but also empowering to incorporate elements of the local architectural tradition into his residences. The dignitaries, travelers, and other visi-

Figure 2.3. House in the village of Derekoy; from Demidov, *Album* (John Hay Library, Brown University Library)

tors who penned detailed descriptions of Crimean estates inscribed these structures into the symbolic landscape of the province; but more importantly, the estates served as daily reminders of the reality of imperial authority to those who inhabited neighboring villages and worked in estate orchards and vineyards. Vorontsov took particular pleasure in the story of a mirza who returned to his native Alupka after a lengthy pilgrimage to Mecca. Arriving home he was overcome with confusion, "thinking Allah had deprived him of his reason. Standing on the shore it seemed he was in the magical garden of a thousand and one nights." The transformative power of the empire could hardly be denied when it was embodied in a physical structure that dominated the physical, economic, social, and cultural space around it.[71]

The power of the empire might not be denied, but it was not uniformly embraced. After decades of tsarist rule, the built environment seemed just as likely as the social landscape to send discordant messages. Residences, for example, could as easily function as sites of resistance as sites for emphasizing imperial power. Mosques could serve as markers of benevolent patronage, or as symbols of indifference to and disengagement from the distant capital. Noble assemblies could function as venues for the resolution or the entrenchment of differences. The essential question of empire in 1853 was the same as it had been in 1783: could a Crimean Tatar be a loyal subject of the tsar?

In early October 1853, the kâtib of the Friday mosque in Evpatoriia delivered a remarkable sermon. Seit Ibrahim Efendi proclaimed that in the seventy years since Catherine I annexed the khanate, the Crimean Tatars "not only had never broken their holy oath of subjecthood, but [had] thrived under the scepter of the Russian monarch," who "not only blessed us with personal freedom and guaranteed our faith, customs, and property, but granted us privileges over other estates." Now, on the eve of the Crimean War, Seit Ibrahim continued, "things are difficult for loyal Tatars, who come under suspicion because of the religion they share with the enemies of our Sovereign. Therefore, Crimean beys and mirzas loyal to Russia have come together" on behalf of the Tatar people to beg Tsar Nicholas I "to accept a new oath of our unshakeable loyalty, knowing that should any man break it for whatever reason, he will be disowned by the Crimean Tatar people." The text of the speech, signed by fourteen of the most powerful beys and mirzas (including members of the Şirin, Krımtay, Khunkalov, Argin, and Kipchat clans), made its way to the imperial capital. Soon, the kâtib from Evpatoriia received commendations from Admiral A. S. Menshikov and War Minister Prince Vasilii Andreevich Dolgorukov, along with assurances that the tsar had never questioned the loyalty of the Crimean Tatars.[72]

Loyalties to empire, clan, faith, territory, and eventually even to nation often overlapped in unexpected ways. Historians have developed a language to try to express the range of possibilities for self-ascribed identity—from "dual loyalty" to "double allegiance"—but it is difficult to capture the complex internal and external dynamics of social cohesion.[73] In Tavrida, where much of the population maintained connections with émigré communities in Ottoman lands and the Mediterranean, or traveled across the border to visit family, fight wars, make pilgrimages, or sell shipments of salt or butter, the boundaries defining community crossed imperial borders too. Greeks looked to the Aegean, Mennonites to Prussia, and Crimean Tatars to the Caucasus and Ottoman Empire for meaningful landscapes of integration. Ultimately, the logic of Russian policy toward the Crimean elite reflected the logic of the empire-building project broadly conceived. This was an empire in which the line between integration and isolation could be maddeningly thin; in which power took on a distinctly formal cast on paper, and a distinctly informal case in practice. This was an empire in which difference—defined in ethnic or cultural terms—could be at once a source of empowerment and grounds for suppression. This was, above all else, an empire that strove for consistency and yet thrived on ambiguity; an empire in which it was always more desirable to maintain a network of linkages, policies, and associations than it was to reduce any relationship to simple black and white.

3 Military Service and Social Mobility

IN 1862 THE journal *Morskoi Sbornik* (*The Naval Collection*) published an excerpt from the memoir of a naval doctor recounting life in Sevastopol in 1831. The doctor related a conversation he had with a Karaite entrepreneur named Leiba Ashurovich, who claimed to have witnessed the only armed uprising of Tatars against Russian rule after 1783. The event, as Ashurovich told it, took place in 1810 against the backdrop of yet another Russian-Ottoman war (1806–1812) and was the result of determined efforts by Ottoman agents to stir up resistance among their coreligionists. The agents found, to their surprise, that the most sympathetic Tatar constituency was neither the elders nor the mullas who had lived through annexation, but rather the young men who for all intents and purposes "appeared calm and even happy," yet inwardly chafed against the tsarist regime. These were the very men Russian officers were recruiting to serve in four specially formed cavalry regiments to be deployed to protect Crimea against invasion. Displeased with the prospect of taking up arms against the Ottomans, the Tatar youth were stockpiling weapons and coordinating with the Ottoman fleet through a network of inconspicuous coastal trading boats and a system of hilltop fire signals.

Ashurovich passed along what he knew of the plan to Jean-François (Ivan Ivanovich) Prevost de Sansac, Marquis de Traversay, Commander of the Black Sea Fleet, and soon to be naval minister. Traversay went straight to the governor-general with the news. Richelieu, however, was hesitant to take aggressive measures against the Tatars, whom he believed to be loyal. Besides, there were seven Russian battalions and four artillery regiments in Sevastopol alone—more than enough to protect the Crimean coast. By June 1810, however, those forces had been deployed elsewhere, leaving Sevastopol with little manpower and no warships. Sure enough, several days later Ashurovich got wind that as many as twenty thousand armed Tatars were massing in the Baydar valley, awaiting the arrival of the Ottoman navy.

Naval authorities in Sevastopol refused to believe Ashurovich until reports to the same effect started coming in and Ottoman ships arrived in port on July 11. In the end it was not the Black Sea fleet that responded, but the small Greek battalion at Balaklava. The battalion's commander, Major Revelioti, had long been suspicious of the Tatars and at the first news of revolt ordered two hundred infantry and cavalrymen north to block the roads leading from Baydar to Sevastopol. According to Ashurovich, the six thousand Tatars who had gathered fled when they saw the Greeks, who gave chase and fired on the retreating rebels.[1]

Armed conflict was nothing new in this corner of the world, and rarely did confrontations end with as little consequence as the purported events in the Baydar valley. During the eighteenth century alone the Russian and Ottoman empires spent nearly two decades under formal declaration of war, with battles raging across the Black Sea littoral. Invasion and civil war wreaked havoc in Crimea in the years leading up to annexation, but had also been an unexpected source of stability and prosperity. In Russia too, the military was an agent of order, albeit a coercive brand of order. After 1783 it proved to be the most flexible and in some ways the most successful medium for working out the place of the former khanate and its people within imperial society. Here, and in many other borderland provinces, local particularities shaped military structures more than any other imperial institution. Just as important, it was through military service that Russian officials forged relationships with non-Russian subjects—relationships that in many places radically altered the calculus of obligations rendered to the regime. In Crimea, military service introduced significant changes in the profile of Tatar society.

Across Romanov territory, the influence of the army extended in one way or another into nearly every nook and cranny of Russian life. Recognizing this, historians have turned their attention from the battlefields and generals who dominated them to the social composition of the army and its influence on civilian life and culture. Military norms, they have found, provided the foundation for the famously pervasive emphasis on rank in Russian society, while military symbols were deployed to impress the strength of the state upon domestic and foreign audiences. Officers often served as diplomats, reformers, administrators, judges, and even kingmakers. Most important, deployment, provisioning, and billeting practices structured many social, fiscal, and administrative relationships within the empire. Conscription in particular was, along with taxation, one of the primary sites of interaction between government representatives and the tsar's subjects.[2]

Until 1874, the taxpaying population represented the conscription pool; while merchants and clergy were technically subject to the onerous obligation, it was for the most part the peasant's burden. And burden it was. Poor nutrition, exposure to disease, lack of access to education, and the often grueling military regimen were high prices to pay for the juridical emancipation that followed a peasant's transformation into soldier. For many peasant families, conscription—this fundamental interaction between ruler and ruled—resulted in economic and emotional trauma. For many nobles, service in the officer corps drew members of privileged households into an even more profitable relationship with the state. In other words, the army clearly replicated the traditional societal division between landowner and serf. But it nevertheless had the potential to function as a powerful integrative institution and a mechanism of social mobility for those able to attain officer rank. In this sense the extremely hierarchical military injected a measure of permeability into the *soslovie* (status) structure of the regime.[3]

In the non-Russian borderlands the military had two potentially contradictory purposes: to act, in the words of Andreas Kappeler, "as an instrument of control and an arm of the administration" on one hand, and, as Mark von Hagen puts it, as "an engine of possible political integration."[4] Military service was critical, for example, to what Bruce Menning describes as the transformation of the "highly volatile Don Cossack host into an obedient and pliant instrument designed to meet the military needs of the Imperial Russian state."[5] Many Baltic Germans, Finns, Poles, and Georgians found a place among the officer ranks, thus easing their transition into Russian subjecthood and revising their relationship with the state.

The army's success as a tool for creating, as well as controlling, the empire depended on judicious application of several techniques at its disposal: integration of indigenous elites into the officer corps, (involuntary) conscription of peasant populations, direct importation of indigenous military structures, and the formation of special or "native" units. As Kappeler and others have demonstrated, the first technique was particularly successful and widely applied throughout the empire. Wholesale importation of non-Russian military structures was far less common. Immediate conscription of non-Russian, and particularly non-Christian, populations was also rare. Instead, over the course of the eighteenth and nineteenth centuries the Russian army created a number of native units that functioned, Robert Baumann argues, as "both a symbol of allegiance to Russia and a tool for the weaving of subject peoples into the social fabric of the empire."[6]

Where do the Crimean Tatars fit into this narrative? Muscovites and Russians had long been acquainted with the military nature of Crimean society. For three centuries the Tatars were a valuable asset to the Porte—a military force that guarded the northern coast of the Black Sea and could be summoned to battle any adversary of the sultan. But the khans had alternately campaigned against Muscovy, raiding Slavic villages and burning towns, and formed alliances with the grand princes. Would conquering Crimea contribute to the security of the frontier? Would military service be the prime benefit of acquiring the Crimeans as subjects, as it had been for the Ottoman sultans? This chapter explores the relationship between military service and the creation of something resembling imperial society in Tavrida. To what extent did local conditions, rather than imperial expectations, determine the terms of Tatar service? Did the medals won on the field of battle represent Crimean allegiance, or was the 1810 Baydar revolt symptomatic of the failure (or irrelevance) of integration?

BEARING ARMS FOR THE EMPIRE:
THE BEŞLI REGIMENTS

Russian officials were relentlessly concerned with the question of security on the Black Sea. As soon as the ink dried on the annexation manifesto, the general staff began revising the military infrastructure of the southern empire. With the acquisition of the khanate, Russia's frontier had become an interior line. New fortified lines stretching from the mouth of the Dnepr northward along the Bug River were needed to defend the new territory. They planned a series of fortified points as well— at Özi (Ochakov), Kilburunu (Kinburn), Kerch, Taman, and Sevastopol— designed both for defensive purposes and to project power into the Caucasus. Orkapısı (Perekop) and Enikale remained the choke points that could control military movement northward into the steppe and eastward into the Caucasus.[7]

They were just as concerned with diminishing or harnessing the threat posed by the Crimeans themselves. For centuries, travelers described the Crimean Tatars as fearsome steppe warriors. As late as 1785, the Italian Francesco Becattini extolled the Tatars' skill with horses and arms, though he correlated their military tendency with barbarism, claiming that "Like the Scyths, they would sooner beat and steal from their parents than obey them." Hans Erich Thunmann, the Swedish historian and geographer who published a thorough study of the khanate in 1784, found that the Tatars had "lost that fierce valor which made them so formidable when they first appeared in Europe." They were not barbarians, but cultivators of the vine and crafters of fine poetry. Yet even he conceded that "every Tatar is a soldier," the rich armed with sabers and pistols, the poor with bows and arrows.[8]

The sources are less consistent in their descriptions of the khan's army, the size and structure of which varied according the purpose of the campaign. While the khan might muster a full-strength force to campaign with the Ottomans, much smaller contingents rode on pillaging raids across the steppe. When Mengli Giray I (1478–1514) claimed, in a letter to Grand Prince Vasilii III, to command over two hundred thousand men, he may well have been exaggerating, but only as much as Vasilii himself did when making the same claim. Sahib Giray brought 70,000 men with him when he invaded Muscovy in 1541 (a contemporary Frenchman put the estimate slightly higher), and English ambassador Giles Fletcher estimated that the khan rode with over 100,000 men in the late sixteenth century. Two hundred years later, the Girays were still capable of raising at least 80,000 horsemen for campaigns.[9]

Whatever the actual size of the fighting force, three crucial elements held relatively constant. First, military service was the right and responsibility of all adult (Muslim) males. The sons of mirzas and common

Tatars alike trained from youth to master the skills of horseback riding and weaponry, and to withstand all manner of weather and fatigue. Second, military service under the khans was irregular. Men mustered to go on campaign and then returned home, their pace slowed by loot or battle wounds. The only standing force was the khan's own *sekban* guard of roughly 1,000 cavalry, provided and funded by the Ottoman sultan. Third, the khan could not raise an army without the approval and aide of the karaçi beys. The khan had his sekban, and could raise a sizeable force from among the inhabitants of Giray lands and the Nogay hordes. But the Şirin and Mansur beys alone had as many as 20,000 men each at their disposal; the Sicivüt and Dair beys could each field 10,000. They were not necessarily storied captains, and seldom led the army on campaign—that task was generally performed by members of the Giray clan. But together the beys were capable of raising a force as large as, or perhaps even greater than, that of the khan. And as the latter's power declined in the seventeenth and eighteenth centuries, the Girays became increasingly dependent on clan leaders to muster an army worthy of the field of battle.[10]

Şahin Giray found this arrangement unacceptable. Anxious to have a regular army under his own command, he set about creating an elite cavalry guard which he called the *beşliler,* or beşli (horsemen) regiment. His initial recruitment efforts yielded approximately 800 volunteers; he used them to conscript several thousand more. Şahin envisioned a standing, well-trained army 20,000 strong, with 1,000 beşlis and 2,000 sekban, though General Prozorovskii, the commander of Russian troops in Crimea, disapproved of the plan. He pointed out that an army of that size could not hope to protect the khan against any of his enemies, and that moreover Şahin had no need for such a force—had Catherine not pledged to defend his throne with her own army?

The khan was undeterred. He outfitted his fledgling army in western military uniforms, and trained them "in the way [he] had observed Russian guard units training in St. Petersburg." Most shocking was Şahin's decision to include Christians in the ranks alongside Muslims. Although he consulted the mufti regarding his right to enforce these measures— and publicly proclaimed the mufti's pro forma approval—Şahin's reforms were rejected by the majority of the population. In fact, they contributed in no small way to the rancor and resentment that fueled the rebellions that plagued his reign, and with his conscription drive stalled, only a few beşlis remained loyal. Those who remained at his side in May 1782 were defeated by Halim Giray, leader of the anti-Russian faction, and fled with the khan to Kerch. Despite (some would argue because of) his weakness, Catherine installed Şahin on the throne yet again in October 1782. Undaunted by the lack of support from his fellow Crimeans, the khan used the depleted beşli force to take revenge against those who had betrayed him, executing and imprisoning so many—including leading members of the elite clans—that Catherine and Potemkin felt compelled to restrain him.[11]

Given this state of affairs, Potemkin might have easily decided to bring an end to the long history of military service in Crimea. After all, the majority of beys and mirzas had fought against Şahin Giray and therefore did not figure to be particularly loyal subjects or soldiers. However, as commander-in-chief of Russian irregular and light cavalry since 1774, the prince was versed in the delicate art of subordinating Cossack forces, and had a vested interest in promoting the use of mobile, flexible units, which he considered vital for the steppe campaigns and colonization programs required in this region. This model was certainly available to Potemkin as he pondered what to do with the Crimean Tatars. But while both Crimeans and Cossacks traditionally fought as light, irregular cavalries, the breakdown of political order, wars, and emigrations had effectively dismantled what had once been a robust military structure and diminished the military value of the Tatar horsemen.[12]

Irregular horsemen were one thing; but what about regularized, conscripted soldiers? Newly acquired subject populations were rarely subject to conscription. Between their annexation by Peter I in 1710 and 1796 for example, inhabitants of the Baltic provinces were permitted to contribute taxes for the upkeep of the army rather than furnish recruits. Russian administrators tread carefully in Poland as well, creating a 100-verst recruitment-free zone along the border. The Grand Duchy of Finland was spared recruitment altogether, as was Bessarabia. By the 1850s, exemptions from conscription "based on social origin removed up to two million men from the pool of possible recruits" and territorial or ethnic criteria exempted another three to four million inhabitants of Siberia, Bessarabia, and the Caucasus, plus Armenians, Serbs, Bulgarians, Greeks, and the Tatars of Astrakhan province.[13]

When Catherine extended the recruitment levy to New Russia in the 1780s, she made "certain modifications necessitated by differences in social structure" in her southern empire. Conscripts, drawn primarily from Slavic farming families, functioned mainly as a Cossack-style local militia, drawing salaries of approximately five rubles—one-fifth the pay of a cavalryman in an imperial Guard regiment. In Tavrida, ethnic diversity, widespread poverty, and the skeletal nature of the imperial administration on the ground forced officials to consider the practical consequences of extracting a percentage of the productive male population to serve in the army. Catherine had still other reasons to proceed cautiously. She had no desire to appear heavy-handed in her treatment of the inhabitants of a region so recently considered an integral part of the Ottoman Empire. No less important were the lessons learned by Şahin Giray (who served in the Imperial Guard Bombardiers before becoming khan), whose attempts to establish a standing army through conscription incited his subjects to revolt.[14]

Nevertheless, Potemkin considered the integration of the mirzas a critical part of the process of establishing the legitimacy of Russian rule and plotted a course that he hoped would lead to a collaborative, mutually beneficial relationship with the native elite. The annexation manifesto had not explicitly granted exemption from recruitment, but Catherine rectified that in a decree of July 1783 in which she declared that "None of these, our new subjects, is to be pressed into military service against his own free will and desire." Four months later, she opened the path to voluntary service by decreeing that Crimean Tatars were eligible for officer rank regardless of whether or not they chose to convert to Orthodoxy. But when Potemkin proposed a distinct structure for Crimean military service (table 3.1), Catherine hastily approved the plan. On March 1, 1784, she ordered the formation of a light horse regiment composed of five squadrons loosely structured along the lines of irregular Cossack units. It was known officially and unofficially as the Crimean Tatar Beşli Regiment.[15]

The prince's plan promised material benefits and enhanced social status to the approximately 10 percent of the Crimean elite who decided to serve in this capacity. This was a dramatic shift from standing policy. In 1713 Peter I had purged unconverted Muslims from the officer ranks and decreed that henceforth the only service for which they qualified was provisioning the navy with timber. Thus for much of the eighteenth century, conversion to Orthodoxy had remained the most reliable path to officer rank for the empire's Muslims. Not in Crimea. The archive

Table 3.1. Proposed Structure of the Beşli Regiment, 1784

Rank	Salary (rubles)	Per squadron	Total (rubles)
Major	300	1	5
Captains (*rotmistry*)	200	2	10
Lieutenants	150	2	10
Ensigns	120	2	10
NCOs	40	10	50
Privates	35	190	950
Totals		8,290	41,450

Source: *PSZ I*, vol. 43, no. 15,945 (March 1, 1784).

of the Tavrida governing board is chock-full of grants of land and villages to Tatar officers; subalterns (class nine through fourteen of the Table of Ranks, including captains, lieutenants, and ensigns) and staff officers (those in class five through eight, including colonels and majors) received substantial salaries from the provincial treasury. Privates in the beşli regiment received as much as thirty-five rubles, whereas infantry soldiers elsewhere were compensated with five rubles, and cavalrymen in the imperial guards might receive twenty-five. John Keep has suggested that the explanation for such discrepancies lies in the social origins of the men in question. While free peasants and settlers constituted the bulk of conscripts in Novorossiia and were therefore at the bottom of the pay scale, the horsemen of Tavrida were "men of privileged background." However, the single extant squadron list suggests that this was not necessarily the case: none of the privates listed bore the title of mirza. Potemkin's justification for providing such compensation to these men is nonetheless clear. Integrating this young, capable segment of Crimean society into the military structure, however loosely, was bound to foster a sense of duty and loyalty to the sovereign who provided such an opportunity.[16]

In the spring of 1784, Potemkin and Governor Igel'strom (and later Governor Kakhovskii) went about the business of recruiting volunteers. They had little trouble enlisting squadron commanders. Captain Mustafa Mirza Kiiatov took command of the first squadron, Major Abdul Velişa Mirza Khunkalov took the second, and Major Batyr Aga Krımtay took the third. Many were seasoned veterans. Abdul Velişa, for example, had occupied a high military post under the khans. Halil Mirza of Karasu-bazar, who requested and was granted appointment as a subaltern, had risen through the ranks of the khan's army to *odo-bashi* (a rank roughly equivalent to that of lieutenant). Even newly minted officers who had not previously served likely possessed many of the skills required of a cavalryman, thanks to the prominent place of horses and military prowess in Crimean culture. In fact, nearly all staff officers, subalterns, and noncommissioned officers were mirzas—men who had fought for their clan chiefs for countless generations.[17]

Filling out the rank and file proved far more challenging. Because few volunteers were forthcoming, Kakhovskii enlisted the help of clan leaders, in hopes that their influence in the community might encourage participation. The strategy enjoyed some success. In September 1784, Bek Mirza, a resident of Akbaş in Perekop district, petitioned for officer rank in Abdul Velişa's squadron. Kakhovskii granted his request on one condition: that Bek Mirza produce thirty privates, complete with uniforms and arms, in return for the rank of captain. A 1788 list of horsemen in Mustafa Kiiatov's squadron also suggests that personal connections between officers and privates were critical to filling the regimental roster. Of the ten noncommissioned officers in Kiiatov's squadron, six came from the same town or village as nine or more of the privates they led. Sergeant Mehmet Bey of Baçal in Feodosiia, for example, served alongside eleven privates from the same village; Mengli Adabaşı served with twelve men from his native Bahçesaray.[18]

In the introductory essay of his collection of archival documents relating to the first Crimean Tatar regiment, M. V. Masaev asserts that the annexation of the khanate was a boon to its inhabitants. They obtained a wider array of rights and privileges under the tsars than they could ever have imagined, he argues, and the 130-year record of military service they proceeded to rack up, all of which was carried out on a strictly voluntary basis, was indicative of their desire to defend this new, beneficent homeland. Archival sources paint a different picture however. Despite the prospect of a respectable salary, grants of land and villages, and the right to wear a military uniform and to enjoy the status of men-at-arms, the lack of volunteers was so pervasive that by January 1785 only two of the prescribed five squadrons had formed. Neither was at full strength. Sixty-six men had volunteered to serve under Abdul Velişa's command, and eighty-six under Batyr Aga. Another year would pass before all three squadron rosters filled with men who in due course overcame either their distaste for serving a Christian monarch or simply their reluctance to leave hearth and home.[19]

RETURN OF THE PRODIGAL SUBJECTS

The beşli regiment's first truly "imperial" experience came in the wake of Catherine's decision to include Tavrida on the itinerary of her 1787 journey through the southern provinces. Members of the regiment played a logistical role, providing horses and curriers at each stage along the route, as well as a symbolic one, participating in the escort that accompanied Catherine across the peninsula in May. Concerned that they make a suitable impression, Potemkin allocated up to three thousand rubles for the purchase of new uniforms and weapons, and issued detailed orders regarding the number and position of beşlis in the procession. At each stage from Kalanchak (on the far side of the Perekop isthmus) to Bahçesaray a fresh officer and twelve horsemen took up their positions to the left of the empress's carriage (Don Cossacks were arrayed on the right). Observers found it simply remarkable that "yesterday's enemies" demonstrated such devotion, even taking care to steady her carriage on the precarious roads.[20]

Three months after Catherine's visit, Sultan Abdulhamid I declared war on Russia. The war was the perfect crucible for testing the Tatars' loyalty. Some, like Ensign Haji Ibrahim Aga Emirov, distinguished themselves. Under orders from the military governor of Novorossiia, General Mikhail Kakhovskii, Ibrahim traveled to Anapa in January 1788 to scout the terrain. Having concluded that there was no way to acquire the necessary information and yet remain unobserved, he made the bold decision to approach Mustafa Pasha, commander of the fortress, presenting himself as a supporter of the Porte who had fled Russian-ruled Crimea. His ruse was successful. Convinced of his loyalty, Mustafa Pasha sent Ibrahim to Constantinople and Ochakov to consult with several high-ranking Ottoman commanders. Eventually he returned to Russia, having gained the respect and gratitude of Kakhovskii.[21]

But most mirzas demonstrated their loyalty—or lack thereof—closer to home. Despite his military rank for example, Major Batyr Aga Krımtay never saw the field of battle. Instead, Catherine granted him the civil rank of court councilor and an appointment to the criminal court chamber. A different fate awaited Lieutenant Colonel Mehmetşa Bey Kantakuzin, former commander of the khan's cavalry and commander of the beşli regiment. General Kakhovskii summoned him, together with Krımtay and Mehmet Aga Balatukov, to execute the resettlement of Tatars dwelling along the southeastern coast to the interior of the peninsula. This decision to enlist Tatar chieftains to implement an unpopular policy demonstrates a judicious—possibly even cynical—willingness on the part of Russian officials to empower local elites. In fact, Potemkin may never have conceived of the regiment or its officers as military assets. Their symbolic value was enough to justify their existence. With the unpleasant task of forced resettlement behind him, Kantakuzin was told to select 120 of the most loyal and capable Tatars to remain under his command. These men, dressed in their standard-issue green kaftans, white *kamzols*, and cornflower blue trousers, would serve as a special escort for Potemkin within the province. The remaining eighty men, along with Mustafa Kiiatov's entire division, received orders to disband and surrender their weapons and uniforms. Officers continued to receive their salaries but were barred from occupying any elected or appointed office without the express permission of the governor-general. For the time being, the government was willing to subsidize their non-participation in public life.[22]

Following a series of victories by forces under Suvorov and Potemkin at Ochakov (December 1788), Fokshani (June 1789), and Bender (November 1789), Russian officials grew more confident in the security of the frontier. Potemkin, who in his correspondence with Governors Kakhovskii and later Major General Semen Semenovich Zhegulin espoused a persistent desire to produce a loyal and integrated Crimean elite, decided the time was right to transform the beşli regiment from a showpiece into an active part of the army. In early 1790, he approved the formation and provisioning of six light horse divisions united under the command of Colonel Prince Mehmetşa Bey Kantakuzin.

With the Ottoman threat abating, Potemkin identified the western frontier as the most appropriate destination for a reconstituted Tatar regiment. While the Russo-Swedish war continued to the north, Catherine devoted a great deal of attention to events in Poland, intent on maintaining Stanislaw Poniatowski on the throne and preventing further partitions of the Polish-Lithuanian Commonwealth. However, when she refused to support Poniatowski's proposed constitutional reforms—a Polish government paralyzed by the nobility's *liberum veto* was far easier to control—the king turned to Frederick William II of Prussia for support. In May 1789 Catherine recalled her troops from Polish territory in order to remove any pretext for a Prussian invasion. But when Frederick moved to "guarantee" the integrity of the commonwealth through a Prusso-Polish defense treaty in March 1790, Russian forces massed along the border.

All six Crimean Tatar divisions, which rapidly mustered under mirza officers, were dispatched to Kiev province and quartered near Pereiaslav, where they settled in to wait with the rest of the forces under General Krechetnikov. They had not been in Pereiaslav long when orders came for the regiment to present itself in Kiev. Almost immediately, Major Mehmetşa Mirza[23] began spreading word among his men that Krechetnikov intended to convert the beşlis into regular army soldiers—a change that would entail the loss of their semi-privileged status and represent a near guarantee of never again setting foot in Crimea. The only way to avoid this fate, the officer counseled his men, was to flee across the border to Poland, and thence to the protection of the sultan.

According to a thirty-two-year-old captain referred to only as Mehmet Bey, Mehmetşa Mirza succeeded in convincing approximately 250 men from the Perekop and Evpatoriia divisions that this was the opening salvo in a wave of repression against Muslim subjects. On the eve of their scheduled departure for Kiev, Mehmetşa gathered his followers— Mehmet Bey among them—and went to the house of a Russian officer, from whom they stole a small sum of rubles, several fur coats and gold watches, and three Circassian-style coats. With goods in hand, Mehmetşa crossed the Dnepr just above Pereiaslav in advance of his men, announcing their intentions to the Polish soldiers stationed there. Whether the Polish commander was bribed with gold and furs or simply found the prospect of weakening the Russian forces by taking in deserters appealing, he gave the order to ferry the Tatars across the river. Unsure of their motives, however, the Poles confiscated the beşlis' horses and weapons, threatening the deserters with return to Russia should they complain about their treatment. The Tatars were transferred to Berdichev, where they spent four months under guard, and then to Vinnitsa.

In the summer of their second year as captives, the beşlis' fortunes improved. After careful preparations, Catherine invaded Poland in May 1792 in order to enforce the restoration of the ancient, politically debilitating Polish constitution. When the Crimeans followed the Polish troops to Warsaw, some fell into the hands of Russian soldiers and were sent up the ranks for interrogation. Meanwhile, news of their predicament reached Colonel Alexander Ulan, commander of the Polish-Lithuanian Tatar regiment. Himself a Tatar, Ulan took pity on Mehmetşa's men and convinced his generals to transfer the deserters to his command. For several months they served as border guards near the small village of Lipa, discharging their duties with varying degrees of reluctance.[24]

Finally, Ulan presented the beşlis with a choice: either enter the service of the Polish king or return to Russian territory, where the deserters could hardly expect a warm welcome. Despite constant encouragement from their own officers to enter Polish service and take up arms against the empress, the majority of the beşlis, long since disillusioned by the realities of deserting both army and homeland for an uncertain future, held out hope for an opportunity to return to Crimea. Sixty gained permission to return to Crimea immediately. Ulan issued passports for safe conduct and restored their weapons, though not their horses, for the journey. "From that point we scattered in all directions, each according to his own desire. The majority went to Crimea, others to Turkey," explained Mehmet Bey, who made his way to Moldavia. In time, like many fellow beşlis, he ended up in Bender. A frequent visitor to local coffeehouses, Mehmet soon heard a rumor that his former commander and forty men who had followed him had all returned to Crimea without suffering arrest or reprisal. He concluded that there was no reason for him not to do so as well. In October 1794, he set out from Bender with three companions, traveling under cover of night.[25]

Beşlis had begun returning home as early as January 1793. Some presented discharge documents from the Polish army; others were picked up by Russian troops in Warsaw; still others trickled in from Kiev or from as nearby as Kherson province. After consulting with his superiors, Governor Zhegulin ordered that all beşlis returning from Poland and internal Russian provinces be allowed to rejoin their families in their native villages. But perhaps as many as half of the deserters returned from Moldavia, other parts of Rumelia, and even Anatolia, and their repatriation posed a challenge to Russian officials: in June 1786 Potemkin had issued a decree stipulating that no one who fled to Ottoman lands from Crimea in order to escape becoming a subject of the Russian Empire would be allowed to return. What should authorities do then with such men? After protracted debate, Field Marshal

Rumiantsev-Zadunaiskii himself who, having heard the beşlis' testimony that they desired nothing more than the opportunity to prove themselves loyal subjects of the empress, concluded that it was inexpedient to punish penitent Muslims.[26]

The beşlis' desertion and return sheds new light on the relationship between the imperial government and its subjects. First, Russian military officials were willing to tolerate possibly treasonous behavior rather than expend the resources necessary to mete out punishment. Surely they harbored suspicions about the Tatars' loyalty, but officials chose to avoid a policy that would lead to social and political unrest. For their part, many Tatars were equally suspicious of Russian intentions: fear of losing their unique status and being reduced to the condition of common peasants was enough for Mehmetşa Mirza's men to desert. But others demonstrated a very practical willingness to adapt to life under Russian rule. Taken by itself, the fact that 13 percent of the approximately 350 male mirzas in Crimea attained officer rank (tables 3.2 and 3.3) might seem indicative of a strengthening relationship between local elites and the Russian administration.

The nature of that relationship and the level of interaction between mirzas and other imperial elites are somewhat obscured by the facade of military rank. The mirzas listed below received ranks, but this alone did not automatically integrate them into the military hierarchy; rank had meaning only when coupled with office—something the vast majority of mirzas did not enjoy. Of the seven men who attained staff officer rank, only Kantakuzin and Ahmet Bey Khunkalov earned that rank through actual military service. Batyr Aga and Abdulla Velişa held command positions in the regiment, but the former resigned his post before the regiment engaged in any military activity, and the latter served as Perekop land captain—a civilian office—during his entire tenure as division commander. Neither Azamat Argin, Seit Ibrahim Aga Taşı-oğlu, nor Abdurahim Aga Mamay held officer posts. Each served as land captain in his respective district. In other words, most were not military officers, though they held military rank. The distinction was important, for it meant that they were not integrated into the culture and society of the officer corps. The mirzas received no Cadet Corps education and spent no time in St. Petersburg rubbing elbows with Russian, German, Polish, and Ukrainian fellow officers. Potemkin bestowed rank upon

Table 3.2. Crimean Tatars with Military Rank, 1784–1796

Colonel	Prince Mehmetşa Bey Kantakuzin, commander of 3rd division 1787; chief of all divisions 1790–1794[a]
Majors	Batyr Aga Krımtay, commander of 3rd division 1784–1787[a]
	Abdulla Velişa Khunkalov, commander of 2nd division 1784–1792[a]
	Azamat Mirza Argin
	Seit Ibrahim Aga Taşı-oğlu
	Prince Ahmet Bey Khunkalov, commander of 5th division, 1790–1792[a]
	Abdurahim Aga Mamay
Captains (*Rotmistry*)	Mustafa Mirza Kiiatov, commander of 1st division, 1784–1792[a]
	Muratşa Mirza Şirin, commander of 4th division, 1790–1792[a]
	Abduveli Mirza Uzdemikov, commander of 6th division, 1790–1792[a]

Captains (continued)	
Abdul Aga Mamay	Mehmetşa Mirza Zujsk
Adyl Bey[a]	Mehmetşa Mirza Şirin[a]
Arslanşa Mirza Dair	Merdimşa Mirza Mansur
Arslanşa Mirza Şirin	Mubarekşa Mirza Şirin
Bek Mirza Aga	Murtaza Aga Nogay
Dzhantemir Mirza	Murtaza Çelebi Emirov
Fetta Aga[a]	Osman Aga Kontugan
Katyrşa Mirza Şirin	Ismail Bey Balatukov
Mehmet Bey Balatukov	Usein Gazy Mirza Şirin

Lieutenants	
Abdul Kadir Mirza Osmanchik[a]	Kasim Mirza Argin
Abdulla Çelebi	Kutluşa Mirza[a]
Ak Mirza Iaşlav	Mehmet Bey Biiarslanov[a]
Ali *bajraktar*[a]	Mustafa Mirza Nogay[a]
Ali Mirza Şirin[a]	Seit Mehmet Çelebi-oğlu
Atay Mirza Şirin[a]	Temir bey Biiarslanov[a]
Dzhien Gazy Mirza[a]	

Ensigns	
Gaidar Çelebi	Mustafa Çelebi[a]
Haji Ibrahim Aga Emirov	Iagia Seit Mirza Ahmetov[a]
Kutlu Giray Mirza Şirin	Dzhelal Mirza Nogay

Source: Data compiled from Masaev, 20–21; and *Mesiatseslov* entries cited in previous tables.

[a] Indicates an officer of a beşli regiment.

Table 3.3. Clan Origins of Crimean Tatars with Military Rank, 1784–1796

	Karaçi	Kapıhalkı	Other/unknown
Staff officers (7)	14.3%	85.7%	–
Subalterns (40)	30.0%	47.5%	22.5%
Total (47)	27.7%	53.2%	19.1%

Source: Data compiled from Masaev, 20–21; and *Mesiatseslov* entries cited in previous tables.

these men purely as a result of their standing in, and ability to influence, Crimean society. The commanders of the beşli regiments hailed from the top military brass under the khans as well from powerful clans, and members of the four karaçi clans alone constituted more than a quarter of those with military rank. The beşli regiments had effectively reinforced the social order and tied mirza status to Crimean territory.[27]

THE HORSE REGIMENTS AND THE NAPOLEONIC WARS

For a decade after Catherine's death, any Tatars who served in the Russian army did so in regiments based in other provinces. Several mirzas entered the naval regiment (*morskoi polk*) as NCOs, including Batyr Bey Balatukov and his brother, Kazy Bey. Aleksandr Ivanov Krymgireev, son of Sultan Krym Giray, served in the Nizhegorod dragoons; Prince Adyl Bey Balatukov entered the Belov musketeers and earned the rank of second lieutenant.[28]

The Napoleonic wars changed that, as they changed so many other aspects of life in the Russian Empire. The Crimean Tatar horse regiments that existed from 1807 until 1817 were an indirect result of Alexander I's November 1806 manifesto summoning a land militia to defend the interior provinces during war with the French. The inhabitants of Tavrida were among those exempt from the obligation to provide militia recruits, but eager to demonstrate their loyalty and reliability, a number of Christian nobles and settlers gathered in informal assemblies to petition Alexander to be allowed to provide men for a provincial militia. At the same time, Governor Mertvago convened an assembly of Tatar secular and religious elites to elect a new mufti (Seit Mehmet Efendi had passed away on November 1). When the assembly members gathered in Simferopol on December 20, 1806, they elected a spiritual leader but also took the opportunity to declare their own patriotic devotion and their desire to form volunteer cavalry regiments. Led by Titular Councilor Kasim Mirza Mansur and Captain Abdulla Aga Mamay, they drew up a formal petition requesting that Alexander indulge their desire to serve and defend Russia.[29]

Provincial Marshal E. I. Notara sent both petitions to St. Petersburg. Both circulated among Minister of Internal Affairs Count V. P. Kochubei, War Minister S. K. Viazmitinov, and Tsar Alexander. The tsar quickly approved the Christians' petition, ordering the formation of two militia regiments under the command of the military governor, duc de Richelieu. This militia, some nine hundred strong, was composed of Russian settlers and landowners of Christian faith, and was charged with preserving order and protecting the inhabitants of the borderland provinces from Turkish incursions on the shores of the Black Sea. They were also tasked with preventing Tatars and Nogays from engaging in any "dangerous activities" that might assist their co-religionists.[30]

Since the Ottoman decision to side with Napoleon, Russian officials had viewed the Muslim population of the Black Sea coast with suspicion. Hoping to defuse the tension (and improve their own position), in early 1807 several mirzas petitioned the governor to temporarily resettle coastal Tatars to the mountain villages "so that no one would be able to unjustly slander" these loyal subjects. Mertvago approved but sent newly elected Mufti Seit Murtaza Efendi into the coastal villages to assess the mood. It was only at the end of March, after hearing the mufti's report that many Tatars met the proposal with approval (or at least complacency) that he ordered the resettlement. Whether or not the mufti and mirzas had the best interests of the common Tatars in mind, they had little to gain from fighting a policy that would likely have been implemented with or without their assistance. It was the common Tatars who felt the impact of these delicate negotiations however. The inhabitants of coastal villages relocated; those not required to move inland were required to turn over their weapons; the nomadic Nogays and Tatars beyond Perekop faced the enforced surrender of all of their horses to the provincial militia—in other words, to the very Christian militiamen assigned to monitor them. In return, they received an official declaration of gratitude from the governor; the secular and spiritual leaders received gifts and ranks for their part in facilitating the process.[31]

Meanwhile, a debate emerged in St. Petersburg within the committee appointed to consider the Crimean Tatar petition. The committee, which included Viazmitinov and Kochubei, was hesitant to duplicate the "failures" of the earlier beşlis. The matter was fraught with complications at every level. Kochubei considered the proposal an ill-fated endeavor. There was no reason to form Cossack-style regiments, he argued in February 1807, "for we have no lack of light cavalry arrayed against the French." And as for organizing units akin to those of the Lithuanian Tatars, "this would be difficult to reconcile," he reasoned, "with the customs and habits of the Crimean Tatars." Emperor Alexander agreed. He informed Kochubei of his desire to see the Crimeans integrated into the Lithuanian Tatar regiment. Perhaps then, wrote the tsar, "having thus gained a kind of military education, [the mirzas] could form a Life Guard hundred or division." Above all, Alexander insisted that "under no circumstances would [the Crimean Tatars] be allowed to form a regular regiment" of their own. Should they resist this arrangement, the whole matter should be dismissed without further ado.[32]

From his vantage point in Simferopol, Mertvago recognized the danger in presenting such a decision to the Crimeans. The governor was convinced that the idea of serving under Lithuanian or Russian officers would be poorly received by a population whose purpose, according to Mertvago, was to dispel the rumors about their lack of devotion and "unite their hearts with those of the devoted sons of the fatherland by contributing to Russia's glory." In a letter to Richelieu, Mertvago elaborated on the practical difficulties of implementing the proposal. The linguistic barrier alone, he pointed out, rendered the use of Russian officers impractical. Even worse, separating Tatar soldiers from their native chiefs would leave them vulnerable to the pernicious influence of Ottoman agents.[33]

Mertvago's reasoning struck a chord. In fact, Kochubei and his fellow committee members had initially dismissed the idea of establishing four regiments precisely because the service of two to three thousand soldiers was not considered significant enough to guarantee the wartime loyalty of the entire Crimean Tatar population of over two hundred thousand. Upon further consideration, Kochubei found the idea of having "at our disposal a hundred young men from the best Crimean families who would serve, in essence, as hostages and little by little be corrupted [by life] in the capital" quite appealing. Mertvago seized on this theme. "The Tatars are a true and good people," he wrote to Richelieu in July. The opportunity to serve would benefit them "but also the army, as well as the situation here in Crimea, for the sons of the great mirzas and Tatars will serve as *amanaty* (hostages)."[34]

The reference to this steppe tradition, whereby khans, chiefs, and other rulers exchanged hostages with the Muscovite grand prince, was anything but arbitrary. Muscovite officials were constantly adapting the amanat institution to suit their own political and ideological needs, often describing the handing over of hostages as an act of submission to Moscow. Most recently, when the governor of Orenburg received instructions to take hostages from among the sons of the Kazakh elite in 1742, he was told to explain to the khan and mirzas that their sons had been invited to serve as officers in the Russian army. And in fact, as Michael Khodarkovsky has shown, the Kazakh amanaty "resided at the imperial court, were educated, awarded a military rank and honors, and often joined the distinguished ranks of the Russian nobility."[35] This was the model Mertvago had in mind: the men of the regiments would be soldiers, sure, but more importantly they would bind the indigenous elite to the court.

In order to demonstrate the quality and potential of these officer-hostages, Mertvago sent Mustafa Machin, whose enthusiasm for the regiment was matched by his fine pedigree, to deliver the governor's letter to Richelieu. In 1801 Mustafa had accompanied the commander of the Nogay hordes to St. Petersburg where, during an imperial audience, Alexander granted him the rank of collegiate registrar. He was therefore already a known quantity when Mertvago selected him to represent the Crimeans' interests. The marquis de Traversay, standing in for an ill Richelieu, found both Machin and Mertvago's arguments persuasive. Richelieu himself agreed that the government had much to gain from approving the petition. He sent Machin along to St. Petersburg, and before long Machin was summoned to a second audience with Alexander. He acquitted himself well. Before he left the capital in April the tsar granted Mustafa the rank of lieutenant and charged him with delivering the order that Richelieu oversee the formation of four irregular Tatar regiments led by mirza officers.[36]

By the end of spring, the mirzas had selected some of their wealthiest peers as commanding officers. Majors Kaya Bey Balatukov (Simferopol) and Ahmet Bey Khunkalov (Perekop), Captain Abdulla Aga Mamay (Evpatoriia), and Lieutenant Ali Şirin (Feodosiia) were all considered to be "personages of demonstrated experience, loyalty and exemplary behavior . . . from among the most well-respected mirzas of Crimea." According to Mertvago, volunteers poured in and "every young [Tatar] nobleman signed up to serve." According to the list of volunteers compiled by the treasury bureau, twelve mirzas signed up to serve—the truth likely lies somewhere in between. Regardless, beneath each staff officer were fifteen subalterns, twenty-five NCOs, and 475 privates. An imam traveled with each regiment, as did a scribe. In the middle of June, the regiments dispatched to Vilnius, only to learn that Russia and France had signed the Peace of Tilsit. Their travels, however, were not in vain. Though they had no opportunity to fire a weapon, each of the two thousand Crimean horsemen secured his freedom from taxes of any kind. More importantly, by August 1807 officials from Simferopol to St. Petersburg had come to see the regiments as effective guarantees of loyalty.[37]

All four regiments mustered for the second time in May 1808. The Simferopol regiment joined the Cossack brigades in Vilnius as border guards. The Perekop, Evpatoriia, and Feodosiia regiments performed the same duties along the western border from Kiev to Zhitomir. For the next six years, all four regiments were stationed along the Prussian border or deployed in campaigns against French and Polish troops. All was not smooth sailing. At first, the horsemen balked at leaving Tavrida, worried about the repressions the provincial government might inflict on the Tatar population in their absence. Both the Simferopol and Perekop regiments suffered minor rebellions, although once they arrived at their destinations the soldiers' mood improved. They made terrible border guards. In August 1808 Major Khunkalov informed Major General Denisov, commander of the Don Cossack regiment, that his men were experiencing difficulties monitoring passports since there was not an officer or private among them who spoke any language other than Tatar. Their inability to process passports and communicate with those who presented them led to numerous misunderstandings and complaints, and Denisov was forced to request Russian-speaking Don Cossack NCOs to assist the Perekop regiment.[38]

Despite such wrinkles, the Tatars' record is impressive. In June 1812, the Simferopol and Perekop regiments saw their first military action when they helped defeat the French near the village of Mir and again at Romanov in July. The fighting resulted in six Tatar casualties, but also resulted in the commanding officer's decision to recommend Kaya Bey Balatukov for the Order of St. Vladimir. They went on to fight at Mogilev (July 20), Smolensk (August 16), and Borodino (September 7), and helped chase the retreating French army to Vilnius, and eventually all the way to Paris. Along the way, Russian officers took note of the contributions of the Tatar horsemen. One general reported that the men of the Simferopol regiment "were a miracle of bravery and in every way deserved to be called the best cavalrymen of their time." Major General Prince Shcherbatov, chief of the 18th infantry division, extolled the courageous fighting of the Evpatoriia Tatars. Count Platov was impressed not only with the horsemen, but with the mullas attached to the regiments who, "in the course of all campaigns have executed their duties and in accordance with their faith have taken part in many battles with the enemy. Moreover, by instilling in everyone the duty of their oath they themselves serve as constant examples of courage."[39]

At home in Crimea, enthusiasm remained high. In July the mirzas made a public declaration of loyalty. "We, the noble class here in Taurica," they declared, "who follow the law of Mohammed and yet are loyal subjects of HIS IMPERIAL MAJESTY, here in the town of Simferopol announce our complete readiness to serve HIS MAJESTY the Padishah, not only at our own expense but also with our lives. Our sons too, who are not bound by obligation, are loyal to the throne and those who can ride a horse do not hold back: all must go to war against the common enemy, the Frenchman." An impressive array of leaders, including Collegiate Assessor Atay Bey Şirin, Majors Merdimşa Mansur and Abduraman Aga Mamay, Court Councilors Mehmetşa Argin and Khaydver Bey Iaşlav, affixed their signatures to the document. But it was the Tatar peasants who bore the cost of provisioning, which ran to 300 rubles per horseman. Between that and the fact that the Tatars and Nogays of the steppe provided horses and saddles, the regiments constituted an enormous physical and financial burden. Five years later, when inhabitants of the province pledged contributions to the continuing war effort, three-quarters of the funds came from the Muslim population (though far and away the largest per capita contributions came from dvoriane) (table 3.4).[40]

The Crimeans' dearest contribution came in the form of lives. In the numerous battles waged in the late summer and early fall of 1812, the Simferopol regiment suffered so many casualties that the commander-in-chief of the Russian army, M. I. Kutuzov, instructed Richelieu to make whatever special arrangements might be necessary in order to maintain a critical mass of bodies in the regiment. By January 1813, the four regiments had suffered 250 casualties: one in four had been killed or wounded. According to some testimonies, when young men hesitated to take the place of their fallen comrades, officers like Esaul Abduraman Çelebi Il'iasov took it upon themselves to rally volunteers. Badly wounded and sent home to recuperate, Il'iasov supposedly busied himself proclaiming the brave deeds of his men to all who would listen, while the Tatar youth responded to his call "with delight," convinced that they would inspire fear in the hearts of the enemy. Governor A. M. Borozdin, meanwhile, reported significant resistance to "efforts to bring the Crimean Tatar regiments up to strength."[41]

Those with the good fortune to return from the field of battle found conditions at home quite grim. In addition to contagious disease, adverse

Table 3.4. Contributions to the War Effort from Tavrida Province

Source	Amount (rubles)	Percentage of total	Rubles per capita
Muslims (Tatars, Nogays, Kirgiz, and ulema)	314,583	75.2	1.6
Christian nobility	50,956	12.2	127.4
Russian state settlers	32,666	7.8	2.5
Black Sea Host	14,378	3.4	0.6
Towns	3,942	0.9	0.5
Russian clergy	1,228	0.3	8.8
Colonists	399	0.1	–

Source: Skal'kovskii, *Khronologicheskoe*, 205–206; RGIA 1281-11-132: 54–64. The per capita figures should be taken as rough estimates. Unfortunately, the records do not differentiate contributions from mirzas and the rest of the Tatar/Nogay population, so it is impossible to say whether they, like their Christian counterparts, were responsible for roughly 60% of contributions from among co-religionists.

weather conditions, and the economic challenges of wartime, Tavrida experienced a major demographic shift. Many of the men, women, and children resettled from coastal villages in 1807 joined the contingent of over three thousand that emigrated to Ottoman lands during the war. An additional seven thousand Nogays abandoned the steppe when Russia annexed Bessarabia in 1812. All seemed to sense that the Ottomans had abandoned them and that life in Russian-ruled Crimea held no bright future for Muslims. The reentry of so many armed men into such conditions might easily have exacerbated the tensions between Tatars and the slowly growing Russian population, but there are no known instances of significant unrest, and the horsemen seem to have earned nothing but praise. More than half of the fifty regimental officers returned with various honors, including monetary rewards, chivalric orders, and silver medals of distinction set on light blue ribbons. The commander of the Perekop regiment, Prince Ahmet Bey Khunkalov, received a promotion to colonel, a golden saber, and the Orders of St. Vladimir (fourth class) and St. Anna (second class). Abdulla Aga Mamay, commander of the Evpatoriia regiment, received the rank of major and the Order of St. Anna (third class).[42]

The most decorated hero to emerge from the Napoleonic wars was Prince Kaya Bey Balatukov, commander of the Simferopol regiment. The son of State Councilor Mehmet Aga, Kaya Bey entered military service in 1786 in one of the Crimean Greek battalions. He next appears in the archival sources after having been elected Evpatoriia land captain in 1804. He served in that capacity until 1807, when he was elected marshal of Simferopol. That same year, he became a regimental commander with the rank of major. He led the Simferopol regiment through countless battles, including the siege of Danzig, and earned the rank of major general as well as the Orders of St. Vladimir (third and fourth class), St. Anna (second class), and St. George (fourth class), and the Order of *Pour le Mérite* from the Prussian king. He was one of only two men of Crimean Tatar origin who reached elite military rank, and the only titled Crimean Tatar in the *generalitet* during this period.[43]

The loyalty, courage, and military skill of such men were not enough, however, to merit a permanent place for the Tatar regiments in the Russian army. In November 1816, Alexander I formed a committee to determine the future of the regiments. Lieutenant General A. Ia. Rudzevich chaired a committee composed of Balatukov, former Tavrida governor Semen Zhegulin, and a general from the Second Army. Rudzevich's final report to the War Ministry recommended against maintaining the regiments, and based on this finding the emperor disbanded them in May 1817. Subalterns and staff officers received a promotion upon retirement and, as their names remained in the army registers, they maintained the right to wear their uniforms. Most received awards or chivalric orders; in the early 1850s one could still "meet retired Crimean warriors who still kept their former uniform as a memento of their deeds."[44]

Ceremonial niceties aside, 1817 marked the end of a decade of military service for many Crimean Tatars. Despite the impermanence of the regiments themselves, many men attained a permanent and very significant benefit by virtue of their service. Balatukov and Rudzevich reached the generalitet; twenty-five became staff officers; thirty-seven became subalterns; nearly one-fifth of all mirzas held officer rank by 1824. Together they made up 95 percent of Tatars who attained rank commensurate with hereditary noble status between 1802 and 1825. After 1817 most served as elected officials or tended to their estates, but a few went on to enjoy successful careers and wield a significant amount of power in both Simferopol and St. Petersburg.

BALATUKOV'S LIFE GUARD SQUADRON

Kaya Bey Balatukov was one of them. In 1818, Prince Balatukov began pressing Arakcheev and Alexander to issue an official confirmation of the privileges Catherine granted the inhabitants of Crimea in 1783 and 1796. He reminded Arakcheev of the Crimeans' "right" to practice their faith, their freedom from the demands of military recruitment and taxes, the importance of recognizing "Muslim beys as Tatar princes and mirzas as Russian nobles," and of confirming the right of "Muslims of all *sosloviia* to own property including arable land, forest, etc. and to buy and sell such property according to their ancient rights." At the same time, he lobbied for the formation of a permanent Crimean Tatar Guard on the model of the Don or Ural Cossack regiments and was likely the only man both willing and able to achieve such a goal. It was his "long years of service in the army and the mass of highly influential friends he had accumulated both in the Corps and in battle" that enabled him to realize the project, but as a highly decorated officer and extremely influential member of the Crimean elite, Balatukov also benefited from personal access to the emperor. During Alexander's sojourn on the peninsula in 1825, Balatukov was a constant fixture in the tsar's entourage, accompanying him wherever he went.[45]

For Balatukov, military service was intimately linked with status and privilege. His rationale for creating a life guard squadron was that by producing a venue for voluntary service, he could prevent the kind of downgrade in status that was then transforming so many Cossacks into military servitors. Voluntary service was preferable to conscription; irregular status was a privilege. When Alexander died at Taganrog in November 1825, the prince had already convinced him of the value of a Crimean Tatar Guard regiment. Luckily for Balatukov, the tsar's brother found the plan appealing as well. In 1826 Nicholas approved the proposal, and in June 1827 he issued an imperial decree announcing the formation of the Crimean Life Guard Squadron within the Cossack Life Guard Regiment. The squadron consisted of three units, two residing in St. Petersburg and one in Crimea, on a three-year rotation. It was staffed with one colonel and nine subalterns, all with imperial guard rank, four NCOs, and 192 privates. Although Balatukov originally intended that the squadron be maintained at the expense of the mirzas, the cost of equipping and maintaining the soldiers stationed in Crimea eventually fell to the non-noble Tatars, while the imperial treasury agreed to subsidize soldiers on duty in the capital. Salaries for subalterns were set at fifty-four silver rubles, while privates earned thirty-seven.[46]

Just before his death in October 1827, Prince Kaya Bey received the Order of St. Anna first class. His brother, Colonel Adyl Bey Balatukov, succeeded him as commander of the Crimean Life Guard Squadron and brought the newly assembled unit to St. Petersburg in August 1827. It was under his watch that the unit passed its official military reviews—first by Grand Duke Mikhail Pavlovich and then by Emperor Nicholas I—with flying colors. Just one year later, the Crimean Life Guard made its debut in the Russian-Ottoman war of 1828–1829. Uniformed in dark-blue jackets and traditional mirza-style hats decorated with gold braids, the Crimeans were positioned near Nicholas on the march from Petersburg to the Black Sea, signaling the trust he placed in this newest addition to the imperial guard.

That trust derived from the service record accrued by the Crimean Tatars during Alexander I's reign. Many of the officers of the new squadron were decorated veterans of the war of 1812 (most notably Lieutenant Colonel Maksiut Bey Biiarslanov), and presumably many of the privates fought in the Napoleonic wars as well. True to their reputation, they fought well again, this time against the Ottomans, and received silver pipes in recognition of their bravery. Their commander, Colonel Prince Ahmet Bey Khunkalov, earned a silver medal of distinction and a large sum of money as a mark of the tsar's favor. When the squadron returned to Petersburg, Khunkalov and his fellow officers settled into lodgings built at the treasury's expense and specifically for them: the top floor consisted of one spacious, well-lit room meant for religious services, complete with a *mihrab* (a niche indicating the direction of Mecca).[47]

The squadron's place in the army was not yet assured. In the wake of this most recent Russian-Ottoman war, the Committee of Ministers paused to reconsider policy toward the Crimean Tatars and the privileges accorded them by Catherine II. The conscription exemption was the most pressing issue, and with good reason: disease and plague, together with the attrition caused by campaigns against Persia (1826–1828), the Ottomans (1828–1829), and the Caucasus, had reduced the strength of Russian army units by more than one-third. Half of the remaining forces were deployed along the empire's borders, and military recruiters were hard pressed to fill the gaping vacancies. As Alexander Bitis points out, "exemptions for various estates, regions and ethnic groups meant that only c. 16.5 million men [out of a population of 47 million] were liable for conscription." Of these, four million were fit for service, meaning that one in every five of these were needed to staff a standing army of 850,000 in the early to mid-nineteenth century.[48]

The need for soldiers was acute, and it rendered Crimean privileges, in the mind of many a minister, obsolete. Moreover, Governor A. I. Kaznacheev assured the Committee of Ministers of what he described as the Tatars' overwhelming desire to serve in the ranks of Russian army. He suggested that the army enlist volunteers without requiring them to convert—a step that might otherwise have put a damper on potential recruits' enthusiasm. The ministers took this one step further, recommending that the Tatar population be subjected to the same military recruitment standards as other state peasants.[49]

Before making his final decision, Nicholas consulted Vorontsov. Vorontsov expressed his doubts about the practical benefits of maintaining irregular Tatar regiments. The Crimean Tatars had no experience with Western-style military service, he explained, and had long since shed their military propensities and "acquired a preference for living peacefully." Yet he felt that Nicholas could not simply forge ahead with the plan to impose conscription, for this policy would most certainly be "misunderstood" by the Crimeans as a revocation of their traditional privileges. Vorontsov concluded that the life guard squadron should be preserved—if not for military purposes, then for the sake of preserving order in the province.[50]

Nicholas agreed. The recruitment regulation of June 1831 did not include a specific exemption for them, but noble and non-noble Crimean Tatars retained their immunity from conscription. Thus, when in June 1829 Colonel Ahmet Bey Khunkalov informed the provincial and district marshals of the tsar's desire to man and arm the squadron, the call went out for volunteers, not conscripts. Six months later, however, the officer ranks were still riddled with vacancies. Khunkalov characterized the tepid response of would-be subalterns as evidence of the "Muslim nobility's disinclination to serve" in general, but it turned out he had glossed over an important concern of his fellow mirzas. This came to light in May 1830 at an assembly of the "Muslim nobility" in Simferopol. When Kaznacheev reminded them of their obligation to produce volunteers for the squadron, they hastened to explain that they had not yet come forward because of concerns about their position in the squadron vis-à-vis that of the enlisted Tatars. Don Cossack nobles served the same twenty-five-year term of service as Cossack rank and file; the mirzas would not tolerate any elision of status or privilege. Eventually, they determined that the tsar's decision to register twelve mirzas in the Cadet Corps effectively redrew the division between elite and common Tatars, since upon completion of their studies the mirza cadets would enter the officer ranks directly, filling vacancies in the squadron and effectively dashing "the hope that a junker [of common origins] might be promoted to officer." Satisfied, the mirzas could accept His Imperial Majesty's "generous invitation" to partake of the "honor of serving in the Guard."[51]

The Crimean Life Guard Squadron provided an important venue for gaining noble rank. Forty-four percent of squadron officers were from hereditary elite clans, including all four officers ranking as lieutenant colonel or higher. Another 26 percent came from well-established service clans. And when the Crimean War broke out in 1853, the portion of the squadron stationed in Crimea under Umer Bey Balatukov took part in the famous defense of Sevastopol, earning accolades from Prince A. S. Menshikov, commander of the Admiralty, for crossing the Black River under cover of night in September 1854 and routing the British dragoons on the opposite bank.

But for most Tatars, war brought hunger, disease, Cossack depredations, accusations of treason and, ultimately, confirmation of their long-held fear that the tsar would forsake them in favor of Russian landowners and settlers. Between 1859 and 1861 roughly a quarter million emigrated, leaving a trail of distrust and antagonism in their wake. There was a foreshadowing of that trajectory in the history of the squadron itself. In 1840, a Lithuanian Tatar of the Ulan Guard Regiment replaced Khunkalov. When Colonel Seit Giray Mirza Tevkelev of Orenburg succeeded him, it was clear that a palpable distance had opened between the mirzas and the military command. In May 1863, Alexander II abolished the squadron. In its place he created a Life Guard Special Command and attached it to the Caucasian Life Guard Squadron—a unit that already included Caucasian mountaineers, Georgians, and Armenians. The Crimean Tatars, in other words, belonged to a Black Sea world they no longer anchored.[52]

SERVICE AND THE CONTOURS OF CRIMEAN SOCIETY

From the point of view of Russian authorities, the purpose of this succession of military units was to contribute to the security of the empire by limiting Tatar involvement in the struggle with the Ottomans for control of the Black Sea. Potemkin created the beşli regiment, for example, not because he wanted to capitalize on the military skills of the Crimeans, but in order to emphasize Catherine's position as the sole source of authority. He knew that doling out military ranks would not transform the mirzas into loyal Russian subjects overnight. Thus, when war with the Ottomans broke out in 1787, he ordered the regiment to assume border patrol duties on the Polish frontier rather than risk the defection of hundreds of armed and able horsemen at Ochakov or Bender. The four regiments of Alexander I's reign followed in the same mold, this time serving with distinction against Napoleon from Moscow to Paris. In each case the units proved an effective way of removing hundreds, sometimes thousands, of horsemen from the Black Sea coast for the duration of hostilities with the Porte; the culminating moment was the decision to deploy the life guard squadron against Ottoman forces in 1827.

What effect did these experiences have on the Crimean community? Did these new units provide opportunities for new men to rise, or for a new generation of the existing clan hierarchy to claim its rightful place? Did the acquisition of officer rank have a long-term effect, or did it amount to nothing more than a pleasant but transitory moment of recognition?

Many of these answers were determined by the distinction between regular and irregular military service. The vast majority of the Tatars who served did so in units created expressly for them; all of these units were irregular. On one level, this was a mark of privilege. Like the Cossacks, most Crimean Tatars were allergic to the idea of integration into the regular army, which they saw (rightly) as the end of any claim to autonomy. In another sense, irregular status was a mark of subordination, disenfranchisement, or devaluation. The military leadership felt no obligation to provision or outfit irregulars. True, Richelieu and Field Marshal Barclay de Tolly toyed with the idea of costuming the Crimean Tatars in enough "national clothing" to produce an exotic and intimidating effect on the enemy, but they eventually settled on assigning the Crimean Tatars a Cossack-style uniform consisting of black jackets and Tatar lambskin caps. Many horsemen reported for duty in their own clothes, while their officers dressed in the uniforms of their previous units. In true irregular fashion, they supplied their own weaponry, which ranged from pikes, knives, and axes, to pistols and guns of Persian or Caucasian manufacture. In this they were no different from other non-Cossack irregular units, such as the Balaklava Greek infantry battalion, the Georgian volunteer infantry detachment, the Dagestani and Transcaucasian Muslim horse regiments, and the Bashkir-Meshcheriak force. Even the life guard squadron was a "foreign" unit (*inorodnoe voisko*). It, however, provided its officers access to the social and cultural world of the Russian officer corps, thanks to Tsar Nicholas's decision to equate squadron officers with guard officers (in other words, the ranks were of equal value, though the units were not). Nicholas also opened the doors of the Noble Regiment of the Second Cadet Corps to young mirzas. The privilege of attending the corps was a long time in coming, and it indicated a new level of integration.[53]

Because proximity to the imperial court was a critical ingredient for a successful military career, one of the most important benefits of admission to the Noble Regiment was that it brought mirzas to Petersburg. Advancement to the rank of major elevated an officer to the level at which further appointments were theoretically made by the sovereign himself. Colonels, majors, and generals could claim "to have entered into a direct personal relationship" with the tsar—a relationship that was far easier to cultivate in the capital. The mirzas were well aware of the benefits of access to the imperial court. After Nicholas approved Balatukov's Life Guard Squadron, they lobbied for the formation of two additional regiments to be overseen by a committee of mirzas. Provincial Secretary Mehmet Mirza Krımtay delivered this petition in 1831. A savvy recipient of imperial favor himself, Krımtay explained that the committee would be filled with competent and decorated men, such as Captain Suan Gazy Mirza Şirin and Esaul Kara Mirza Edige. The post of regimental commander required no less a man than *rotmistr* Prince Maksiut Bey Biiarslanov, who boasted military credentials and a mastery of the Russian language rare among mirzas. The proposal failed to gain traction, but a handful of young men were able to cash in on the opportunity to live in the capital. Only two (Major Generals Balatukov and Ahmet Bey Khunkalov) rose to the generalitet—the level at which officers were considered part of the ruling elite based on their service record, material wealth, education, and the honor of their family name. Nineteen reached the level of staff officer, while 157 remained subalterns.[54]

Considering that there were nearly 27,000 officers in the Russian army on the eve of the Crimean War, it is clear that Crimean Tatars did not have a significant presence among the imperial military elite. Nor did they represent a significant part of the military establishment within Tavrida itself. Since before annexation, the region had played host to large numbers of Russian soldiers. Between 1782 and 1783, Suvorov's Fifth Corps maintained order in the khanate, and from April 1783 until November 1784 at least 20,000 soldiers were stationed there at any given time. Large infantry and Cossack forces moved into the province during each of the Russian-Ottoman wars, and by 1811 over 20,000

Black Sea Cossacks were in residence. Moreover, architects and engineers were busily constructing a military landscape in which the native population played little or no part: Sevastopol quickly emerged as an important harbor and naval base populated with Englishmen, Frenchmen, Jews, Greeks, Sardinians, Italians, Swedes, Germans, and Ottomans, but no Crimean Tatars.[55]

The significance of Crimean military service lies in the influence it had on the structure of indigenous society. It remained a far more common occupation than civil service, and a more effective path toward rank: more than 73 percent of the mirzas who earned rank did so through the military (table 3.5). Military service afforded important access to wealth. Paul Heineman has demonstrated that those Don Cossack officers allowed to serve in Guards regiments in the late eighteenth century constituted a core elite who "remain[ed] wealthy and influential actors in Don society until the fall of the Empire." Salaries were the most

Table 3.5. Tatar Servitors, 1783–1853

Highest rank attained	Military rank		Civil rank		Total
	#	percentage	#	percentage	#
4	2	100.0	0	–	2
5	0	–	4	100.0	4
6	3	42.9	4	57.1	7
7	3	37.5	5	62.5	8
8	13	72.2	5	25.0	18
9	47	64.4	26	35.6	73
10	5	83.3	1	16.7	6
12	49	90.7	5	9.3	54
13	3	100.0	0	–	3
14	53	77.9	15	22.1	68
Total:	178	73.2	65	26.4	243
With hereditary rank:	178	100.0	18	27.7	196

Source: Data compiled from the *Mesiatseslov, Adres-kalendar'*, and *Rodoslovnaia kniga* entries cited in previous tables, as well as RGIA f. 1343, op. 51, d. 664; DAARK f. 49, op. 1, d. 417; DAARK f. 49, op. 1, d. 1026. If a mirza held both military and civil rank, he is included only in the rank for which he was approved for the noble register.

immediate material benefit of service. Early in Catherine's reign, an infantry colonel earned 600 rubles a year; a lieutenant colonel earned 460 rubles, and a major earned an average of 350. From the early days of the beşli regiments, Tatars received salaries that exceeded the average for their rank. This source of income was critical after 1783, when the Crimean economy lay in ruin after decades of war and civil unrest. In fact, Potemkin may well have paid generous salaries to his mirza officers in order to help them recoup their economic and social positions. Officers and soldiers also reaped rewards for demonstrations of skill or bravery on the battlefield in the form of chivalric orders or medals of distinction, together with the purses, golden sabers, and diamond rings that came along with them. Land grants accompanied promotions, particularly during Potemkin's tenure as governor-general. Whether these grants conferred new property or simply confirmed an individual's right to his traditional lands, a strong correlation grew between landownership and military rank (table 3.6).[56]

Military service was, more than anything, a pathway toward local power. While not averse to rising to the upper echelons of the imperial elite, the mirzas proved far more concerned with maintaining their positions in the former khanate. They were not the only segment of the Russian elite to harbor such "provincial" ambitions. According to Menning, while the Don Cossack starshyna initially sought prestige and glory, by the late eighteenth century they sought noble status precisely because it entailed the privilege of retiring "to a quiet, sedentary life on a mod-

Table 3.6. Landownership of Mirzas with Rank Inscribed in the Noble Register, 1804–1853

Type of rank	Mirzas	Mirzas owning land	Approximate total amount of land (desiatinas)	Average (desiatinas)
Military	20	11 (55%)	125,000	6,250
Civil	8	3 (37.5%)	20,000	2,500
None	12	5 (41.7)	25,000	1,991

Source: RGIA f. 1343, op. 51, dela 485–496; RGIA f. 1343, op. 51, d. 664.

est estate carved out of some portion of the Don steppe." Since the storied emancipation of the nobility in 1762, a large number of Russian nobles also angled to parlay military rank into comfortable appointments in the provinces. In 1794, as many as 73 percent of Russian nobles in middle-ranking positions, including the great majority of land captains and nearly every governor appointed after 1775, had held military rank. A similar picture emerges in Tavrida, where men like Seit Ibrahim Aga Taşı-oğlu (1751–1830?) and Halil Mirza Ulan (1785–1836) made the transition with great success.[57]

Ibrahim Aga's grandfather was from an Anatolian family in the service of the Ottoman sultan, and his father served as adjutant (*kapuci başı*) under Selim Giray. Potemkin appointed him kaymakam of Perekop shortly after annexation, and he quickly made an impression on Baron Igel'strom, who recommended promoting Ibrahim to the rank of captain in 1784. Catherine elevated him to major during her visit to Crimea three years later, though he never served as an officer—he served instead as land captain in Perekop (1788–1791) and Evpatoriia (1791–1794) and higher land court deputy (1794–1796), participating in noble assembly elections through 1827. Along the way, he accumulated over 6,000 desiatinas inhabited by nearly one hundred households in Perekop, a series of orchards in Simferopol, and a residence in Bahçesaray, all of which his son, who made his way to the rank of lieutenant, inherited.[58]

Born a generation after Seit Ibrahim, Halil Mirza Ulan also descended from an important kapıhalkı clan. His father, Ak Gazy Mirza, was kaymakam under Şahin Giray before acquiring the rank of court councilor and serving as a member of the temporary government and civil court assessor (1785–1796). But in contrast to Taşı-oğlu, who was a military man in rank only, Halil's rank of *esaul* (captain) referred to his service as commander of the Simferopol Tatar regiment. An educated man literate in both Russian and Turkish, Halil entered service in 1804 and subsequently fought in the battles of Smolensk, Borodino, and Danzig. He received the Order of St. Anna (third class) along with a golden saber and a silver medal. After retiring from the regiment in 1817, Halil won election as Perekop lower land court deputy, and participated in subsequent noble assembly elections. His landholdings were not as extensive as those of Seit Ibrahim Taşı-oğlu, but Halil claimed over 1,000 desiatinas in Perekop district plus other lands in Feodosiia.[59]

The careers of these two men are not unique. Many mirzas were able to translate military rank into positions in the provincial administration, extensive landholdings, and social prestige. Interestingly enough, of the two dozen men who followed this trajectory, all were from hereditary elite clans. Among the karaçi clans, the Şirin were far and away the most successful, both in terms of wealth accumulation and military accomplishments. Ali Mirza Şirin's biography illustrates the way in which members of this clan capitalized on both traditional and imperial sources of power particularly well. Ali was one of those mirzas who entered military service during Catherine's reign but did not transcend the ranks of subaltern until the early nineteenth century. Born in 1773 into a lateral branch of the Şirin clan, Ali first served as a lieutenant on Count Zubov's staff in 1796. Zubov rewarded this promising member of Crimea's most powerful clan with a grant of 3,500 desiatinas of land and a mill in Feodosiia, as well as five desiatinas of vineyards in Sudak. Thus comfortably established, Ali married the daughter of Mehmetşa Bey Şirin and was subsequently elected commander of the Feodosiia regiment in 1807. He served with the cordon patrol along the Dnestr River, and though he did not see combat, Ermolov recommended Ali for promotion to army captain in 1810. He earned a series of chivalric orders, and upon return to Crimea after the war served a three-year term as marshal of Feodosiia, by which time he had extended his land holdings to some 10,000 desiatinas spread between Feodosiia and Perekop districts. By that point he was also the bey of the Şirin clan. The Heraldry enhanced his status with its 1829 decision to inscribe him in the noble register, and with wealth, rank, and nobility in hand, Ali and his descendants had secured their place among the provincial elite.[60]

Thanks to men like Ali, the karaçi clans comprised a large proportion of Tatars with military rank. The Şirin, Argin, Mansur, and Iaşlav clans each produced an average of 7.5 military servitors, two civil servants with rank commensurate with nobility (eight or better), and just over two in ranks nine or lower. Each non-karaçi clan could lay claim to only 2.6 military servitors, 0.2 civil servants in rank eight or above, and 0.8 in ranks nine through fourteen. Without corresponding data on the composition of the eighteenth-century Giray armies it is impossible to say for sure whether the karaçi constituted a larger percentage of officers under the tsars than they had under the khans, but their share of the mirza population rendering military service to the tsars clearly dropped over time (table 3.7).

In part, that downward trajectory is explained by the withdrawal of the bey clans from interaction with Russian institutions and the comparatively strong presence of a different segment of the hereditary elite: the "princely" clans, that is, the foreign (Caucasian) elite of the khanate. The Khunkalovs were the only princely clan to produce three individuals who attained staff officer rank of higher. Their success began with Abdulla Velişa, the son of an important advisor of Selim Giray and himself a high-ranking official at the Giray court. Potemkin made Abdulla Velişa first adjutant and later commander of the second beşli squadron with the rank of major. His eldest son, Prince Ahmet Bey (born 1767), entered the Tambov musketeer regiment as a sergeant in 1784. Potemkin appointed him adjutant in November 1787 and promoted him to lieutenant three years later. In August 1790 Ahmet received the rank of *rotmistr*, as well as command of the fifth beşli squadron (1790–1792). He rose to major in May 1796 and took command of the Perekop regi-

Table 3.7. Ranks Obtained by Mirzas, According to Clan Type (All figures are percentages of the total)

	Karaçi	Kapıhalkı	Other/unknown clan
1783–1796			
Military	27.7	53.2	19.1
Civil	42.9	42.9	14.3
Civil (non-hereditary)	46.2	38.5	15.4
1801–1825			
Military	12.7	40.8	46.5
Civil	50.0	25.0	25.0
Civil (non-hereditary)	11.1	63.0	25.9
1825–1855			
Military	11.7	48.3	40.0
Civil	0.0	0.0	0.0
Civil (non-hereditary)	0.0	42.9	57.1

Source: Data compiled from the *Mesiatseslov, Adres-kalendar'*, and *Rodoslovnaia kniga* entries cited in previous tables, as well as RGIA f. 1343, op. 51, d. 664; DAARK f. 49, op. 1, d. 417; DAARK f. 49, op. 1, d. 1026.

ment in July 1807. This impressive beginning led to an even more successful career than that of his father. Ahmet Bey earned the rank of colonel during the Napoleonic wars, was awarded the Orders of St. Vladimir (fourth class) and St. Anna (second class), and commanded the Crimean Life Guard Squadron (1828–1832), eventually attaining the rank of major general (1832) before his death in Crimea in 1842.[61]

As stellar as his accomplishments were, Ahmet Bey did not enjoy a monopoly on success among Abdulla Velişa's sons. Ahmet's brother, Seliamet (b. 1774), became a titular councilor in 1796 and an esaul in the Perekop regiment a decade later. In return for his efforts on the battlefields of 1812, Seliamet received the Order of St. Anna (third and fourth class). Later, he served a three-year term as land captain of Perekop district 1819–1821. The Heraldry confirmed his noble status, along with that of his son, in 1837. Mehmet Bey (b. 1817) represented the third generation of Khunkalovs in the Russian military. He served as life guard squadron commander for six years (1834–1840) before becoming Governor-General Vorontsov's adjutant and, like his uncle and grandfather, ascending to the level of staff officer.[62]

The Balatukov clan also capitalized on the opportunities represented by service in the various Tatar regiments. Major General Kaya Bey's success remained unmatched by any mirza of his generation. His son Batyr Bey followed suit, and at least two nephews served as lieutenants in the life guard squadron, while two cousins served as esauls in the Tatar horse regiments. Kaya's younger brother, Prince Adyl Bey (b. 1780), began his career in the Belev grenadier regiment and reached the officer ranks two years later. He commanded the Simferopol horse regiment from 1808, where he earned the rank of major and became a cavalier of two orders. Decorated with several gold sabers, he rose to the rank of lieutenant colonel in July 1813, a mere seven years after entering military service. Adyl also made the transition to provincial life easily, serving as Evpatoriia marshal for almost a decade (1815–1824) and accumulating over 3,000 desiatinas of arable land, a large fruit orchard, several small vineyards, and two mills in Simferopol district, plus an additional 15,000 desiatinas in Evpatoriia.[63] Clearly, the Şirin, Khunkalov, and Balatukov clans were adept at rising through the military ranks and using that success to either acquire or protect material assets, ranging from salaries and grants of land to medals and other valuables made of precious metals and gems. Together, wealth and rank helped fortify their place within post-1783 Crimean society.

Was this the intention of the officials who administered Tavrida? When Potemkin convinced Catherine to form the beşli regiment, did he intend to preserve the channels through which the hereditary elite clans derived their authority? Perhaps he did. At the same time, military service had an integrative function. Of the forty mirzas inscribed in the noble register for example—one of the key indicators of social integration—all but four cited their military rank or that of their father. There is even some evidence that as high-profile a Tatar leader as Kaya Bey Balatukov converted from Islam. The Commission on Muslim and Greek Clans approved him under his Muslim name, Kaya (not Kiril), for inscription in the noble register in 1820, on the strength of his descent from the Cherkess prince Balatuk. Kaya Bey's own sons, Batyr (a Guards lieutenant) and Mehmet, bore Muslim names, and Kaya Bey is included on every list of members of the "Muslim nobility" compiled during his lifetime. However, he is identified as "Kiril" in the imperial grant of princely title issued in 1830, and he married a Christian woman, Ol'ga Aleksandrovna Gedenshtrom. In his case then, it would seem that conversion (if it did occur), altered his identity in the imperial, but not the local, context.[64]

Even Balatukov's resume pales in comparison with that of the most influential Crimean Tatar to serve in the Russian army: Alexander Iakovlevich Rudzevich (1775–1829). Rudzevich was the son of Iakub Aga, a native of Karasubazar who made his career in Potemkin's chancellery and as a crucial player in the machinations leading up to annexation. When Iakub died, Potemkin provided his daughters wife dowries, his wife with a pension and an estate at Sarabuz, and all four of his children with a new life in Petersburg, where they were baptized and raised under Catherine's protection. A beneficiary of imperial favor, Rudzevich enlisted in the Preobrazhenskii Regiment at the age of eleven, studied at the Greek Cadet Corps, and began active service in 1792.[65] He fought in the 1794 campaign in Poland, but spent the next four years working on topographical studies of Vyborg and Kazan. In the course of his illustrious career Rudzevich rose through the ranks to lieutenant-general (1813) fighting in the Kuban and Caucasus, and later against the French. He served as military governor of Kherson from November 1814 to

January 1816, and then as chief of staff of the Second Army until 1819. He commanded numerous corps and divisions, accumulated innumerable orders, and became an infantry general in 1826. Rudzevich died in Wallachia during the Russian-Ottoman war of 1828–1829 and was buried on his estate in Karasubazar.[66]

This native son of Crimea was more accomplished, and to a far greater extent integrated into both the military hierarchy and imperial society, than Balatukov. However, as a convert to Christianity from early childhood, Rudzevich was never considered a member of the Tatar elite—either by the Tatar elite or by his Russian peers. His official service document (*formuliarnyi spisok*) identifies him as "a member of the Tavrida gentry and son of a state councilor." His entry in the *Brokgaus-Efron Encyclopedia* describes him as an infantry general who served in the Caucasus and pulled off a number of military feats, such as leading the assault on Montmartre in 1814, before dying in Wallachia (no mention of his birth or burial in Crimea). His entry in the *Russian Biographical Dictionary* mentions that his father was a Tatar and that Alexander himself was buried near Karasubazar; otherwise one would never know "one of the greatest generals" of the day was anything but a Russian hero. The glory he earned for himself and for his country did not translate to Crimea or its inhabitants, though he certainly claimed a place there. Rudzevich married Marfa Evstaf'evna Notara, daughter of one of the most powerful men in Crimea and, as the proprietor of over 70,000 desiatinas, was one of the largest landowners. An obituary praised him as "a true and loyal son of the fatherland" and the Tavrida noble assembly posthumously inscribed him in the noble register along with his sons, Guard Lieutenant Nikolai (b. 1810), Izmailov Life Guard Ensign Alexander, and Court Page Mikhail Alexandrovich.[67]

Many men with less land and fewer accolades claimed membership in the elite ranks of imperial society. They too recognized the value of military service; they simply defined its value differently than Potemkin or Rudzevich might have. For most Crimean Tatars, military service was (potentially) a tool for enhancing wealth and status. But it was useful only so long as the wealth and status it generated could be converted into social capital at home in Tavrida. This is why there is no contradiction in the Tatars' lack of enthusiasm to muster and their spectacular performance on the field of battle. They fought, died, and marched to Paris not to prove themselves subjects of the tsar, but to prove themselves worthy members of Crimean society. They used the ranks they earned to enrich and empower themselves and their kinsmen at home, rather than to gain entry into the illustrious Guards regiments of the capitals. From a certain perspective, their goals were modest, perhaps even provincial. Their success was modest as well. But unlike the Cossacks, Kalmyks, or Bashkirs, who similarly started out as irregular cavalrymen, the Crimean Tatars were never assigned a military caste status, and they never rendered obligatory service. This was enough to preserve the fragile veil of privilege—and isolation—that defined their place within imperial society.

4   The New Domain

> Like most barbarians, their own country is to [the Crimean Tatars] at once
> the pattern of excellence and the boundary of knowledge.
> —William Eton, *A Survey of the Turkish Empire* (1799)

> We find it impossible to imagine that the Crimean steppe, if claimed in its
> entirety, would be doomed to present an empty, uninhabited, sunburnt
> landscape as it does now.
> —Iu. E. Ianson, *Krym, ego khlebopashestvo i*
> *khlebnaia torgovliia* (1870)

THIS CHAPTER BEGINS and ends in the gardens of Crimea. It begins
with the idea that establishing imperial rule required not just imagining
a new landscape, but asserting authority over the measure, use, ownership, and meaning of land itself. Previous studies have built a narrative
of dispossession, according to which the appropriation of land from
Tatar owners began in the earliest days of Russian rule with Catherine's decision to claim all land belonging to the khan for the imperial government. In subsequent years the remainder of the former
khanate—the portion claimed by mirzas, peasant communities, and
Muslim pious endowments—gradually fell into the hands of Slavic
pomeshchiki (landowners) and a handful of German settlers. The dispossession of the vast majority of native Crimeans, complete by the
outbreak of war in 1853, was a prime motivation for their mass emigration to the Ottoman Empire in the early 1860s.

It is indisputable that throughout these decades a vast number of fields,
pastures, gardens, and vineyards came under new ownership. The rules
governing landownership changed. New institutions for measuring,
assessing, and managing access to land emerged. Agricultural methods changed. And the government involved itself in all of this. But the

story of Tavridan land is far more than a tale of dispossession. It is a story about the intricacies and limits of imperial rule and about the dynamic shifts in the administrative character and social composition of the fin-de-siècle empire. It is a story about evolving practices of governance and the reconsideration of the relationship between social status and landownership that was ongoing throughout the Catherinian and Alexandrine periods. And it is a story about the development of new legal and social vocabularies, the laborious creation of a coherent system for administering the territory of the empire's southernmost province, and the reimagination of what constituted Russian space.

At first blush, the relationship between land and space might seem quite straightforward. Territory under the sovereign authority of the Romanov tsar was Russian land, and Russian space. However, the terms are not coterminous. Land is significant in this story not solely because of the chemical compounds that compose its soils, the slope of its terrain, or even its location; it is significant because of its productive capacity, the claims made on it by historical actors, and the role it plays in shaping a range of cultural practices and identities. It is one of the many possible manifestations of Russian space, but it might well be the most important one. As Valerie Kivelson has shown, the physical environment was a crucial venue for the articulation of individual, community, and imperial identity. "Muscovites found social and political identity in the rocks, forests, and fields of the places they inhabited," she explains, and because of that "The landscape took on both a political and theological significance far beyond its objective geographic features and contributed to defining and enacting the meanings of belonging to an Orthodox Muscovite realm." This chapter adopts a similar perspective on the significance of land, considering it as an actor in its own right: a constantly evolving force which, susceptible as it was to radical renovation by human hands, could nevertheless enable or constrain opportunities for cultural interaction or economic exchange. In the southern empire, the land did not simply absorb the significance attributed to it by longtime residents or by new settlers; it helped define patterns of experience, knowledge-creation, discourse, and policy. In an effort to buttress that claim, this chapter explores the process of reorganizing Crimean land in the wake of annexation. It argues that this process involved far more than simply summoning particular governing bodies into existence or implementing a new toponymy. It meant confronting the complex materiality of daily life on a variety of scales. It required reinventing the land.[1]

The idea of scale is crucial here. This chapter argues for the significance of micro-landscapes for understanding imperial history. It does so not out of conviction that the dynamics of empire building replicated themselves in every grain of sand, but because at any moment in time empire building occurred in innumerable locations and at every scale imaginable. The institutions and rules intended to standardize basic features of governance across a massive continental empire were meant to render the most exotic and mundane nooks and crannies of that empire legible to the men who exercised authority over them. This was the purpose, for example, of the attempt to conduct a general land survey that luxuriated in the specificity of place and sought to translate that specificity into the universal language of cartographic representation. This was also the motivation for the voluminous documentation of property disputes. Behind each carefully crafted discussion of legal precedent and social hierarchy lurked personal attachments to quite particular terrestrial spaces. In Tavrida as elsewhere, possessing new land meant knowing it. It meant describing, measuring, and mapping places like the Baydar valley, the orchards of Beshui, and the vineyards of Otuz. It also meant striking a functional balance between the demands of the physical environment, local practices, and imperial interests. The pages that follow explain the attempts to pull off this feat. They examine the use of the dacha system to imprint imperial authority on the former khanate, the subsequent administrative and legal wrangling over landownership, and the emergence—thanks to the herculean efforts of surveyors, geodesists, and naturalists—of a new calculus for defining the value of Russian land and the meaning of imperial space.

GEOGRAPHIC KNOWLEDGE AND DACHA LOGIC

Whether it took cartographic, narrative, or statistical form, geographical knowledge was a means of producing and projecting power. And like its fellow imperial states, the eighteenth-century Russian Empire sought the kind of geographical knowledge that would allow it not just to connect discrete and bounded enclaves, but to seep outward from them into the nebulous spaces in between: to convert the sprawling constellation of tsarist sites into a sovereign territory with defined, though certainly not fixed, boundaries. Routes and bounded provinces could be leveraged to this end, but the project required a third tool: the property map.

The history of Russian land surveying, like that of Russian mapping more generally, extends back to late fifteenth-century Muscovy and gathers steam with the establishment of the *Pomestnyi Prikaz* (Service Lands Chancellery) in the mid-sixteenth century. Elsewhere in Europe cadastral maps became important instruments for the management of natural resources in the early sixteenth century and for reforms in land taxation from the seventeenth century, spreading in both cases from Dutch lands to Venice, the German states, Sweden, England, and France. Enclosure mapping came into its own in the eighteenth century and gathered steam throughout the nineteenth. Muscovy, which began to produce large quantities of property sketches or drawings (*chertezhi*) along with standard statistical descriptions in the second half of the seventeenth century, fits neatly into this chronology. There, as elsewhere, the cadastral map was an increasingly important instrument for facilitating "the regulation of privileges and obligations of both officialdom and subjects" and the mobilization of human and natural resources in service of the state.[2]

The difference was that Russian property maps developed within the context of the Muscovite moral economy: a moral economy grounded in a complex form of consensus between ruler and ruled. As the Petrine state bureaucratized, developed a regular army, shifted the unit of taxation from the household to (male) soul, and otherwise shed its reliance on the notion of reciprocal obligations flowing back and forth between tsar and subject, the foundation for that consensus eroded and land surveys became less and less important. Agents of the government focused their attention on cataloging the service rendered by members of the elite and on compiling inventories of forests, rivers, and political borders; they paid precious little attention to the demarcation or use of landed property.[3]

All of that changed in the second half of the eighteenth century. The Petrine reforms had created a growing service elite, and members of that elite were eager to consolidate their claims to landed property. Meanwhile, a woman obsessed with developing both the cultural and economic resources of her empire had ascended the throne. Over the course of her reign Catherine II confirmed her late husband's decision to emancipate the nobility from required service, secured their private property, granted them full use of all that could be found underneath or emerging from the soil, and reinvented the nobility as a corporate entity endowed with rights and privileges along with obligations. Historians have long debated whether these policies were motivated by political necessity or Enlightenment-era philosophy, but regardless of her motivations, these maneuvers paired nicely with Catherine's push to expand and secure her southern frontier. To that end Catherine and Potemkin recruited a motley assortment of foreign colonists, Old Believers, sons of clergy, and a smattering of officers and nobles to populate the steppe.[4] This meant that the southern economy in general and the land regime in particular—which had up to that point been defined by Cossack *khutors* (small, often single-homestead rural settlements) and *slobody* (villages), military settlements, Nogay pastures, coastal towns populated by Greeks and Armenians, and a great many Tatar farms, villages, and towns— was suddenly subject to significant revision. As the forces of integration, reform, and preservation collided, land and landownership took on new significance.

Grigorii Potemkin shared Catherine's belief that knowledge (along with a preponderance of military power) was the foundation of imperial rule. In Crimea, that belief was transformed into a nearly unquenchable thirst for information about this new territory—one that bore so little resemblance to the rest of the empire. Between 1762 and 1796 the peninsula figured on the itineraries of four Academy of Science expeditions, making it the second most visited region (Siberia took the honors).[5] But these expeditions pursued carefully defined scientific agendas; Potemkin's needs were more immediate. Intent on compiling as complete a documentary record of the new province as possible, he commissioned an administrative account (*kameral'noe opisanie*) in late summer 1783, just months after annexation. The account would be composed of reports on the hierarchy and territorial organization of the khan's administration, tax and customs revenues, the number, size, and location of Christian and non-Christian households, churches, and mosques. In addition, he ordered newly installed Governor Vasilii Kakhovskii to produce a systematic description of the land itself, paying particular attention to vineyards, orchards, and all lands appropriated by the treasury, complete with accompanying plans and maps attesting to the area and qualities of each parcel.

Meanwhile, Potemkin commissioned an altogether different accounting of Tavridan space from Karl Gablits (1752–1821), a Prussian-born, Russian-educated naturalist and longtime resident of the Caspian region. On receiving Potemkin's orders Gablits moved to Simferopol in the spring of 1784. Within a year, the Academy of Sciences published his *Physical Description of Tavrida Province*. The volume, in keeping with the tradition set out by earlier academy expeditions, describes everything from the location of lilac trees and watermelons to the locations of caves and wells, moving fluidly between sweeping generalizations about the nature of Tavridan space and indulgence in the climatic and botanical minutiae that made the peninsula an object of fascination to a man of Gablits's training—and to the growing number of educated readers consuming accounts of the botanical expeditions that fanned out across Europe and its colonial territories in the late eighteenth century. Throughout the text Gablits compares Crimea's topography with that of Provence, Italy, Anatolia, and Iran, creating a clear referential space for his readers. More important, he provides the Russian, French, and Latin names of each specimen along with notes on the plant's domestic and foreign (mainly Mediterranean) habitats, translating each leaf, shrub, and berry into terms familiar to a reasonably well educated audience. Gablits thus made an invaluable contribution to the ideological renovation of the former khanate. By applying the Linnaean approach to the new province he correlated it not with the colonial territories of the New World and Asian subcontinent, but with the physical world of Enlightened Europe and classical antiquity.[6]

But the truly seductive power of this particular text was rooted as firmly in Crimean soil as in scientific metonymies. The *Physical Description* created a deeply influential spatial hierarchy based on its assessment of the fertility and value of the terrain. Gablits dispensed with the huge expanse of land between Perekop and Gözleve in a few brief paragraphs, noting that other than the prolific gardens near Gözleve and Tarkhanskii Kut, the region that had commanded the attention of cartographers a few decades earlier offered little of interest beyond ample swaths of pasture that might be converted into farmland. Instead, he devoted the bulk of the monograph to the previously unpossessed, unmapped portion of the khanate. His thick descriptions of the geological, hydrographical, and botanical particularities of the foothills, valleys, highlands, and coast played a significant part in re-orienting the imperial gaze from steppe to seacoast.

This was no small task. Many of the travelers, officials, and settlers who spent time in Crimea over the next century were puzzled by what seemed to them its discrepancies and incongruities. "There is hardly any-thing consistent and uniform in it," complained Anthony Grant, who traveled the region in the early 1850s. "In its physical condition there is no harmony or uniformity . . . it resembles rather a collection of het-erogeneous plants, than a native woodland . . . a heap of disconnected links, and not a continuous chain." But in the Catherinian age, many Russian elites, officials, and writers took pleasure in this unruly abun-dance. Sergei Pleshcheev, author of one of the first geographic descrip-tions of Russia, exalted in the "instances of perfection" to be found in the highlands, while Pavel Levashev, who published his *Description of All the Predations of Turks and Tatars in Russia* in 1792, glorified the "ineffable fertility" that made Crimea "not only one of the most wonder-ful of Russia's possessions, but one of the truly superior possessions in all Europe."[7]

Relentlessly systematic, Gablits's *Physical Description* constructed a topographical logic of the peninsula, rooting it not in the salt lakes of Perekop or the harbor at Caffa, but in the heights of Chatyr Dag, the highest peak in the Crimean range. In his text, the sloping highlands and narrow river valleys radiating northward from that mountain dis-placed the even-pitched steppe—and its promise of black earth—as the ideal southern topos. His catalogs of fruit trees, medicinal grasses, gar-den flowers, and grains created an evocative series of micro-landscapes of fertility and productivity mapped onto the southern littoral. It was possible, according to Gablits, to find apricots, apples, dogwood, and rowan trees in nearly every orchard. True, only those on the south-facing slopes of the mountains offered dates, olives, and pomegranates: if Rus-sia's Eden-seekers craved diversity and rarities, they would find them in the crescent-shaped coast stretching from Balaklava to Sudak. But that exalted coastal terrain, as well the hinterland extending north past Man-gup and Akmeşit and along the banks of the Alma, Kacha, and Kabarda rivers, occupied the second rung of his spatial hierarchy. Gablits identi-fied the Karasubazar region and the upper Iandal, Burulcha, and Zuia rivers as the most desirable spaces for settlement and cultivation, and therefore the area most worthy of Potemkin's attention. The Salgir, which flowed northward from Chatyr Dag, hemmed in these lesser rivers, each of which flowed toward the Azov, while a far gentler ridge line separated the relatively broad and well-irrigated valleys from the ports at Sudak and Feodosiia. Away from the Mediterranean climate of Alushta and Yalta, the midlands could not boast of grape vines and laurel thickets. Instead they offered oaks, aspens, and stone pines growing in abundance alongside the field maples, hornbeams, and ash trees found on the increasingly idealized coast.[8]

Over the next half century, the Russian and European elites who documented their impressions of Crimea almost without exception defined the region in terms of its ecology and the promise of abundance. Pavel Sumarokov, a writer and local judge inspired by the potential for cultivating grapes, figs, almonds, and olives, wrote with excitement that "Tavrida [was] a vast, aromatic garden, a storeroom of treasures, and a pleasing and above all promising servant (*usluzhnitsa*) for the empire." To those who had caused "the invention of a thousand ill-natured lies about this new country, in order to lessen the share of praise" due Prince Potemkin, Baroness Elizabeth Craven countered that she saw nothing that might "justify the idea of the country's being unwholesome." Even the highlands harbored delights, rather than rebels. While the Caucasian range was already a site of resistance to Russian rule—the Giray princes enhanced their reputation by fleeing there in 1783 to gather support among the Circassians—Chatyr Dag and the lesser peaks arrayed around it provided good sport for mountaineers and, in the words of an enamored French traveler, "an infinity of trees." With its lush forests, orchards, grassland, and gardens, Crimea, these writers suggested, was nothing less than a nature preserve; an untamed but endlessly fertile environment.[9]

In reality of course, it was neither untamed nor endlessly fertile. Agricultural activity had been a mainstay of the khanate's economy for centuries, and by the early eighteenth century the vast majority of inhabitants of the peninsula had long since settled into the rhythms of agricultural pursuits. Gardening and viticulture predominated among Tatars, and slave labor allowed members of the elite to produce large quantities of wheat, barley, sorgo, and other grains on their estates. By the 1770s the population numbered over half a million and the mosques, gardens, markets, and palaces of Bahçesaray ("garden-palace"), Eski

Kırım, and Karasubazar had displaced the steppe as loci of prosperity. Hans Erich Thunmann, who traveled the region in 1777, found the extensive practice of agriculture diametrically opposed to the standard western image of the Tatar as by turns rapacious and indolent. In other words, the spatial hierarchy Gablits proposed had distinct cultural as well as geographical foundations.[10]

While Potemkin was not familiar with the general contours, let alone the nuances of the Tatar land regime, he saw no need to delay the introduction of a fundamental tool of empire building: the *dacha*. The dacha was in simplest terms a portion of land given out by the tsar. The apportioning of land to servitors and favorites was hardly an innovation, but over the course of the eighteenth century the dacha became increasingly differentiated from institutions such as *pomest'e* and *votchina* and ever more closely associated with the expansion of the empire. Early in the century, as he did with so many other elements of Russian statecraft, Peter I imbued the dacha with a distinctly strategic character, distributing grants both as a form of incentive and a coercive strategy for affecting the physical transformation of his new capital at St. Petersburg. Devoid of any associations with wellness, leisure, comfort, or domesticity—this came later in the nineteenth century—the earlier iteration of the dacha referred to a plot of uninhabited, unbuilt, uncultivated land located some distance away from the proprietor's primary residence. A diligent proprietor might convert it into an *usad'ba* (country estate), with formal or mature gardens and permanent dwellings, or into an agriculturally productive site—a farm, an orchard, a cultivated woodland. The essence of the dacha was that it implied a dynamic relationship between owner and property and the conversion of empty spaces into usable, definable places.[11]

These characteristics made the dacha an indispensable tool throughout the southern empire and particularly in the former khanate, where it served as a mechanism for distributing state-owned (in other words, recently appropriated) land and thus subsuming the newly acquired territory within larger imperial structures. Since its establishment in 1764 all of New Russia had, in fact, been defined through the distribution of land. The Plan for the Distribution of State Land in Novorossiia Province for Settlement promulgated in March of the same year stipulated that anyone willing to become a military settler was to be compensated with hereditary rights to between twenty-six and thirty desiatinas. The quantities and terms of ownership varied in subsequent decades, but the fact remained that in the Catherinian period members of the nobility in New Russia did not enjoy the signature monopoly on landownership they did elsewhere. In New Russia landownership was a tool for settling and cultivating land, and in so doing expanding imperial space, rather than buttressing the *soslovie* system.[12]

The dacha was designed to work from the inside out. It was akin to the insertion of a bit of genetic coding into a protean mass: the desirability of cultivated land and permanent dwellings was expected to replicate and spread, increasing the stability, as well as the legibility, of the new territory. This system revolved around a category of land that has received relatively little attention from (particularly Western) scholars interested in untying the Gordian knot of landownership policies and practices. Most studies have focused on the settled estates that formed the backdrop for Russian serfdom, and there are excellent reasons for this. But the implication that land bereft of enserfed inhabitants was less valuable or less significant is misleading, particularly in the context of the empire's southward expansion. Over the course of half a century Russia's rulers dissolved the Cossack Hetmanate and Zaporozhian Sich, swallowed vast portions of the Polish-Lithuanian Commonwealth, and helped themselves to a generous slice of the Ottoman Empire. The continually reconfigured southern empire absorbed layer upon layer of legal and cultural infrastructure, from Roman Catholic canon law and the Lithuanian statute to Ottoman *kanun, sharia,* and customary practices derived from Eurasian steppe tradition. Demographic patterns varied on either side of the Dnepr River, as did systems of land use and tenure. Much of the steppe was devoid of the usual markings of permanent habitation and cultivation—roads, homes, fields, pastures, and all other manner of agricultural enclosure. Yet nearly every acre from the Dnepr to the Kuban was of value within its respective micro-environment, and the desire to possess every inch of it changed both the way the Russian empire assessed property rights and the value of land itself.

The logic of Potemkin's dacha system was derived from two fundamental ideas. First, in an effort to cultivate a sense of familiarity and kinship with Tavrida among the ruling elite, Potemkin granted chunks of property to admirals and ministers, academics and princes. These were substantial grants. Potemkin himself claimed over 86,460 desiatinas (mainly in Melitopol) and allotted over 120,000 to his chief of staff,

Vasilii Popov. Catherine's procurator general, Prince A. A. Viazemskii, received 30,268 desiatinas; her minister of foreign affairs, Count A. A. Bezborodko, received 18,006; the head of the provincial government and ranking member of the Crimean elite, Mehmetşa Bey Şirin, received 27,334. By the time of Catherine's death in November 1796, the empress and viceroy had distributed 350,000 desiatinas on the peninsula alone, with another 276,358 desiatinas distributed north of Perekop. To put this in perspective, these figures represented 15.1 percent of the land available for cultivation (that is, excluding areas occupied by waterways, roads, ravines, etc.) on the peninsula proper, and 8.9 percent of land available for cultivation in the districts north of Perekop. A whopping 92 percent of all dacha grants and 81 percent of the total area allocated went to settler elites, which would seem to confirm the general narrative of dispossession that runs through Crimean history. Historical records are rarely so straightforward, however. The same register that speaks of the dominant place of pomeshchiki also suggests that the dacha grants had some benefit to the Tatar population. After all, the size of the average dacha awarded to settlers was 2,477 desiatinas, while grants to Tatars averaged 5,988 desiatinas. The discrepancy suggests that local men of power had a role to play, and that Potemkin felt they would play it with more skill if satisfied with the empress's largesse.[13]

In addition to using the idea of property—and for most elite recipients of remote Tavridan properties the land was never more than an idea—to embed the new province in the elite's mental map of the empire, Potemkin reinforced the idea of community by clustering grants on the southern portion of the peninsula. He distributed dachas almost exclusively between the northern flank of the Taurian mountains and the right bank of the Salgir River (figure 4.1). In fact, just under 50 percent of dachas distributed on the peninsula during Catherine's reign were located in Simferopol district and another 37 percent were in Feodosiia. As if he had a copy of the *Physical Description* ever at his elbow, Potemkin's dacha properties clustered not around urban centers such as Bahçesaray or Karasubazar but in the fertile valleys and around the headwaters of the Karasu, Iandal, Salgir, Belbek, Kacha, and Alma rivers. And apart from the handful of spectacularly large grants, most dachas were of modest size, between 2,000 and 3,000 desiatinas, meaning that the landscape of ownership—on paper anyway—had a distinctly regular aspect in terms of scale and location.

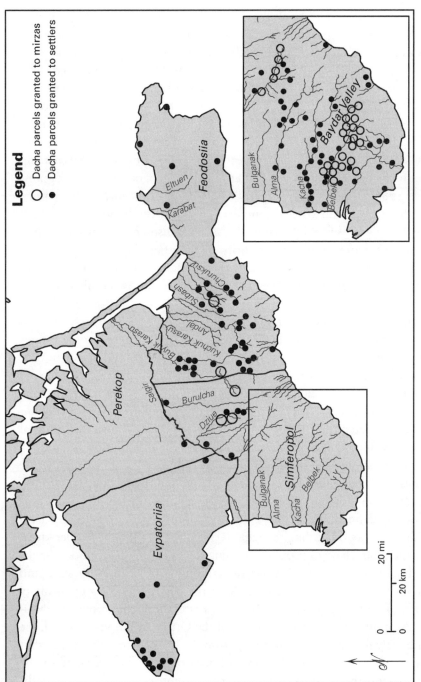

Figure 4.1. Distribution of dacha properties granted to mirzas and settlers, 1784–1802; with inset of Simferopol district (Source: Lashkov, "Sbornik dokumentov," part 4: 145–158)

This would seem to be clear evidence that Potemkin indeed had a carefully considered spatial policy, or at least that a spatial logic guided his allocations. Then again, each of these grants was carved from the territory Catherine claimed for her treasury: a land fund that included some 357 peninsular estates that had belonged either to the khan or to mirzas who had emigrated, as well as the "empty" (uncultivated) lands of the mainland steppe. As Alan Fisher rightly points out, in the first decade after annexation the Russian treasury appropriated land from very few native Crimeans. In other words, the geography of landownership that had existed prior to 1783 determined the geography of dacha grants after 1783. Disputes over property would erupt by the turn of the century, but for now, Tatar-owned lands remained in the hands of Tatars. If the dacha grants proved an effective tool for dismantling the connection between territory and the authority of the khan, it would be because they reiterated the spatial logic of the khanate; and because they reinforced the connection between owning land and owing allegiance to one's sovereign.[14]

On the ground, however, the outcome of Catherine's largesse was not an organic expansion of large, productive, well-ordered noble estates from Crimea's river valleys outward toward steppe and coast. In fact, Dmitrii Borisovich Mertvago, governor of Tavrida province (1802–1807) and never one to mince words, declared in no uncertain terms that the awarding of dachas "carried out by the unscrupulous governor [Potemkin], completed the ruin of Crimea." His superior, Minister of Internal Affairs Count V. P. Kochubei, agreed that "the distribution of land . . . was carried out in a decidedly unclear and poorly defined manner."[15] What was their cause for complaint? How had things gone so wrong?

In the common parlance of eighteenth-century officials, the dacha was a loosely defined institution: a quantity of unsettled, uncultivated land with no owner other than the imperial treasury. In 1783 the former khanate had a fair share of property seeming to match this description, thanks to three landmark events. First, fifteen long years of inter-imperial and civil war (1768–1783) brought about the destruction of a great many fields, orchards, and vineyards, and caused the flight of tens of thousands of inhabitants to other parts of the Ottoman Empire. Second, the withdrawal of Ottoman authority from the khanate in 1774 meant that the southern coast from Caffa to Foros became the property of the khan—and therefore the property of the empress after 1783. Finally, perhaps emboldened by his sudden possession of the prized coast, Şahin Giray Khan pursued an aggressive policy of appropriating hereditary estates from elite clans in order to improve the revenue streams flowing into his treasury. Crimean land tenure, in other words, was anything but stable when Catherine and Potemkin began handing out dachas.

Rather than injecting a measure of order into this disordered landscape, the dacha grants caused further destabilization. The documentary regime accompanying the grants proved an endless source of frustration for the provincial officials tasked with facilitating the development of the local economy. As far as they could tell, more than a third of the dachas existed only on paper, as ascribed quantities of land, with little or no accompanying geographic information. Grant documents associated most of the others with specific villages—one described 637 desiatinas near the village of Kapsikhor in Feodosiia district and another 1,678 desiatinas near Suuk-Su, for example—but said nothing about the actual location or boundaries of the properties. Newly arrived landowners therefore had a tendency to treat their grants as guidelines rather than specifications. After acquainting themselves with the region, they simply claimed the best parcels: parcels which, more often than not, were the same lands inhabited, cultivated, and claimed by Tatar peasants, pious endowments, and mirzas. Undeterred, the new pomeshchiki (Russian, or occasionally Ukrainian, landowners) set about the work of demarcating and enclosing their property behind fences and other barricades, gradually designating clear boundaries between what they claimed for themselves and what may or may not belong to others. They then sought out the few harried government surveyors, knowing full well that more than anything else, a confirmed survey document would secure the boundaries they had carved out and ascribe legal, as well as geographical, meaning to their dachas.[16]

Almost immediately the provincial government began fielding complaints from every possible corner. Pomeshchiki, mirzas, and Tatar peasants alike complained about improper seizures of land, inaccurate boundary lines, and even conflicting notions of ownership. In 1791, with yet another Russian-Ottoman war (1787–1792) winding down, and in the wake of Potemkin's death, Governor and Major General S. S. Zhegulin decided the time had come to address the slowly mounting confusion in Tavrida. The first step was to obtain an authoritative account of the privileges bestowed on various strata of the provincial population. The civil chamber decided that the best way to obtain such an account was to request it from the Imperial Senate, and so in 1791 officials in Simferopol asked the senators ensconced in far off St. Petersburg to define the rights of Tavrida's Tatars, Greeks, Armenians, and Jews to own and bequeath arable land, gardens, mills, and other forms of immovable property.[17]

The Senate did not respond. Tensions mounted in Crimea until finally, in late summer 1794, Zhegulin demanded a response to the civil chamber's request. The response came in the form of an opinion issued by Potemkin's successor as governor-general of Novorossiia, Count Platon Zubov. Zubov argued that based on the terms of the annexation manifesto, which promised to "preserve and protect the persons, property, houses of worship, and native faith" of the indigenous population, the traditional property rights of all Crimeans—even those who would not have enjoyed such rights in Russia—must be respected. "All merchants, *meshchane* [lower-middle class townspeople, craftsmen], simple Tatars, and others who are of Muslim faith or other national origin, who are inhabitants of Tavrida and who acquired lands under the khans through purchase, inheritance, or other legal manner shall remain landowners," he declared, "and this right shall be conferred on their heirs." He offered only one modification to what he identified as Crimean precedent. Non-nobles could own land, Zubov argued, but they could not sell or transfer immovable property to anyone who did not meet the criteria for landownership laid out in Catherine's 1785 charters to the towns and nobility. The implications of this policy were clear: in time, property would be channeled away from the Tatars into the hands of pomeshchiki, and the particularity of Crimean land tenure would fade.[18]

Catherine approved Zubov's opinion and news soon reached Simferopol that the imperial government had no intention of seizing lands or supporting the seizure of lands held by non-noble Crimeans. Buoyed by the decision, many Tatars grew bolder in their dealings with pomeshchiki over disputed estates. In December 1795, Evstafii Notara, president of the civil chamber and owner of a significant amount of property, submitted a petition to the newly installed governor, I. I. Khorvat, outlining some of the illicit dealings in the Crimean land market. First, he complained that members of the ulema and other non-noble Tatars were selling properties without first establishing the legitimacy of their ownership rights. (They often did this, Notara noted, with the encouragement of land-hungry settlers.) Second, Tatars had begun demanding the return of properties sold before 1794 on the grounds that they were themselves worthy of nobility and had not known that selling their land would jeopardize official confirmation of their elite status. Notara argued that under no circumstances should the integrity of a Russian landowner's estate be violated by such claims and, on behalf of the chamber, suggested that in cases where Tatars claiming elite status could provide conclusive evidence of having sold land they possessed as a result of legal purchase or inheritance, they should be compensated with lands of similar value elsewhere.[19]

Khorvat pondered the matter while making a tour to acquaint himself with the province. Finally, having received countless complaints from Tatars during his travels, the governor decided to advocate on their behalf. As a result of his input, together with copious petitions from mirzas and the influence of Zubov himself, in September 1796 Catherine approved what would henceforth be known as the Zubov Rescript. The rescript upheld the terms of the 1794 opinion and announced that all land either seized by or improperly granted to settlers must be returned to its rightful (Tatar) owner. It confirmed Crimean Muslims' right to follow Islamic law pertaining to inheritance and to seek arbitration in kadı courts. It did not, of course, provide specific instructions for identifying "rightful owners," nor did it explain the nuances of Islamic law. Yet the rescript, which would serve as the legal foundation of the land regime in Tavrida for the next half century, captured the essence of Catherine's imperial logic in two ways. First, it asserted the legitimacy of Russian rule by demonstrating its compatibility with existing institutions. According to the language of the rescript, Islamic and Crimean laws were understood to supplement—possibly even to enhance the efficacy of—imperial legislation. Just as important was the rescript's affirmation of the local institutions as a generative site of authority. By empowering authorities in Simferopol to resolve conflicts among overlapping systems of law and practice, Catherine left open the possibility that the resulting landownership regime would operate according to principles and interests that transcended the boundaries she had imagined.

Armed with what seemed to him a reasonably coherent explication of both Tavridan land tenure and his own responsibilities, Khorvat did what most fin-de-siècle Russian administrators would have done. He convened a commission to see to the settlement of property disputes once and for all.[20]

SETTING THE TERMS OF OWNERSHIP

Over the next thirty years the real work of establishing authority over Tavrida was conducted by local officials and the inhabitants of the province: by men and women who saw the land not as a sum of desiatinas but as an assemblage of idiosyncratic meadows, fields, orchards, and groves, each with its own history and purpose. Perhaps the best source for reconstructing their visions of and relationships to the land is the set of complaints lodged with the offices of the governor, district land courts, and the commissions convened for this purpose between 1797 and 1820. Taken together, these documents make two important arguments about the relationship between landownership and imperial rule. First, while landownership remained intimately bound up with social status, after 1783 ethnicity and confession provided new means of mobilizing social difference in order to pursue (and often to protect) economic interests. Second, the painstaking process of sorting out rival claims and deeds of ownership—of simultaneously demarcating legal and absolute space—fundamentally altered the way Russian officials viewed Tavrida and its relationship to the physical space of the empire.

For over a decade, many of the dachas doled out by Potemkin and Catherine were little more than a collection of imagined spaces that reproduced—on paper only—social and political hierarchies determined in St. Petersburg. Many grantees were reluctant to invest the necessary resources in establishing estates in the distant borderland, and those who did claim their property often found it difficult to convince local inhabitants that anything had changed. The Prince de Ligne once asked the local "good Mussulmans" whether they were aware that they were now tenants on land that he owned. "They answer that they know in general that they have been parceled out," Ligne explained, "but they do not wholly understand what it means. They are happy now, and if they cease to be so they shall embark on the vessels they have built for themselves and take refuge with the Turks in Roumania."[21]

It is not hard to see why on one level local inhabitants were skeptical about the permanence or authority of the pomeshchiki: the annexation manifesto had guaranteed the right to own land according to local laws and customs, and the 1796 rescript only confirmed this state of affairs. In practice this meant that Tatar claimants had a new set of (Russian) institutions, rules, and arbiters to enlist in the resolution of old disputes. Meanwhile, they could bring the weight of Crimean law and practice to bear in their disputes with pomeshchiki. Thus in the last days of Catherine's reign, the Tatar hold on property seemed relatively secure.

But on November 6, 1796, the empress died. She was succeeded by her son, Paul I, whose brief reign had extraordinary consequences for the inhabitants of the former khanate. Within a month Paul had begun reorganizing the administrative boundaries of the empire, and as part of this project he abolished Tavrida's provincial status, folding it, along with the neighboring provinces of Voznesensk and Ekaterinoslav, into the newly formed province of Novorossiia. The dismantling of Tavrida's provincial government meant the expulsion of many "scoundrels" from office and, in an attempt to right what he saw as his mother's wrongs, Paul approved the formal investigation of illegal seizures of land by pomeshchiki. By July 1798, Military Governor Count M. V. Kakhovskii (who succeeded Khorvat) had recruited a veritable who's who of local elites, both Tatar and settler, to examine the complaints that had been pouring into his office as soon as word escaped that such a commission might be formed.[22]

Before any serious work could be done, Kakhovskii decided it would be helpful to know something of the laws and practices that were sanctioned, but not described, in the 1794 and 1796 rescripts. He therefore asked Mehmet Aga Biiarslanov, who had served as *khaznadar*, or treasurer, of the khan and was the ranking elder of one of the most powerful Crimean clans, to provide a detailed explanation of the khanate's land tenure regime. The governor wanted to know which strata of society had been eligible to own land, and whether property could be owned collectively. Could non-elites own the land itself—and therefore have the right to sell, exchange, or inherit it—or was "ownership" in their case akin to usage rights? Did peasants or mirzas pay taxes of any kind in exchange for such rights? Finally, how did officials establish the legitimacy of claims?[23]

In September 1798, Biiarslanov duly submitted a report signed by representatives of the most influential clans. In it, he explained that both Muslim peasants and mirzas enjoyed rights of perpetual and hereditable ownership under certain circumstances. The properties of mirzas almost always originated in firmans of the Ottoman sultan or *iarlyks* issued by the Giray khan. Kadıs (sharia court judges) drew up deeds of purchase and sale. All of these documents resided in the khan's archive in Bahçe-saray. Aware that the former system of taxes and rents was a crucial element of the defense of Tatar rights within the Russian empire, Mehmet Aga took particular care to explain it: Peasants who inhabited lands owned by the sultan (before 1774) or by the khan, paid taxes and tithe (*uşura*) either to the mirza who held the *timar* (a form of Ottoman tenure that granted the tax revenue of a given land in return for military service) or to the khan directly. Those who owned freehold paid no land tax of any kind.[24]

In theory, the khan was the most important landowner. In practice, the beys—the leaders of the most powerful clans—were the dominant force. The Şirin, Argin, Barin, and Kipchat clans had all laid claim to extensive properties well before the Giray dynasty established its dominance in Crimea, and they supplemented their holdings over the centuries through the acquisition of timars. In the Ottoman Empire the timar system allowed the state to retain ownership of land while military servitors gained the right to collect special property taxes—taxes that eventually replaced their salary. Timar grants were technically revocable, but elites succeeded in converting them to freehold from time to time.[25] Such was the case in Crimea as well. From at least the mid-sixteenth century, the khan issued two types of grants: grants of *mevat* (unsettled, uncultivated) lands which, once settled and cultivated, were treated as freehold, and timar-style grants that allocated the right to collect revenues from settled land. The khans, like the sultans, preferred to assign timar-holders shares in scattered villages in an attempt to prevent them from consolidating economic and social power. However, in time powerful clans converted timar and other holdings into beyliks, or independent hereditary lands over which the khan had no control. Even among lesser service clans the vast majority of mirzas had converted their holdings to freehold by the eighteenth century, which meant that they, like the beys, no longer paid rents to the khan. Mirzas could cultivate their lands or rent them out to peasants, and they had the right to pass them on through direct inheritance, sale, or the establishment of pious endowments.[26]

Mirzas and beys did not enjoy a monopoly on landownership, Biiar-slanov explained. Before 1783 individual Tatar peasants could own homes, the kitchen gardens or other enclosed gardens and orchards sur-rounding them, and other small parcels located within the boundaries of properties belonging to mirzas, beys, pious endowments, and even the khan. Common Tatars also owned land collectively through the *cemaat*, a Crimean institution resembling the village commune and far more prevalent in the steppe than in the mountains or coastal region. Com-munal land usually included pastures and hayfields, and often wells, fountains, orchards, vineyards, and beehives. Arable land was less impor-tant, but could be claimed as cemaat if demarcated and cultivated. As was the case among Russian peasants, many Tatars asserted a deeply held belief that the land belonged to those who cultivated it, rather than those who collected revenues from it, and that cemaat was a form of freehold, or collective private landownership.[27]

In this way the deft administrator defined the right to own land in the broadest possible terms, claiming it as an attribute of nearly every stratum of Tatar society and laying the groundwork for a vigorous de-fense of Tatar claims. Biiarslanov's equation between being Tatar and enjoying the right to own land challenged one of the core organizational principles of Russian society: that is, the association between noble sta-tus and landownership. To be sure, by the turn of the nineteenth century not all landowners—and more specifically, not all owners of settled land—were noble, but the vast majority certainly were. If Biiarslanov's report were to be accepted as an accurate accounting of Crimean prac-tice and the proper foundation for imperial policy, it might well lead to one of two problematic outcomes. First, the regime might declare all Tatar landowners to be Russian nobles in an effort to preempt com-plaints that the elite's stranglehold on economic resources was being undermined along the periphery. Alternately, officials might choose to disassociate landownership and noble status, effectively preventing the wholesale inclusion of Crimean Tatars within the dvorianstvo.[28]

The potentially explosive impact of any decision taken with regard to land tenure in Tavrida would need to be defused by articulating clear spatial and social boundaries: accommodations required to facilitate Russian rule in Tavrida could not be allowed to erode the entrenched system of privileges operating elsewhere in the empire.

If this seems perfectly obvious to historians, it was neither apparent nor persuasive to the disputants. In fact, Biiarslanov crafted his report in response to arguments advanced by a subset of pomeshchiki who felt the fundamental correlation between landownership and elite status was in jeopardy and who feared the tectonic shift sure to follow its collapse. Appalled at the notion that two signature pieces of legislation—the annexation manifesto and Zubov Rescript—accommodated local precedent, their complaints revolved around two crucial issues. First, they argued that rather than simply guaranteeing the status quo the Zubov Rescript actually ascribed the right to own land to those who had not previously enjoyed it. Aleksandr Stepanovich Taranov, one of the most powerful men in Tavrida, sent a memorandum to this effect to the governor of Novorossiia in January 1801. In it he made the case that the simple fact that the vast majority of Tatars paid tithe and other taxes stood as incontrovertible proof that they were in fact cultivators who occupied and used land owned by the khan or by mirzas with legitimate rights to freehold.[29]

Second, many pomeshchiki found the notion of collective ownership diametrically opposed to the basic principles of the tsarist regime. According to Admiral Nikolai Semenovich Mordvinov, vice president of the Admiralty, soon-to-be minister of the navy, and owner of a magnificent property in the Baydar valley, the government's toleration of Crimean particularities was extraordinarily problematic. "Property," he proudly declared, "is the rock upon which all statutes are founded. Without it, and without a firm set of rights defending it, all other laws, the fatherland, and even the sovereign are meaningless." Eliding the difference between use and ownership altered the fundamental relationship between land, nobleman, and sovereign. Even worse, the cemaat (like all forms of collective ownership) contradicted the notion of "one property, one owner" that Mordvinov felt ought to describe the land regime throughout Russia. For Mordvinov, maintaining the twin pillars of accommodation and ambiguity—the very strategies Empress Catherine II held as intrinsic to empire building—would hobble any attempt to create a modern and presumably more powerful state.[30]

Mordvinov's advocacy of singly owned properties animated much of the struggle that ensued over the next several decades, but it was Karl Gablits who made the most ambitious contribution to the debate. Long years of service on the local criminal court and treasury expedition, together with his formidable skills as a naturalist, meant that he was among the most well-informed voices in the debate. He was also the owner of a lovely dacha at Chorgun, near Foros. In his capacity as both pomesh-chik and man of science, Gablits proposed a strategy for addressing the problem of disorder in the Tavridan countryside. He flatly rejected the notion that misappropriated lands should be returned to Tatar claim-ants. Moreover, he believed that the provincial government ought to em-bark on a massive redistribution program—one that would consolidate ownership of all "valuable land" in the hands of those with the ability and desire to cultivate it.

The simplest way to promote this project, Gablits explained, was to renovate the tax system. Rather than rely on the poll tax, the funda-mental unit of the Russian economy, Gablits proposed wiping the slate clean and implementing a single tax based on the quantity and quality (though not on the yield) of land each individual owned. He believed this would not only encourage landowners to sow their fields, but would transform the demographics of landownership. The "Tatar mirzas now own the vast majority of land in Tavrida, but they are ill-disposed toward farming," Gablits assured his peers and colleagues. "When suddenly obliged to pay a land tax, they will quickly limit themselves to small dachas and sell off their vast estates." With pomeshchiki (the presumed buyers) in control of increasing acreage, agricultural production was sure to improve. This would mean higher government revenues, while a homogeneous body of landowners would mean fewer challenges to Russian authority.[31]

This was the sort of proposal a man like Johann von Michelsohnen, military governor of Ekaterinoslav, could sink his teeth into. For Mi-chelsohnen and many of the military and civil governors who succeeded him, tsarist power derived not from a commitment to reformist ideals or even rational systems, but from the ability to maintain order, stabil-ity, and security. Michelsohnen was disturbed by the flood of disputes that inundated his office. From his vantage point, continuous abuse of Tatar peasants by pomeshchiki, rather than Tatar agricultural practices, was the root cause of simmering unrest in the region. In a carefully worded report, he explained that the government was justified in seiz-ing unsettled, uncultivated lands from ne'er-do-well landowners and had every right to appropriate land that had belonged to the Ottoman sul-tan, Crimean khan, and mirza émigrés. However, he was convinced that

along the way officials had sanctioned many illegal or impolitic seizures
of property that rightfully belonged to the empire's newest subjects and
that this was a breach of order that must be rectified.[32]

Emperor Alexander and his State Council agreed. In September 1802
Grigorii Petrovich Miloradovich, the first civil governor of the newly
reconstituted Tavrida province, received orders to open the "commission for the resolution of disputes over land in Tavrida province" under
the chairmanship of Senator I. V. Lopukhin. According to the commission guidelines, Tatars had the right to sell or inherit land on which they
resided, so long as it had belonged to the khan. Neither the government
nor any landowner had the right to seize or redistribute such properties, and they must be returned to whoever owned them before any such
illegal transactions took place. The commission was to approve appropriation of property only if the owner emigrated without providing documentation of sale or transfer. In that case inhabitants could remain on
the land, now state property, which they would hold in tenancy. In general, the guidelines muddled matters considerably by reaffirming the
state's right to appropriate lands that were unsettled at the time of annexation or that were determined to be unsettled by the commission,
particularly since land qualified as empty even if only part of a village
population had emigrated. Finally, the guidelines charged the commission with guaranteeing the Tatar right to access and use gardens, orchards, pastures, and other such parcels held as freehold under the khans
and purchased from those with right to sell it.[33]

In essence, the imperial government had turned the problem of ownership back to the province and bound it up with local practice. Disputes
between Tatar owners and pomeshchiki thus became a prime site for
working out new ideas about landownership and more broadly about
the functional relationship between place and people. The legitimacy of
peasant and collective ownership remained a contentious issue, but it is
the articulation of new notions of land use and the evolution of a new
geography of property ownership that make the legal wrangling over
several hundred small, inaccessible dachas in the southernmost corner
of the empire such a significant moment in Russian history.

Six hundred and seven complaints arrived almost immediately; the
content of the resulting disputes varied wildly. In some cases the boundary line between two properties was at issue; in others it was the authenticity of deeds, the character of the property, the manner in which

it was acquired, the legitimacy of the rules that governed grants and sales, or the social status of the claimants. Disputes cropped up among siblings, pomeshchiki, and Muslim clerics, between mirzas and Tatar peasants, pomeshchiki and mirzas, and between pomeshchiki and Tatar peasants. Policemen, admirals, generals, provincial secretaries, judges, foreigners, unranked settlers, and Tatar women—often the wives of elite mirzas—figured as plaintiffs and defendants, deploying a dizzying array of arguments in an effort to advocate for their rights as landowners. To the handful of men serving on the various land commissions and land courts it must have seemed that all of Tavrida was demanding satisfaction. And if those stakes weren't high enough, they were all keenly aware that with so many members of the ruling elite personally invested in its outcome, the resolution of the land tenure crisis on the peninsula was bound to serve as a prominent articulation of nothing less than Russia's "imperial manner."[34]

It is tempting to read the disputes as thorough-going evidence of the willingness of newly minted subjects—Muslim Tatars no less—to engage Russian legal institutions, participate in the inevitable redistribution of resources, and perhaps even recognize the legitimacy of tsarist rule. They certainly were a response to the dacha grants and the early articulations of imperial authority emanating from St. Petersburg. But to read the sources that way would give dangerously short shrift to the role played by individual appetites for economic resources, the strength of locally derived systems of meaning and authority, and the remarkably circumscribed power of officials to control some of the most important elements of daily life. Establishing authority over the land of the former khanate was not simply a matter of fitting Crimea to an existing imperial model: it was one of several processes through which the imperial system was generated, valley by valley, estate by estate.

Insofar as each case represented an opportunity to recalibrate relationships between and among newcomers and natives, property disputes were crucial. The advantage fell to those who knew both the region and the rules, and N. S. Mordvinov was among the most notorious of those who fit this bill. Mordvinov, known in Catherine's reign for his shortcomings as an admiral—he was relieved of his duties as admiral of the Black Sea Fleet—successfully reinvented himself as a vociferous advocate of private property and one of Alexander I's most trusted advisors. The tsar appointed him to his permanent council and to committees set up to investigate everything from the land regime in Novorossiia to trade in the Caspian. In the interim, he spent four years in Crimea (1797–1801). An early recipient of a dacha, Mordvinov gradually expanded his holdings to include much of the sprawling, fertile Baydar valley, largely by pressuring local Greeks and Tatars into selling their properties for shockingly low prices. But Russian settlers were not the only ones to take advantage of the relative lack of regulation in land transactions. In fact it was social status, not ethnicity, that correlated with the ability to convert claims into either large amounts of money or official ownership. Tatar elders and Muslim clerics were among the opportunists who brokered the purchase of everything from garden plots to whole estates without the knowledge—let alone the cooperation—of those who owned them. Pomeshchiki and mirzas alike busied themselves flipping properties, charging anywhere from 25 to 100 percent more than what they paid to the peasant sellers.[35]

Ultimately, ownership of any amount of land was a function of one's ability to document a given claim. Savvy members of the Tatar elite forged deeds of purchase or inheritance in order to appropriate land from peasants or rival clans; Muslim clerics and mirzas seized properties dedicated as pious endowment (waqf) by simply preventing the iarlyks and firmans attesting to their endowed status from seeing the light of day. Tatars who owned land collectively under the khans or couldn't afford to have deeds drawn up by Russian officials had little chance of holding on to disputed property, while those with the right connections and the wherewithal to pay a small bribe had dramatically better luck. When the inhabitants of Toigush in Feodosiia district, for example, found out that Katyrşa Bey, member of the powerful Şirin clan and a captain in the Russian army, claimed to have inherited the village from his father before selling it to Halil Giray Sultan, they immediately petitioned local authorities. Katyrşa had never owned the land, they explained, and therefore had no right to sell it. They themselves had a document attesting to their ownership of Toigush; it was kept by a cleric in the nearby village of Monat. Realizing that they were perilously close to losing their land, the villagers appealed to Major Velişa Aga, another Tatar elite and former adjutant of none other than Prince Potemkin, to come to their aid. He investigated, recovered the document in Monat, and used it to procure the deed from Katyrşa Bey. The grateful Tatars of Toigush paid Velişa the healthy sum of 130 rubles.[36]

Meanwhile, members of the commission on land disputes had perilously little information at their disposal. They had yet to establish the location of most contested properties, and decades would pass before they managed to translate the extensive body of Ottoman and Tatar documents referenced by local claimants. It took a handful of Greek and Tatar officials two years just to produce a report detailing the proper conversion of Crimean units of measure (including the *zan, arkan,* and *bostan*) into their Russian equivalents (desiatinas and sazhens) and thus enable officials to get some sense of the scale of the land involved in each dispute.[37]

Faced with such a daunting workload, the commission made little headway in those early days. By the time Dmitrii Mertvago took the reins as governor of Tavrida in December 1803, the commission had essentially ground to a halt, having resolved only twenty of the 607 registered disputes. Mertvago was sure he could do better than that and in 1804 Senator Lopukhin happily relinquished his role as chairman. Mertvago was convinced that he knew the secret to resolving land disputes. To his mind defining social status, documenting local custom, cataloging deeds of purchase, and lobbying for imperial legislation all paled in comparison with the most authoritative tool of all: the cadastral survey. Mertvago believed that by sending out a small army of men to walk property lines, measure angles, set up boundary markers, plot estate plans, and compile a register of landownership and use, he could impose order on the landscape and imbue the idea of Russian authority with local meaning.

MAPPING A CONTESTED LANDSCAPE

The Tavrida Survey Department opened in 1804 and with this renewed focus the commission found a rhythm. In the summer and fall of 1805 two surveyors covered more than fifteen hundred miles. They mapped twenty-four dachas, outpacing in a matter of months what the commission had accomplished in two full years of work. After similar success the following year, Mertvago set about lobbying Count Kochubei, minister of the interior, to send as many as a dozen surveyors to Simferopol in all haste. It had become apparent to the governor that property disputes could not be resolved without them, and with only two surveyors chipping away at the task—and hampered by everything from incapacitating and often fatal seasonal fevers to incapacitating (though less fatal) shortages of astrolabes—it would take more than thirty years to survey all the contested properties. Despite the fact that he was willing to pay salaries upwards of 400 rubles, Mertvago found to his utter frustration that the few surveyors stationed between Ekaterinoslav and St. Petersburg were otherwise occupied. In desperation, the governor issued public advertisements in hopes of hiring private individuals on a contract basis, though he admitted to Kochubei that there were "few who know what geometry is" and thus there was little hope of accelerating the pace of work.[38]

Meanwhile the authority of survey documents grew steadily. By 1810 the process of establishing ownership hinged on the production of survey plans and books (*mezhevye knigi*). In September of that year Kochubei announced that in an effort to stem the tide of appeals that threatened to undermine the authority of the land commission, survey documents would become a collaborative and binding element of the dispute process. Henceforth each time a decision was taken, one member of the commission would travel to the site along with deputies representing the parties involved in order to review the disputed property. Each claimant was then asked to review the survey documents, and could either challenge their accuracy then and there or attest to the survey's validity by affixing their signatures. In order for the resolution to go into effect, the party to whom ownership was awarded then had to present proper documentation of either purchase, inheritance, or imperial grant; or swear a traditional oath (*uç talak*) in the presence of all who had gathered to approve the survey (along with a Muslim cleric if not already present). In this system, the legitimacy of the process depended both on the survey's scientific accuracy and on its function as a consensual, socially constructed document. The survey map promised to make land tenure coherent and legible; to reflect existing relationships between owners, users (often inhabitants) and the physical environment.[39]

Governments had relied on different variations of the cadastral survey as a foundation of fiscal order for millennia. The Ottoman method of delimiting villages, according to which kadıs conducted interviews and documented the physical boundaries of each village's land, was typical of cadastral practice throughout much of early modern Europe, but by the sixteenth century changes were afoot. Innovations in cartography led to the rise of the property map as a bastion of land tenure regimes, first in the Netherlands, and soon thereafter everywhere from Norway to Venice. The Muscovite government's attempt at a general survey in the 1680s generated a significant amount of geographical information on the local and regional level, but it was Peter I who recognized the correlation between mapping and improving the government's capacity to mobilize resources, be they military recruits or ship-grade forests. He initiated the first attempt at a systematic cadastral survey as early as 1720. The implications for Russian subjects were potentially vast, particularly for non-nobles in de facto possession of serf-inhabited estates which they were not, by law, entitled to own. However, the illegal seizures, undocumented sales, and other irregularities that pervaded the tsarist land tenure system meant that officials had their work cut out for them. By 1735 responsibility for the cartographic study of the empire was vested in the Academy of Sciences. In 1754 Empress Elizabeth ordered another survey of private and state lands in a further attempt to reclaim property for the treasury. But it was not until Catherine II inaugurated the general land survey in 1765 that the administration fully committed itself to mapping the space of the empire.[40]

The Catherinian survey paired the traditional narrative account of bounded spaces with visual representation. It was designed to register the boundaries of properties, produce corresponding plans and "economic notes," and compile them in county and provincial-level atlases. The empress had at least two motivations for opening the survey. First, when she confirmed the emancipation of the Russian nobility from obligatory service (initially decreed by her ill-fated husband, Peter III, in 1762), Catherine furthered the evolution of the elite into an estate defined by its right to own land. Her decision in 1764 to initiate the secularization of land owned by the Orthodox Church further emphasized the growing convergence between the boundaries of landed property and the geography of political authority. Up to that point authorities had found it nearly impossible to establish the boundaries between secular and monastic properties or even to disentangle the allotments of villages from the inherited estates of noble families. Disputes over land were rampant. Ignorance of property boundaries was endemic, applying to at least fifty million desiatinas (an area roughly the size of Texas) of land granted to pomeshchiki over the years. Both the disputes and the misunderstandings were a dangerous source of instability in the Russian countryside. The new survey was intended to resolve such matters. It would implement the territorialization of Russia's social structure through a system of survey books and maps.[41]

Catherine was a relative pioneer in this regard. Her 1765 decree came just a year after Empress Maria Theresa inaugurated the cadastral survey of the Hapsburg Empire and less than a decade after Cassini's *Carte géométrique de la France*. It was followed by Portugal's decision in 1788 to compile a general map, Britain's Ordnance Survey in 1791, the mapping of India from 1799, and Napoleon's famous survey of Egypt. Even this short list suggests a link between cadastres and empire building. And indeed, surveyors contributed to the articulation of "colonizing visions" and imperial policies implemented everywhere from New Zealand to the Middle East. But mapping projects could mitigate geographical and cultural distinctions as easily as they exacerbated them, and this increased their appeal to Catherine. She intended her general survey to render the vast space of her empire as a set of discrete, legible units that could be governed by a standard set of rules just as they could be measured by a standard set of tools. Her stated goal was simple: to "confirm the order of things as they were"; her ulterior, and admittedly long-term, motive was the creation of a uniform socioeconomic landscape.[42]

What Catherine did not anticipate was that the survey process would localize the scale and meaning of imperial rule. Yet privileging the local was an intrinsic part of survey methodology. Following the instructions laid out in May 1766, surveyors began their work by mapping the district town (*uezdnyj gorod*). They moved outward from there to map the territory of the surrounding villages, after which it would be possible to establish the boundaries of the district itself.[43] A similar progression from micro- to macro-level work ordered the eventual compilation of small-scale maps and atlases. The province, which served as the organizing mechanism of every general atlas of the empire, also served as the container for the bundles of cartographic material generated by the survey. However, the fundamental unit of analysis was not the province. Nor was it was the village. The fundamental unit of analysis of the survey was the dacha. It was the dacha that provided the space in which individual, community, and imperial interests were inscribed. As much as survey work subjected the territory of the empire to standardized, state-prescribed processes of documentation and legitimation, it also meant acknowledging and formalizing the specificity of each parcel of terrain, the individuality of each abutter and claimant, and the set of relations among them. Each dacha map reiterated the idea that imperial power was a function of place.

The techniques of the modern land survey broke with Crimean tradition. There had been a surveyor among the officials at Bahçesaray, but landownership within the khanate tended to be an unwritten affair. In practice, courts seldom produced documents in instances where mirzas, individual peasants, or cemaats cultivated empty land and claimed it as freehold, or where land was exchanged through sale or inheritance. And when disputes arose, the oral testimony of respected members of the community carried as much weight as written evidence from the kadı registers in accordance with Islamic law. However, the Giray khans did mark the distribution of heritable property or the right to collect revenues from villages or salt lakes by issuing decrees, and Tatar elders assured Russian authorities that in the late fifteenth century the sultan had guaranteed permanent possession of land by issuing firmans to each inhabitant of the khanate on the occasion of the khan's submission as vassal.[44]

In the late nineteenth century the formidable scholar F. F. Lashkov published a large number of surviving iarlyks and firmans in several issues of the *News of the Tavrida Scholarly Archival Commission*. The documents range over three centuries and detail the various mechanisms for property acquisition, including inheritance through maternal and paternal lines, pious endowment, clan succession, purchase, and grant. Many deal with disputed properties and without fail these include—in fact they hinge on—precise descriptions of boundaries. Saadet Giray Khan's iarlyk granting land to Ibrahim Efendi (Dzhamin) in 1530 describes the boundary "bordering a stream along the middle ravine and from the *kişla* [winter sheepfold] called Mufti Efendi among the shrubs of Orta *çair* up to the road to Ulakly; and from the western side from Kurulu and Sayke to Iurliubitere."[45]

Documenting landownership, in other words, was not entirely new. But it was only in the 1790s that surveyors produced the first visual representations—maps—to accompany the spatial narratives of Crimean properties. Very few of these early maps survive in the archives, but those that do, together with the decrees, petition documents, and many hundreds of maps and survey books produced later in the nineteenth century, suggest that Crimean land tenure was distinguished by three main features. First, the estates of elite Tatars tended to contain properties dispersed across multiple noncontiguous locations (this was rarely the case among settlers). Second, while roughly one-third of property belonged to individual owners, the vast majority belonged to a combination of elite, peasant, and religious entities—an arrangement I call composite ownership. Third, the smallest properties were often the most lucrative.

The scattered nature of Tatar holdings had the potential to undermine both the integrity of settler estates and the coherence of the landownership system. Clan status often determined the geography of ownership, albeit not in the way one might expect. Until the middle of the eighteenth century, it was generally the case that the more powerful the clan, the greater the geographical distribution of its land (figure 4.2). The Şirin bey, for example, second in importance only to the khan, owned fifteen properties spread across more than two thousand square kilometers in Feodosiia district alone, while a single member of the ruling dynasty endowed a set of properties including farmland and pasture at Kipchak (near Gözleve), vineyards in the Belbek valley, a çair and vineyard at Inkerman, and a forest parcel near the south coastal village of Alupka. Even after 1783 a branch of the Giray dynasty that elected to remain in Crimea claimed to have inherited twenty-five properties spread from Kerch to Feodosiia. When Russian officials appropriated and distributed these properties to settlers on the grounds that they had belonged to the khan, the family showered authorities with petitions. They argued that because they resided on and cultivated a handful of the properties included in the estate *all* of the properties must be considered inhabited and cultivated. Though not geographically contiguous, they were legally bound together and thus could not be appropriated or partitioned. (Remarkably, they won the return of many of their properties.)[46]

Wills and testaments suggest that wealth in noncontiguous property accrued to members of lesser clans as well, through inheritance or the reclaiming of land vacated by émigrés.[47] In the first decade after annexation many mirzas and beys joined thousands of peasants, craftsmen, merchants, ulema, and Nogays in emigrating to Ottoman lands. This led to a massive redistribution of property as significant as that constituted by the dacha grants. The mirzas who remained in Tavrida tended to enjoy lesser political and economic status than those who left, and these

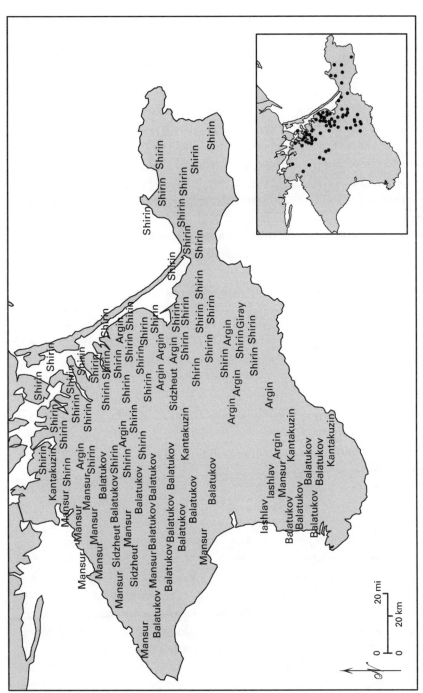

Figure 4.2. Villages in which members of the Tatar hereditary elite owned land, 1805–1806; with inset showing Şirin clan properties (Source: Lashkov, "Sbornik dokumentov," part 5: 84–154)

younger brothers and distant cousins recognized the opportunity to improve their fortunes by claiming the properties of their kinsmen. Some ended up with diverse and scattered holdings—an orchard near Kazasker in Feodosiia district and a large pasture at Kodagay in Perekop—but the scramble to collect abandoned morsels of land did not always lead to the disaggregation of adjacent pastures and orchards. In fact, in the decades after annexation it became common practice to claim as inheritance or purchase a small amount of land—often a field or mill—from Tatar peasants and subsequently leverage ownership of that parcel into a claim to the surrounding orchards, gardens, vineyards, and forests.[48]

Tatars and some Greeks used these techniques to greater effect than settlers, as they were more familiar with the physical terrain and had connections with local peasants to parlay or exploit, but this was a relatively widespread manner of acquiring land. Profit potential and weak oversight by Russian officials (most government offices were severely understaffed through the early nineteenth century) created plenty of leeway for dishonest or heavy-handed tactics. In one case documented in 1818, Sadyk Çelebi, son of the highest-ranking member of the Crimean ulema and himself a member of the Feodosiia land court, sold farmland and pasture to the villagers of Bashpek for 1,000 rubles. He also sold it to a local mirza, who in turn sold the property to a Greek. Meanwhile, Pashuk Hanim, the wife of Major General Kaya Bey Balatukov, claimed that she had purchased the land from Sadyk Çelebi, who appears to have pocketed three payments for the same property. In another case from the same year, after buying up small parcels from eight villagers at Sultan Bochala in Perekop, Mehmet Krımtay drafted a deed of purchase claiming that the property in question extended over 696 *khans* (2,088 desiatinas)—an area far greater than that covered by the village in its entirety, let alone the area of the purchased parcels. Oftentimes buyers took advantage of the fact that estates were owned by several members of a single family. It was relatively easy, for example, for Krımtay—who comes through in the archival record as land speculator extraordinaire—to purchase land from Asan Çelebi near the village of Boran in Perekop district, claim ownership of the property of Asan's brother and sister, and then sell the illegally cobbled together estate to a newly settled Russian official.[49]

Already by 1805, a heady mix of government appropriation, private seizure, and transactions of all sorts resulted in a land tenure regime full of parity and disparity. Just over 307,000 desiatinas had been awarded in dacha grants and surveyed between 1784 and 1802 (leaving over 40,000 desiatinas of property to be surveyed and fully claimed). Ten of the 120 dachas listed, consisting of a total of 59,877 desiatinas, belonged to Tatars. In fact, they belonged to five individuals: Mehmetşa Bey Kantakuzin, Mehmet Aga Biiarslan, Batyr Aga Krımtay, Abdulla Velişa Mamay, and the widow of Iakub Rudzevich. Their land amounted to 12 percent of the dacha territory on the peninsula. The concentration of wealth in the hands of this small circle of men with the rare combination of lineage and willingness to serve in either civil or military office seems clear. Then again, the register notes that in the case of half of these dacha grants—and in the case of 48 percent overall—the grantee owned land in combination with (other) mirzas or Tatar peasants; or rather, that their land was interspersed with lands owned by (other) mirzas and Tatar peasants. In sum, only ninety-eight properties existed as continuous spaces that could be claimed, without interruption, by an individual pomeshchik.[50]

We get a very different picture too from the registers of inhabited villages compiled in 1805 and 1806 for each of the peninsular districts. According to the registers, settlers owned lands that were associated with 15 percent of the 1,207 inhabited villages of Crimea (they did not own the inhabitants or the villages themselves). Mirzas owned land in 39 percent of inhabited villages, while the state claimed 4 percent (figure 4.3).[51] What this means is that while members of the Russian nobility were scooping up large swaths of territory, they laid claim to less than one-fifth of the inhabited land in Crimea. After two decades of Russian rule, roughly three-quarters of the elite landowners who owned inhabited land were mirzas. Mirzas were also far more likely than settlers to own land in more than one location (36 percent of mirzas owned property in more than one location as opposed to 21 percent of settlers).[52]

When it comes down to it, the significance of almost any pattern is easy to exaggerate, in large part because of the prevalence of composite ownership: instances in which an individual held land either in common with peasants or other elites (Tatar or settler), or in "composite ownership" (v chrezpolosnom vladenii). In cases of composite ownership a dacha was fragmented; each of its pieces might have a different owner. This condition was not unique. Across Russia, composite ownership was most common in provinces with high serf populations. The average

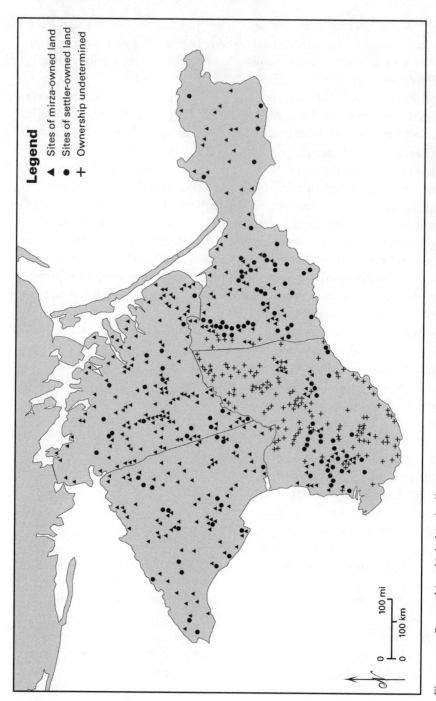

Figure 4.3. Ownership of inhabited villages, 1805–1806 (Source: Lashkov, "Sbornik dokumentov," part 5: 84–154)

composite property (*chrezpolosnitsa zemel'naia*) consisted of thirty to fifty segments (though officials in Iaroslav province recorded instances in which the number exceeded 120). This almost mind-boggling level of fragmentation made it nearly impossible to either demarcate boundaries or pursue efficient agricultural practice. In Tavrida, properties tended to split in less than a dozen parcels, but the situation was exacerbated by the multiethnic and multiconfessional profile of landowners. According to the dacha registers prepared in 1802, in fifty-nine of the 110 cases where settlers were registered as dacha recipients, their properties were in fact interspersed with those of mirzas or Tatar peasants. According to the 1805–1806 registers of inhabited villages, more than half of the properties owned by individual mirzas or settlers were sites of composite ownership as well, and Tatar peasants owned property in 48 percent of all inhabited locations (the status of a healthy chunk of the remaining locations was unknown).[53]

The system was messy, and it was nearly impossible to eradicate. The general land survey had it in its sights, as did decrees of 1806, 1833, 1839, 1853, 1875, and 1886. But the extraordinary level of ambiguity built into both the Russian system of land tenure and the Crimean system (before and after 1783), combined with the equally extraordinary lack of documentation, meant that Tatar ownership of much of the settled, productive space of the province continued not just for months or years, but for decades.

Survey plans like the lushly colored map of Duvankoy capture the spatial and legal complexity of what this meant. In November 1795 Second Lieutenant Aleksandr Karabtsov put the finishing touches on his survey work. The map he produced painstakingly recreates the forests, pastures, orchards, vineyards, ravines, ponds, households, and even the cemetery located on this sprawling 3,784-desiatina (11,352-acre) dacha. It shows the connective tissues—the streams and roads—as well the boundary lines that defined the various properties within the composite terrain. As was so often the case, the boundaries of function and ownership are generally coterminous, with clearly defined fields, orchards, and vineyards allocated to Tatar villagers, two individual Tatar peasants, a mosque, a Karaite man, and three mirzas. Vice Admiral Ushakov controlled the majority of acreage; more importantly, he controlled the roads that connected Duvankoy to surrounding villages, and thus access to the entire dacha.[54]

It was the issue of access that put Duvankoy on the list of disputed properties and led to the November 1795 survey. Ushakov was among the many pomeshchiki who attempted to convert composite dachas into single-ownership properties by denying access and thus the ability to demonstrate residence and cultivation. But mirzas and Tatar peasants played the same game, and they played it well enough that in November 1801 provincial secretary and landowner V. S. Chernov penned a petition to Procurator General Bekleshev himself. On behalf of seventeen prominent Russian landowners he described the systematic oppression of pomeshchiki by "Crimean Muslims." In addition to devastating the former's gardens and hay fields, Chernov explained, the latter "helped themselves to timber, and, contrary to religious law, broke down and stole the survey markers and posts" set up to delimit dacha boundaries. By humoring—in fact by protecting—the legitimacy of Crimean Tatar claims to land, imperial policy in Tavrida seemed to be working against the rational vision of empire articulated in any number of other Catherinian initiatives as well as the ideal pursued elsewhere in New Russia of large, well-defined estates owned by individuals whose rights were documented and uncontested.[55]

What Chernov and others like him perceived as Tatar sabotage was only one cause of Tavrida's negligible agricultural transformation. Another was the fact that despite Tavrida's popular image as an almost obscenely fertile land, Russians did not immediately flock there. The prospects of either making due with local labor or incurring the expense of transporting serfs from interior estates dissuaded many competent, well-to-do landowners from resettling. In 1798 Paul I held out a proverbial carrot to potential Christian settlers, promising that those who moved to the peninsular districts—Simferopol, Feodosiia, Evpatoriia, Perekop—would receive free land, allotments of state-owned forests, and even the use of stones from the ancient Greek ruins for building. Some took up the offer, but not enough to tilt the scales away from the bureaucrats and craftsmen who formed the majority of the settler population and had less of an impact on the agricultural landscape than officials had envisioned.[56]

Most of the pomeshchiki who did make their way to Crimea were low-ranking bureaucrats and retired soldiers with hardly enough resources to maintain their own residences, let alone invest in the labor and tools necessary to make their newfound estates productive. Dmitrii Mertvago complained that almost all grants "went to fools and boot-lickers who owned no souls with which to settle [their lands]." The problem, explained the governor, was that the valets, military officers, and clerks induced to become Tavridan landowners were simply not interested in making a long-term investment in the cultivation of the new province. Instead, "in order to increase their own revenues, [they] began to oppress the ancient inhabitants, causing much dissatisfaction, grumbling, and danger." A decade later, A. I. Mikhailovskii-Danilevskii concurred that pomeshchiki in Tavrida were "of the lowest sort." Sensing a slack rein, they oppressed Tatar peasants, seized their lands, and bribed judges to shelve complaints. The further one got from Simferopol, Mikhailovskii-Danilevskii concluded, the more "incredible" the corruption and abuses of power.[57]

"And so this Palestine, this paradisiacal country," lamented Vladimir Bronevskii after his travels in 1815, "which produces everything to satisfy the most extravagant taste and luxurious gaze, produces no revenue for the landowner. It provides for the native inhabitants in great abundance, and with no labor on their part. But then [Tatars] are content with little and live only the life allowed them by local conditions." Ivan Matveevich Murav'ev-Apostol, a well-known writer, advisor to Alexander I, and visitor to Crimea in 1818, likewise concluded that the Tatars did not appreciate the advantages of hard work. "For that they must learn to love property," he explained, "and in order to love property they must learn to love the fatherland, and in order to love the fatherland it is necessary that each of them possess the mind and heart of a [true] subject."[58]

Bronevskii and Murav'ev-Apostol had no notion that the Tatars knew well what agricultural labor meant and that for them determining who owned a specific piece of property in many cases meant determining who used it. The remnants of the khan's archive attest to this. In 1704 for example, inhabitants of the village of Bora near the Dair River complained that a neighboring mirza had begun to farm portions of their commonly held forest and pasture. To make matters worse, he was barring the villagers from using the land. When presenting his side of the case, the mirza argued that the land had belonged to his great-grandmother and that she had converted it into a private trust which passed to her son, grandson, and now to him and to his brother. "For the past twenty years we have cultivated many places, collected and sold forest products without [incurring] protest, grazed our sheep in many places suitable for pasture, and collected hay from the meadows," argued Ilias Mirza. This testimony was enough to convince the kadıasker that the inhabitants of Bora had no claim to the land. Following the same principle, he decided a similar dispute, this time concerning a group of peasants from villages surrounding Duvankoy. The peasants had protested a mirza's attempt to claim their land as private trust, arguing that "the moment we . . . felled and uprooted the trees, and sold them without interference, [the land] became our property." The kadıasker found this clear and compelling evidence and ruled in their favor.[59]

Cultivating, felling, grazing, and collecting: such pursuits were crucial to establishing a claim to landownership long before Russia began building an imperial framework for the former khanate. But there is an important subtext here. The winning litigants demonstrated not just a record of agricultural activity, but the ability to commodify the fruits of their labor. Selling timber and other products of the forest could be as effective a method of establishing a legitimate claim as producing a tattered, finely lettered grant for inspection, for embedded in the act of sale was the authority to define the value of one's work and one's property; embedded in the act of purchase was an acknowledgement of that authority.

THE POLITICS (AND PRICE) OF A WELL-TENDED GARDEN

Most Russian sources from the nineteenth century ascribe the ability to tend the land exclusively to Tavrida's settlers. Officials and settlers seem to have had unabashed faith in their ability to improve on the agricultural practice of the Tatar population. Grigorii Potemkin's famous attempts to transform the landscape were emblematic of this attitude. Despite increasing tensions between St. Petersburg and the Porte, he could not resist sending an officer to Constantinople, Izmir, and Chios in 1787 to purchase olive trees, lilies, and a host of other flowers and vines he intended to cultivate in Crimean soil. Such was his desire to prove Russia the kind of enlightened state that could fill even a wild and empty borderland with botanical gardens, English parks, and alleys of tropical trees. The potency of such images often led settlers to treat Crimea as a landscape, rather than land—as a beautiful abstraction rather than a material realm. For many, like Chernov and Mordvinov, the Crimean Tatars detracted from the beauty of that landscape and reduced the luster of Russia's image as a great imperial power.[60]

On the other hand, a few deplored the destruction of the "natural" balance they believed the Tatars maintained between themselves and the surrounding environment. "Only the Tatars could work the soil of the steppe," admitted one commentator, for only they knew how to coax water out of it and find their way to the best pastures. Their very bodies, according to Baron von Haxthausen, suited the climate so perfectly that they needed to exert little effort to meet their needs. "Why should [they] heap up stores and collect supplies, when nature is constantly preparing new gifts for [them]?" asked Haxthausen. "The deep blue heaven above, the rich nature around, invite them to enjoyment and contemplation, not to labour. They have lost their ancient proud freedom and independence; but modern life, with its labour and industry, its railroads and commercial travelers, its taxes and soldiers, has not yet penetrated so far." Maria Guthrie, after issuing a light critique of the Tatars' lack of enthusiasm for planting corn, commented on the hard, salty quality of the soil, "which shows the folly of galloping travelers condemning the inhabitants of a country for many things that appear the result of ignorance, laziness, &c.; when, in fact, the imputation of ignorance lies on ourselves, for judging lightly of what we do not thoroughly understand; and of laziness, for not being at the trouble to investigate the truth, before we decide with all the pride and self-sufficiency of conscious superiority."[61]

There was another explanation for the apparent inactivity of the Tatars many travelers encountered in Crimea. E. D. Clarke described the steppe between Enikale and Aktiar as one continuous "campaign country, covered with grass and locusts; capable, it is true, of the highest cultivation, but entirely neglected. The Tahtars and the Greeks refuse to till the land, because they fear to be plundered by the Russians; and the Russians are too indolent to speculate upon the advantages of industry." Haxthausen pointed to the contrast between the Tatar peasant's willingness to work for a mirza but not for a pomeshchik. After all, Tatars often associated Russian landowners with the wholesale destruction of crops, cattle, horses, and whole villages during the years of military conflict prior to formal annexation, as well as its aftermath. In other words, the emptiness that served as a core attribute of Crimean cartography well into the nineteenth century was not an intrinsic physical element of the region's geography but rather a function of its political legacy.[62]

The lack of water was, by contrast, an intrinsic element of local geography. Mikhailovskii-Danilevskii found it endlessly amusing when, over lunch in Karasubazar in 1818, the prince of Hessen-Homburg told Tsar Alexander I that the peninsula "ought to be called the garden of Your Imperial Majesty's empire," despite the fact that the Prince had seen little in the way of cultivated land in his travels across the steppe. Water was precious in the mountains, let alone the steppe—so precious that almost every extant will dating from the pre-1783 period defines the property in question in relation to nearby rivers and wells, and nearly every travelogue penned after 1783 lingers in description of fountains and irrigation systems. The Tatars were renowned for their irrigation skills, and justifiably so. Their skills made the Baydar valley one of the most highly valued regions of the province, provided the city of Caffa with a dense network of water sources, and created the sequences of canals and fountains that watered the "garden-palace" (Bahçesaray) and filled poets with romantic inspiration.[63]

Intimate knowledge of the land informed the way it was managed by the Giray government. Under the khans the distribution of property to beys and mirzas depended on the revenues a property generated. After 1783 Russian authorities viewed the same terrain from a different vantage point. They were primarily concerned with acreage rather than revenue, and with apportioning properties whose area was commensurate with the rank or status of the recipient. In time they came to see that a mammoth dacha in Dneprovsk or Evpatoriia—steppe dachas often ranged from 10,000 to 20,000 desiatinas—without irrigation held little value, and that across the variable terrain of Tavrida province some of the most diminutive spaces—orchards, gardens, and vineyards—were in fact the most valuable. Extant registers of the Crimean kadıaskers show that the vast majority of lawsuits prior to 1783 pertained to just such properties, and in the early years of the nineteenth century pomeshchiki began initiating property grabs with the purchase of a garden, vineyard, or orchard. Officials were often reluctant to interfere. Many shared Admiral Mordvinov's belief that maximizing the wealth of the province meant cultivating the mountainous regions where these small, productive spaces thrived. It was here that the composite nature of Crimean

Figure 4.4. Women returning from the fountain at Derekoy; from Demidov, *Album* (John Hay Library, Brown University Library)

land tenure was acutely problematic. "A garden cannot be communal property," argued the admiral. "A garden must belong to a single owner, and a worthy one at that, capable of waiting patiently for the yield of a vineyard for no less than five years and from fruit trees no less than fifteen or twenty years." The Tatars, Mordvinov felt, had proven themselves incapable of such skill and patience. Therefore, if the government persisted in its policy of satisfying their demands, "the grand vision of Tavrida that once existed—of a province providing an abundance of grapes, olives, pomegranates, and other rich produce for the Russian empire" would be replaced by "a Crimea left unsettled, uncultivated, and undeveloped by labor and craft, poor, wild, doleful, and rushing toward its own destruction."[64]

Despite Mordvinov's spirited eloquence there is little evidence that wanton neglect by Tatars had reduced the productivity or value of Crimean gardens. On the contrary, the owners of garden and vineyard properties certainly enjoyed healthy profit margins. According to deeds of sale for Tavridan properties executed between 1803 and 1805, when the price of a desiatina of land exceeded ten rubles the property in question consisted primarily of vineyard and/or orchard in all but two cases. A general appraisal of land values conducted in 1805 by the Tavrida provincial government also drew a clear correlation between gardens and property value, with parcels planted with vineyards and fruit orchards worth far more than those without: prices for the former ranged from 100 to 1,000 rubles per desiatina; prices for the latter started at fifty kopeks and topped out at fifty rubles per desiatina.[65]

In 1806 the land commission, led by deputies of the provincial noble assembly, compiled a similar report describing the qualities and values (rubles per desiatina) of various "classes" of land. The authors, however, attempted to deflect the interest of the imperial treasury by reducing their estimates. According to the report, a desiatina of forest (whose most likely buyer would be the Naval Ministry) was worth fifty rubles; a desiatina of high-elevation forest, that is, accessible only by horse or mule, was valued at fifteen rubles; a desiatina of gardens or land with sufficient irrigation for gardens was worth thirty rubles; a desiatina consisting of arable fields was worth ten rubles; and the pasture land of the steppe was worth a single ruble per desiatina. This helps explain the otherwise oddly tenuous link between the acreage of a given property and the income derived from it (table 4.1). It also explains why Batyr Bey Balatukov's paltry 500 desiatinas, which consisted entirely of vineyard, enjoyed far and away the highest value per desiatina.[66]

Vineyards and gardens held an important aesthetic value as well. Tavrida was not isolated from the rest of the empire, and in the post-Napoleonic era the embrace of romanticism fostered both a new acceptance of the spectacular nature of Crimea and a tension between dueling desires to transform and to preserve. Memoirists and artists were part of the cultivation of Crimea's "wild sylvan appearance," busily building the image of an idyllic space at the same time that surveyors were turning their purportedly objective gaze on the province, recording their geometries and calculations. Writers such as Bronevskii

Table 4.1. Landholding and Income of Mirza Nobles, 1833

Name	Inhabitants	Area (desiatinas)	Income (rubles)	Land value (rubles per desiatina)
Provincial Secretary Mehmet Krımtay	991	21,044	12,700	0.6
Lieutenant Batyr Bey Balatukov	500	500	11,000	22.0
Lieutenant Kazi Bey Balatukov	466	8,634	10,000	1.2
Provincial Secretary Sale Kipchat	600	6,700	8,000	1.2
Major Abdurahim Aga Mamay	650	14,500	5,000	0.3
Lt. Colonel Adyl Bey Balatukov	1,000	8,700	5,000	0.6
Titular Councilor Osman Abdullov	300	5,000	5,000	1.0
14th class Ahmet Mansur	200	4,600	3,000	0.1
14th class Dzhelial Kipchat	150	2,500	3,000	0.7
Guard Rotmistr Murat Argin	400	25,637	3,000	1.2
Esaul Ak Bochalin	0	1,500	3,000	2.0
Titular Councilor Ali Ulan	206	5,100	2,200	0.4
Khorunzhii Mehmet Bey Teketov	107	2,000	1,000	0.5

Source: DAARK f. 49, op. 1, d. 1086, ll. 35–82.

swooned over places like Alupka, with its abundant pear, fig, and cypress trees, its laurel forest, and "everywhere wonderful rose bushes, lavender, jasmine, and lilies, such that I thought I was in Italy." Madame de Hell too took pleasure in the "luxuriant vegetation" and coastline that "everywhere presents an amphitheatre of forests, gardens, villages, and country houses, over which the eye wanders with delight. The almond, the cythesus [sic], the wild chestnut, the Judas-tree, the olive, and the cypress, and all the vegetation of a southern clime, thrives here with a vigour that attests the potency of the sun." Others delighted in the rich garden culture of Bahçesaray where "Men and women were everywhere employed in damming up the water with planks and stones, and in other places letting it flow to water the land."[67]

There was an undeniable attraction to the idea of inhabiting, rather than transforming, this landscape. In towns like Balaklava, the "wild, gigantic landscape" infiltrated the built environment, covering facades with vines and flowers and shading streets with thick foliage. Laurence Oliphant, who traveled through Crimea in 1852, was delighted to find the fertile Salgir River valley descending from Chatyr Dag and expanding "into a richly cultivated plain, where the white houses and handsome churches of Simpheropol seemed half buried amid luxuriant vegetation." Some property owners incorporated the natural world into their architectural plans. At a country house on the Alma River guests could dine in "a spacious hall, formed by a clump of venerable oaks, that kindly unite their lofty branches to construct such a dining-room, as was worthy of the roast-beef and plum-pudding which graced the table." A manor home near Simferopol boasted an arrangement of "flower beds and gravel walks, lilac and rose bushes, acacia trees, exotic plants" and begonias reaching to the roof that together formed an open-air summer drawing room. Floriant Gille reached the height of sentimentality with his description of "the magnificence of trees, lawns, and beautiful plants" at Livadia. "What any traveler can admire and comprehend," he wrote, "is the discernment and taste that directed the distribution of trees and plants such that they form here and there masses of greenery and flowers within which the texture and tone vary, where the nuances offer contrasts that are so pleasing to the eye. For this many years are required, during which the proprietors must be men in possession of taste and enormous fortune in order to realize, each season, the dream of the lover of nature and all its pleasant or rare fruits."[68]

Anyone judging a landscape by such criteria was bound to recognize the Baydar valley as one of the most aesthetically pleasing corners of the entire south. In the words of Lady Craven, it was an "enchanting and magnificent spot intended by nature for some industrious and happy nation to enjoy in peace." Baydar won accolades as a "Tauric Elysium" blessed with abundant water and cultivated such that "everywhere there are ploughed fields, *bahçe* and shady forests of oak and *kizil*; walnut-

Figure 4.5. The valley of Uzembaş; from Bossoli, *Beautiful Scenery* (Courtesy of George C. Gordon Library, Worcester Polytechnic Institute)

Figure 4.6. View of the River Salgir in 1837; from Bossoli, *Beautiful Scenery* (Courtesy of George C. Gordon Library, Worcester Polytechnic Institute)

trees; everywhere springs and sources babble; everywhere nature is charming and everywhere there is abundance, richness, and a pleasantly varied landscape." But not everyone was thoroughly charmed. Some discerned that imperial control over ecologically valuable spaces such as the fine oak and pine forests of the valley led to "astonishingly rapid" deforestation. Some posited causal links between the greed of pomeshchiki, the diminishing volume of Crimean rivers, and skyrocketing costs for firewood. Such perceived linkages between deforestation, climate, and health were seeping into the discourse of empire in a variety of other contexts as well, and when the Marquis de Castelnau declared the Tatar claim that after Russian conquest "the winters became colder and longer" ridiculous, it was not the substance of the claim but the Tatars' reasoning that perplexed him. "They do not accuse their conquerors of changing the temperature by culling forests, destroying villages, redirecting rivers and streams," he mused. "Instead they accuse men born in a cold climate of having brought with them a germ that causes the difficulties of winter."[69]

The Tatars, in what Castelnau characterized as flawed reasoning, had in fact anticipated a theme—that of acclimatization—that would worry practitioners of European settler colonialism for much of the century. The implications of the relationship between environment, imperial authority (the "germ" that had descended from northern climes), and daily life were of immediate relevance and the Tatars' appraisal of the shift in that relationship helps explain the new wave of emigration that accompanied the Russian-Ottoman war of 1806–1812. During these years roughly three thousand peninsular Tatars and seven thousand Nogays from the steppe north of Perekop emigrated to Anatolia or Rumelia. Many sold their property to help finance the trip, as did many of those who stayed and suffered the hardships of wartime disease and adverse economic conditions. They sold their land to an assortment of military settlers, merchants, low-level officials, and mirzas in such quantity that in several years' time 100,000 desiatinas in Crimea and over 343,000 desiatinas in Tavrida as a whole were under new ownership.[70]

The government was concerned with these sales for three reasons. First, in many cases it was not clear that the seller owned the property in question. Individuals often sold lands they had dedicated as pious endowments or that had remained empty as a result of emigrations and to which they therefore had no claim. Second, while some sales were contracted voluntarily, many were the result of abusive tactics by constables, town governors, and private individuals. Finally, as had been the case since Potemkin began distributing land grants, most of the would-be landowners could not muster the means either to settle or to cultivate their newly acquired properties.

The antagonistic disputes that would inevitably flow from these transactions were bound to have an impact on order, and therefore security, in the province—an undesired outcome, to be sure. Catherine, after all, had presented the 1783 annexation as the act of an enlightened state: one that tolerated cultural difference and would guarantee the privileges of the population even if they were grounded in Islamic, rather than Orthodox, traditions. It fell to Alexander I, who maintained this carefully honed ideology, to address the situation. In May 1816 he therefore appointed Count Aleksei Andreevich Arakcheev, the infamous overseer of Alexander's military settlement project, to investigate cases of abuse of authority and seizures of land belonging to individual Tatars, cemaats, pious endowments, or those who had not yet reached their majority. Arakcheev was nothing if not serious about establishing order, and prolonged his stay in Simferopol in hopes of bringing his work to a satisfactory conclusion. It was not to be.[71]

The closest the imperial government came to resolving the thorny problem of landownership came in September 1827 in the form of a Senate decree. The decree "on the position of Tatar peasants and landowners in Tavrida province" was of immense interest and eagerly consumed: the first 500 copies were snapped up immediately, and authorities requested a thousand more for distribution through their offices, with another 250 to be distributed by the mufti. In the text of the decree, Nicholas I (who succeeded Alexander in December 1825) confirmed the right of Tatar peasants to hold properties collectively, although such lands could not be sold or transferred to a private owner. It also confirmed the right of non-noble Muslims, as well as other merchants, meshchane, and raznochintsy (people of various non-elite ranks), to own fields, meadows, gardens, forests, and other properties as private property, to be sold or transferred at their discretion (assuming they could present documentation of ownership). The message seemed clear. The decree equated Tatar rights with those of other state peasants who, beginning in the reign of Alexander I, could purchase and enjoy full ownership over uninhabited land. By extension, it brought land tenure in the former khanate in line with Russian practice. In fact, in the following months the State Council explained that the terms were not retroactive and that any previous purchases of land from Tatar peasants, whether made under duress or not, were irrevocable.[72]

But the 1827 decree was an aspirational document. On the ground, the territorialization of soslovie envisioned by Catherine II was unfolding over generations, rather than over the handful of years the empress anticipated. How could it be otherwise? The Imperial Senate, forty years after annexation, had again undermined the ability of its own policy to renovate the landscape of ownership in Tavrida by confirming the right of Tatar peasants and Muslim institutions to own parcels of land—gardens, çairs, orchards, forest parcels, and other sites—located within the dachas of "ancient and new pomeshchiki." Despite the efforts of Russian landowners and the government's own desire to curb the particularities of the borderland land regime, the Senate could not—or chose not to—disregard the policy that Catherine and Zubov had formalized in 1794 of grounding imperial rule in the protection of local institutions. Rather than signal a watershed in imperial policy, the 1827 decree rearticulated the tension between the government's undeniable tendency toward standardization and the simultaneous localization of empire.

In the end, the task of untangling the snarl of legal, cultural, ethnic, and geographical variables undermining the imperial project fell to a handful of surveyors. The Tavrida Survey Department had managed to produce excellent maps for the purposes of the general survey—which it completed in 1843—but could never marshal sufficient staff or funding to make significant headway against the backlog of property disputes and more complex cases. In this, Tavrida was not unique. When survey work spread to the Baltics, the Volga, Malorossia (Ukraine), and the southern empire early in the reign of Alexander I, the incompatibility of the original instructions with conditions in the non-Russian borderlands compounded with resource scarcity to bring the process to a halt. Special instructions for Bessarabia arrived in 1818; the rules for the special land survey of Tavrida province were issued in January 1829 and a special bureau opened in Simferopol, charged with surveying the peninsular districts. "On account of the local conditions in Tavrida province, the origins of its inhabitants, and the unique characteristics and variety of privileges regarding landownership, the boundaries and rights to privately owned and treasury property have not been appropriately clarified," explained the Senate. Because the preparation of property plans on the peninsula required "particular knowledge and expertise," the Ministry of Justice decided to appoint the very best surveyors and place them under the authority of an officer of the General Staff. But despite such careful preparations, the surveyors encountered obstacles of all kinds, from the logistical to the cultural. And so, in 1833, the Senate changed course, opting to streamline the survey process, reduce the number of special circumstances, and reorganize the survey bureau under the governor-general of New Russia.[73]

Over the next seven decades the survey bureau generated thousands of books and plans, obsessively documenting the contours of each property line and the acreage of arable and nonarable land. In so doing the bureau resolved disputes, one square sazhen at a time, and produced an extraordinary visual and textual archive of the process of empire building. That archive offers eloquent testimony to three key ideas.

First, property maps serve as an index of the socio-spatial relations that defined the southern empire. Valerie Kivelson has demonstrated the curious power of the seventeenth-century Muscovite property map to at once document and defuse disputes between litigants (or between litigants and the state), a power derived as much from the local meaning of the land as from the structure of authority imposed on it by imperial officials. "A forked pine and a decapitated aspen, a spot that once held a church but no longer did, a thicket of raspberries and thistles" whose significance extended no further than their own root systems nevertheless found a place on maps, she explains, maps "drawn on an obviously local scale, documenting issues of strictly local importance, but subsumed into the broader state vocabulary, symbolic abstraction, and administrative mechanisms." This holds true in the Tavridan context as well, where survey maps located each property in relation to adjacent properties, their owners, the environment, and the imperial administration. Take for example the 1835 map of a Sudak valley vineyard owned by a pair of brothers named Mehmet and Iag'ia. The vineyard, which covered 2,221 square sazhens (2.5 acres) along the left bank of the Sudak River, is depicted as a lush green field of color hemmed in by a series of straight-ruled and (intentionally) wavy lines. Working from south to east, the property abutted vineyards owned by an army captain, a Frenchman, a pair of Tatar brothers from the village of Taraktash, a Russian noblewoman, and finally, a parcel owned by the State Viticultural School. Meanwhile, the map of a sizeable orchard in Simferopol district describes its owner as a Tatar craftsman and the owners of adjacent properties as the children of a Greek official, a Karaite merchant, and the town of Bahçesaray. Of course, survey books could communicate the riotous patterns of landownership just as effectively. The 1789 survey of V. V. Kakhovksii's large estate at Arginchik (it covered over 9,300 acres) went to great pains to delineate the boundaries between the governor's property and that owned by the daughter of a Tatar official and the Tatar residents of three different villages, while countless other survey documents mapped the spatial relationships (accidental or intentional, long-standing or new) between bureaucrats, foreign settlers, Russian pomeshchiki, Tatar peasants, and various religious and educational institutions. All of these relations were documented, attested by signatories, set down on oversized sheets, embossed with the imperial stamp (the two-headed eagle), and archived.[74]

But there is even more to it. In addition to documenting the often fascinating geographies exposed through claims to landownership, survey maps emphasize that the vast majority of properties were not noble sanctuaries, set apart and inaccessible except on the landowner's terms. Roads, paths, and rivers transected them, and parcels owned by Tatar villages or dedicated as pious endowments interrupted their coherence. The 1795 survey of the dacha at Iamichi (in Perekop), for which Gentleman of the Bedchamber Ivan Mikhailovich Tiul'pin received a grant in 1792, revealed that the estate contained within it not only land belonging to Tatar peasants but also a property endowed to a nearby mosque. Working in the other direction, the survey of an orchard at Ay Serez (in the foothills above Sudak) identified the tiny parcel (less 162 square sazhens) as a tidy intrusion into an otherwise uninterrupted stretch of state forest.[75]

Tavrida was certainly not the only province with widespread instances of collective and common ownership. By the mid-1840s, surveyors had mapped 82,410 dachas across thirty provinces with more than one owner, and filed at least 189,831 plans associated with the special survey work that had been under way since 1806. What distinguished this case was the multiethnic and, by extension, ideological nature of the irregularities and intrusions. Nowhere else in the empire did Russian nobles find their properties crossed by centuries-old horse trails leading to the ancient capital of the Giray khans; nowhere else in the empire were pomeshchiki forced to grant access to groves of hazelnut and plum trees embedded in their estates and yet dedicated to the financial well-being of mosques and medreses. And nowhere else did they have to defend the integrity of their newly acquired property against the claims of men (and women) whose tenure as owners extended back generations and even centuries, steeped in the culture of the Turkic world.[76]

Finally, the survey maps remind us of the specificity—and significance—of physical space. The tsars distributed quantities of land in the south just as they did elsewhere, but in Tavrida the land grants took different forms, draped as they were over different elevation profiles, ecological zones, and hydrographic features. Rivers, ravines, and trees appear with some regularity, for they were the core vocabulary of Crimean properties, but in most cases the lack of topographic detail on the survey maps makes it nearly impossible to know, simply by looking at the map, whether (or how) a property was shaped by mountains, lagoons, or coastlines, let alone soil quality. The Geometrical Special Plan of the Dacha of the Villages of Bahçe Eli, Abdal, and Bike Eli, produced in 1847, is a glorious exception. The dacha was owned by the villagers, together with Prince Aleksei Petrovich Shakhovskoi and Evdokiia Semenovna Grilovaia (née Zhegulina), wife of a general and hostess of one of Tavrida's few renowned salons. It was a good-sized property: almost 3,234 desiatinas (8,732 acres), over 90 percent of which was suitable for cultivation. Most of the land consisted of arable fields and pasture (961 and 1,906 desiatinas, respectively), but the plan describes—and depicts—areas of deciduous forest (thirty-four desiatinas), mixed shrubs (seventeen desiatinas), fruit and mulberry trees (five desiatinas), and kitchen gardens (twenty-five desiatinas) as well. We can tell from the crude symbolization (the map relies on watercolor strokes instead of hachures for relief) that the wooded areas were at slightly higher elevation than the villages and gardens, which nestle near the rivers, and that the pastures and fields spread across a plateau rising northwest of the main post road. The map does not show the canals and channels described in the title text, but it illustrates the washes and exposed beds of the Little Salgir and Choiunchu rivers. This is not a trivial detail. When the Russian army produced a topographical map of the province in 1817, it noted that the Salgir was "only knee deep except in heavy falls of rain and snow in the mountains," but it offered no way to distinguish a deep river from a seasonal channel, depicting both—as well as anything in between—with a standard black line. A plan like the one from 1847, with its rich if selective detail, allows us to get a sense of how relief and climate determined the irrigation potential of a river, and therefore the agricultural value of the surrounding terrain.[77]

At Bahçe Eli, the features located in closest proximity to the Little Salgir River were the kitchen gardens, the fruit and silk trees, and a rectangular parcel surveyed with extraordinary care (every possible angle measurement is recorded on the map) but then left blank. At Abdal, the fields—map areas adorned with nothing but washes of pale apricot color—stand adjacent to the main road, but the village is set back on the far side of the river along with two more carefully surveyed but otherwise unidentifiable parcels. The same holds for Bike Eli, the village at the northern end of the dacha.

These precisely measured parcels are waqf properties. Six supported local mosques; two—the parcel closest to Abdal and the parcel at the very center of Bahçe Eli—remained charitable trusts overseen by individual Tatars. Each of them stands as striking evidence of important continuities in the spatial dimensions of land tenure. On the eve of annexation, between 14 and 30 percent of land in the khanate was dedicated to the financial support of mosques, schools, shrines, and other Muslim institutions. The annexation manifesto and subsequent legislation ruled that waqf properties could not be expropriated by the Russian treasury, but little was known about their quantity or location. The 1805–1806 register of inhabited villages, which was to that point the most authoritative demographic accounting of the province, recorded the existence of waqf in 212 locations. But because only Perekop—the district with the lowest population density on the peninsula—reported systematically on waqf (202 of the 212 locations in the register fell within that district), the number of sites was in reality far higher. After more than half a century of Russian rule, some remained ciphers, like those at Bahçe Eli, illegible (at least on some level) to Russian officials. We can only assume, based on their purpose and their proximity to water sources and cultivated gardens, that these parcels held significant economic value. Meanwhile others exploded into view in a riot of crimson, gold, and green on the map, the trees and vines that populated them articulated with geometric precision, their boundaries narrated, their scale recorded, their locations fixed, their values assigned.[78]

Either way, by the middle of the nineteenth century it was clear that it was the vineyard, the garden, and the orchard that structured the space of an imperial dacha. Russian authorities believed that on both a symbolic and a fiscal level controlling this subset of diminutive properties was the key to establishing authority and absorbing Tavrida into the social and cultural fabric of the empire. This was no easy task, but it was made easier by the implementation of the survey—"one of the most important and most beneficial institutions of civil societies," according to the influential journal *Messenger of Europe*. In an ebullient article published in 1822 the journal informed readers that this tool, which brought order and clarity to an otherwise undifferentiated and unenlightened world, had been contributing to the evolution of the Russian state since the tenth century. If it had yet to impose true order and clarity on the tsar's domain, that was the fault not of grand princes or lowly surveyors; it was the fault of the Tatars of Crimea, who for centuries had destroyed villages and emptied the land. Now, the political landscape had changed. The chore of empire was to fill the empty lands, tame the unkempt forests, and produce the kind of deep knowledge that would render the southern empire legible, accessible, and close to the heart of Russia.[79]

5 Intimacies of Exchange

RUSSIAN OFFICIALS RARELY lost sight of the economic implications of empire building. The desire for new markets or materials often supplemented expansionist agendas, and once the maps were redrawn the materiality of imperial rule manifested itself in everything from provincial budgets to tariff policies. Integrating the economy of a newly acquired territory took time: it could take decades for officials to fully grasp the complexities of production, consumption, and trade in any one region. But they had no need to wait that long to use the economy as a medium for empire building. With or without tailor-made policies, economic activity created sites of interaction that penetrated deeply into daily life: into decisions about what to wear and what to eat, where to travel, and what to produce.

The fact that production, consumption, and trade were core elements of daily life did not distinguish Tavrida, but the particular balance among that triad of activities, as well as the fact that the networks through which they moved were deeply embedded in a strategically sensitive transimperial regional system, certainly did. In an attempt to understand the impact of Russian rule on the economic landscape, this chapter mines the significance of local and trans-regional patterns of exchange and consumption. Economic life throughout the southern empire was bound up with a long-cherished plan to reorient the supply lines and market relations of the southern steppe away from Gdansk and the Vistula River, and instead funnel the productive potential of a huge swath of territory southward toward a strand of military installations and commercial ports on the Black Sea. The central node of this network of exchange was Odessa. It was through Odessa that millions of bushels of wheat, plus large quantities of everything from Chinese rhubarb to Caspian caviar, made their way each year from the fertile steppes of Novorossiia to Levantine and Mediterranean markets. Capital was concentrated there; Italian and Greek merchants dominated the city's astonishingly cosmopolitan cultural life.[1]

The novelty of this plan was striking. During three centuries of Ottoman domination, Kefe (Caffa, Feodosiia) had functioned as the commercial hub of the Black Sea. But the political renovation of the northern littoral demanded economic restructuring as well, and Catherine II created the city of Odessa to express her own imperial vision. The new city was a platform for growth; a venue carefully constructed to project Russian power—commercial, but also political—outward toward Constantinople and the Mediterranean. And it was wildly successful. In terms of tonnage, customs revenue, and ship traffic, the Crimean ports figured as little more than backwater harbors in a booming maritime economy whose center of gravity lay just over a hundred nautical miles to the west.

Yet quantities can be as misleading as they are revealing, and one of the premises of this chapter is that such figures yield only a rough approximation of the significance of any given port, trading house, route, or commodity. Helpful as those numbers are in assessing economic vitality, the apparent correlation between larger numbers and greater historical significance can mask important subtleties and structures within a given market system. And as it happens, beneath the gleaming surface of international commerce swirling through Odessa there was an economic *corrente sottano*—a thriving coasting trade moving single- and double-masted vessels along the familiar routes of a long-established regional economy. The trade volumes following this current were modest, but they offer a great deal of insight into what I think of as the intimacies of commercial life—the daily practices of consumption and production that imbue economies with social and cultural significance. Far from the din of Odessa's wharves, the import and export traffic at

Crimean ports enabled inhabitants to convert hides full of cow butter and skeins of silk into consumable pieces of wealth and meaning that embedded their households in layered geographies of exchange.

Scale was not the only difference between ports like Odessa and Feodosiia. In Odessa, Richelieu and his lieutenants were building a world-class emporium from the ground up: constructing wharves, recruiting merchants, developing new markets. Meanwhile, their counterparts in Simferopol were attempting to restore a badly damaged but deeply rooted economic system. Over time, the lands of the former khanate took on two rather unique functions within the imperial economy. First, they emerged as the garden of the empire, a paradise of unsurpassed beauty studded with lush meadows, exotic orchards, and prolific vineyards. Unlike the grain traded at Odessa, Crimea's walnuts and pomegranates would not disappear into the holds of foreign ships: they would be transported to Moscow and St. Petersburg, to the tables of Russians eager to consume those delicacies. Crimean wine would grace the homes of nobles from Kherson to Kiev, securing Crimea's status as a domestic source of gastronomical luxury. Likewise, its horses would end up in the stables of Moscow, rather than being sold to the Ottomans as they had been for centuries. Second, it would anchor the coasting trade linking Novorossiia's Black Sea ports with those on the Sea of Azov and along the Caucasian coast—a trade often driven by politics rather than profit margins. The question is, do these developments tell a story of integration or isolation? Where was the center of gravity? Is it possible that the logic of these networks of exchange originated anywhere but the desks of the Finance Ministry in Petersburg?

Skeptics will argue that the particularities of economy and environment in Tavrida—an ensemble of gardens, fields, bazaars, pastures, workshops, salt mines, and harbors—held only marginal relevance to the development of the imperial economy, and that reconstructing its idiosyncratic coherence is little more than an exercise in self-indulgent micro-history. But most contemporaries of Catherine II and her grandsons would have disagreed. To them the goods, ports, and markets of the south held inherent value. Princes and botanists alike devoted themselves to revealing the south's potential. It was a borderland after all, vulnerable to wind and war, shaped by passages and migrations, and a prime site for demonstrating the civilizing capacity of Russian rule. This chapter delineates two basic arguments. First, the coasting trade along the Black Sea littoral preserved a great deal of continuity across the 1783 divide and thus shaped the evolution of Russian coasting. This trade was dominated by Karaite, Turkish, and Greek traders, was oriented toward luxury goods, and was highly susceptible to illicit activities. Second, the myriad small-scale transactions and local markets examined here coalesced not into an imperially determined or even an insular provincial market, but rather into a series of overlapping and interdependent micro-economies.

THE IMAGINED ECONOMY

Officials and observers in Petersburg were preoccupied with what they believed to be the unique qualities of the peninsula and by the belief that the Giray khans had squandered the potential of one of the most fertile chunks of imperial space. In 1783, Tavrida was little more than an economic wasteland: an expanse of overgrown fields, untended orchards, ruined villages, crumbling wharves, and abandoned villages. This was the result, though ideologues preferred not to admit it, of nearly two decades of invasion and occupation by tsarist forces, incessant civil war, and the debilitating effect of mass emigration, rather than the ignorance or "Asiatic indolence" of the khanate's inhabitants. In their correspondence and memoirs, officials projected an imagined economy onto this imagined tabula rasa. In his exultant account of conquest, Pavel Levashev assured his readers that the littoral provinces would "flourish to the extent seen elsewhere in Europe and bring us abundance and wealth, particularly if we are able to attract part of the Indian trade to the Caspian, Azov, and Black seas." Foreign observers also anticipated expanding infrastructures of trade and mobility. In his 1805 account, William Eton speculated that Russia's ongoing canal projects would soon provide "water carriage from the Black Sea to the Baltic, to the Caspian, to Siberia, and to every province in the Empire." To Eton, the commercial geography was clear. While Odessa would dominate the grain trade between Poland and Constantinople, "the trade of Caffa [would] comprehend all that of the Don, Taganrok [sic], and other parts as far as Astrakhan, &c. and Siberia," as well as Persia, Bukhara, and the Anatolian coast. Caffa would, according to this scenario, reclaim its role as a gateway for the caravan routes and sea passages that had linked Eurasia to the Mediterranean (and beyond) for millennia.[2]

Officials serving in the region tended to hold a different vision of economic vitality: one that redirected Crimea's untapped potential toward the Russian core and focused on the productive capacity of soil rather than sea. In the early 1790s, General M. V. Kakhovskii encouraged Russians to revisit the notion of a foreign and dangerous terrain. "If you can," he wrote, "paint yourself a picture of the open space from Perekop to the Salgir River, spreading out over 100 versts, surrounded on the western side by the Black Sea and to the northeast by the Sivash and Azov seas. Sometime in the future," Kakhovskii assured his audience, "this vast plain will be filled with villages, embellished with churches, palaces and other buildings, and around them will be gardens." A great many military and civilian officials, landowners, and travelers cherished similarly ambitious hopes for the province, though most were drawn not to the steppe north of the Salgir but to the mountains and coast south of it. It was there that gardens would proliferate. It was there that the majestic terrain would, in the words of admiral, statesman, and local landowner Count N. S. Mordvinov, provide "abundant grapes, olives, pomegranates, and other rich produce for the empire."[3]

The expectation that a newly acquired territory should in some way support the imperial core is a common enough theme in the history of empires. But this garden-variety colonial notion represented a radical reconceptualization of the economy of the former khanate and with it the Black Sea region. From roughly 1475 until 1774, Kefe was an Ottoman *sancak* (administrative district); it was also one of the four Ottoman customs zones in the Black Sea, with authority extending through the Azov to the Abkhazian coast. For the most part though, the Crimean economy was decentralized. It was organized around the bazaars and workshops of Bahçesaray, Karasubazar, and Eski Kirim, the residences of the Girays, the vast (but diversified) landholdings of the bey clans, and a dense network of waqf properties. The products of both agricultural and trade activity coursed through innumerable social and commercial channels, many of which led to the port cities of Kefe (Caffa) and Gözleve, the khan's port. These were the commercial nodes that connected Crimeans to markets throughout the Caucasus, Anatolia, and the Danubian principalities. If imperial officials believed that "all [economic activity] must be directed to the good of the nation," they had a choice to make. They could attempt to create a colonial economy built to serve the interests of the government and its agents (the pomeshchiki), or work to restore the regional economy long since designed to serve local (non-Russian) elites—who would in turn be expected to serve the interests of the empire.[4]

The first choice appealed to men like Potemkin. Nothing if not ambitious, the prince sketched out a plan for Tavrida's economy during the harried months leading up to Catherine's ceremonial procession in spring 1787. The provisioning needs of the empress and her entourage were overwhelming. For just the nine luncheons and nine overnights scheduled for Crimea, the movable court required sufficient quantities of kvas (*polupiva*) and sparkling water, and seven hundred bottles of Sudak wine. Even if the prince could find that much wine, finding the bottles to pour it from would be an enormous challenge. To build the triumphal arches and "palaces" in which the empress would rest overnight—or sometimes just for an hour, to take the view—officials brought timber from Taganrog, across the Azov Sea. Potemkin sent men to Moscow to purchase mirrors, tables, silverware, and candles, and to Constantinople, Scutari, Smirna, and Chios to buy chocolate, coffee, and wine. Labor and materials of various kinds came from Kharkov, Kherson, and Kiev. Craftsmen in Bahçesaray and Akmechet produced the required clay tiles. The village of Kuchugur, near Aleshki, provided some ten thousand trees in order to build an appropriately pleasant grove at the palace at Kamennii Most'.

The frenzy of provisioning activity went hand in hand with infrastructure projects. Potemkin fretted endlessly (and for good reason) about the quality of existing roads in some places, and the utter lack of roads in others. Work began on a road that would connect Sudak with Akmeçet, Bahçesaray, and Karasubazar—important stops on Catherine's itinerary—as well as on bridges and stone mile-markers. The governor-general put soldiers to work laying a new road from Alma to Bahçesaray. Engineers had to widen the main street in Bahçesaray to allow for the passage of the procession. Potemkin enlisted the Don Cossacks to help provide the 10,500 horses to be kept on hand at Tavrida's post stations (the prince wanted 420 horses at each of the twenty-five stations). He assigned building work to the local kaymakams and merchants, as well as the local Greek battalions, but personally inspected every inch of the resulting route, adjusting the itinerary when local roads proved resistant to the kind of improvement he felt was necessary.[5]

The top-down nature of this project is undeniable; moreover, much of its funding came from the sale of Crimean salt, giving the endeavor a distinctly colonial cast. Then again, salt had long been a mainstay of the khan's government. The sums paid to lease the right to collect the salt tax, together with the customs duties generated at Perekop, Göz-leve, and Kefe, had together composed nearly 70 percent of the khan-ate's revenues in the years leading up to annexation. In fact, officials with experience on the ground recognized the importance of working within the constraints of the historical and environmental factors that had structured trade in the region for centuries. Richelieu, for example, content as he was to advocate for the introduction of foreign trees and vines along the southern coast of Crimea, opposed plans to privilege Taganrog over Feodosiia. Feodosiia's position near the Azov had distinct advantages, he informed Tsar Alexander in 1810. Richelieu was inspired by the recent arrival of a fleet of boats from Taganrog and Rostov bearing products of the Russian interior, including furs, butter, tallow, and caviar. With coasting traffic gravitating toward the south coast, "It seems far too absurd to want to sacrifice the good of the state for a village," he chided. Taganrog had been Russia's toehold in the region for nearly a century, but Feodosiia was the natural entrepot, the harbor that could handle the lion's share of the trade that would, as Czartoryski declared, "make the peninsula one of the richest provinces of the empire."[6]

If there were rival visions focused on Taganrog and Feodosiia, all agreed that Tavrida's main commercial function was to act as way station or customs house for trade moving between the rival imperial capitals of Petersburg and Constantinople. The Ottomans were never far from Catherine's mind as she laid out a plan to gradually map Russian commercial policy onto her new littoral territories. The first step in this process came just two months after she issued the annexation manifesto, when she announced a new commercial treaty with the Porte. The treaty was mainly concerned with reaffirming the capitulation-style privileges of merchants conducting trade in the Ottoman Empire, but Russian negotiators took pains to define the status of, and each party's obligations toward, merchant vessels, crews, and cargoes. The treaty required Russian and Ottoman officials in any port or harbor to do everything within their power to aid a ship in distress and provide necessary repairs and stores; and to recover goods from any ship wrecked in nearby waters, restore those goods to the ship's owner, and transport them to the nearest port without assessing duties of any kind. Adhering to such international

codes of maritime conduct might seem to cut against the grain of border demarcation along the Russian-Ottoman frontier. In fact, it simply
added to the complex layering of jurisdictional spaces that characterized the Black Sea region.[7]

Those ambiguities, created both by imperial policy and by regional
practices, were a precondition for the generation of wealth and power.
Catherine recognized this. In February 1784, in the same figurative breath
in which she confined the Crimean elite to their own social and legal
niche within Russian society, the empress issued a "manifesto on free
trade" that threw open the harbors of Kherson, Sevastopol, and Feodosiia to any ship flying the flag of a friendly nation. For a time, these ports
figured to be the prime locations for lucrative trade. Of course, Catherine herself was not bound by constraints of any kind: her own order
for Levantine coffee came in from Constantinople through Ochakov,
where customs officials consigned the shipment directly into the hands
of Vice Admiral Mordvinov for safe transit on to Petersburg. Officially,
Catherine declared that the principles of free trade had motivated her
from the earliest days of her reign but here again, a conflict arose between principled policies and exigencies on the ground. Free trade was
one thing, but increasing the income of the treasury was a pressing matter,
and one hampered by the outdated Black Sea tariff that had been in place
since 1782. In 1794, Prince Zubov insisted that Zhegulin conduct a careful examination of the tariff. "It has always been my intention to support trade and allow it to thrive," explained the governor-general, but
"fairness demands that those who are engaged in trade and enjoy the
associated privileges pay for the security and profits of their endeavors."
Zhegulin's task was to confirm that the items listed were still viable
commodities, and to recommend appropriate increases in the associated
customs duties.[8]

In July, Zhegulin convened a group of powerful men to consider the
necessary revisions. They included Tatar and Karaite merchants from
Bahçesaray, the overseer of Feodosiia, a Feodosiia merchant named Al-
liadzhi Aga, the overseer of Evpatoriia, and Tatar, Armenian, and Karaite merchants of Evpatoriia. Together, the merchants agreed that most
linens and other textiles could easily be subjected to an import duty of
thirty kopeks (per ruble); the same held for pearls, which had been duty-
free. The duty on fine morocco leather ought to double, they reasoned
(bringing it in line with similar goods), in order to protect local pro-

ducers from Ottoman competitors, while the duty on black olives ought to be cut in half as their price was low and they were much in demand by the local population (green olives were another matter entirely). The import duty on nuts of various kinds ought to rise from ten to forty kopeks per ruble since "the gardens and forests of the Tavridan peninsula abound with nuts" and the population was simply too lazy to harvest them. A similar logic applied to imported fruit syrups. The merchants took a harder line on export duties. They deemed a nominal duty appropriate for felt and fish oil, as demand was such that the market for both could sustain the introduction of an export duty, but proposed more robust duties for wax, black caviar, honey, cow butter, beluga, salmon, horse tails, and grain, all of which did very well in the markets of Constantinople and Greece. Ox and ram hides were an interesting case. These fetched good prices, but the 1782 tariff prohibited their export. Given the boom in cattle and livestock farming in Tavrida, suggested the merchants, the difficulty of transporting the hides into Russia, and the customs revenue to be gained, they ought to be added to the tariff with a nominal duty attached. The same held for wool. With no appetite for Crimean wool in Russia, livestock farmers needed to cash in on the foreign market; the merchants therefore requested permission to export the product with a minimal duty, from any port in Tavrida.[9]

Their tariff plan articulated a clear, if multilayered vision of the economic logic of the southern empire. This was a space in which forms of agricultural activity common across the empire—grain production, for example—had their place, but where the tastes of the majority population demanded access to a vastly different basket of goods than one would find in Ekaterinoslav, let alone Novgorod. Prices were different here; value was defined in different terms. Textile and leather production were increasingly lucrative occupations, but primarily because they met the needs of consumers outside the boundaries of the empire and as far away as the Greek archipelago. At the same time, Crimeans were used to having access to luxury and everyday items—from precious stones to fruit juice—that Russian markets simply did not offer.

This was how things looked from the vantage point of the governor's mansion in Simferopol, the piers of Evpatoriia and Feodosiia, and the coffeehouses and shops of Bahçesaray. The Tavridan economy looked quite different from the imperial capital. Paul I, the ill-fated emperor who prided himself on reversing his mother's policies, initially followed

Catherine's lead. In 1798 he granted free-port status to the entire Crimean peninsula for a period of thirty years, abolishing all customs houses and barriers. He did this not in order to realize the goals of Tavrida merchants or satisfy the needs of the Tatar population; Paul was motivated by a mental geography that had little to do with local conditions and culture. He conceived the designation of free-port status as the logical extension of a formula for commercial success under way in the Baltic and White seas. His main goal was to increase the profitability of southern commerce by eliminating the substantial contraband traffic moving to and from Crimea. His approach appealed to Karl Gablits, the influential vice governor. "Tavrida's harbors," Gablits wrote with palpable enthusiasm, "will serve as the warehouses for all the goods which to this point have come to the Anatolian coast via caravans from Smyrna and Persia with great difficulty, danger, and no small amount of losses."[10]

Though it was obvious to Gablits that Russians, Ottomans, and Persians would benefit by moving their goods through the maritime routes linking Tavrida with Trabzon and Sinop (eschewing the hazards of the overland trade through Tokat and Erzurum), in December 1799 the tsar revoked Crimea's free-port status, citing the "troubling events in Europe" which required heightened vigilance along the empire's borders. The notion that the unique produce of the peninsula—wine, salt, horses, sheep, grain, fruit, silk, fish, caviar—suddenly required a customs seal in order to be imported into Russia proper (*vo vnutr Gosudarstva Nashego*) did not sit well with ideologues or landowners. They felt that by shifting the customs infrastructure northward to Perekop, Paul had effectively wrested the "pearl" in his mother's crown from the economic territory of the empire and ceded it to Ottoman markets. At the turn of the nineteenth century, it remained to be seen whether old patterns would persist or adapt; it remained to be seen also whether the provincial government would be able to tell the difference.[11]

MARITIME ITINERARIES

The Black Sea's commercial geography was as dependent on currents and prevailing winds as it was on the evolution of Russian policy. The tattered, imperfect record of ship traffic in the early decades of Russian rule attests to the regularity with which ill-tempered winds forced Ottoman vessels to seek safe haven in Crimean harbors. Mariners' tales of an "inhospitable" sea had circulated for millennia by the time a Russian governor replaced the Giray khan, and though human activity had dramatically altered the estuaries spilling into the sea's western coast, much of the art of sailing the Black Sea remained unchanged. Writing from his unique vantage point as superintendent of the quarantine at Malta and with the aim of convincing his readers that Britain stood to gain from investing in Black Sea trade, William Eton assured readers that "the navigation is very simple and easy to skillful seamen; nor is there perhaps anywhere a sea of such an extent so free of dangers." "From Constantinople eastward to the Phasis there is neither rock nor sand-bank," he explained, and any skipper worth his salt would make short work of the soundings near the Danube, which "decrease so gradually and exactly, that you may know . . . to half a mile your distance from the shore." As if that were not enough to entice legions of merchants, he finished with a description of the "deep and clear" Crimean coast, obstructed only by two rocks nestled somewhere "between Caffa and Kertch, not far from the latter [and] . . . nearer the shore than any vessel has occasion to go."[12]

This must have been welcome news to many. Eton, who had himself surveyed part of the coast, knew of no accurate chart of the whole sea. "The Turkish charts show the ports with tolerable correctness," he admitted, but they were "often more than ten times the size they should be [. . .] according to the scale of the chart." For their part, Russian maps might guide a ship from Odessa to Constantinople tolerably well, but otherwise nautical knowledge of the Black Sea was scant until the publication of the *Atlas of the Black Sea* in 1807, complete with soundings and detailed harbor maps. Armed even with a reliable nautical atlas, merchants and sailors remained vulnerable to the particular dangers of a sea that so often played host to "sudden gales and impenetrable mists [that] frequently produce shipwrecks, even within sight of the lighthouses."[13]

Reducing one's chances of perishing at sea could be as simple as confining maritime activity to the summer and autumn months when storms were less frequent and the winds less capricious. In fact, seasonality was a clear feature of ship traffic throughout the first half of the nineteenth century, with northeasterly winds speeding vessels from Crimea to Constantinople in the summer months and southerly winds prevailing the rest of the year. Many captains sailed regardless of prevailing wind of course, and port logs record the arrival of their vessels in all seasons.

But the vagaries of Black Sea navigation often marooned ships in inter-
mediate ports—a particular misfortune for skippers with holds full of
perishable goods, such as the cargoes of oranges and high-quality Turkish tobacco regularly imported from Constantinople to Evpatoriia in
the early nineteenth century. Treacherous weather was so common that
in the 1830s and 1840s more ships sailed into Akmeçet harbor (on the
northern coast of Tarkhanskii Kut) due to poor weather than because
they intended it as a port of call. Akmeçet's customs logs are replete
with instances of ships seeking safe mooring and essential provisions.
The *Mariato Slaviano*, for example, one of the mainstays of the coasting fleet, entered the harbor with a major leak after taking heavy seas
in September 1846, while the *Brik*, an Ottoman ship sailing for Evpatoriia from Brailov, was pushed northward to Akmeçet by another
severe storm.[14]

The Sea of Azov presented an entirely different set of challenges. Silt
and runoff from the Don was accumulating at an alarming rate at the
turn of the nineteenth century, rendering the sea too shallow for most
seagoing ships. "Thirty years ago vessels drawing twelve feet water
loaded at Taganrog," observed Eton, while "at present they load twenty
miles from it." Navigation by smaller vessels looked increasingly attractive to Eton and many fellow foreign observers, who felt quite strongly
that trading interests were best served by eschewing the straits at Kerch
and making instead for the small (thinly staffed) harbor at Arabat,
whence the overland connection to Feodosiia was easy and well-
established.[15]

The challenges to mobility posed by topography and weather explain
why published descriptions of the Black Sea lingered over the advantages and disadvantages of its various ports, cataloging harbor depths,
freeze-thaw patterns, hidden sand banks, estuary hazards, lighthouse
locations, conveyance facilities, and land-carriage rates. Scrutinizing
the same landscape, imperial officials agonized over how best to effect
what they believed to be the necessary transformation of the region's
maritime infrastructure, pouring millions of rubles into facilities at
Odessa, Kherson, Nikolaev, and Taganrog in an attempt to impose a
new commercial architecture. Such infrastructural changes and even
the circulation of new nautical charts might mitigate some of the hazards of maritime trade, but wharves and quarantines could not com-
pensate for the idiosyncrasies of the coast's geomorphology. Feodosiia

won praise for its protected, spacious harbor—Terristori proclaimed that "no ship was ever known to have been wrecked there"—and mariners agreed that Sevastopol was far and away the best harbor in Crimea if not in the entire Black Sea region. But most everywhere else, sailors faced peril in some form or another: shipwrecks were so common that merchants found it impossible to obtain insurance in the early decades of the century.[16]

If the risks and frustrations of navigating these seas occupied the minds of imperial officials, merchants and sailors focused on the logic of supply and demand. Their itineraries reinforced commercial relationships forged long before 1783. The territory that now constituted Russia's southern empire was bound to the great emporium of Constantinople by the taste for Crimean goods cultivated on Ottoman and Russian palettes during the Porte's long tenure in the region, but also by commercial relationships extending back to the days of the roads leading quite famously "from the Varangians to the Greeks." For centuries before Russia gained its foothold in Crimea its merchants conducted a healthy trade in Ottoman markets. As recently as 1782 they exported iron and furs worth 337,398 rubles to Constantinople and imported fruits, cotton, silk, and wine worth 190,561 rubles. Throughout the Ottoman tenure on the Crimean coast, Caffa regularly drew ships from Constantinople as well as Trabzon, Sinop, Burgas, and Alexandria; even after 1783 merchant vessels (often relatively small one- and two-masted ships) called daily at Crimea's main harbors. In April 1784 alone, thirty-nine ships called at Caffa, thirty at Gözleve, and twenty-one at Balaklava.[17]

Over the next several decades these maritime relationships remained the mainstay of the local economy. Hundreds of small Crimean vessels were constantly under sail laden with salt, wool, butter, hides, wax, honey, caviar, and barley bound for the bazaars of the (Ottoman) imperial capital, while Feodosiia and Evpatoriia (still known as Gözleve and Caffa in many European sources) supplied markets in Anatolia and Rumelia with large amounts of wheat, butter, salt, and mohair, as well as tallow, hides, and the famous Crimean honey. The density of exchange was such that a Turkish merchant might easily arrange to purchase furs at a Feodosiia bazaar on behalf of a relative in Trabzon.[18]

It is easy to miss these linkages: they tend to fade into the vast terrain of commercial statistics. Tavridan ports handled a small percentage of the overall value of foreign trade carried out at Russia's Black Sea ports, varying between 4 and 8 percent from 1826 to 1836. In an average year they received less than one-fifth of the total volume of maritime traffic (table 5.1). But there are some juicy nuances embedded within these figures. Most importantly, Evpatoriia, Feodosiia, and Kerch together claimed from a quarter to just over a half of the annual fleet of ships arriving from the Ottoman Empire in a given year. "Turkish" ships—and by extension their cargo and the markets they served—played a relatively minor role at Odessa and Taganrog, but had a much stronger presence in Bessarabian ports and served as the very foundation of trade in Crimea, where they constituted 75 percent of ships calling at the ports of Evpatoriia and Feodosiia in the late 1820s.[19]

It is probable that the actual number of Ottoman vessels calling at all Russian ports was much higher, in large part because accurate data on coasting is notoriously difficult to come by. For decades if not centuries, ship captains snapped up opportunities to hire themselves out for purposes of local transport, ferrying wine, lumber, and tobacco short distances along the Crimean coast, often beyond the reach or knowledge of the bare-bones customs administration. The *Sv. Nikolai*, for example, did a brisk business as a ship-for-hire to residents of Feodosiia needing to transport materials or goods to Evpatoriia or Kerch, yet the documentary record of its activities is largely anecdotal. Coasting in the Black Sea involved shorter distances, smaller volumes, and vessels that more easily evaded quarantine (and often notice of any kind) than those involved large-scale commercial activity. It was in many ways a highly localized institution, and for that reason coasting has attracted little attention from historians of empire. In the British field, maritime histori-

Table 5.1. Ship Arrivals at Russian Black Sea Ports

Region	1827	Percentage of total	1830	Percentage of total
Kherson	855	46	885	49
Azov	342	18	486	27
Crimea	276	15	344	19
Bessarabia	383	21	96	5

Source: Terristori, *Geographical*, 42–43.

ans have tended to associate railways with domestic modernization, and shipping with overseas commerce, leaving little space for coasting. But those who have dug into the record of coastal shipping have found that rather than being displaced by new transportation infrastructures it increased in importance over the nineteenth century, growing incrementally within the economies of both Britain and Spain. Meanwhile, a number of scholars have begun to unearth the myriad functions of coastal trade, from facilitating industrial development and agricultural commercialization, to monetarizing local economies and integrating domestic markets.[20]

In the context of the Black Sea it makes sense to speak of both coasting and cabotage. Coasting can be understood relatively broadly as maritime trade within a particular region or environment; some historians use the term to describe trade over relatively short distances, or without trans-oceanic passage, that might nevertheless involve crossing an international boundary. Cabotage tends to have a more restricted meaning, referring to trade conducted within the rivers and coastal waters of a single state. In the Black Sea, coasting and cabotage had been largely synonymous since the late fifteenth century, with merchants sailing an "Ottoman lake" dominated by Constantinople. Having made incursions along the northern littoral from 1774 onward, Russian officials were happy to have the Ottoman capital remain a market and entrepot for the produce of Novorossiia. But by 1797 the Admiralty College felt the time had come to begin differentiating the forms of trade moving across the waterways of the south. Henceforth the term "large voyaging" (*bol'shoe moreplavanie*) would describe the passage of ships sailing from the Black Sea through the Dardanelles to the Aegean and Mediterranean, while "small voyaging" (*maloe moreplavanie*) would refer to traffic moving along Russian rivers and within the Azov and Black seas as far as the Sea of Marmora.

If the language of the decree was inelegant, it acknowledged the coherence of the Black Sea as a unified trading zone. In fact, the Admiralty College explained that not only Russian subjects but foreigners who had settled within the empire or otherwise enjoyed the right to maritime trade at Russian ports could participate in small voyaging. Thus "small voyaging" amounted to a unique form of cabotage that invented a commercial space that transcended the Black Sea and opened the possibility of projecting Russian power through and past Constantinople.

The requirements for large voyaging were more stringent. Only ships built in Russia and purchased by subjects or foreign settlers who had invested in Russian goods qualified for patents. If sailing under a Russian skipper, half the crew could be foreign; otherwise two-thirds must be Russian subjects.[21]

In 1826 the Ministry of Finance began to include in its annual statistics a table describing cabotage. Customs records occasionally drew the distinction between domestic and foreign trade, and it was subtly inscribed in the finance ministry's annual "survey of maritime trade" (*vid torgovago morekhodstva*). According to the survey, the average tonnage of ships sailing to Odessa was consistently well over 100 *lasts*. Taganrog received vessels between ninety-five and 135 lasts, while the tonnage at all other Black Sea ports ranged between thirty-eight and eighty-five lasts (these were the one- and two-masted vessels typical of the coasting trade). The smaller vessels were suited to carrying less tonnage over shorter distances, and they could prove elusive even to otherwise diligent customs officials. The port of Evpatoriia, for example, saw foreign imports worth 22,639 rubles in 1826 despite the fact that all ships represented in the ministerial survey arrived under ballast.[22]

Given the volatile nature of the Russian-Ottoman frontier in the eighteenth and nineteenth centuries, the elusiveness and ambiguity inherent in maritime trade raised concerns. Officials were well aware that such a deeply rooted and dispersed regional network might eventually work against the interests of empire building, and they tried to exert control over its merchants, vessels, and cargo. In the second half of the eighteenth century they made concerted attempts to enforce customs regulations (merchants from Crimea and the Kuban habitually avoided paying Russian duties simply by skirting the customs house at Taganrog) and even maintained agents in Constantinople charged with reporting on the inventories and itineraries of ships hailing from Caffa. The Russian government's sense that maritime trade and political destabilization were linked was substantiated in 1782, when the Russian resident in Bahçesaray advised the commandant of Yenikale not to allow the passage of commercial vessels from Circassia and the Kuban on the grounds that economic relations between the Crimeans, Cherkess, and Abkhazians represented too great a threat to Russian interests in the region.[23]

The extension of sovereignty over Crimea did not dispel these fears. In the decades after annexation, Tatars maintained social and economic connections that undercut the potency of the political borders separating the newly created Tavrida province from the north Caucasus. Those connections presented opportunity as well as danger. In June 1804 Minister of Internal Affairs Viktor Kochubei informed residents of the Crimean coast that they had the right to take the produce of their farms by boat to any port and that such voyages would be exempted from quarantine requirements so long as the skipper swore under oath that he had neither encountered nor communicated with Ottoman vessels. The intervention of one of the most powerful figures in all of Russia might seem a disproportionate response to the trading practices of coastal Crimeans, but the minister and military governor had grown concerned about what they feared to be a widespread and potentially dangerous mode of economic exchange. While Armenians, Greeks, and Karaites had a much higher profile in the merchant ranks, reports compiled in 1783 suggest that roughly one-fifth of Tatar males were traveling on trade-related business; Tatars were prevalent enough among Tavrida merchants that Igel'strom printed sixty copies of the February 1784 decree on trade in Crimean ports in Tatar, and ten copies in Greek. Governor-General Bekleshev worried over the spread of plague, but even more so over collaboration between Tatars and Ottomans determined to restore the dominant position of the Porte. Maritime trade could serve as a vehicle for either or both, but Kochubei decided that the risk posed by market disruption was greater than that of potential covert collaboration between disgruntled subjects and their co-religionists on the opposite shore. Surprisingly, Russian officials generally followed suit, seeing the trade network they had inherited as a mechanism for extending influence well beyond the borders of their empire, particularly into the Caucasus.[24]

CONTRABAND AND CABOTAGE

The necessary maritime itineraries were already in place. In the early years of the nineteenth century Ottoman vessels like the *Shaika* sailed regularly between Samsun, Amasra, and Evpatoriia. Others charted courses between Evpatoriia, Galats, and Constantinople. One of the most common itineraries of the 1820s—one that involved cargoes of tobacco—ran from Redut Kale on the Georgian coast, through Feodosiia, to Odessa. Russian officials and foreign merchants alike waxed enthusiastic about what would happen when they tapped into the maritime trade networks accessible from the ports of Crimea. Many pinned their hopes on Feodosiia—still called Kefe or Caffa by nearly everyone save Russian officials—because of its long history as a major commercial hub. "Caffa affords an opportunity of procuring any quantity of oak, of a kind inferior to none in the world, from the coast of Anatolia . . . and from the coast of Abassa [Abkhazia] and Mingrelia," explained William Eton. With such stores, ships could be built "of any size, and copper bottomed, and sail fit for action" faster and more cheaply than they could be by ferrying timber to Malta, as the British navy currently did.[25]

Richelieu recognized the political potential of maritime trade. In fact, he threw his weight behind a plan to use it to facilitate the expansion of Russian rule in the north Caucasus. Officials had known for decades that many inhabitants of the Caucasus were dependent on salt imports: it had long been a staple of Crimean and Ottoman trade with the Adyge (contemporaries called them Circassians), who often obtained it in trade for female captives or the daughters of poor families desperately in need of income and essential goods. With the productive salt lakes of Crimea now part of Tavrida, officials recognized an opportunity to draw Caucasians into the tsarist orbit. Richelieu returned to France before seeing the plan carried out, but in 1817 the Department of Foreign Affairs commissioned a Genoese attaché to sail with one thousand pounds of salt to Abkhazia, trade it for timber, and thus inaugurate regular trade relations. The scheme was not an overnight success, but Prince Vorontsov, who was both governor-general of Novorossiia and viceroy of the Caucasus, and Nikolai Raevskii, commander of the Black Sea defensive line, continued to champion the cause. Their patience paid off when in 1839 word came that the mountaineers had begun offering wine instead of women in exchange for salt. Meanwhile, in 1826 inhabitants of Circassia and Abkhazia had gained the privilege of entering Russian territory through Feodosiia without paying customs. Two years later, the imperial government further sweetened the deal by reducing the customs duty on silk and woolen goods from "Little Asia" entering Russia through Crimean ports.[26]

Yet much of the maritime traffic circulating between Anatolia, the Caucasus, and Crimea operated according to the whim of merchants and skippers rather than according to the letter of the latest decree from tsar or sultan. Ottoman vessels were widely known to sail cargoes of cotton, coffee, Greek wine, tobacco, dried fruit, and silk from Turkey to Crimea and to return with salt, leather goods, butter, caviar, and wax, all regardless of bans or prohibitions. Often alongside or wedged in among these goods were choice bits of contraband, such as the diamond-studded harness plates and ruby-encrusted saddles hidden away under the neatly folded fur coat of skipper Tersane Mehmet Ali Emin oğlu, who sailed into Feodosiia in November 1826 only to have the items confiscated (and later pocketed) by a local customs guard. Contraband and unapproved goods often made up over 80 percent of the total value of goods any given merchant traded, in no small part because the Russian government was forever amending the tariff, adding to the dazzling array of prohibited goods, which included knives, silks, rings, buttons, inkwells, copper mirrors, snuff boxes, and candlesticks. Confiscated contraband was sold at public auction, with the proceeds split between the customs officer who found it and the local chamber for public oversight. Merchants—even those not intentionally violating the tariff—were simply out of luck.[27]

As the list suggests, contraband cargoes were often quite modest. In September 1806, for example, customs officials caught a group of thirteen traders—eleven residents of Bahçesaray and two of Evpatoriia, all of them Tatars—importing prohibited goods from Constantinople. On average, the contraband imported by each man was valued at less than ten rubles. Abdul Kerim of Bahçesaray brought in two white fur jackets, ten shirts, five saucers, seven coffee cups, and a small copper kettle. Agmet Umer, also of Bahçesaray, imported a hand mirror, four children's coats, and eight toy drums. Tikidzhi Abit's contraband consisted of an iron scale and a kettle. Copper pitchers and skillets, coffee pots, coffee cups, saucers, braziers, and lanterns rounded out the list of confiscated items—the kind of household wares precious to a housewife but not likely to bring down a regime. They were so precious to their would-be owners, in fact, that the traders petitioned all the way up the ladder to Finance Minister N. P. Rumiantsev to have them restored.[28]

Contraband came in more extravagant packages as well. In 1806 the *Shekhtie,* an Ottoman merchant vessel, sailed into Evpatoriia harbor with silver buckles and necklaces, wool and silk garments, and an assortment of raspberry-colored brocades: altogether a horde worth more than 182 rubles. Ottoman Armenians and Turks, Karaites, and Greeks residing in Crimea continually imported suspect goods such as "asiatic" tools for shaving and jewelry. In 1802 Menish oğlu, a Karaite merchant from Gözleve, outdid most of his rivals by attempting to trade 450 rubles worth of contraband as well as a few ambiguous cover items such as wooden combs and Turkish dyes (table 5.2).[29]

Brocades and copper buttons were not the only commodities moving clandestinely across the water. Late one evening in April 1793, Magmut Reis, an Ottoman subject residing in Feodosiia, sailed from that harbor bound for nearby Koktebel, accompanied by two sailors. There they brought on board six men and four women who had been waiting on shore, all of them natives of the Caucasus who had been sold into slavery at Anapa and registered as the serfs of Second Major Tumanov. After

Table 5.2. Contraband Confiscated from Menish oğlu

Item	Quantity	Value (rubles)
small mirrors	80	20.8
decorated snuffboxes	7 dozen	7.0
wire	60 bundles	5.4
dyed cloth	19 quires	4.8
decorative wall paper	3 quires	2.3
copper pendants for a girdle (*kushak*)	90 pair	15.7
copper saucers used under Turkish coffee cups	2 dozen	6.0
copper thimbles	30	0.6
copper necklaces	75	7.9
copper rings	1,200	9.0
tin rings	950	7.6
small round Turkish buttons	1,400	4.5
iron flints	2,790	30.0
silk ribbon (in 250-arshin bundles)	13	15.0
lace ribbing	10 *funty*	65.0
combs made of bone	22	7.7
bowl of hammered silver	1	7.6
iron door locks	7 dozen	15.0
iron scale (*kantar*)	1	5.0
copper washbowl weighing 21 *funty*	1	14.7
high-quality wooden boxes	60	9.0

Source: DAARK f. 369, op. 1, d. 28, ll. 3–70b

stealing property worth 300 rubles, Magmut Reis and his men joined the former slaves in the *sandal* (a small sailing vessel). The overseer of Tumanov's estate got word of the escape and rushed to the shore, demanding that the boat turn back. Reis's sailors opened fire, then made for Anapa. A month later, Vice Governor Gablits asked Prince Zubov to increase patrols of the coast near Feodosiia in order to guard against the "pernicious danger" of illegal maritime traffic.[30]

It would take another decade for the emperor to intervene. In November 1803, the Melitopol procurator's assistant submitted a report to his superior detailing his recent travels through the district. Along the way, Popov had been surprised to find a Russian woman (*velikorossiiskoi porody zhenshchina*) living in the home of the Nogay chief, Bayazet Bey. When he asked locals about her, they explained that she had converted to Islam and married Bayazet, and that four more young women lived with him as well. Bayazet Bey had obtained all of them through purchase, though the locals were quick to explain that there were many converts to Islam living among them, their Christian identities obscured by Muslim names. Popov decided to pursue the matter. He was able to establish that the Nogays were regularly importing Cherkess slaves (*plenniki* and *iasyry*) trafficked through locations in Astrakhan province, well away from the watchful eyes of customs inspectors. They kept some (roughly a thousand) and sold the rest in Crimea.[31]

The sale and possession of human souls might not have been problematic in a society grounded in serfdom if not for the fact that the slaves in question were Christian and their owners Muslim. This, Popov pointed out, violated the terms of a February 1784 decree that had guaranteed the status and privileges of the mirzas *other than* their right to own Christian souls. Officials were just as bothered by the notion that there were robust trade networks linking the Caucasian highlands to Feodosiia— networks that they did not have the manpower to subject to customs duties—as they were about the fact that Nogay traders were selling Christian women into Tatar households throughout the region. As if that were not bad enough, there was the possibility that those networks might bring in Muslims disenchanted with Russian rule. In the 1820s, during his several voyages along the Caucasian coast, Eduard Taitbout de Marigny often met Tatar merchants in the coffeehouses of Kuban. They were, according to the Dutchman, well traveled and literate in affairs of the day, and "many of them, after having served in Russia, preferred

Circassia to their native country. The sentiments which these people must cherish might render very dangerous the relations which they continue to have with their countrymen, through the channel of the merchants of the Crimea, who come every year to Anapa."[32]

The need to regulate small-scale, regional trade led to the elaboration of an official cabotage regime. The first step in this direction came in 1798, with Paul I's decision to give Crimea free-port status: a move that closed the existing customs outposts (*zastavy*) at Balaklava and Sudak and displaced all customs activity to Perekop and Arabat, the small harbor on the southern end of the Sivash Sea (known to many contemporaries as the Putrid Sea). He recanted that decision a year and a half later, closing the new customs at Arabat and Perekop, and reestablishing customs houses at Gözleve, Aktiar, and Feodosiia, with customs outposts at Kerch and Enikale. One of the unintended consequences of the tsar's flip-flop was to draw attention to the Azov corridor to the Caucasus. By 1808 the Senate showed a willingness to address the challenge of navigating and policing the Azov by creating the office of Chief Overseer of Merchant Shipping. The Senate appointed the city governor of Taganrog, Baron Balthasar von Campenhausen (Kampengauzen), to the job of inspecting wharves and lighthouses and collecting data on shipping and wrecks. Meanwhile, work was under way on the piers at Feodosiia, extending them into deeper water in order to receive ships under precautionary quarantine (that is, those with plague on board), but also those not subject to quarantine, such as ships arriving from other Russian ports in the Black Sea.[33]

The infrastructure of the coasting trade developed slowly but surely. In 1816 Evpatoriia had some 1,000 households, of which the majority were Tatar merchants and craftsmen, Greek and Armenian traders (*torguiushchie liudi*), and the Karaite merchants who dominated commercial activity. The harbor had until recently held two hundred vessels and been connected by good roads to the markets of the southern and interior provinces. Despite the relative decrepitude of the port in the early nineteenth century, Nogays still sent grain, leather, butter, salt, and wool to Evpatoriia for export to Anatolia. At Feodosiia meanwhile, nearly half of the export duties were collected from wool (12,312 rubles from goods valued at 450,885 rubles in 1826; proof that the group convened in 1794 to discuss the tariff knew what they were talking about). The larger source of revenue, though, was the import trade. Small amounts of vodka and wine came to Feodosiia from Mingrelia, but most everything else, including large amounts of grapes and figs, came from the Ottoman Empire. By the mid-1820s, improved record keeping made it possible to establish that at least 44 percent of customs revenue at Feodosiia came from cabotage.[34]

This indicated a remarkable change. At the turn of the nineteenth century, seven or eight hundred merchant vessels frequented Russia's Black Sea ports. Most were foreign built. But the shipyards at Kherson were hives of activity, turning out hundreds (as many as fifteen hundred) of flat-bottomed boats designed to ferry merchandise from the ports of the Azov to Feodosiia. According to Henry Dearborn, precisely 132 sailing vessels coasted between Taganrog, Crimea, and Odessa, while barges operated in the estuaries at Mariupol and Taganrog, in the shallows around Arabat and, daringly, around Feodosiia, Kerch, and Enikale. Like Feodosiia, Kerch served as a hub for both foreign commerce and cabotage. Merchants there could find "great facilities . . . for building coasting vessels": the kind that drew no more than thirteen feet, carried no more than two hundred tons, and thus navigated the shallow Sea of Azov with relative ease. In 1830 Kerch customs officials recorded foreign imports (primarily lemons, oranges, cotton and silk goods, and wines from the archipelago) worth 205,027 paper rubles, and foreign exports (corn, flour, salt, dried fish, and iron) amounting to 133,649 paper rubles. By contrast, coasting vessels took salt alone worth 227,697 paper rubles from Kerch to the Azov ports. Russia had its own maritime economy in the south.[35]

MAPPING MARKETS

Maritime trade was flourishing, feeding off the emerging port network as well as the river traffic that had long ferried goods across and through the Black Sea littoral. Elsewhere in Russia, an even more significant change was in the works: by the middle of the nineteenth century, overland routes had emerged as an appealing complement to water-based trade. Until the arrival of railways later in the century, landowners and merchants alike complained incessantly—and with good reason—about the lack of good quality roads in Novorossiia. Be that as it may, a network of annual fairs had taken shape in the provinces of Novorossiia, consisting of 545 fairs in 220 locations throughout the governor-generalship. This network facilitated the exchange of produce from coastal orchards and the farming settlements of the steppe, foreign goods (mostly wine and tea), and the movement of merchants from as far as Moscow and Kharkhov. In some cases the markets in this network tapped into much older trade routes. Those at Elizavetgrad (Kherson province), for example, resuscitated the trade that had linked Constantinople with northern markets via the wharves at Hadzhi-bey (the future site of Odessa). Once frequented by Armenians selling linens, vodka, tobacco, and rope, Tatars and Zaporozhian Cossacks selling horses, cattle, and leather goods, and Karaite merchants of Crimea selling lambskins and Sudak wine, Elizavetgrad temporarily fell into the shadow of Kherson but had found new life by the middle of the nineteenth century. At Novii Mirgorod, a key link to the large markets of Podolia and Kiev since the 1750s, one could purchase horses and livestock from the steppe but also groceries from the interior and fish and caviar from Kerch (sold by Tatars). By 1850 trade was so well established at Novogeorgievsk (also in Kherson province) that merchants had extensive warehouses, wharves, and depots to store forest products and the salt that came both by water and overland from Perekop.[36]

Anchoring the eastern end of the network, Rostov drew trade from the Kuban and Don lands, and from as far away as Siberia. Armenians from Nakhichevan, Taganrog Greeks, Don Cossacks, and Kalmyks dominated trade, selling everything from Siberian iron and timber from Saratov to grains from Penza, butter from Perm, and increasing amounts of Crimean wine. Rostov was a site for internal trade, with goods coming from the great markets of Kharkov, Moscow, and Nizhegorod but only a few items (lemons and oranges, tea, coffee, wine, and dyes) funneling through Taganrog from abroad.[37]

Most fairs were annual events lasting roughly a week. They attracted diverse crowds and a wide range of goods, from basic provisions to luxury items. Word of newly established or soon-to-open markets circulated through official channels: notices fill the archives of various provincial bureaus. Dozens of new fairs opened throughout the 1820s and 1830s as the pace of settlement in Novorossiia increased and the scope of commercial interest broadened to include not just Ekaterinoslav and Kherson, but Poltava, Orenburg, Omsk, and Tiraspol (Moldavia). Market days were chosen carefully. Some coincided with Orthodox feasts, such as the fair at Kerch on April 23 (the day of St. George the Victory-Bearer and Wonder-Worker) and August 29 (the day of the beheading of the Glorious Prophet John the Baptist).[38]

To be sure, the fairs of Novorossiia paled in comparison to the famous fairs at Nizhnii Novgorod, Kharkov, and Irbit, but they need to be seen as a meaningful space of production, consumption, and trade. After all, each interregional fair functioned "as a single, moveable (ambulant) market" arranged according to a cyclical schedule that covered a vast terrain without ever taking merchants too far from their home bases for too long a period. Seen in this light, the *chumaky* who transported salt overland from Perekop to Kharkov did not simply create a local dynamic of exchange between two points; instead, their work connected into a vast economic network.[39]

Tavrida's biggest fairs took place in the Dneprovsk and Melitopol districts, where landowners and Tatars bred livestock and horses in large quantities. The best known was the fair held at the village of Kakhovka. Owned by Colonel Ovsianiko-Kulikovksii, a former provincial marshal, Kakhovka was a fifteenth-century Tatar fortress (Islam Kermen) conveniently located on the banks of the Dnepr River and on the postal road running from Kherson to Simferopol. Named for Governor Vasilii Kakhovskii, Kakhovka received a constant stream of oak trees sent downstream from Kremenchug and Ekaterinoslav, and also hosted week-long markets in May and October. Though Kakhovka became predominantly a woolens market by the end of the nineteenth century, in 1832 merchants there offered Russian goods and wares worth 772,950 rubles, livestock worth 308,465 rubles, European imports worth 30,620 rubles, and tea worth 8,604 rubles. Textiles (cottons, woolens, silks, felt, and hemp goods) generated the most revenue, followed by livestock (cattle and sheep), leather goods, and furs (table 5.3).

The Kakhovka fairs catered to a wide range of tastes and budgets. One could spend eight rubles on a *pood* of soap, fifteen rubles on an *arshina* of high-quality wool cloth, or as much as 400 rubles on a single marten fur. If forty-five rubles per pood of Turkish tobacco was too steep for one's pocketbook, simple tobacco was on sale for five rubles per pood. If a fox cub fur cost 160 rubles, an adult fox fur could be had for seven. Wool ranged from three to twenty rubles per arshina depending on quality; wines ranged from three rubles forty kopeks per bucket of Crimean wine to forty-five rubles for Sauterne and 240 rubles for champagne. The complexion of goods on offer is significant,

Table 5.3. Sample of Russian Goods at Kakhovka Fair, 1832

Item	Value (rubles)	Amount sold	Percentage sold
cattle	233,550	–	
cotton goods	146,960	77,674	52.9
leather goods	123,432	60,135	48.7
silken goods	116,240	62,635	53.9
felt and hemp goods	70,528	29,205	41.4
woolens	43,512	30,292	49.4
furs	60,664	29,544	48.7
alcoholic beverages	31,269	31,269	100.0
metals	44,013	17,101	38.9
fish and sturgeon	5,560	2,964	53.3
crystal and glass	4,629	2,487	53.7
marble	3,180	1,460	45.9

Source: DAARK f. 26, op. 1, d. 8113, ll. 2–11.

for while Tavrida hosted one-fifth as many fairs and moved goods worth 37 percent of those sold in Ekaterinoslav, Tavrida's market towns averaged sales nearly double those of Ekaterinoslav (140,415 rubles as opposed to 78,947 rubles in 1850 for example). In other words, the goods on offer in Tavrida had value, if not volume.[40]

Kakhovka was an important market for local farmers, craftsmen, and winemakers. Much was expected from the prized vineyards arrayed along the narrow stretch of coast, but unlike hemp, tallow, wheat, salt, wax, wool, canvas, horse hair, flax, tobacco, and leather products, wine did not find its way onto the list of exports from Russia's southern ports in the early nineteenth century. On the contrary, it was among the main imports at Kherson, Taganrog, and Feodosiia, along with sugar, West India coffee, silks, velvets, spices, olive oil, almonds, dried fruits, syrups, cheese, jewelry, and rum. Some visitors were astonished to find many of the Crimean wines "poor and hungry," and the grapes with which inhabitants made brandy imported from Trabzon and Sinop. Others, like Maria Guthrie, who visited the Sudak valley during the 1796 harvest, found the grapes pleasant and the wine "the best in the peninsula," remarking that it "somewhat resemble[d] that of Hungary in lightness and flavour, especially when well made, and kept a proper time." According to Guthrie sales were already generating substantial enough revenues that the production of syrups from local fruit—a traditional practice of the Crimean Tatars—had largely ceased.[41]

Over the following decade enthusiastic Russian officials and patrons of enlightened agriculture opened grape nurseries. In 1803 the interior ministry directed that each colonist receive five to ten vines, which they would be responsible for cultivating. In cases where recipients knew something of viticultural methods these policies met with success. But Pavel Sumarokov, a senator and member of the Russian Academy of Sciences who traveled through Tavrida in 1803–1805, found that most farmers did not bother to research the suitability of the vines they planted; they demonstrated equal ignorance of proper harvesting techniques. They lacked the presses, cellars, and casks needed to produce decent wine from the grapes they were able to coax from their vineyards, and instead "decanted it into casks [recently] emptied of grain vodka." Stubbornly optimistic, Sumarokov insisted that with substantial investment the cultivation of grapes would thrive in what he saw as "a vast, aromatic garden, a pleasing pantry of treasures" capable of producing well over 300,000 buckets of wine each year.[42]

By 1808, wine production exceeded 100,000 buckets, and production more than doubled in the next two years. The market for Crimean wine kept pace, pushing prices from a ruble and a half to three rubles per bucket in 1811. In 1831, Crimean vintners produced 472,000 buckets (5.8 million liters). They sold an average of 85 percent of their total vintage through the 1820s, but their wine had not yet found a place in the regional wine trade. Sinop and Trabzon continued to supply Constantinople, Odessa, Crimea, and Taganrog with wines ranging from the sherry-like whites of Amasya to the claret-like reds of Tokat, as well as olive oil, Angora wool, dried figs, hazelnuts, copper, Persian silks, and saffron. Greek wine poured in through Feodosiia and Taganrog, and champagne arrived from Odessa.[43]

Governor-General Vorontsov offered an explanation. On account of its distance from the center of the empire and its lack of population, he posited, "Crimea [could] not become an important point of external trade." Those who argued the opposite, citing the legacy of the Genoese, Turks, and Tatars in Caffa/Feodosiia, did so, suggested Vorontsov, without considering factors such as the proximity of booming ports such

as Odessa and Taganrog. Moreover, in previous centuries Crimea's lucrative trade had been driven by the consumption of luxury goods by
the khan's court. Unless another elite group took up residence on the
peninsula, there would be no local market.[44]

It just so happened that the upper crust of noble society was beginning to build estates and summer dachas on the coast and in so doing
created a nascent consumer market. Local demand had always been crucial to the Black Sea wine trade, though it did not come exclusively from
elites. Throughout the eighteenth century the biggest consumers of
Crimean wine (other than Crimeans themselves) were Zaporozhian and
Don Cossacks, and they remained a thirsty market. The arrival of the
naval and foreign populations of Sevastopol, which consumed as much
as 300,000 buckets per year, helped sustain producers as well. As winemakers sought new customers, they looked to the vibrant commercial
centers in neighboring provinces as the most promising proximate markets. Bessarabian wine made an appearance when, in 1826, the Committee of Ministers took Vorontsov's advice and approved the import
of Bessarabian wine through all customs points in Novorossiia. (Prior
to that, imports were limited to Dubossar and Mogilev in order to prevent Moldavian and Wallachian wine being passed off as Bessarabian.)
In Tavrida, when engineers and soldiers finally devoted themselves to
the herculean task of extending the main postal road along the southern coast of the peninsula in the 1830s, they did so at the behest of officials intent on connecting Crimean vineyards to the trading hubs of
Novorossiia as well. Slowly but surely, Crimean wine began to penetrate Novorossiia and beyond. It was plentiful and blissfully cheap, especially in comparison with champagne or a nice glass of Sauterne
(table 5.4).[45]

In 1843 Minister of State Domains Pavel Kiselev appointed a com-
missioner to sell a small quantity of Magarach wine in St. Petersburg.
Charged with this task, A. D. Kniazhevich, the ambitious owner of the
vineyards at Kuru Uzen near Alushta, almost single-handedly created a
domestic market for Crimean wine. Kniazhevich sent his wine by sea
to Petersburg—it took three months to arrive at Kronshtadt—where a
merchant from Simferopol claimed it and promptly sold the entire shipment. The wine fetched a purchase price of between three and eight
rubles, and the experiment was deemed a success. Sales in the imperial
capital climbed from 3,896 buckets in 1844 to 5,287 in 1846 and, en-

Table 5.4. Value and Volume of Alcoholic Beverages Sold at Kakhovka Fair in 1832

Drink	Quantity	Price (rubles, kopeks)	Total value (rubles)	Quantity (buckets)	Unit price (rubles/ bucket)
Rum	1,170 bottles	2r, 50k	2,925	73	40
French vodka	980 shtof	2r, 30k	2,254	98	23
Vodka	850 buckets	12r	10,200	850	12
Crimean wine	50 casks	120r–150r	6,000–7,500	2,000	3 to 3r, 75k
Rhone wine	80 boxes	40	3,200	?	?
Madeira	1,000 bottles	3	3,000	63	48
Sauterne	800 bottles	2.25	1,800	50	36
Champagne	65 bottles	12	780	4	195

Source: DAARK f. 26, op. 1, d. 8113, ll. 40b & 90b. The fairs took place on May 9 and in early October 1832.

couraged, Kiselev appointed commissioners for Kharkov and Kiev as well. From there sales spread to Orenburg, Saratov, Samara, and Kazan, reaching 300,000 buckets per year by the end of the decade. The Crimean War interfered with this trajectory, but Kniazhevich was not to be deterred. He set his sights on Odessa, where his efforts attracted the attention of the Russian Society of Steam-Navigation and Trade. Soon Crimean vintners were sending wine across the Black Sea on steamships, while Kniazhevich himself spent a good part of the 1860s traveling to Saratov, Nizhnii Novgorod, Omsk, Tobolsk, Krasnoiarsk, Perm, Uralsk, Orenburg, and Ufa to introduce these new markets to Crimea's signature product.[46]

The wine market had a discernible geography. French and Spanish wine entered Russia through St. Petersburg, Riga, and Odessa. Taganrog dealt in Greek wine until 1851, when its merchants began importing other European wines as well. All was destined for eventual sale at Kharkov, the main wine market of the south, and this made good sense as Taganrog was 250 versts closer to Kharkov than it was to Odessa and boasted a more efficient transportation infrastructure. Consumers willing to pay for high-quality wine could make their purchases through Lemaire and Company in Kharkov or subscribe to wines from trading houses in Moscow or Petersburg. Those who cared less about quality, if they lived in provinces east of Kharkov, might be supplied by merchants from Nizhegorod and Iaroslavl; those living north of Kharkov looked to Moscow; while inhabitants of the Don and southern Russia purchased and drank local wine. In fact, at midcentury half of all wine brought to Kharkov markets was from Crimea or Bessarabia.[47]

A good portion of the output of Crimean wine was purchased in Tavrida itself, of course, much of it sold at the autumn harvest fair in Simferopol or in towns such as Alushta and Sudak, which emerged as key sites for the sale of pears, apples, walnuts, and wine to merchants provisioning interior provinces. Town markets and fairs complemented the annual fair system. The Tuesday and Friday markets in Staryi Krym, for example, served as conduits of foodstuffs, textiles, candles, furs, and alcoholic beverages, and drew merchants, traders, and producers of the surrounding area into the urban economy. In 1826 Governor Naryshkins opened a Wednesday market in Alushta as part of his plan to make that town the way station between Simferopol and the southern coast, complete with a new road, post station, and shops. Though they made fewer infrastructural and fiscal demands on the local government, fairs too embedded patterns of exchange in the commercial landscape. Local officials expected the two fairs established at Feodosiia in 1810 "to strengthen the town's economy and cultivate connections between it and the interior provinces." The dates (May 21 and September 14) were scheduled to coincide with the arrival of ships bearing foreign goods, in hopes of maximizing the appeal of Russian manufactured goods (*krasnye tovary*) and thus enhancing merchant profits and customs revenue. Similarly, the opening of a Sunday market in Akmechet (north of Evpatoriia) was designed to entice the mountain Tatars further south to bring their fruits, tobacco, woodwork, and pottery to the otherwise much neglected town.[48]

Tatar towns were already centers of trade and craft production. Throughout the peninsula the significance of trade was reflected on town balance sheets and in the distribution of workshops. In 1837, for example, the lease of weights and measures generated 33 percent of town revenues in Bahçesaray, 58 percent in Evpatoriia, and 51 percent in Karasubazar. There were thirteen workshops in Feodosiia but twice as many in Bahçesaray and a whopping 128 in Karasubazar. Together they turned out an assortment of leather goods, bricks and tiles, candles, soaps, shoes,

Figure 5.1. The bazaar at Kerch; from Demidov, *Album* (John Hay Library, Brown University Library)

and knives. Mikhailovskii-Danilevskii complained of the town's chaotic aspect, with streets "overflowing with Muslims" and filled with flat-roofed houses and a riot of minarets. Somewhat less sensitive to urban aesthetics, Henry Dearborn found Karasubazar's most remarkable feature to be that one could purchase absolutely anything—"all the commodities of the Crimea"—at astonishingly low rates. "A long street of shops extends the whole length of the town," he reported, "where are sold leather, particularly of the morocco kind, prepared by the inhabitants, pottery, hard ware, soap, candles, fruit, and vegetables."[49]

Even a man like Pavel Sumarokov, who looked disparagingly on Crimean Tatar culture, was impressed by their second city, Akmeçet (Simferopol), where people of so many customs and backgrounds converged. Having walked its streets feeling "as much a foreigner as [he] would in Tunis," Sumarokov cataloged the institutions of urban living, including twenty bakeries, 197 shops, twelve coffeehouses, thirteen khans, two taverns, nine *bouza* houses (shops selling a fermented beverage made by Tatars from millet, buckwheat, or barley), and eleven blacksmiths. But travelers were more often drawn to the charms of Bahçesaray: "one of the most remarkable cities in Europe, for the novelty of its customs and costumes, which are absolutely oriental and offer no trace of European taste, as much as for the setting of the city itself." By the mid-nineteenth century Bahçesaray was home to more than 600 master craftsmen, 309 shops, and seven mills, whose goods reportedly brought in more revenue than in any other town in the province save Berdiansk.[50] Coffeehouses and taverns were ubiquitous, and three dozen orchards and vineyards supplied inhabitants with wine and brandy. Baron Haxthausen's description just of Bahçesaray's fountain system conveys the sense of productive energy pervading the town in the 1840s. "On every side were seen small watercourses, brought down from the surrounding heights, from which channels flow for the irrigation of the meadows, gardens, and even corn-land."[51]

The merchants of Bahçesaray imported a range of goods—chests of medicine and sacks of herbs, almonds, *bekmes* (concentrated grape juice), olives, halva, incense, and books—through their peers in Evpatoriia and Feodosiia. Maintaining close relationships with the merchants of those towns was important. After all, though few in number—in the 1830s Feodosiia was home to only forty men registered in the merchant guilds, for example—they handled 40 percent of all commercial traffic passing

Figure 5.2. Merchants and tradesmen of Bahçesaray; from Demidov, *Album*
(John Hay Library, Brown University Library)

through Crimean ports. Maintaining close relationships with the skippers of coasting vessels was absolutely essential, as almost all imports
came from the Ottoman Empire on coasting vessels from the Anatolian
ports of Trabzon and Sinop. Generally speaking, commerce along this
route flourished under the terms of the 1799 Russian-Ottoman commercial treaty. By 1817 there were 104 merchant houses in operation
in Russia's Black Sea ports (sixty-five of them in Odessa alone). By 1809
even a relatively small port such as Evpatoriia racked up over three-
quarters of a million rubles worth of revenue each year from the trade
of Karaite merchants with their counterparts in Anatolia (table 5.5).[52]

Much of that commercial activity—and the revenue it generated—
centered around one man in particular: Sima Bobovich. For decades,
Evpatoriia was more or less his own private harbor. Seemingly at his

Figure 5.3. The main street of Bahçesaray in 1837; from Demidov, *Album*
(John Hay Library, Brown University Library)

bidding ships arrived with Turkish tobacco, dates, dyes, lemon juice, vin-
egar, squash, lumber, canvas, and wine. Most of them sailed away with
cargoes of salt on the order of 100,000 kilograms (roughly 6,000 poods)
even in a modest year. For in truth it was salt, and not Sima Bobovich,
that was king of Crimean commerce. Salt now funded the provincial
treasury as it had that of the Giray khans, paying officials' salaries and
funding construction projects throughout the province. Russian ships
brought an average of over 55,000 poods of salt each year to the Caucasian coast for trade with the mountaineers, and filled hundreds of barks
to send upriver to Smolensk and along the tributaries of the Dnepr.[53]
Salt was, more than anything else, Crimea's currency in the Russian and
Black Sea economies, and this was obvious to far less careful observers
than Henry Dearborn. In his *Memoir of the Commerce and Navigation of
the Black Sea* (1819), Dearborn describes the scene at the Perekop salt

Table 5.5. Value of Goods Traded by Crimean Merchants, 1826

Port	Merchants listed	Imports	Exports	Average trade per merchant	Imports within port total
Taganrog	24	3,379,617	8,428,726	492,014	28.6%
Mariupol	2	6,155	801,636	403,896	0.8%
Tiflis	4	0	807,433	201,858	0.0%
Feodosiia	5	1,550,782	889,299	488,016	63.6%
Evpatoriia	3	571,344	921,687	497,677	38.3%
Kerch	1	91,892	96,156	188,048	48.9%

Source: *OVTR*, (1826), tables 5 and 6.

works, bringing out the mundane and sublime qualities of the salt trade and capturing the geography of commercial activity with journalistic flair:

> Throughout the whole summer [Perekop] is a scene of great bustle and commerce. The shores of the isthmus, and all the neighboring stepes [*sic*], are covered with caravans, coming for salt, consisting of wagons, drawn sometimes by camels, but generally by white oxen, from two, to six, attached to each vehicle. . . . The driver of each wagon pays a tax of ten rubles to the crown. Among the various reservoirs of salt in the Crimea, those of Perecop, used from time immemorial, are the most abundant, and they are considered as inexhaustible . . . it was sent as it is now, by the Euxine, to all the territories on its border, to Constantinople, and to the Archipelago; by land to Poland, and all over Russia, to Moscow, to St. Petersburgh, and even to Riga. The oxen, after their long journeys, are sometimes sold with the cargoes they have brought, and sometimes they return again, the whole of that immense distance, with other merchandise . . . presenting a picture of the internal commerce, carried on by Russia, throughout all parts of her vast empire.[54]

In 1804, revenues from salt reached 800,901 rubles; by 1811 revenues from the sale of over two million poods surged to over one million rubles. Three decades later, Crimean salt lakes produced roughly seven million poods per year, selling it in Novorossiia, Malorossiia, Belorussia, Kursk, Voronezh, and throughout the Caucasus. But as Dearborn's text suggests, salt was only one sector of the economy. The *Military-Statistical Description* published in 1849 explained that actually there was no "monotony" in the Tavridan economy due to the "unusual abundance in the realms of animal life and vegetation, all of which was rooted in the physical formation of the province" with its distinct geographical and ecological zones. The northern reaches were blessed with rich grasses and soils, and thus lent themselves to farming and the pasturing of livestock. By the middle of the nineteenth century, grain production was sluggish on the peninsula but booming in the steppe districts. Dneprovsk, Melitopol, and Berdiansk provisioned southern Tavrida and had vast quantities to spare for the wharves at Berdiansk. Fishing was a significant industry along the Dnepr River and the shores of the Black and Azov seas: each year four million fish—fresh and salted—sold for something on the order of 40,000 silver rubles in markets near and far. Horse breeding and the raising of oxen and sheep were important as well. This was particularly true in the steppe, though many contemporary sources insisted that livestock constituted "the principal property of the Tahtar gentlemen," among whom the possession of horses in particular was a mark of prestige as much as a source of wealth. Several mirzas were renowned for their stables, none more so than Mehmet Krımtay, whose stables near Eski Kırım were home to countless horses "of the beautiful breeds of this country and of Circassia."[55]

But if a Tavridan was concerned with profit per square inch, then his place was in the orchards and vineyards. Gardening remained the most profitable activity on the peninsula, and its allure was spreading throughout the province. The peasants and pomeshchiki of Dneprovsk had set to work planting pear and apple trees, and the Molokan and Mennonite colonists of Melitopol and Berdiansk had planted large gardens. Two Nogay villages had planted alleys of mulberry and white acacia under the direction of the chief of the Molochnaia Mennonite agricultural society. Even in arid stretches of Perekop gardens were emerging, watered by deep wells. But the most lucrative sites were in the valleys of the Salgir, Alma, Belbek, and Kacha rivers in southern Crimea. Each year, gardeners in Simferopol sent 1,000 wagons of apples and 5,000 bins of pears each to Moscow, Kherson, Kharkov, and other provinces. Merchants from Moscow leased large gardens for anywhere between 1,000 and 5,000 silver rubles (though local Tatars and Karaites from Bahçesaray held a majority of gardens). Annual revenue from a single desiatina of grain amounted to between ten and fifteen rubles; from a desiatina of vineyard, annual revenue stood over 220 rubles.[56]

The natural world of the south was nothing if not abundant. However, the wealth derived from it was vulnerable to any number of threats.

Figure 5.4. Domestic interior near Kapsikhor; from Demidov, *Album* (John Hay
Library, Brown University Library)

Outbreaks of disease could (and did) hobble farmers. Locusts could
(and did) destroy whole crops; drought, frosts, fogs, extreme variations
in temperature, beetles, caterpillars, and the dread *Otiorhynchus tauri-
cus* (a local weevil) could do the same. Torrential rains could be just as
catastrophic to the economy. They rendered roads impassable, preventing producers and consumers from getting to market. Severe flooding
was common. In 1805, flooding damaged fountains and buildings, and
in Bahçesaray, wreaked havoc on the network of stone walls that ter-
raced the land and held the famous gardens. In 1811, floods caused so
much damage to Crimean gardens that the governor lobbied for a
100,000-ruble loan to finance the restoration of the industry.[57]

It is no wonder, then, that disputes over landownership grew as heated
as they were common. The precarious nature of the environment—and

the wealth generated from it—put a premium on both ownership and access. In fact, by the 1840s, disputes over access (to water sources as well as plots of land) were almost as common as disputes over ownership. And it is no wonder that mirzas were known to spend extraordinary sums outfitting their wives and daughters in elaborate girdles, layered bracelets, and long delicate necklaces of gold, silver, copper, and colored glass: the value of gold and gems was at least somewhat less subject to the vagaries of Russian courts and the inconsistencies of Black Sea weather.[58]

More important than the clashes, catastrophes, and idiosyncrasies of economic life in this part of the world was the spatial logic lurking just below the surface. By its very nature, economic activity created relationships among individuals, communities, goods, and the places where they were produced or consumed. It created zones of commonality, networks of exchange, and landscapes of wealth. We see aspects of all of this at Kakhovka. We see it in a relatively insignificant district town such as Aleshki, where by midcentury inhabitants were busily tending vegetable gardens and fisheries, raking in 10,000 rubles each year from the herring catch and the same amount from the sale of watermelons (consumers from Perekop to Odessa gobbled them up with astonishing alacrity). They spent a good deal of time transporting goods to Kherson in small boats, and an equal amount of time battling mosquitoes, fevers, and whooping cough. They attended fairs stocked with a wide range of goods. In the whole town there was only one house made of stone—the rest were wood and thatch—but the library held some five hundred volumes. There was a coffeehouse, a hospital, and ten storehouses full of Crimean wine. In other words, Aleshki had its own microeconomy, but it was also a node in the network of exchange connecting the vineyards of Sudak with the great houses of Odessa. In that sense it had the same value as Feodosiia, though the latter operated at a much different scale. Feodosiia too was a district town; it too had a long history, and a new toponym thanks to Empress Catherine II. Its resident population was twice that of Aleshki, however, and there were more than six thousand temporary residents in the city as well. Feodosiia was home to a distinctly cosmopolitan population, with Russians, Greeks, Armenians, Tatars, Italians, Germans, Frenchmen, and Roma among them. Roman Catholics, Orthodox Christians, Dukhobors, Old Believers, Muslims, Jews, Protestants, and Karaites all lived and worshipped in Feodosiia. There were 109 customs officials and two naval officers in the town. There was a sophisticated built environment, with everything from barracks to Turkish baths, seventeen coffeehouses, sixteen bakeries, an apothecary, an infirmary, more than 500 private homes, six fountains, 372 shops, a customs house, two dozen khans (inns), and numerous wharves. Residents produced leather goods, brandy, bricks, and tallow candles.[59]

This was a bustling, thriving port city. It had farmland, gardens, and vineyards at its disposal. The roads to Karasubazar and Kerch were good. Ships arrived and departed by the dozen. What it lacked was funds. As a *gradonachal'stvo*, the city was its own administrative unit, separate from the rest of the province. And as a gradonachal'stvo perched on the Black Sea, it was subject to policies aimed at assuring the security of the empire rather than the financial well-being of the city. When Alexander I established the gradonachal'stvo in 1804, revenues from vodka-tax farming, salt-tax farming, and customs duties all went into city coffers. In 1812, the war effort required a redirection of the vodka revenues into the state treasury. In 1819, the government redirected salt revenues to Simferopol, leaving Feodosiia to rely on only one-fifth of the customs taxes it collected. In 1830, in the aftermath of the Russian-Ottoman war of 1828–1829, Feodosiia's governor, Alexander Kaznacheev, claimed it was impossible to drum up the million rubles the city needed for operating expenses on an annual basis and that the moment was ripe for a reconfiguration of revenue flows. If only Governor-General Vorontsov would see fit to endow Feodosiia with the revenue from the city's own humble salt lakes, in addition to its modest slice of customs revenue, the city might begin to find the resources it needed. Otherwise, without annual infusions of funds from St. Petersburg, Feodosiia would be ruined.[60]

Kaznacheev meant this quite literally. This city, which was so deeply connected to ports and markets far and near, was endangered by the proximity of the sea. Fresh water normally came from wells up in the mountains, but the aqueducts were crumbling. Where just a decade ago there had been dozens of fountains, only six remained—and these were in disrepair. Many of the ditches that channeled waste to the sea were damaged, and the pilings along the embankment that once protected the city had come loose, casualties of strong seas. The firehouse lacked proper equipment; there was no jail; and perhaps worst of all, the city was without shade, relentlessly subject to the salt wind and southern sun. It needed proper greenery as much as it needed clean water and financial support.[61]

Kaznacheev's petition found a sympathetic audience. Though Feodosiia never rose to the top of his priority list, during his long tenure Vorontsov never wavered in his conviction that Odessa, Nikolaev, Kherson, and Kerch were natural centers of trade, and that "the fertile steppe was meant for production of rich grains," while Crimea was "created for the raising of sheep and of grapes" and nothing more. Looking out over the same landscape in 1815, writer Vladimir Bronevskii expressed confidence that in a few years Russia would no longer have to import wine, apricots, bay leaves, peppers, capers, or olives at all, and would be able to drastically reduce imports of silks, merino wool, horses, and cattle. On his way to becoming one of the most prominent vineyard owners in the empire, Vorontsov came to attach far greater importance to the goods produced, rather than those consumed by the inhabitants of Crimea. And he speculated that one day, the region's economy might transcend its local boundaries and reconnect with the commercial networks linking the northern coast of the Black Sea with the Ottoman Empire, Persia, and the Mediterranean world.[62]

What he meant, of course, was that one day the region's economy might take on a scale and shape that would meet the expectations of the Russian government. For the connections he spoke of had long been in place. Wine, salt, textiles, grain: these had never stopped flowing. The problem was, as we have seen, that they flowed through channels that did not lead straight into the coffers of the state treasury. They were instead borne on Turkish *kocherma*—one- and two-masted ships that excelled in skimming coastlines and nipping in and out of harbors before customs officials had taken their morning tea. The simple fact that Greek and Turkish captains could sail to Evpatoriia, fill their holds with salt at eight kopeks per pood, and sell it for fifty in Constantinople was definitive proof that the economic landscape retained its own logic and vitality.[63]

When the clouds of war began gathering yet again in 1853, the southern empire had expanded its sphere of influence in two directions: it had moved further into Russia's economic space in meaningful ways (as Bronevskii had hoped); it had also moved deeper into the economic space defined by the Black Sea (as Vorontsov had predicted, but not necessarily understood). It was no garden paradise, but those who governed and inhabited its terrain had found ways to define patterns of exchange and consumption that connected them to a broad terrain of commercial spaces while never losing sight of the local spaces—the intimate landscapes—in which their everyday lives played out.

Conclusion

Rethinking Integration and Imperial Space

MIKHAIL VORONTSOV, GOVERNOR-GENERAL of Novorossiia from 1822 until 1854, and Dmitrii Naryshkin, civil governor of Tavrida from 1823 until 1829, took their respective offices at a particularly difficult time. In 1823 nearly all of southern Russia was plagued with drought, and the misery of Crimean farmers was compounded by locusts. Food and fodder ran short. In desperation, Colonel Ahmet Bey Khunkalov, one of the most prominent members of the Tatar elite, requested permission to send his brother Isliam Bey, a landowner of means in Simferopol district, to their family estates near Constantinople to collect water to help ease the suffering in Crimea. Both Naryshkin and the provincial marshal approved Khunkalov's petition in late summer.[1]

When Isliam Bey returned a month later, he brought not barrels of fresh water, as Russian authorities may have anticipated, but eleven Sufis. He had in fact traveled to the site of a holy well that, according to Crimean legend, yielded water capable of restoring lands laid waste by locusts and drought. Isliam Bey, a traveling companion, the sheikh of the shrine lodge, and ten dervishes arrived at the port of Feodosiia bearing thirteen copper vessels of holy water. The water, when sprinkled over the soil, would produce starling eggs; these would hatch in spring and eat the locust larvae buried in the soil before they could unleash a new

259

wave of destruction. The harvest would thus be saved by Khunkalov's act of devotion.[2]

Sheikh Ali Efendi and the other Sufis traveled to every Crimean town and many villages. Everywhere they went they were honored by large crowds that followed them to the local mosque for special prayer services. Russian officials—Governor-General Vorontsov in particular—regarded the unfolding situation with consternation. "Although the government must not hinder the Muslims in the practice of their customs and religion," Vorontsov wrote to Naryshkin, "I believe it to be entirely judicious for local authorities to avoid facilitating [the Sufis' procession], and for the police to avoid any semblance of participation in the rites."[3]

Despite Vorontsov's misgivings, all reports from the district chiefs indicated that the Sufis had come for purely religious purposes and neither they nor the Crimean Muslims were violating Russian law in any way. The overseer of the khan's palace even reported that the visitors were having a positive effect on local morality: Tatar men were spending less time in cafes drinking spirits and were instead filling the mosques. But in March 1824, Governor Naryshkin sent a small contingent of police to Bahçesaray to secretly observe Ali Efendi's movements. The men—mostly Greeks from Balaklava—did everything short of "dressing in Tatar clothes" in order to maintain a low profile in the mosques and coffeehouses. They found no evidence to support the governor's suspicion that the Sufis were laying the groundwork for a major revolt. On the contrary, they dined with Ahmet Bey Khunkalov and other eager hosts, prayed at the mosques, spoke with the people, and led quiet lives on the outskirts of Bahçesaray. Nevertheless, the Greek commander recommended removing the Sufis immediately on the grounds that the presence of Ottoman spiritual leaders among the Tatars posed a risk to security. Vorontsov ordered Naryshkin to take action. Ali Efendi had no choice but to comply with the subsequent Russian "request" that he and his companions leave for Odessa—and the ship to Anatolia—immediately.[4]

Four decades had passed since annexation. In the intervening years many Crimean Tatars had lost their lives fighting for the tsar. Mirzas dominated the provincial nobility, the ulema were ensconced in the tsarist administrative structure, and Sevastopol projected naval power across the Black Sea just miles from the Tatar capital that used to send waves of armed horsemen across the steppe to raid and pillage Slavic settle-

Figure C.1. In the coffeehouse in Karasubazar; from Demidov, *Album* (John Hay Library, Brown University Library)

ments. The administrative space of the former khanate had been reorganized, and surveyors were slowly converting its territory into measured, mapped, governable parcels. Why then did Russian officials still perceive Islamic institutions, practices, and peoples as a threat to security and order in Tavrida?

There are several reasons. First, by their very nature Sufi brotherhoods remained largely outside the scope of state control. While we know relatively little about Sufism in the region, there is evidence that from the sixteenth century onward Crimeans were associated with the Halveti and Mevlevi orders, and that lodges were reasonably widespread. Sufis played an active role in keeping Islam alive in Crimea during the upheavals of the eighteenth century and even in the nineteenth century. Despite the government's consolidation of authority in the hands of the Spiritual Board in 1791, the Department of Foreign Confessions reported

Figure C.2. Dervishes at the Istrim Cami in Karasubazar; from Demidov, *Album* (John Hay Library, Brown University Library)

that in 1826 there were fourteen sheikhs and sixty-one dervishes residing in the province. Whether as a result of improved bookkeeping or the popularity of Sufism, by 1830 the number of sheikhs alone had tripled; they represented 9 percent of those taking part in the kadıasker election of that year. By that time Crimean Sufism included members of the Naqshbandi order, which originated in Bukhara in the fourteenth century and emerged as a radical challenge to the purported orthodoxy established by the ulema. Sheikh Mansur was the first in a succession of Naqshbandi leaders in the northern Caucasus that culminated in Imam Shamil, who famously led a war against Russia from 1834 until his defeat in 1859.[5]

The fact that great crowds turned out to pray with Ali Efendi in their moment of need can be read any number of ways. While Russian authorities correlated Sufi practice with the rejection of Russian sovereignty, the holy water episode suggests instead that the Crimeans were simply part of a different sort of geography—a geography of cultural practice that spread across much of the Tatar-inhabited steppe. Agricultural festivals, rain prayers, and prayers to protect crops against rodents and locusts were not formally part of Islamic tradition: these were Muslim rituals in the sense that they were performed by Muslims and incorporated Islamic elements. Throughout the Volga-Ural region and Siberia it was quite common for visiting sheikhs and local religious leaders to lead prayers, collect stones, and make pilgrimages to local shrines even while members of the Muslim Spiritual Board denounced such activities as "innovations" or deviations from the "correct" practice of Islam. Uncomfortable with the implications of this, and unwilling to set aside the political implications of Islam in the context of the Black Sea, Vorontsov and Naryshkin determined that it was in the best interests of both borderland security and administrative uniformity to purge Islam of anything that might fall into the category of "innovation" or "unorthodoxy."[6]

Russian officials were aware of the spatial component of imperial power. They poured a great deal of energy and resources into controlling certain sites—palaces or ports, for example—from which they could project power in symbolic and geographical terms. Sacred sites were key in this regard, for they forged intimate ties between Crimea and the steppe and Islamic worlds, both of which continued to challenge Russian authority along the empire's frontiers. In the eyes of Russian officials, any site associated with Islamic practice or Tatar tradition—be it a fountain, mosque, coffeehouse, or shrine—had intrinsic political content. After all, this was certainly the case with their own sacred sites. Just as "the belvederes and columns of provincial manor houses" symbolized a nobleman's wealth and "external allegiance to western culture," explains Roosevelt, "the spires and bell towers of estate churches, rising above the belvederes, reflected the precedence given to Russian Orthodoxy" by the Russian nobility.[7]

Building churches had been a fundamental mechanism for articulating the power of the tsar for centuries. In the aftermath of the conquest of Kazan in 1552 one of Tsar Ivan IV's first acts was to build an Orthodox church on the ruins of the central mosque. He followed that with establishing a new bishopric, commissioning more than a dozen monasteries, and building the Church of the Intercession on the Moat just outside the Kremlin. In the southern empire, Catherine II occasionally used local church leaders as proxies for imperial power; churches, however, were few and far between. According to 1776 synodal reports there were only 293 churches in the New Russia and Azov *guberniias* combined. Two years later, the archbishop of Slaviansk and Kherson reported that nearly four thousand Orthodox Christians in his diocese lived without an accessible church. Just a year after annexing Crimea and securing her hold on the Black Sea littoral, Catherine addressed the problem of church distribution throughout the empire. "For the general welfare," she wrote in a message to the over-procurator of the Holy Synod, churches must be built "such that their number corresponds to the parishioners attached to them, and so that those serving at them can have adequate support free from popular control." A thoroughly political creature, Catherine subscribed to the notion that fortresses may defend borders by keeping people out, but churches, with their awe-inspiring tent roofs and frescoes, had the ability to draw people into the Christian fold. These consecrated spaces established, as Gregory Bruess has argued, "a spiritual universality which connects those assembled in or around the sacred space to an experience which transcends local space and time. . . . The new lands are joined through the ritual act of church construction to the imperial center in St. Petersburg. Church building and empire building thus went hand in hand, with cupolas and crosses delineating Russian space as no meridian or map could."[8]

Religious structures were abundant in Crimea. Greeks had settled the northern Black Sea coast by the fifth century BC, building temples that Christians would convert into churches in the second century AD. Long home to practitioners of Orthodoxy and Catholicism, Karaite and rabbinical Judaism, Crimea received Islam by the thirteenth century. The built environment reflected the resulting religious mosaic, with the distribution of churches and mosques serving as a constantly shifting map of political and cultural authority. In 1784 Russian officials counted thirty-three churches, plus an additional fifty-seven in ruins, as part of their assessment of the economy and infrastructure of the former khanate (figure C.3). At the same time, they documented the existence of 1,540 mosques and twenty-four dervish lodges.[9]

In the spirit of her decree on the toleration of all faiths (1773), Catherine II declared in 1783 that Crimean Muslim institutions would be preserved and respected, and Potemkin went to great lengths to prevent

Figure C.3. Ruins of a church at Cherkes Kermen; from Uvarov, *Sobranie* (General Research Division, The New York Public Library, Astor, Lenox, and Tilden Foundations)

soldiers under his command from destroying or desecrating mosques.[10] After all, though in many cases "younger" than the khanate's churches, Crimea's mosques also held significant cultural value within the local and broader Muslim landscape. Without them—without places where Muslims could engage in communal religious practice—Muslim identity could not have persisted in the Russian empire.

One of the oldest and most important was the Özbek Khan (Uzbek Khan) mosque in Eski Kırım (Staryi Krym, Solhat; figure C.4). The existing structure dated to the turn of the sixteenth century but incorporated a portal, *mihrab* (niche indicating the direction of Mecca) and other elements from the 1314 original. Together the square floor plan, monumental entrance, and carved wooden door spoke of the influence of Seljuk-period Anatolian architecture, and provided material evidence of the complex cultural and economic linkages between Crimea and the Turkic world. Despite its symbolic significance, the mosque remained intact after annexation. In fact, Potemkin insisted on allowing the system of pious endowments to provide funding for this and other Muslim institutions throughout the province and even restored control of revenues that had been hastily confiscated by the Russian treasury to the suddenly bereft mosques, fountains, and schools. At the same time, the prince knew full well that the chaos of war, rebellion, and emigrations had reduced the ability of many such endowments to produce revenue. By shifting the fate of the Özbek Khan mosque and others like it into the hands of the Muslim population, in what he likely meant as a gesture of understanding and respect for Islam, Potemkin guaranteed that the empire's policies toward Islam in Crimea would be expressed in the built environment.[11]

Between 1787 and 1800, Russian authorities began restoring many of the churches left in ruin after the exodus of Greek and Armenian Christians in 1778. They also built new churches in Bahçesaray, Kerch, Sudak, Feodosiia, and Balaklava. The first Orthodox church in Sevastopol, the Cathedral of Saints Peter and Paul, was built in 1792. In 1805, Governor Mertvago received 30,000 rubles earmarked for the construction of a cathedral church in Simferopol, plus an additional 12,367 rubles for churches in larger villages, but funds from the imperial treasury earmarked for church building were otherwise limited. The lack of skilled craftsmen and architects, the vagaries of the provincial budget, and the scant Christian population also hampered construction. Planning for the Simferopol cathedral, for example, began in 1804, but workers did not lay the foundation until 1823 and they completed the church only in 1832. Smaller projects also got mired in bureaucratic and logistical delays. One group of local landowners petitioned the diocese in 1807 for permission to restore an abandoned stone church (a converted mosque) near Sudak. They assured the archbishop that sufficient land and 6,000 rubles in funding were already in place, but without official approval the would-be peasant parishioners could not begin building. They spent years waiting for a response, the old mosque remaining a silent reminder of the limits of imperial power.[12]

At the same time, Russian officials themselves built mosques when and where it served their interests. This policy began in 1767, when Catherine II approved the construction of mosques in Siberia and then

Figure C.4. Ruins of the mosque of Sultan Baybars at Eski Kırım; from Uvarov, *Sobranie* (General Research Division, The New York Public Library, Astor, Lenox, and Tilden Foundations)

Kazan. By the end of the eighteenth century, there was a mosque in each of the 116 villages of Kazan district, and a total of approximately 250 mosques in Kazan province. In 1782, the empress issued a decree calling for the construction of mosques for the use of the Kazakhs along the borders of Orenburg and Simbirsk provinces, describing the project as an effective way to lure nomadic and semi-nomadic peoples into Russian territory and provide them with a measure of "civilization." Alexander I continued where his grandmother left off. At the start of his reign, Interior Minister Count Kochubei took a similar interest in settling—and therefore more effectively controlling—the nomadic Nogays. Kochubei supported Governor-General Richelieu's proposal that the government build mosques, schools, and houses for mullas, and he allocated almost 13,000 rubles to this end in 1806. Work began right away. Provincial officials divided the vast expanse of pastureland into portions, and in each built a small number of houses and a mosque, careful to meet the interior ministry's stipulations that each mosque be in a central location, with open space on all sides. By 1842, whether they wanted them or not, the 31,662 Nogays remaining on the steppe had 139 mosques and 5,479 houses at their disposal.[13]

Empire building did not always facilitate mosque building. In the rest of Tavrida, responsibility for building and maintaining mosques fell to the Muslim Spiritual Board, which had neither the authority nor the funding to pursue a construction agenda until receiving its statute. It built only two mosques before 1831, both in Simferopol, and even after 1831 managed only a handful of new projects. Meanwhile, one of the most prominent architectural sites in Crimea was the Mufti Cami (or "Sultan Selim") mosque in Feodosiia. The mosque dated from 1623, when its patron built it on the site of a Greek church. Russians and Europeans alike extolled its beauty. Dubois de Montpereux described it as "large, with elegant white marble columns and chess-board marble floors, thirteen cupolas and two nine-*sazhen* high multicolored minarets"—a structure that "elicited a sense of wonder in the traveler." This "noble specimen of simple architecture," as Peter Simon Pallas called it, was neglected for decades until a handful of influential men determined to convert it into an Orthodox church in the early 1820s. According to Felix Lagorio, the former Italian consul, they convinced Vorontsov to tear down the mosque, employing Muslim inhabitants to do the work. Outraged, the Tatars immediately protested. The governor-general reconsidered, but not soon enough: when word of his change of heart reached Feodosiia three days later, the minarets, domes, and columns lay in heaps on the ground. In an ironic twist, the funds pledged for building the church did not materialize, and the ill-fated mosque remained in ruins for years.[14]

Tsar Nicholas I understood the symbolic value of sacred sites as well as Vorontsov or Potemkin. One of his elder brother's final acts had been to open an empire-wide subscription to sponsor the construction of "a church of exquisite architecture" at Chersonesos, the site of Prince Vladimir's conversion to Orthodox Christianity in 988. In 1829, with his armies triumphing against Ottoman forces in the Danubian principalities and on the Caucasian coast, and advancing within a hundred kilometers of Constantinople itself, Nicholas dipped into his personal coffers to pay not for the planned cathedral but instead for the restoration of Crimea's most important *existing* architectural site. The object of his generosity was the Friday mosque in Evpatoriia's main square. Commissioned by Devlet Giray khan and designed by the famous sixteenth-century Ottoman architect Sinan,[15] the mosque boasted a series of large and small domes and multiple minarets that together seemed oblivious to more recent buildings that encroached on its visual space. The cost for restoring this lovely monument was, according to the provincial architect, 19,828 rubles and 20 kopeks—a sum far in excess of what the pious endowments supporting the mosque could afford, but easily within the personal budget of the tsar.[16]

Clearly, the tsar felt that the days of mullas climbing the minarets to incite the Tatar population to revolt had passed (at least one was shot for this behavior in Bahçesaray in 1783), and that the prestige that accrued to him by claiming authority over a site that had up to that point expressed the cultural linkage between Crimea and the Ottoman world would far outweigh the disapproval of those who sought to define this terrain in exclusively Orthodox terms. Indeed, imperial officials were generally willing to sacrifice homogeneity for the much greater goals of order and security. If they could solidify the allegiance of subjects by preserving and co-opting local institutions—even mosques or muftis—they did so. Thus while so much of the character of Russia's longstanding mode of imperial rule changed in the 1830s, Nicholas I continued the institutionalization of difference in at least one medium. In fact, the crucial shift came in meaning more than in method. In the eighteenth century, the relationships between the sovereign and subject groups were often bundled in the language of privilege. Inclusion in a social category such as "Crimean Tatar" distinguished its members from the rest of the population, and this specificity of status often had its advantages (exemption from taxation or military recruitment, a more capacious set of economic rights, access to a broader set of judicial or administrative institutions, etc.). From the Nicholaevan era onward, the institutionalization of difference generally implied a diminished scope of privilege and status.

The restoration of the Sinan mosque in Evpatoriia and the decision to build a monument to Russian Orthodoxy at Chersonesos served as tangible reminders of Russia's ability to impose its authority over any cultural landscape. They can easily be read into one of the narrative arcs of the nineteenth century: the integration of Crimea through a combination of church building, settlement, and colonization, massive waves of Muslim emigration, and the implementation of the Great Reforms certainly takes root under Nicholas. But these are stories of the postwar period—the long years after the devastating siege of Sevastopol and Russia's eventual defeat in the Crimean War (1853–1855). For the first seventy years, Tavrida was nothing if not a work in progress.

Until the 1840s, for example, when Archbishop Innokentii Borisov began laying the groundwork for what Mara Kozelsky calls the "Christianization of Crimea," Tavrida was a distinctly Muslim terrain with over one-third of all mosques in the Russian empire within its borders. According to the Department of Foreign Confessions there were 536 Friday mosques, 1,110 ordinary mosques, and thirteen Sufi lodges in the province through midcentury, serving the spiritual needs of Muslim men and women and providing focal points of social and economic networks. Bahçesaray, together with Evpatoriia and Karasubazar, claimed 76 percent of all religious structures located in Tavrida's towns in the early 1830s: there were ninety-one among the three of them, the vast majority of them mosques. By contrast, in the early 1840s there were only eighty Orthodox churches and a lone monastery in all of Tavrida, constituting less than 5 percent of religious structures in the province. Constrained by anemic annual revenues, the major towns of the province could barely support their police and courts, let alone fund construction of the government buildings, palace squares, and churches expected to provide tangible proof of the efficacy and enlightened nature of Russian rule. Instead, urban landscapes remained marred—as provincial officials and many dvoriane saw it—by "architectural disorder" and the "Asiatic" influence of Tatar construction.[17]

Pavel Sumarokov, a senator, writer, and member of the Russian Academy of Sciences who served as a judge in the provincial government 1803–1805, offered a very different appraisal of the transformative influence of Russian rule. Sumarokov, waxing poetic, found it remarkable that only twenty years before his sojourn "dense forest [had] covered the land, packs of rapacious wolves roamed everywhere, and only the turbulent, melancholy wind interrupted the silence that had settled" in Crimea. The region Sumarokov imagined to have been a wilderness was so utterly transformed by the early 1840s that fashionable ladies could sip tea and catch up on the latest Parisian news while sailing from Odessa to Yalta. Once there, they could admire the splendid noble estates set along the southern coast like a string of pearls, "adorned with vineyards and orchards and handsome houses, varied by thickly wooded mountain declivities and groups of rocks, and views of the sea." Madame Hommaire de Hell astutely observed that the presence of Russian nobles had changed even the width and quality of the roads—now "made expressly for the dashing four-horse equipages that are continually traversing it"—and that the boundaries between properties, once so difficult for surveyors to discern, were marked by posts "bearing the blazonry of the proprietor."[18]

The power of provincial estates was not only visual; these were truly interactive spaces where, according to Priscilla Roosevelt, no matter what his status in St. Petersburg the provincial noble "was expected to be endlessly hospitable and to display a certain indifference to how much this way of living cost, particularly if he was a marshal of the nobility." Hospitality was, after all, a mechanism for displaying the authority of the tsarist regime as well as personal wealth and status. To the extent they were able, nobles therefore opened their gardens for public enjoyment or used them as sites for staged amusements and lavish entertainments. Their homes included (sometimes vast) interior spaces designed specifically as ballrooms or reception halls, as well as other devices for impressing visitors, such as parquet floors, sunrooms, and windows onto the surrounding park or garden.[19]

The "local solidarities" that grew in these spaces were not always inclusive, and in Tavrida there was little camaraderie among Christian and Muslim elites, who moved in distinct social worlds. Dvoriane rarely set foot, for example, inside the urban venues frequented by mirzas (and Tatars more generally), such as mosques and coffeehouses. Most travelers seem to have visited a coffeehouse at some point in their travels though, and their memoirs paint an unambiguous picture of a distinctly non-Russian institution with its "picturesque old Tartars, seated cross-legged in little wooden pens, incessantly smoking chibouks or nargillehs, and drinking their thick coffee out of cups resembling large brass thimbles." Nor is there much evidence that celebrations such as weddings and circumcisions provided opportunities for inter-elite mingling despite the fact that mirza weddings were elaborate multiday affairs. Even the pre-wedding luncheon hosted by Kazy Bey Balatukov days before his wedding in 1820, an event attended by no less than three hundred Tatar villagers, included only one Russian—a visitor to the province, not a fellow landowner. Nor did Russians attend the religious holidays or guild festivals that filled the Tatar social calendar.[20]

The events that did bring Russians and Tatars together included the major fairs held twice a year (in October and April), as well as the races held each October near Simferopol. Competitors in the races vied for a silver cup worth over a thousand rubles, provided by the emperor. In the mornings, they rode Tatar horses mounted without saddles, and at the end of the day raced on camelback. "Almost every Mourza of the peninsula, along with a large number of other Tatars, attends the races," reported Montandon, and their presence produced "the curious spectacle of a great variety of customs" brought together in a single amphitheater.[21]

Of course, not all landowners were wealthy enough to build *usad'by* that could accommodate lavish public spectacles. The majority of those who commanded that level of wealth were members of the ruling elite who owned summer estates in Tavrida but neither registered in the local noble register nor otherwise participated in daily life in the province. Most members of the provincial noble class were mirzas or small-time Little Russian nobles, or Polish szlachta who owned between five and thirty-five serfs. The low population density of the province, together with the freedom of the Tatar population from serfdom, prevented landowners from accumulating wealth in the form of souls until well into the nineteenth century. Even noble wealth in land trended downward from 1815, when 96 percent of non-Tatars and 88 percent of mirzas owned land of some kind, to the outbreak of the Crimean War: of the 225 nobles registered between 1830 and 1853 for whom I have property data, only 65 percent owned either arable or pastureland, and another 12 percent owned land in the form of orchards, gardens, or vineyards. The remaining 23 percent owned houses and/or household servants and peasants, but did not mention landed property among their assets.[22]

Counting the number of desiatinas or types of land owned by mirzas and settlers is very a crude way of getting at the question of how Russian rule impacted daily life. Disaggregating information according to clan and even individual can be far more revealing. The remarkable rise of the Balatukovs signaled an important shift within the Tatar hereditary elite. Prior to 1783, a certain clan-based geography shaped the khanate. According to this geography the Argins dominated the region around

Caffa and Sudak, the Mansurs were associated with the steppe surrounding Gözleve, the Iaşlavs with Akmescit, the Kipchat with the Perekop steppe, and the Şirins with a swath of land that stretched from Perekop to Kerch and southwestward to Staryi Krym (Eski Kırım). The Cherkess princely clans, of which the Balatukovs were one, did not have regional affiliations. However, between 1783 and 1796 none of the mirzas who served as marshals or land captains in Simferopol hailed from the Iaşlav clan: members of the Zuisk, Kantakuzin, and Uzdem clans rotated as marshal, and Argins monopolized the land captaincy. In Evpatoriia, members of the Mamay clan held the latter position, while Şirins and Mansurs took turns as marshal. And from 1804 onward, Balatukovs dominated the marshalships and land captaincies in both districts. This is particularly striking given that according to the district-level residence lists, there were three times as many Mansurs as Balatukovs in Evpatoriia, and twice as many Iaşlavs as Balatukovs in Simferopol. If the Balatukovs' success is any indication, the association between territories and the clans that had traditionally held sway had begun to disintegrate.

At almost every turn however, Russian rule preserved as much as it changed. Owning land was not in and of itself grounds for mirza status, but both the status of one's clan and one's own position within the clan were critical to the resolution of any dispute over land brought before Russian courts. In 1823 the Evpatoriia district land court and Tavrida civil and criminal chambers both ruled that Abdişa Bey Mansur could not legally alienate a fifteen-desiatina parcel near the village of Bakal because the land was part of the Mansur beylik: as bey, Abdişa had the right to use, but not alienate the land, which belonged to the clan and must be passed on intact to the eldest Mansur upon the current bey's death. Mirzas who took note of such decisions successfully tailored their own arguments, grounding them in Crimean custom rather than Russian law. Thus in 1847 Nietcha Bey Iaşlav informed the noble assembly of his right to inherit the lands held by his forefathers without documentation because "the custom was for land to be inherited by the eldest of the clan. There was therefore no need for deeds of sale," Nietcha explained, though he took care to point out that according to the land survey of 1801 the Iaşlavs had held the area in question "from ancient times and without challenge." When Russian policy on Crimean landownership crystallized in 1827, Nicholas I showed little compunction in reducing the privileges of Tatar peasants—a necessary step, as he saw it, in developing agricultural production—but did not diminish the rights of the province's unofficial nobility.[23]

If the mirzas found ways to defend their economic interests against incursions by Russian settlers (and at the expense of Tatar peasants), they were even more successful at controlling the terms of inclusion in local noble society. Russian officials were determined to ascribe noble status only to members of the "traditional" elite, but they could not identify legitimate members of that group without the help of local intermediaries. Thanks to the gatekeeping of marshals, land captains, members of the Commission on Muslim and Greek Clans, noble assembly deputies, and men whose prestige and standing in Crimean society was universally accepted, with very few exceptions a Crimean Tatar became a dvorianin only by virtue of first being a mirza. When the Tatar-dominated assembly approved Menglişa Mirza Ulan and Samedin Çelebi Karaman as nobles in 1804 for example, they did so not on the basis of service rendered to the Russian sovereign, but on the strength of their forefathers' status and service to the khans. As former inhabitants of the khanate and vassals of the Ottoman sultan, these men were slated for inscription in the fourth part of the noble register—that reserved for nobles of foreign origin. The noble assembly came to the same conclusion when considering Captain Usein Gazy Şirin in 1805: despite having achieved a Russian military rank commensurate with hereditary noble status in 1793, which would seem to place him in the second part of the register, he was approved for entry in the fourth. A host of others gained similar approval in the first quarter of the century, establishing a pattern culminating in the recommendations of the Commission on Muslim and Greek Clans.[24]

Crimeans could theoretically translate mirza status into Russian noble status, but the reverse did not hold. Elite status in the former khanate was based on kinship. The importance of clan affiliation and lineage cropped up again and again in mirza petitions for noble status, many of which contained genealogies composed with the express purpose of establishing an individual's legitimate descent from an honorable and occasionally glorious ancestor. These genealogical claims were vetted by the petitioners' peers, tested against their shared memory and interests.

This does not mean that the Crimean elite remained insulated from the demands of the empire. By the 1820s the rules of the game—and criteria for inclusion—were changing, and some mirzas were willing and able to adapt. Kutlu Giray Edige, for example, applied for noble status on the basis of his grandfather's service to the tsars, as did Murat Mirza Argin, who grounded his claim on his father's status as a court councilor rather than the prestige of his clan. Others simply knew how to spin their arguments. The assembly rejected Mufti Seit Murtaza Çelebi Kontugan's petition on the grounds that members of the religious elite were not eligible for inscription in the noble register. The son of Mufti Seit Dzhelal Çelebi drew a different ruling by convincing the assembly that his status depended not on his father's rank as mufti, but on his uncle's receipt of a pension from Sultan Mahmud I in 1738 in recognition of service to Mengli Giray II. "Although in the khanate *çelebis* constituted a separate class from the beys and mirzas," concluded the assembly, "because of their lineage and service they enjoyed the rights of nobility." Seit Dzhelal became a "foreign" noble, and his son entered Russian service with that status as well.[25]

As the terms of inclusion in Russian society narrowed in the 1830s and 1840s the responses of provincial nobilities varied. Zenon Kohut has shown that in Ukraine, the gentry of the former Hetmanate fought hard against what they perceived to be the loss of their traditional rights and privileges, eventually convincing the Council of Ministers to confirm the hereditary noble status of the upper echelons of Cossack society in 1835. "By questioning the most cherished symbols of the elite's collective identity," Kohut writes, "the Heraldic Office greatly strengthened the traditionalist sentiment among the Ukrainian nobles and helped nurture a spirit of opposition to St. Petersburg which lingered well into the 1830s." According to I. I. Krivosheia, the similarly exclusionary policy of the Senate "laid the foundation for the emergence of dissatisfaction with the contemporary order" in the Polish provinces as well.[26]

As long as Russia was willing to pursue a non-assimilative integration strategy, as it was under Catherine, most mirzas felt they had a place in the imperial system. But by the 1830s, imperial policy had shifted. Russian officials had never focused on the cultural integration of the mirzas, and by that point they felt it was unnecessary. As Governor Kaznacheev pointed out in his 1835 report to the interior minister, the Russian population in Tavrida was growing, the formerly nomadic Nogays had begun to "settle in the European fashion" on the steppe, agricultural production was increasing, major roads now radiated out from Simferopol through the peninsula, and markets were flourishing. Authorities saw no need to court the mirzas: they considered the development of the province a sufficiently compelling reason for the tsar's subjects to be content with whatever status he might accord them.[27]

From their vantage point on the margins of imperial society, the mirzas pondered whether their future lay in Russia-ruled Crimea. Together with the rest of the Tatar community they watched the Crimean War unfold and by the time the dust and smoke had cleared, many concluded that they would be better off elsewhere. Between 1856 and 1862 approximately 130,000 Crimean Tatars (possibly more) and over 46,000 Nogays—together roughly two-thirds of the combined Tatar population of the province—ended their ambiguous relationship with the tsarist regime and emigrated to the Ottoman Empire in a singular gesture of disengagement with the process of Russian empire building. Their departure shifted the ethnic and cultural balance in Tavrida and radically altered the layered geographies that constituted the southern empire. Exports from Evpatoriia and Feodosiia plummeted by 97 and 70 percent respectively from 1862 to 1864; when they began to climb again in 1865, it was thanks to the arrival of English and Italian, rather than Ottoman ships. Crimea's role as a crucial trade partner with the Ottoman Empire had ended; the center of gravity in the Black Sea had shifted yet again.[28]

The land the Tatar emigrants left behind remained little more than a myth to many in the interior. According to Skal'kovskii (writing in the 1830s), "many . . . saw little difference between it and China. They thought Odessa was in Crimea itself . . . Many were convinced that the lands and settlers sent to populate them existed only on paper."[29] Even for the scores of adventure-seekers, merchants, diplomats, and travelers who documented their journeys through the region, Crimea was a place apart from the Russian mainland; a littoral entity defined by a spectacular coast and harbors that had earned their fame among the ancients. The pages of these memoirs, many finely wrought, describe a maritime landscape in which barges, fishing vessels, *chaiky*, *kochermy*, large-hulled ships, and (eventually) steamers made their way, some coasting from port to port, others charting an intrepid course across the Black Sea from Constantinople, Trabzon, Batumi, Anapa, or Odessa. For these Russian visitors Crimea remained an imagined landscape of lighthouses and shipwrecks, Tatar coffeehouses and vineyards.

As early as 1807 Governor Richelieu had begun to doubt that Crimean Tatars would become good Russian peasants. "Judging by their customs and the fundamental laws set out by their faith," he wrote in a report to the minister of war, "[the Tatars] cannot be good farmers. Their women do not emerge from the walls of their houses and therefore all agricultural labor must be performed by the men." The fact that Tatars living in other provinces had taken Russian customs as their own was the only source of hope. Richelieu proposed that two divisions from each of the four Crimean horse regiments be sent to Saratov, Simbirsk, and Kazan to observe the way of life of the Tatar inhabitants there. In summer months, the Crimean soldiers "could be used for mounted patrol, and in winter they could be quartered in Tatar villages where, observing the household activities of their co-religionists, they would be assured that they will not lose their religion by changing their customs." This sort of exposure to a way of life in which both sexes participated in agricultural production "would acquaint the Crimeans with Russia and would forge a more appropriate and more useful relationship between them and [their new] fatherland."[30]

Richelieu's plan never came to fruition. Though a few Crimeans did assimilate, the vast majority retained their cultural identity and sought acceptance within imperial society on their own terms. A man like Major Seit Ibrahim Aga Taşı-oğlu, a member of the Crimean kapıhalkı with a tradition of service extending back at least three generations (and eventually to Anatolia), could rise to noble rank and secure his right to own approximately 7,000 desiatinas of orchard, pasture, and arable land. His son Emin Bey and grandson Arslan Bey, who were inscribed in the noble register, both held officer rank in the Crimean regiments, but like their forefather felt no need to convert or otherwise change their cultural identity. While they did not necessarily see this as a way of subverting Russian authority, as the nineteenth century progressed Russian officials grew increasingly averse to the persistence of a separate mirza culture, and by the end of the 1840s determined that mirzas no longer satisfied the terms of inclusion in noble society.

That turn toward exclusivity and the new mode of imperial rule it accompanied ought not obscure the fact that as much as tsarist institutions strove to impose hierarchical relationships or centrally defined jurisdictions, they thrived when the boundaries between them overlapped or grew indistinct. Negotiating and exploiting the ambiguous terrain of authority was a central part of the Crimean experience of empire, and a crucial characteristic of the dynamics of Russian imperial rule.

SPATIAL LOGIC AND THE SOUTHERN EMPIRE

One of the main contentions of this book is that the relevance of empire to its inhabitants varied not only according to religion and status, but also according to the depth and breadth of the connections between an individual and the administrative, cultural, social, and physical landscapes in which daily life unfolded. It was a network with as many nodes as it had subjects. And it had a spatial logic.

By midcentury anyone willing to read a geography could learn that Tavrida province stretched roughly 400 versts (268 miles) from east to west between Berdiansk and Kinburn, and 360 versts from north to south between Orekhov and the Cape of Ai Todor. It was the southernmost of the empire's European provinces and a highly strategic one, thanks to its proximity to the Caucasus, Anatolia, and Constantinople itself, which lay less than two days away by sea. Officials, settlers, and soldiers had built towns and fortifications, roads and libraries, and yet officials were deeply frustrated by how little was known about the province and its basic geography. According to the 1849 volume of the *Military-Statistical Survey* devoted to Tavrida, the fields, meadows, and pastures had not been counted, nor was there any systematic documentation of the province's roads, marshes, or wells. If the Ministry of State Domains was capable of differentiating forests suited for firewood from those suited for shipbuilding—and that was an open question—it had not shared those reports with the army's general staff. To add insult to injury, civilian and military officials were still debating the area of the province, with many believing it to be roughly 20,000 square versts (8,780 square miles or 5.6 million acres) larger than it really was.[31]

The scope of official ignorance would have infuriated Catherine and Potemkin. Both were thrilled to have altered Russia's strategic position in the Black Sea, but neither was content with geopolitical victory. Like their counterparts in Vienna and Berlin, they were deeply concerned with cultivating enlightened absolutism within their domains. In fact, the attempt to establish a rational, civilizing order capable of improving the functionality of the state has long been the most celebrated aspect of Catherine's reign. It is the conceptual thread that binds the provincial reforms of 1775, the 1785 charters to the nobility and towns, her liberal attitude toward publishing and literary activities, educational reforms, urban planning decrees, and the policy of religious toleration formally articulated in 1773. Above all else, Catherine wanted a powerful, governable state, and such were the tools she chose to deploy to this end.

The fact that the fundamental arts of imperial governance—cultivating land, collecting taxes, establishing postal roads, securing frontiers— required the empress to assess Russia's territory as well as its taxable souls put a premium on policies designed to mitigate the figurative and literal distance between sovereign and subject, governor and governed. For this reason, some of the most important activities she and her subordinates undertook were among the least glamorous. The glamorous scientific expeditions and the decidedly unglamorous general land survey, both of which were under way in the 1760s, attest to the fact that from the earliest days of her reign Catherine placed a premium on collecting information about the empire she had wrested from her husband. During her reign, the Academy of Sciences commissioned twenty-seven expeditions to various corners of the empire and beyond, including Staraya Russa, the Ural Mountains, the White Sea, Orenburg, Moscow province, Constantinople, Lake Ladoga, Finland, Japan, Astrakhan, and Crimea. The expeditions varied in purpose and produced results ranging from the mineral to the astronomical, but all were charged with preserving "the common good of the state and the spread of science." As Christopher Ely has argued, they were less "voyages of discovery" than attempts to find "a new way of understanding the land in terms of its distinct geographical features and its economic value."[32]

In this sprawling continental empire, proximity was as much a function of knowledge collection as it was a measure of versts. Over time, the familiar places—those that had been studied, measured, described, and cataloged—came to be recognized as not only well known but also, by extension, closer to the imperial center than they might otherwise have been. In fact, proximity became one of the fundamental organizing principles of the administrative system. Sergei Pleshcheev's 1787 *Survey of the Russian Empire* reflects this emerging spatial logic. Pleshcheev begins by systematically describing Russia's borders, its distinguishing geographical features (mountains, seas, lakes, and navigable rivers), and the various "nations" inhabiting the country. The second, far more substantial part of the book divides the empire into northern, middle, and southern (*poludennye*) belts, and then into respective arrays of administrative units—gubernii for the most part, with the lands of the Don Cossacks and Kirgiz "hordes" and Tavricheskaia oblast' the only exceptions.[33]

Pleshcheev could hardly have described the empire otherwise in the wake of Catherine II's reforms. The signature piece of legislation, the Fundamental Law for the Administration of the Provinces of the All-Russian Empire (1775), entailed a massive reorganization of administrative space. It was, among other things, an attempt to align the territorial size of administrative units with the size of their resident populations (20,000–30,000 males per district, 300,000–400,000 males per province). It established the administrative-spatial hierarchy that would persist until 1917, nesting districts within provinces and designating district towns based as much on the centrality of their locations as on their level of urban or economic development. In other words, the statute formalized the idea that proximity to a static seat of authority—rather than to a human, and inherently mobile, representative of authority, which had sufficed in the past—was an essential attribute of governance and the organizing logic of the physical space of the empire.[34]

As if that were not enough, full implementation of Catherine's administrative reform also required local officials to produce cartographic documentation of the new boundaries and toponymy summoned into existence. Officials in a great many provinces left this rather daunting task unfulfilled and so, in May 1781, Catherine outlined the procedures for mapping the boundary lines separating one district from another and one province from the next. Commissions composed of land surveyors and representatives from both noble and peasant organs set to work. Having installed markers in prominent locations, surveyors were to draw up plans and send copies to the civil court, treasury chamber, higher land court, and Imperial Senate. Remarkably, they acquitted themselves well enough that in 1792 cartographers working under Aleksandr Vil'brekht in the Geographical Department of Her Majesty's Own Chancellery were able to publish, for the first time in history, a comprehensive atlas of the Russian Empire complete with district-level boundaries (figure C.5).[35]

Pleshcheev and Vil'brekht were not the first men to articulate the idea that Russian space ought to be imagined as a series of polygons; nor was Catherine the first ruler to attempt to enact such a large-scale

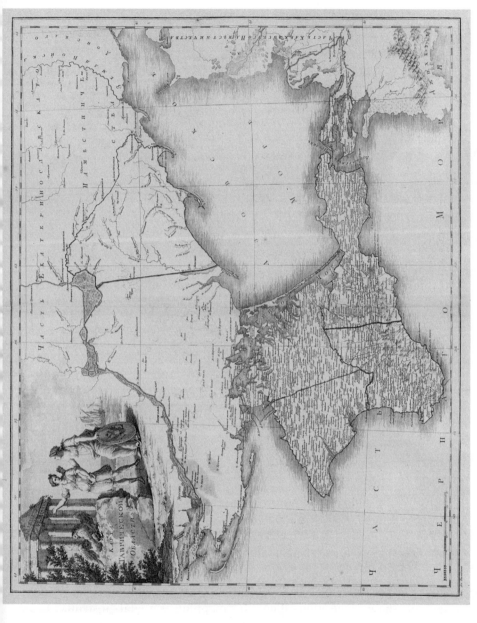

Figure C.5. Map of Tavrida Province in 1792; from Vil'brekht, *Rossiiskoi atlas* (Harvard Map Collection, Harvard Library)

reorganization. Peter I laid out his own provincial reform in statutes of 1719 and (posthumously) 1727—a reform one prominent nineteenth century historian memorably described as "an attempt to build on quicksand or take flight without wings." Whether or not Peter's legislation was doomed to failure by the utter lack of a "new brand of men" steeped in Enlightenment principles, it certainly did not help matters that Russia's adoption of European cartographic science was still in its infancy. In the mid-sixteenth century Tsar Ivan IV's desire for a comprehensive general map of his domain had gone unfulfilled because, as Steven Seegel explains, "pictographs in the form of sacred icons and fortress plans were printed as substitutes for geometric space"; Russian mapmaking had not changed very much in the intervening century and a half.[36]

Valerie Kivelson has brilliantly shown the rich meaning of Muscovite maps, demonstrating that despite the lack of projection and scale, spatial thinking was a crucial element of Muscovite culture and a necessary tool for articulating one's place in the (Orthodox) religious and secular realms of the seventeenth century. Similarly insistent on the value of maps and mapmaking both for better understanding early modern Russia and for critiquing Eurocentric narratives of modernization, Denis Shaw points to the breathtaking cartographic and geographic ambition of the *Book of the Great Map*—the textual accompaniment to the set of (lost) late fifteenth-century maps depicting the realm from the Kola peninsula in the west to the Black Sea in the south and Yenisei River in the east. Shaw carefully unpacks the implications of the scrupulous attention given to relative location, general direction, and topographical features. "One reads of features being 'above' or 'below' other features along the rivers," writes Shaw, "of features being located on the 'right,' 'left,' or 'high' bank, on 'the Moscow side' (that is, the Russian side) of a southern defensive river, or on 'the Crimean' or 'the Nogai' side," but also of old settlement sites, stone formations, wells, monasteries, and forests that might be used to navigate an otherwise unmarked terrain. Despite the book's decidedly pre-modern cartographic style, Kivelson and Shaw argue compellingly for mapping as a vital "instrument in the modernization of the state."[37]

For Peter I, who was both a student and devotee of European cartography, this was a woefully inadequate utilization of the map. His top-down, highly centralized approach to the cultivation of cartographic science was embodied by Ivan Kirilovich Kirilov, the secretary of the Senate and point man for Peter's project for mapping every square inch of the empire with unwavering precision. Hamstrung by a painful lack of both material and financial resources, the project fizzled out and Kirilov died in 1737 without producing a complete version of the gloriously detailed map of the empire Peter had commissioned. But he did manage to pull off the monumental feat of documenting the governmental, social, and cultural features of Petrine Russia in exquisite detail. His two-volume tour de force opens with an exhaustive catalog of information about St. Petersburg province before radiating outward from the northern capital to describe the provinces of Moscow, Smolensk, Kiev, Voronezh, Riga and Revel, Nizhegorod, Kazan, Astrakhan, Arkhangelogorod, and Siberia.[38]

Kirilov's spatial logic starts with the capital city and moves outward, while Pleshcheev's 1792 variant is latitudinal, embedding Petersburg and Moscow in the text's inexorable march southward from the White Sea to the Black. But the crucial difference lies in the way the two men conceptualize provincial space. Both texts identify the province as the organizing mechanism—the fundamental unit—of governance. Kirilov constructs each province as a litany of government offices and office holders, monasteries and cathedrals, schools, hospitals, and factories which, taken altogether, describes the density and distribution of official and cultural linkages from Petersburg to Iakutsk. Pleshcheev, having acknowledged the authority of the governor and governor-general of St. Petersburg, launches into a descriptive geography of the province's borders. St. Petersburg province "is bounded," Pleshcheev writes, "on the north side by the Gulf of Finland and the gubernii of Vyborg and Olonets; on the east by Novgorod guberniia and Lake Ladoga; on the south by Pskov guberniia; and on the west by Lake Chuda, Revel', and the Gulf of Finland." In other words, he describes provinces as bounded spaces—polygons, in the language of spatial geometry—while Kirilov describes them as accumulations of places, sites, or points.

This is important. If in Kirilov's day the boundaries depicted on official maps were more rough indicators than authoritative lines, this was not only because of the vast differences between traditional Russian mapmaking and the increasingly scientific approach taken in much of Europe. It was also because of the particular geometry and scale of Russian spatial culture. Like their Muscovite predecessors, as well as their coevals in seventeenth-century France and the Holy Roman Empire, Petrine officials conceived of the tsar's domain not as a neatly circumscribed territory but as a constellation of points; an array of particular, often small but significant locations whence tsarist authority radiated outward across a vast but unnarrated expanse of terrain.[39]

In time, through exposure to foreign expertise, and motivated by the exigencies of managing a remarkably expansive empire, Russian cartographers began acquiring the skills necessary to apply Cartesian coordinates, scale, and mathematical projections. It was not until the 1780s, however, that the ability to represent a province (or a district, or an entire state, for that matter) as something more than an assemblage of towns and villages became feasible. Catherine's territorial reforms capitalized on the ability to translate the idea of bounded space from the mind to the map consistently, and with great accuracy, marking a watershed in Russian cartography, statecraft, and in the conceptualization of Russian space.

From that moment forward, each province possessed a recognizable, reproducible shape; a shape formed according to an assortment of geographic and demographic considerations, but above all a shape that reflected Catherine's idea of governable space. The province thus became an essential cartographic container. It provided shape, structure, and scale. In fact, the advent of the authoritative administrative map of the empire introduced a new array of attributes to the catalogs of information compiled by the Kirilovs and Pleshcheevs of the world. Previous government surveys offered systematic coverage of the empire and attempted to capture and present the same kind of information (number of inhabitants, notable geographic features, economic activities, historical events, etc.) for each and every feature. In the wake of Catherine's territorial reforms, geographical surveys proliferated. Officials could count the number of souls inhabiting a certain region as they had in the past, but now they could also calculate population density. Now they knew not only where shipyards and fortifications were located; they could calculate the distances between such strategic locations and the nearest provincial town or port.

As important as this shift was, the province did not displace the other items in Russia's cartographic lexicon. After all, the ability to represent administrative boundaries did not remove the need to represent the myriad other spatial relations that described a location and/or its place within a broader geographical system. Chief among those was the sequencing of locations along a route. Aleksei Postnikov has shown that in Russia prior to the eighteenth century the mechanism for conveying movement through space was not a Cartesian grid but a "cartographic canvas . . . composed of structurally heterogeneous materials, which were spatially arranged around the 'skeleton' of routes." These routes might describe sacred, military, administrative, or economic mobility, but regardless, Russian cartographers represented them all in terms of "positional features relative to each other within a certain area." These topologies, together with copious texts that informed the viewer of the area of estates or the number of versts or days needed to cover distances between locations, constituted the map. This meant that in Russia the gap between map and text was not as great as it had become in Spain, France, Holland, and England, where cartographic elements replaced textual inscriptions as repositories of information by the early eighteenth century.[40]

In the wake of the Petrine period, Russian cartography gradually fell into step with Enlightenment standards, though the prominence of textual description as a form of mapping refused to recede into the margins. Producers and brokers of information preserved traditional forms, such as post-route and pilgrimage itineraries, while at the same time ushering in the age of topographical descriptions, ethnographies, geographical surveys, and travel literature. In this sense Russia was not alone. Throughout Europe writing about place grew ever more common across the eighteenth and nineteenth centuries, producing a range of sequencings and experiences—mappings, really—of the variable, perceived connections between one place and another. Lauren Benton has argued that these routes, or "corridors," were the mechanism for understanding the system of interconnected "enclaves" that constituted imperial space. Travelers, imperial agents, and settlers, after all, shared a preference for geographic information "in forms that mirrored the likely experience of new geographies, and these were subjectively grasped less as broad regional segments than as discrete destinations that were distributed along strings of at least imagined imperial control." Itineraries, whether they took the form of lines on maps or narratives in travel accounts or military records, facilitated the movement of people, objects, ideas, and even authority. As a consequence, they structured imperial space in tangible and intangible ways, often long after the initial phases of acquisition and integration.[41]

The official *Post Route Itinerary, or Description of All Post Roads of the Russian Empire, the Kingdom of Poland, and Other Annexed Regions* published in 1824 offers eloquent testimony to the persistent significance of corridors and enclaves in Russia's spatial culture. The Post Department issued this new itinerary after recognizing the need to incorporate the changes to both provincial boundaries and the network of post stations in the twenty-three years since the release of the previous itinerary, and to distribute crucial geographic information in a more accessible, more portable format than the six-volume behemoth issued in 1801. The new itinerary weighed in at a relatively svelte 454 pages. Even better, it organized post routes into three tiers: those connecting the capitals (St. Petersburg and Moscow) to provincial and frontier towns, those connecting provincial and frontier towns to one another, and those connecting the capitals, provincial, and frontier towns to all district towns in the same province. The itinerary said little about the routes themselves, other than to identify the distances between post stations and number of horses available at each one, and thus bore resemblance to the *Hydrographical Atlas of the Russian Empire* published six years later. Both were compendiums of geographical information, catalysts for physical mobility, and above all else sophisticated tools for collapsing staggering distances into manageable lengths with predictable, if not completely homogeneous, temporal and material attributes.[42]

The real game-changer in the south was the *Atlas of the Black Sea* published in Nikolaev in 1841. This milestone in maritime cartography came thanks to studies conducted between 1825 and 1836 by Captain Egor Manganari, and no less a figure than Nikolai Nikiforovich Murzakevich, one of the most prominent historians of the day, swooned in his assessment of the results. "How many prayers of thanks must be raised to kind Providence," he enthused, "for causing our wise government to gift humanity and science with this absolutely essential and useful book." Up to that point, Russian sailors had relied first on the maps of Cruys (1699) and Bellin (1772), and then on a series of maps published by the Naval Ministry and Admiralty between 1804 and 1817. The twenty-six maps and sixteen relief views of Manganari's atlas were a godsend for ship captains partaking in the relative boom of Black Sea trade, for they detailed the harbors, currents, depths, and coastal topography of the entire littoral. Captured in precise swirls of ink and neatly formed

numeric inscriptions, the sea appeared static, predictable, and highly regularized, its vagaries and idiosyncrasies muted by cartographic conven-
tion. But the sea, of course, was anything but static, predictable, and
highly regularized, and the atlas, authoritative as it was, was little more
than a pale shadow of the multidimensional experience that resulted
from any attempt to move across it.[43]

However inadequate they might be, maps, guides, itineraries, and the
infrastructures of mobility they described mattered a great deal to a great
many people. Mobility was an inescapable feature of life in the southern empire. Not every corner of the empire was equally connected, nor
was every place in the empire a desirable or common destination. The
southern empire—Crimea in particular—was one of the most desirable
and most common destinations. Travel to Crimea for pleasure began in
1785 with the journey of the sensational Lady Craven, and over the
course of the next century generated a flood of descriptive text rivaled
only by writing about the capitals and the Caucasus. Travelers to the
south reveled in what they perceived to be the exoticism of the landscape and the heady combination of pleasure and danger they encountered within it. They strove to mark Crimea as distinct, and in many
ways succeeded. And yet the more they saw and wrote, the more recognizable, even familiar, the region became, not only to the small army of
well-heeled thrill seekers who could afford the journey, but to those who
consumed their accounts from a distance.

The paths travelers took through this space varied tremendously. Some
moved slowly and methodically, exploring each grove and every curious
pile of stone. Others made a beeline for Sevastopol or Yalta. Some, like
Nikolai Sergeevich Vsevolozhskii, made their way overland. Vsevolozhskii, an aristocrat and accomplished man of letters, traveled southward
in 1836 from Kharkov through Ekaterinoslav and Berislav, across Perekop to Simferopol, along the valley of the Salgir as far as Chatyr Dag
and then along the southern coast from Alushta to Yalta, where he finally boarded a steamship bound for Odessa and Constantinople. By
contrast, Anatolii Demidov, a member of one of Russia's most prominent
entrepreneurial families and of the Academy of Sciences, made an expedition to Novorossiia in 1837 focusing on the mineral and geological
endowments of the region. Demidov traveled by steamship from Odessa
to Yalta and then made haste along the coast to Feodosiia, northward to
the Arabat Spit and eastward beyond Crimea to explore the mouth of

the Don. By the 1830s most itineraries were well worn and what was known to that point about the region's history, geography, and culture was becoming well entrenched. Like many others, Demidov cribbed from the accounts of those in whose footsteps he followed. In the process he made errors of his own and recycled others; accepting, for example, the poetic yet inaccurate popular etymology of *bella chiave* ("beautiful key") for Balaklava rather than the Tatar-Greek hybrid meaning "*balyk*-catching place," and offering a novel interpretation of the Nogay use of thatching as an expression of unique "national" identity rather than recognizing it as a technique used by Ukrainian peasants and a great many other inhabitants of the south.[44]

No one seemed quite able to master the region's toponymy or geography. Vsevolozhskii identified the village of Chevki as "Chafki," Vorontsov's estate Massandra as "Marsanda," and Trekh-Ablam (a post station on the road from Perekop to Simferopol) as "Ablana." Demidov placed Ovidiopol at the mouth of the Danube instead of the Dnestr. Even a source as authoritative as Manganari erred, complained one reviewer, as a result of his attempts to faithfully record place names according to the pronunciation of locals. But such errors could easily be forgiven. Some merely highlighted the constantly changing demographic landscape. Vsevolozhskii, for example, was not wrong to describe the village of Taushan-Bazar as "an uninhabited valley," though his reviewer, writing in 1844, was quite right to report that the site had been "enlivened" by the presence of a post station in the few intervening years. This was a place where time folded in on itself: where one could reach out and touch Ottoman mosques, Genoese fortresses, Byzantine churches, and Greek temples. While some of the so-called errors rife in travel writing, scholarly accounts, and official records might reflect incompetence or ignorance, a good many of them reflect the difficulty of describing a space that had been indelibly marked and layered long before 1783, and continued to evolve in substantial ways.[45]

Russia's investment in the significance of the southern empire and the meaning of particular sites within it grew exponentially in the wake of the Crimean War. This was a global war, with troops from Russia, France, Britain, the Ottoman Empire, and Sardinia, and it was a bloody one, with military casualties running well over a half million and perhaps as high as three-quarters of a million men. It was also a distinctly modern war, documented by journalists and photographers whose pieces studded the headlines of newspapers on either side of the Atlantic between the outbreak of hostilities in October 1853 and the signing of the Treaty of Paris in March 1856. Suddenly a rather out-of-the-way peninsula in the middle of the Black Sea found itself in a glaring international spotlight. Indeed, the level of press and popular attention in those years went unrivaled—with the exception of the swirl of attention surrounding the Yalta Conference in 1945—until March 2014.

The war put Crimea on the map, so to speak. The heroics and idiocies of the battlefield caught the international imagination, inspiring Tennyson and sparking fashion innovations such as the balaclava. But the grandeur of the landscape and tsarist opulence shone through as well. One eloquent, if unique, testament to the reach of Crimea's reputation is the decision in 1856 by Thomas DeKay Winans, a chief engineer for the railway project connecting St. Petersburg to Moscow, to build his own summer estate at Leakin Park near Baltimore, Maryland. The estate was known as "the Crimea," and its centerpiece was an Italianate stone mansion called "Orianda" in honor of the Romanov estate near Yalta. Crimea had, in other words, in the span of a few short years become a site of suffering and at the same time an exotic portal into the intimate world of a great dynasty.

Within Russia itself, the arrival of the age of tourism in the 1870s meant that growing numbers of tsarist subjects began traveling hundreds and thousands of miles to experience the former khanate: to take in its charming landscapes, its stunning architecture, its lavish displays of elite wealth, its fascinating web of caves and ruins, beaches and vineyards. The first *Travel Guide to Tavrida Province*, published in 1872, bemoaned the fact that Crimea had suffered such bad press during the war, but was equally appalled by the fact that up to that point the only publications describing the region had been scholarly in nature. These, explained the guide, while "respectable, were now and then quite boring" and in no way met the demands of a public thirsting to know more about this "picturesque, delightful little corner of Russia." The *Guide* sought to slake that thirst. But in addition to providing colorful sketches of Crimean life, it included itineraries for short tours on and off the beaten path, as well as up-to-date schedules for the steamship lines connecting Crimea to Odessa and to the Caucasian and Azov coasts. Subsequent travel guides followed, the most popular of which came out in 1888, when Grigorii Georgievich Moskvich added

Crimea to the list of Russian travel destinations for which he published guides. In 1913 he issued a twenty-fifth anniversary "illustrated practical guide" complete with steamship schedules and a Russian-Tatar dictionary.[46]

Just a few years earlier, the Ministry of the Interior had dutifully compiled the authoritative *Lists of Populated Places of Tavrida Province,* and in 1867 the provincial statistical committee produced its *Memorial Book of Tavrida Province,* brimming with thick descriptions of the region's geography, demographic composition, economy, history, educational institutions, and industrial production. But Evgenii Markov stole the show when he published his famous *Crimean Sketches: Portraits of Crimean Life, History, and Nature* in 1872. Markov served as head of the Simferopol gymnasium from 1866, and in his spare time visited "every nook and cranny, inspected every monument, and read everything he could get his hands on." In his sketches Markov celebrates Crimea's curative waters and wines, its vistas and its people. He worked, by his own admission, "as an artist or landscape painter, flinging onto the canvas everything that amazes him: here a scene from domestic life, there a landscape, here the portrait of a passerby, there a scrupulous copy of an ancient monument." He sought to capture Crimea's brilliant essence and bring it to life on the page for those who had not experienced it for themselves. He was thrilled when the popular book was republished in 1883 to mark the centenary of annexation. "In this context a Russian book about Crimea," he wrote in the preface to the second edition, "is a relevant and natural expression of Russian society's brotherly attitude toward Crimea; an attitude which inevitably now lies at the foundation of any political union of our times regardless of what the origins [of that union] might have been."[47]

Taken together, these texts represent the integration of the former khanate into imperial space with remarkable eloquence. They stand as a gleaming promise that, given time, everything would be documented, counted, measured, and explained. Indeed, after a long century under Russian rule, the work of documenting the southern empire was promising. Statisticians, archaeologists, archivists, landowners, and countless others were busy accruing information, drawing maps, and meticulously documenting grain prices and horse thefts, the comings and goings of trading vessels, the trickle of Tatar conversions to Orthodox Christianity, the incidence of heavy rains and seismic activity along the coast. The former khanate's place in the imperial imagination was slowing becoming fixed.

CODA

Markov's words and motivations remain as relevant in the early twenty-first century as they were in the late nineteenth. For regardless of the form Kremlin policy ultimately takes, Crimea is back on the map: its layered history exposed, its relationship with Russia reconfigured, its geostrategic value matched by the ideological potency of its ruins and harbors. Inevitably, some will read this book in the context of twenty-first century geopolitics. Others will read it in the context of familiar narratives of the last century, ranging from civil war to collectivization, Nazi occupation, Stalin's brutally swift deportation of the Crimean Tatar population in May 1944, Nikita Khrushchev's infamous transfer of control over Crimea to the Ukrainian SSR, the collapse of the Soviet Union in 1991, and Moscow's subsequent struggle for an economic and naval foothold in the Black Sea. Still others will read it in the context of an arc spanning millennia and extending deeply into the worlds of Greco-Roman or Turkic civilization. This book describes, after all, a contested and all-too-often imagined space as much as it does one with a distinct material reality. Crimea is a classic object of desire and of memory, an ideological platform and nationalist playground, a sacred space, a UNESCO World Heritage Site, a geological wonder, an enological curiosity, a multiethnic landscape, a homeland. In a place where only the sea and sky—and perhaps the grandeur of Chatyr Dag— remain constant, inhabitants wait patiently while power brokers and mapmakers decide how to redraw the lines of possession and dispossession. As their neighbors just over the Ukrainian border told me in January 2015, "we will wait and see. And we will live."

Notes

Abbreviations

AGM	Arkhiv grafov Mordvinovykh
DAMO	Derzhavnii arkhiv Mikolaivs'koi oblasti
DAARK	Derzhavnii arkhiv Avtonomnoi Respubliki Krim (liquidated in October 2014 and reestablished as the Gosudarstvennyi arkhiv Respubliki Krym)
ITUAK	Izvestiia Tavricheskoi uchenoi arkhivnoi komissii
OVTR	Obzor vneshnei torgovli Rossii po Evropeiskoi i aziatskoi granitsam
PSZ I	Pol'noe sobranoe zakonov Rossiiskoi Imperii, sobranie I
PSZ II	Pol'noe sobranoe zakonov Rossiiskoi Imperii, sobranie II
RBS	Russkii biograficheskii slovar'
RGADA	Rossiiskii gosudarstvennii arkhiv drevnykh aktov
RGIA	Rossiiskii gosudarstvennii istoricheskii arkhiv
RGVIA	Rossiiskii gosudarstvennii voenno-istoricheskii arkhiv
TAK	Tavricheskii adres-kalendar'
TGV	Tavricheskiia gubernskiia vedomosti
VSOb	Voenno-statisticheskoe obozrenie Rossiiskoi Imperii
ZOOID	Zapiski Imperatorskago Odesskago obshchestva istorii i drevnostei

Introduction

1. *PSZ I,* vol. 21, no. 15,708 (April 8, 1783).
2. *PSZ I,* vol. 16, no. 12,099 (March 22, 1764); Skal'kovskii, *Opyt statisticheskago opisaniia,* 206; Sunderland, *Taming the Wild Field,* 89.

3. See for example Lazzerini, "The Crimea Under Russian Rule," and his more critical take on the relevance of colonialism in Lazzerini, "Local Accommodation and Resistance to Colonialism in Nineteenth-Century Crimea"; Williams, *Crimean Tatars;* Vozgrin, *Istoricheskie sud'by.*

4. For a concise discussion of the "turn" and notes on essential readings see Michael David-Fox, Peter Holquist, and Alexander M. Martin, "The Imperial Turn." Influential studies of multiethnicity and the nature of imperial rule by scholars in the west include Thaden, *Russia's Western Borderlands;* Khodarkovsky, *Where Two Worlds Met* and *Russia's Steppe Frontier;* Slezkine, *Arctic Mirrors;* Barrett, *At the Edge of Empire;* Gvosdev, *Imperial Policies and Perspectives Towards Georgia;* Geraci, *Window on the East;* Martin, *Law and Custom in the Steppe;* Jersild, *Orientalism and Empire;* Werth, *At the Margins of Orthodoxy;* Crews, *For Prophet and Tsar;* Dolbilov and Miller (eds.), *Zapadnye okrainy Rossiiskoi imperii;* Burbank, Remnev and von Hagen (eds.), *Russian Empire.* On conceptual geographies see Sunderland, "Imperial Space"; Leonid Gorizontov, "The 'Great Circle' of Interior Russia"; Morrison, "Metropole, Colony, and Imperial Citizenship in the Russian Empire"; and Bassin, "Geographies of Imperial Identity."

5. Lieven, *Russia: Empire and Its Rivals;* O'Neill, "Rethinking Elite Integration."

6. Pravilova, *Finansy Imperii;* Werth, *Tsar's Foreign Faiths;* Lohr, *Russian Citizenship.* A major strength of much of the most recent work is its insistence on placing Russia in the much broader context of world empires. See the exemplary integration of Russia into world history in Burbank and Cooper, *Empires in World History.*

7. Bukhteev, "Opyt statisticheskago opisaniia," 466; "Otryvok povestvovaniia," 91; *Putevoditel' po Krymu* [1872], 3; Levashev, *Kartina ili opisanie,* 150.

8. The society's most recent conference was on "The Crimean Factor in Russian History and Culture," held at Moscow State University in December 2014, just months after the second Russian annexation. On *kraevedenie* in the imperial era see Berdinskikh, *Uezdnye istoriki;* "Prikhodskoe dukhovenstvo Rossii," 134–138; Sevastianova, *Russkaia Provintsial'naia Istoriografiia;* Nepomniashchii, *Arsenii Markevich;* Nepomniashchii, *Muzeinoe Delo;* Nepomniashchii, *Zapiski puteshestvennikov;* Nepomniashchii, "Novye Istochniki," 25–28.

9. Smith-Peter, "How to Write a Region," 528–530, and "Bringing the Provinces into Focus," 835–848; Catherine Evtuhov, "Voices from the Regions," 883.

10. LeDonne, "Frontier Governors General," 29; LeDonne, "Building an Infrastructure," 598. On the provincial reforms see Got'e, *Istoriia oblastnogo upravleniia v Rossii.*

11. LeDonne, "Administrative Regionalization," 5–33.

12. Bassin, "Inventing Siberia"; Bassin, *Imperial Visions;* Bassin, "Geographies of Imperial Identity," 46.

13. Remnev, "Siberia and the Russian Far East," 446. On the ideological implications of agricultural colonization see Sunderland, "Empire Without Imperialism?" 101–114.

14. Remnev, "Siberia and the Russian Far East," 427.

15. Evtuhov, *Portrait of a Russian Province.*

16. Baron, "New Spatial Histories," 374. I define place in simplest terms as an area (a relatively small one) on the surface of the Earth that is imbued with meaning by human thought and/or activity. For the geographers and anthropologists responsible for theorizing place, it is a way to refer to location, locale, and various forms of affective attachment and consciousness; to notions of stasis and dwelling; to the site and the consequence of social processes. For excellent introductions to theories of place see Withers, "Place and the 'Spatial Turn'"; Cresswell, *Place: A Short Introduction*. Place is a common analytical framework in urban studies as well. Among the best examples from the field of Eurasian studies are Buckler, *Mapping St. Petersburg* and Paperny, *Kultura dva*.

17. Remnev, "Siberia and the Russian Far East," 437–438.

18. "Protokol otkrytiia Tavricheskoi uchenoi arkhivnoi kommissii v g. Simferopole," 1–2.

19. Among them were the marshal of the nobility, the head of the treasury chamber, the secretary of the statistical committee, the medical inspector, surveyor, the inspector of Tatar schools, an assortment of priests, teachers, nobles, scholars, and representatives of district noble assemblies and town governing boards. The final signature belonged to a newspaper publisher and emerging leader of the Tatar cultural reform movement—a Crimean Tatar named Ismail Bey Gasprinskii (Gasprirali). See "Protokol otkrytiia," 12.

20. By the third installment the bibliography ran to 10,811 items. It was organized into sections covering 1) history, archaeology, numismatics; 2) geography, ethnography, statistics, travel literature; 3) memoirs, biographies, literature; 4) natural sciences, anthropology, medicine; 5) agriculture, industry and trade; 6) zemstvo affairs; 7) education; 8) sectarianism; 9) public life; 10) military and naval affairs; 11) maps, atlases and plans; and 12) periodical literature. See Markevich, *Taurica;* "Opyt ukazateli sochinenii"; and "Opyt ukazatelia knig i statei."

21. De L'Isle, *Malaia Tatariia.*

22. Ascherson, *Black Sea,* 1–3. The *corrente sottano* was identified by a young Italian fisherman in 1680.

23. According to Charles Peysonnel, the formal title of the khan reiterated this claim, extending Giray authority as far as Dagestan. See Peysonnel, *Traité sur le commerce,* vol. 1, 4–5.

24. Only in 1808 did Nikolai Bantysh-Kamenskii, director of the archive of the ministry of foreign affairs, compile the "Register of Crimean affairs from 1474 to 1779," which provided the first systematic scholarly index of the documentary material. The register was published in Simferopol in 1893 by the eminent historian of Crimea, F. Lashkov, who was himself responsible for the publication of a trove of late sixteenth–seventeenth century documents in at least thirteen of the fifty-seven volumes of *ITUAK*. Meanwhile the Imperial Russian Historical Society published documents related to Crimea in their *Digest (SIRIO,* volumes 41 and 95 in particular). See also Broniouij, *Martini Broniouij, de Biezdzfedea, bis in Tartariam nomine Stephani Primi Poloniae Regis legati, Tartariae descriptio.* The Odessa Society published an excerpt—in a fresh translation from the Latin—describing the region around Ochakov ("Opisanie Kryma Martina Bronevskogo," *ZOOID* 6

[1867]: 333–367). Several decades later Ellis Minns in his *Scythians and Greeks* accused Bronovius of cribbing excessively from Strabo.

25. Travelers rarely failed to mention that the tsar rendered tribute to the khan each year until the treaty of Karlowitz in 1799. See for example Thounmann, *Description de la Crimée*, 17.

26. "Sbornik sobytii v Novorossiiskom krae," 297–305. Russia reclaimed control of Azov in 1739.

27. Manstein, *Contemporary Memoirs*, 101–122. Manstein's memoir was first edited and published by David Hume in 1770.

28. "Doklad Imperatritse Ekaterine II po vstuplenii Eia na Prestol," 190–193.

29. "Mery o privedenii v izvestnost' Novorossiiskago i Kavkazskago kraia," 225–229; Shugurov, "Dnevnik puteshestviia," 180–203; "Astronomicheskoe polozhenie gorodov v Krymu," 257–264. Güldenstädt (1745–1781) was born in Riga and studied at the Berlin medical college. The Academy charged him with studying soil, waterways, farming, silk production, and crafts, and he spent time studying oil and mineral deposits in the northeast Caucasus as well as compiling a dictionary of Ossetian and tending to the medical needs of the locals. After an audience with King Irakli in October 1771 he spent two years traveling the Caucasus, in part as a Lezgin captive (Zuev's assistant would die in captivity), before moving on to Cherkassk in July 1773 to begin his study of the Don and Azov coast. See *RBS*, vol. 5: 187–190; and Gnucheva, *Materialy dlia istorii ekspeditsii Akademii Nauk*, 104–106; "Podennaia zapiska puteshestviiu," 182–187; "Topograficheskoe opisanie dostavshimsia po mirnomu traktatu," 166–198; Tott, *Memoirs*; Craven, *Journey Through the Crimea*. For a fantastic trove of official documents see Dubrovin, vols. 1–2; and the microfilmed collection from RGVIA published as the "Potemkin Papers."

30. Eton, *Survey of the Turkish Empire*, 315; Dolgorukii, "Stikhi na Mishenskuiu dolina"; Sarandinaki, "Tavrida"; Pushkin, *Bakchesarian Fountain*; Dickinson, "Russia's First Orient"; Schönle, "Garden"; Zorin, *Kormia dvuglavogo orla*.

31. Bellin, *Le petit atlas maritime*. The map of Crimea appears as No. 126 in volume 4.

32. Druzhinina, *Severnoe Prichernomor'e*; "Gorod Aleshki," 217; Pearson, "Littoral Society," 354; Sosnogorov, *Putevoditel' po Krymu*, 19–20. This is a republication of the 4th edition of the guidebook, published in 1883. The first edition was published in 1871.

33. The sea was dubbed a "maritime desert" because of its lack of islands. On the fascination with its etymology see Smolin, "K voprosu o nazvanii," 90–95. Mentions of illness run rife through archival and published sources: "Dnevnik puteshestviia v iuzhnuiu Rossiiu," 180; numerous reports can be found in the archive of the governor of Nikolaev (DAMO, f. 230). Cholera outbreaks were widely blamed on the consumption of watermelons. Despite John Snow's discovery of the link between contaminated wells and the spread of cholera in London in 1854, it was not until the early twentieth century that the science was well understood by the public.

34. Pallas, *Travels*, 141–145; "Floods in the Crimea."

35. *Spiski naselennykh mest*, vol. 41: v.

36. "Abrikosovoe derevo, posazhennoe Imperatritseiu Ekaterinoiu II," 607–608.

37. Lashkov, "K voprosu o kolichestve naseleniia," 158; *AGM* vol. 3: 212; Kakhovksii, "Kratkoe primechanie," 593–594.

38. The majority of settlers were state peasants, ex-soldiers, Old Believers, and runaway serfs, in addition to Orthodox immigrants from the Ottoman Empire and Poland. Between 1803 and 1806, 362 Mennonite families came from Prussia. They were joined by over 800 Lutheran and Catholic families from Würtemberg, Nassau, Baden, and Bavaria, all administered by a committee on colonial affairs in Odessa. See RGIA f. 1281, op. 11, dela 131, 132, and 133; Florovskii, "Neskol'ko faktov," 33; Lashkov, "K voprosu o kolichestve naseleniia," 169; *Pamiatnaia knizhka Tavricheskoi gubernii na 1914 god,* 29–33.

39. *AGM,* vol. 3: 532–543.

40. Eliseeva, *Geopoliticheskie proekty,* 125.

41. Nolde, *La Formation de l'Empire Russe,* 177; Druzhinina, *Severnoe Prichornomor'e,* 146; Fisher, *Russian Annexation,* 139–150; Fisher, *Between Russians, Ottomans and Turks;* Fisher, "Şahin Giray"; Fisher, *Crimean Tatars;* Andreev, *Istoria Kryma;* Magocsi, *This Blessed Land;* Kozelsky, *Christianizing Crimea.*

42. Gaiman, "Iz Feodosiiskoi stariny," 96–97.

43. *Simferopoliu 200 let,* 37–38; Lebedintsev, "Stoletie tserkovnoi zhizni Kryma," 216–217.

44. *Vysochaishie Reskripty Imperatritsy Ekateriny II,* 1. Muslims made up over 75 percent of the provincial population until the Crimean War.

45. *Bumagi Imperatritsy,* 245; Potemkin, "Rasporiazheniia," 262 (May 16, 1783), 266 (June 14, 1783).

46. *Bumagi Imperatritsy,* 246; Potemkin, "Rasporiazheniia," 262 (July 1, 1783), 264 (May 26, 1783), 265 (May 31, 1783), 272 (July 1, 1783), 287 (October 16, 1783). On treaties and oaths in steppe politics see Khodarkovsky, *Russia's Steppe Frontier,* 46–75; Martin, "Kazakh Oath-Taking," 483–514.

47. RGVIA f. 52, op. 1, d. 295, l. 70; RGVIA f. 52, op. 1, d. 336, ch. 3, l. 74. Lt. General Suvorov and Lt. General Potemkin administered the oath of allegiance to the Nogays and nomadic Tatars on the right bank of the Kuban in late June. Suvorov arranged festivities to accompany the oath-taking, including "abundant fare" and horseback competitions. See Aleksandrov, "Sheikh Imam Mansur," 1; Druzhinina, 95.

48. RGVIA f. 52, op. 1, d. 300, l. 37; RGVIA f. 52, op. 1, d. 295, l. 118 (July 26, 1783); "Ob orderakh kniazia Potemkina i grafa Zubova," *ITUAK* 3 (1897): 25.

Chapter 1. Geographies of Authority

1. Montandon, *Guide,* 102.

2. Eliade, *Myth of the Eternal Return,* 22; Seed, *Ceremonies of Possession,* 2. On the deployment of ritual and ceremony by the Russian state, see Richard Wortman's classic *Scenarios of Power* and Guzel' Ibneeva's excellent *Puteshestviia Ekateriny II: Opyt "osvoeniia" imperskogo prostranstva* (2006).

3. Milner, *Crimea,* 84; Rostovtzeff, *Iranians and Greeks,* 213.

4. Discussed in Panchenko, "Potemkinskie derevni."

5. Druzhinina, *Severnoe Prichernomor'e;* Madariaga, *Russia,* 359–365; Raeff, "In the Imperial Manner," 201–202.

6. In fact, Russians renamed Ak Kaya *Shirinskaia gora* ("mountain of the Şirins") in recognition of the role that clan played in laying plans for many a revolt against the khans. See Potemkin, "Rasporiazheniia," 266; Sumarokov, *Dosugi krymskogo sud'i,* part 2, 71; Telfer, *Crimea and Transcaucasia,* vol. 2, 162–163.

7. Milner, *Crimea,* 248–250; O'Neill, "Ashlama," *Beautiful Spaces,* http://dighist .fas.harvard.edu/projects/beautifulspaces/item/588. The Cossacks did destroy some of the palace's most precious treasures, including the remarkable library founded by Selim Giray I, as well as that of the resident Jesuits. At the approach of the Russian army, the Jesuits hid the texts in a wine cellar, where it was discovered by Cossacks who apparently proceeded to uncork as many bottles as they could lay hands on, drinking much of it and bathing the precious manuscripts in what remained. See Seymour, *Russia on the Black Sea,* 28; Markevich, "K istorii khanskago," 132–133, 136.

8. After his 1818 visit Alexander I had the eagle placed atop a triumphal column erected in Catherine's honor and the crescent returned to its original position. See O'Neill, "Constructing Russian Identity," 186–187.

9. Schnitzler, *Description de la Crimée,* 101; Milner, *Crimea,* 252; Ligne, *Prince de Ligne,* 18; Parkinson, *Tour of Russia,* 193; Gazley, "Reverend Arthur Young," 385; Kohl, *Russia,* 460.

10. In June 1784 Potemkin ordered Governor Igel'strom to use all salvageable building material from Ashlama for the construction of two residences designed "in the Asian manner": one for himself at Akmechet, the other for the governor at Karasubazar. See Seymour, *Russia on the Black Sea,* 35–36; Pallas, *Travels,* vol. 2, 19; Schnitzler, *Description de la Crimée,* 72; Fisher, "Şahin Giray," 344; Potemkin, "Rasporiazheniia," 301–302; *Simferopoliu 200 let,* 23.

11. Gazley, "The Reverend Arthur Young," 385; Pallas, *Travels,* vol. 2, 17. Reginald Heber described Tatar towns as rabbit warrens with well-maintained irrigation systems (Heber, *Life of Reginald Heber,* 268). Jeff Sahadeo describes similar fears about Tashkent in his *Russian Colonial Society in Tashkent* (Bloomington: Indiana University Press, 2007).

12. *Simferopoliu 200 let,* 27, 32, 35; Guthrie, *Tour,* 68; Pallas, *Travels,* vol. 2, 16–18; Heber, *Life of Reginald Heber,* 272; Murzakevich, "Poezdka," 629; *Sto let zhizni Tavridy,* 246. The city population exceeded 9,000 in 1811, but fell to 1,200 in 1814. It then grew to 11,300 in 1825 and 12,891 in 1851. See Schnitzler, *Description de la Crimée,* 93; Polonskaia, "Pervye desiat' let Simferopoliia," *ITUAK* 55 (1918): 135–141.

13. Clarke, 160; Craven, 184; Schnitzler, *Description de la Crimée,* 92–93; RGIA f. 1409, op. 1, d. 2854, ll. 1–2; *Simferopoliu 200 let,* 40–42; M. B. Mikhailova, "Sobornye ploshchadi novykh gorodov iuga Rossii perioda klassitsizma," *Arkhitekturnoe nasledstvo* 36 (1988): 193.

14. Sumarokov, *Dosugi krymskogo sud'i,* part 2, 61–62.

15. There were a total of seventeen governor-generalships all of which, with the sole exception of Moscow, were located in the borderlands. See LeDonne, "Frontier Governors General"; Gryzlova, *Gubernii Rossiiskoi Imperii,* 11–33.

16. Alan Fisher characterizes the khanate as "an oligarchical system which maintained a titular monarch, if not one with absolute authority." See Fisher, *Russian Annexation,* 6–15; İnalcık, "Khan and the Tribal Aristocracy," 445–466; Seidamet, *Crimée,* 17; Kharkhatai, "Istoricheskye sud'by" (1866): 209–214.

17. A council that functioned as the highest court of appeal as well as the forum for determining domestic and foreign policy. It was composed of the *khan agasi* (vizier), *defterdar* (treasurer), *haznedar* (chief accountant), *kapıcı başı* (steward of the household) and *silâhtar* (chief sword bearer), *kadıasker, seraskers* (commanders of the Nogay hordes, usually Giray sultans), and most importantly the *baş karaçi* (head of the bey clans), who was almost always a Şirin.

18. Potemkin, "Rasporiazheniia," 264, 276, 284, 314; Skal'kovskii, "Zaniatie Kryma," 19; Lashkov, "K voprosu o kolichestve," 160; Markevich, "Pereseleniia krymskikh tatar," 387; RGVIA f. 52, op. 1, d. 295, ll. 41 and 98; RGADA f. 1261, op. 1, d. 2789, l. 9. The Şirins enjoyed a series of exclusive privileges such as the right to address the Porte directly, summon the divan without the khan's approval, and marry daughters of the Giray dynasty. Leading members of the clan had actively resisted Russian influence in Crimea for years, culminating in their rebellion against Catherine's chosen khan, Şahin Giray.

19. Fisher, *Crimean Tatars,* 73.

20. Lashkov, "O kameral'nom opisanii," 22–24.

21. Tavrida's mainland was organized into three districts with the creation of Berdiansk in 1842; the peninsula was reorganized with the establishment of Yalta district in 1837. See O'Neill, *Beautiful Spaces.* Maps are located in the "Mappings" section of the site.

22. Taganrog was the first gradonachal'stvo (1802). It was followed by Odessa (1803), Feodosiia, Kerch, and Izmail. Sevastopol became a gradonachal'stvo after the Crimean War, as did Baku, Derbent, Kiiakhta, Rostov, Nikolaev, St. Petersburg, and Moscow.

23. Ziablovskii, *Geografiia,* 36–39; *PSZ I,* vol. 25, no. 18,533 (May 26, 1798): 254–255; *PSZ I,* vol. 25, no. 18,534 (May 26, 1798): 255; *PSZ I,* vol. 30, no. 23,996 (November 20, 1809): 1305–1339.

24. The idea that an individual's worth ought to be measured by the value of his service to sovereign and state rather than (pre)determined by birth or wealth was prevalent in Europe, particularly among practitioners of "enlightened absolutism." See Dickson, "Monarchy and Bureaucracy," *English Historical Review* 110, no. 436 (1995): 323–367.

25. Raeff, "18th-Century Nobility," 770; Marasinova, *Psikhologiia elity,* 77; Givens, "Eighteenth-Century Nobiliary Career Patterns," 106–129.

26. Kakhovskii, "Pis'my pravitelia," 243; *PSZ I,* vol. 22, no. 15,925 (February 8, 1784): 21; *PSZ I,* vol. 22, no. 15,988 (April 24, 1784): 137–138.

27. Lashkov, *Kniaz' Grigorii A. Potemkin-Tavricheskii,* 6; Lashkov "O kameral'nom opisanii," 25–26; RGVIA f. 52, op. 1, d. 336, ch. 12, ll. 48–49; RGVIA f. 52, op. 1, d. 336, ch. 8, l. 12.

28. Nolde, *Formation de l'Empire Russe,* 179.

29. *PSZ I,* vol. 44, *Kniga shtatov,* ch. 2, no. 17,494 (8 August 1796), table VI; Fisher, *Crimean Tatars,* 83.

30. Azamatov, "Russian Administration," 100–101; Crews, "Empire and the Confessional State," 50–83. Igel'strom was assisted in this project by D. V. Mertvago, who would serve as governor of Tavrida from 1803 to 1807.

31. Funding for salaries did not come until Mufti Seit Mehmet Efendi petitioned in 1801. Military Governor Michelsohnen agreed to provide a building in Simferopol but suggested that it be funded by pious endowment rather than the treasury. Nor did he see any need to provide salaries for five chancellery staff who, in his view, would likely "drown in the unfamiliar waters of Russian law." His superiors in St. Petersburg saw things differently. Other than reducing the mufti's salary to 1,000 rubles, they approved Seit Mehmet's request. See *PSZ I,* vol. 23, no. 17,174 (January 23, 1794); RGIA f. 1374, op. 4, d. 231, ll. 8 and 21; Khairedinova, "Vozniknovenie i razvitie," 54–55, 65; Aleksandrov, "O musul'manskom dukhovenstve," 212–214.

32. These numbers are likely an underestimate. See Fisher, *Crimean Tatars,* 77; Kharkhatai, "Istoricheskye sud'by" (1867): 142–143.

33. RGIA f. 1286, op. 1, d. 132, ll. 1–7; Mertvago, *Zapiski,* 197–199. On the similarly contentious kadıasker elections of 1820 and 1830 see O'Neill, "Between Subversion and Submission," 71–72. For examples from Kazan see Azamatov, "Muftis of the Orenburg Spiritual Assembly," 364–365.

34. All matters related to spirituality and ritual observance remained within the sphere of ulema authority. See *PSZ II,* vol. 6, otd. 2, no. 5,033 (December 23, 1831); Aleksandrov, "K istorii uchrezhdeniia," 316–355; Khairedinova, 67–69. The statute was prepared by the Department of Spiritual Affairs for Foreign Faiths, apparently from a compilation of "opinions and plans" submitted over time by provincial officials and most likely by the mufti or other Crimean Muslims. The significance of "foreign faiths" is expertly explained by Paul Werth in *Tsar's Foreign Faiths.*

35. RGIA f. 1286, op. 4, d. 102, l. 35; DAARK f. 27, op. 1, d. 3559, ll. 1–21; *PSZ II,* vol. 9, no. 6,774 (February 2, 1834); Crews, *For Prophet,* 100. Volost' kadıs and others associated with the kadı courts were not included in ulema statistics.

36. Article 81 of the 1831 statute charged the board with keeping metrical records. In November 1832 the Senate applied the terms of an 1828 decree addressed to the Orenburg board in order to reiterate that responsibility. See *PSZ series II,* vol. 7, no. 5,770 (November 24, 1832); RGIA f. 1263, op. 1, d. 787, ll. 159–161.

37. Steinwedel, "Making Social Groups," 68–69.

38. Velychenko, "Identities, Loyalties and Service," 189. The Charter to the Nobility stipulated that all nobles must be entered in the official noble register of the province in which they resided. It also formalized the idea of the nobility as a self-regulating estate and assigned the primary responsibility for compiling and maintaining the register to the assembly under the leadership of an elected marshal.

39. LeDonne, *Ruling Russia,* 57; Fisher, "Enlightened Despotism," 542–553. On the election of marshals see *PSZ I,* vol. 22, no. 16,187 (April 21, 1785).

40. Kakhovskii, "Pis'my pravitelia," 260; RGVIA 52-1-547, svod 232: 139.

41. Korelin, "The Institution of Marshals," 6–8.

42. Korelin, "The Institution of Marshals," 17. Traditionally, the most powerful clans (karaçi clans) were the Şirin, Mansur, Argin, and Sicivut.

43. DAARK f. 327, op. 1, d. 277, l. 16; Korf, *Dvorianstvo,* 210; Marasinova, *Psikhologiia elity,* 66; DAARK f. 49, op. 1, d. 6600, l. 178.

44. *PSZ I,* vol. 27, no. 20,449 (October 8, 1802); Rudnev, "Lichnii sostav," 228–229.

45. RGIA f. 1409, op. 1, d. 165, ll. 1–6.

46. Mikhailovskii-Danilevskii, "Iz vospominanii," part 1, 94; RGIA f. 1409, op. 1, d. 2643, ll. 5–7.

47. *PSZ II,* vol. 4, no. 2,808 (April 6, 1829).

48. *PSZ II,* vol. 4, no. 2,808.

49. DAARK f. 49, op. 1, d. 6600, ll. 195, 222, 241; DAARK f. 49, op. 1, d. 404, l. 43; DAARK f. 49, op. 1, d. 1203, ll. 1–2.

50. *PSZ II,* vol. 6, no. 4,989 (December 6, 1831), especially articles 21–39. The terms of the decree are also reproduced and discussed in Korf, *Dvorianstvo,* 534–588.

51. DAARK f. 49, op. 1, d. 1086, ll. 14–15.

52. DAARK f. 49, op. 1, d. 1086, ll. 18–19, 25; RGIA f. 1263, op. 1, d. 1003, ll. 52–56; DAARK f. 13, op. 1, d. 515, ll. 4–29; *PSZ* series II, vol. 10, no. 8,676 (December 17, 1835).

53. DAARK f. 26, op. 4, d. 928, ll. 5–6.

54. Masaev, *Tavricheskie tatarskie diviziony,* 166–167, 170, 179, 234–235; Menning, "Emergence," 137; Ransel, "Bureaucracy and Patronage," 154–178.

55. Masaev, *Tavricheskie tatarskie diviziony,* 209–210, 215–219.

56. RGADA f. 286, op. 1, kniga 120, d. 30, ll. 338 and 343; *AKTG,* 1785; *AKTG,* 1796.

57. RGVIA f. 52, op. 1, d. 547, svod 232, l. 84; *AKTG,* 1812 through 1820; DAARK f. 49, op. 1, d. 6596, l. 18; DAARK f. 49, op. 1, d. 1975, ll. 1–32; DAARK f. 49, op. 1, d. 1408, ll. 1–10.

58. Guthrie, *Tour,* 222–223; Wortman, *Development of a Russian Legal Consciousness,* 15–16; Wortman, "Russian Monarchy," 150–151.

59. Martin, *Law and Culture,* 34–35; Bartlett, "Russian Nobility," 235; Thaden, *Russia's Western Borderlands,* 123–126, 210–211; Kohut, "Ukrainian Elite," 78–79. See chapter 3 of Kappeler, *Russian Empire,* for an excellent description of Russian policies toward the legal systems of the western provinces. On the notion of "multicentric legal orders" see Benton, *Law and Colonial Cultures,* 11.

60. Fisher, *Russian Annexation,* 13; Smirnov, *Krymskoe Khanstvo,* 310–314; Martin, *Law and Culture,* 58–59; Jersild, 92–97. No one has yet produced a detailed study of the khanate's judicial system, but the recent discovery of kadı court registers in St. Petersburg might make this possible.

61. O'Neill, "Between Subversion and Submission," 84; Crews, "Islamic Law," 468–469. The Ottomans themselves pursued a policy of protecting orthodoxy under Sultan Abdülhamid II (1876–1909). On the documentation of "orthodoxy" elsewhere see Deringil, *Well-Protected Domains,* particularly chapters 2 and 3; and Mani, *Contentious Traditions.*

62. Kutscheroff, "Administration of Justice," 131–136; Pomeranz, "Justice from Underground," 324.

63. RGIA f. 1263, op. 1, d. 1849, ll. 306–313.

64. Ruzhitskaia, "Sudebnoe zakonodatel'stvo Nikolaia I," 45–48.

65. *PSZ II,* vol. 6, no. 4,974 (November 28, 1831). On "the pursuit of justice as a creative process of legal and political contestation, rather than a quest for blind, impartial, and therefore, irreproachable justice" see Ergene, *Local Court, Provincial Society,* 107–108.

66. GARK f. 49, op. 1, d. 1086, ll. 35–82; Kohl, *Russia,* 456.

Chapter 2. Elusive Subjects and the Instability of Noble Society

1. RGVIA f. 52, op. 1, d. 336, ch. 2, ll. 12 and 43; RGVIA f. 52, op. 1, d. 295, l. 127; RGVIA f. 52, op. 1, d. 300, l. 15; RGVIA f. 52, op. 1, d. 336, ch. 2, l. 9; RGVIA f. 52, op. 1/194, d. 336, ch. 3, l. 40; Markevich, "Pereseleniia," 388. It is difficult, if not impossible, to ascertain the actual number of émigrés, as the governor's office records are far from complete. See DAARK f. 799, op. 3, d. 3, ll. 1–21; RGVIA f. 52, op. 1, d. 336, ch. 4, ll. 21–22.

2. Fisher, *Between Russians,* 9; Desaive, "Deux Inventaires," 416; Fisher, "Şahin Giray," 344.

3. RGVIA f. 52, op. 1, d. 336, ch. 8, ll. 24 and 39–40; DAARK f. 799, op. 3, d. 233, l. 55.

4. DAARK f. 799, op. 1, d. 106, l. 1; Kırımlı, *National Movements,* 8.

5. RGVIA f. 52, op. 1, d. 336, ch. 3, ll. 36–37; RGVIA f. 52, op. 1, d. 336, ch. 3, ll. 73–74; RGVIA f. 52, op. 1, d. 336, ch. 4, l. 23; "Pis'my Kakhovskago," 300.

6. DAARK f. 27, op. 1, d. 905: 1–371; DAARK f. 27, op. 1, d. 640, ll. 1–5; Mertvago, *Avtobiograficheskiia zapiski,* 214–219.

7. "Pis'my Kakhovskago," 289; Aleksandrov, "Sheikh Imam Mansur," 26; Bennigsen, "Un Mouvement Populaire au Caucase," 159–205.

8. Krichinskii, *Ocherki russkoi politiki,* 4–5.

9. Krichinskii, *Ocherki russkoi politiki,* 5; "Pis'my Kakhovskago," 289–290.

10. "Pis'my Kakhovskago," 288–289, 293; Krichinskii, *Ocherki russkoi politiki,* 7.

11. "Pis'my Kakhovskago," 288, 294; Lindsay, *Daily Life in the Medieval Islamic World,* 255–256; Kurtiev, *Kalendarnye obriady krymskikh tatar* (Simferopol: Krymuchpedgiz, 1996); Aleksandrov, "Sheikh Imam Mansur," 27; Krichinskii, *Ocherki russkoi politiki,* 7–8.

12. "Pis'my Kakhovskago," 291–294; Krichinskii, *Ocherki russkoi politiki,* 8. For the list of seventy-one exiled mullas see RGVIA f. 52, op. 1/194), d. 500, ll. 18–19.

13. Krichinskii, *Ocherki russkoi politiki,* 9; "Pis'my Kakhovskago," 294.

14. Khodarkovsky, "'Not by Word Alone'": Missionary Policies and Religious Conversion in Early Modern Russia," 267–293; *Bumagi Imperatritsy,* 240; Bronevskii, *Obozrenie iuzhnago berega,* 71; Holderness, *New Russia,* 173, 252–253; Heber, *Life of Reginald Heber,* 275.

15. "Pis'my Kakhovskago," 278. On previous Christian missionary work in Crimea see Veinstein, "Missionnaires Jésuites et Agents Français en Crimée au Début du XVIIIe Siècle," 414–458.

16. Potemkin, "Rasporiazheniia," 318–319; Lebedintsev, "Stoletie tserkovnoi zhizni Kryma," 209–211; Pallas, *Travels,* part 2, 260–261; Sumarokov, *Dosugi krymskogo sud'i,* 159; Skal'kovskii, *Khronologicheskoe obozrenie,* 12–13.

17. Markevich, *K voprosu o polozhenii,* 11–17; DAARK f. 134, op. 1, d. 132, l. 3.

18. RGIA f. 797, op. 3, d. 12,632, l. 3. See also the cases of Seit Samedin (baptized Nikolai) and Bek mulla (Dmitrii) of Kerch-Enikale (1835) in DAARK f. 27, op. 1, d. 3869, ll. 1–8.

19. RGIA f. 797, op. 3, d. 12,632 ll. 1–5.

20. Markevich, *K voprosu o polozhenii,* 18–19.

21. DAARK f. 799, op. 1, d. 456, ll. 1–3.

22. RGIA f. 797, op. 2, d. 8142, ll. 10–11. Clement Augustus Gregory Peter Louis, Baron de Bode, traveled extensively through Central Asia and Persia.

23. Kırımlı, "Crimean Tatars, Nogays, and Scottish Missionaries," 67–81; DAARK f. 49, op. 1, d. 5640, ll. 1–73; Turhan, "XIX Yüzyılda Kırım," 932–936. The Russian Bible Society (originally the St. Petersburg Bible Society, founded in 1809) established 196 branches and produced copies of the Gospel in Russian, Kalmyk, Armenian, Finnish, Persian, Georgian, ancient and modern Greek, Tatar, Turkish, Chuvash, and other languages by 1821. See Tompkins, "Russian Bible Society," 251–268.

24. RGIA f. 1409, op. 1, d. 2667, ll. 155 and 162; Mikhailovskii-Danilevskii, "Iz vospominanii" [July], 97.

25. RGIA f. 1409, op. 1, d. 2667, ll. 2–3 and 143; Kırımlı, 87–95. On the missionary work of Anna Sergeevna Golitsyna, the daughter of Lieutenant General S. V. Vsevolozhskii and wife of Prince Ivan Aleksandrovich Golitsyn, on her estate of Koreiz, see Bragina and Vasil'eva, *Khoziaeva i gosti,* 88–90.

26. Holderness, *New Russia,* 128.

27. RGIA f. 1343, op. 51, d. 487, ll. 10–11; "O prosheniiakh deputatov," 12; RGIA f. 1374, op. 4, d. 231, ll. 14 and 32; Muftizade, "Ocherk voennoi sluzhby," 10; DAARK f. 49, op. 1, d. 2438, ll. 45–52.

28. Bennett, 173 and 185; Muftizade, "Ocherk voennoi sluzhby," 13–14. The inscription referred to God, not the tsar, though the meaning remains the same.

29. "Pis'my Kakhovskago," 282 (emphasis mine). Kantakuzin did remain a Muslim.

30. *PSZ I,* vol. 20, no. 14,816 (November 25, 1778); *PSZ I,* vol. 22, no. 16,187 (April 21, 1785), articles 76–82. On emancipation see Jones, *The Emancipation of the Russian Nobility* and Faizova, *"Manifest o volnosti" i sluzhba dvorianstva v XVIII stoletii.* Among the classic works on the dvorianstvo are M. T. Iablochkov, *Istoriia dvorianskago sosloviia v Rossii* (St. Petersburg, 1876); Baron S. A. Korf, *Dvorianstvo i ego soslovnoe upravlenie za stoletie 1762–1855 godov* (St. Petersburg: Tip. Trenke i Fiusno, 1906) and A. Romanovich-Slavatinskii, *Dvorianstvo v Rossii ot nachala XVIII veka do otmeny krepostnago prava* (The Hague: Mouton, 1968). Marc Raeff's review article describes recent work in this vein: Raeff, "The 18th-Century Nobility and the Search for a New Political Culture in Russia," *Kritika* 1, no. 4 (2000): 769–782.

31. *PSZ I,* vol. 22, no. 16,187 (April 21, 1785): 344–384 (articles 76–82).

32. *PSZ I,* vol. 22, no. 15,708 (April 8, 1783); *PSZ I,* vol. 21, no. 15,798 (July 28, 1783): 985–986; *PSZ I,* vol. 21, no. 15,861 (November 1, 1783): 1030–1031.

33. Skal'kovskii, *Opyt statisticheskago opisaniia,* 304; "Istoricheskaia spravka ob obrazovanii," ch. 3: 41–43; İnalcık, "Khan and the Tribal Aristocracy," 447; Manz, "Clans of the Crimean Khanate," 284; Fisher, *Russian Annexation,* 3.

34. *PSZ I,* vol. 22, no. 15,936 (February 22, 1784): 51–52.

35. Potemkin, "Rasporiazheniia," 304; Madariaga, *Russia,* 310–312; Kohut, *Russian Centralism and Ukrainian Autonomy,* 238–245; Kohut, "The Ukrainian Elite," 65–97.

36. Potemkin, "Rasporiazheniia," 238, 304; Lashkov, "Statisticheskiia svedeniia," 93; Lashkov, *G. A. Potemkin,* 6; RGVIA f. 52, op. 1, d. 332, ch. 1, ll. 150–158; Iablochkov, *Istoriia dvorianskago sosloviia,* 517; Zubov, "Ordera," 29. For details on the compilation of the early lists and on the ennoblement process in Tavrida see O'Neill, "Between Subversion and Submission," chapter 4.

37. RGIA f. 1343, op. 57, d. 146, l. 36; Iablochkov, *Istoriia dvorianskago sosloviia,* 583–585.

38. "O prosheniiakh deputatov," 10–11.

39. "O prosheniiakh deputatov," 10–11, 16–17; DAARK f. 799, op. 1, d. 445, l. 3; *AGM,* vol. 3, 519; RGIA f. 1374, op. 4, d. 231, l. 9.

40. Savitskii, *Vedenie dvorianskoi rodoslovnoi knigi,* 24–25; DAARK f. 327, op. 1, d. 36, ll. 1–2.

41. Lashkov, "Arkhivnyia dannyia," 96–110; Lashkov, "Istoricheskii ocherk," part 1, 69–70.

42. DAARK f. 49, op. 1, d. 5, ll. 8–9.

43. Figueirôa-Rêgo, "Family genealogical records," 2–3; Confino, "À propos de la Notion de Service," 48; DeWeese, "Politics of Sacred Lineages," 507–530.

44. Fedorchenko, *Dvorianskie rody,* 254–255, 429–430; Baskakov, *Russkie familii,* 79–80, 235–236; Lashkov, "Sbornik dokumentov," part 2, 123–126.

45. DAARK f. 49, op. 1, d. 359, ll. 1–5.

46. DAARK f. 49, op. 1, d. 698, ll. 1–11; RGIA f. 1341, op. 7, d. 695, l. 101.

47. RGIA f. 1341, op. 7, d. 695, ll. 71–72.

48. RGIA f. 1341, op. 7, d. 695, ll. 46–48; RGADA f. 286, op. 2, d. 120, ll. 230–253.

49. DAARK f. 49, op. 1, d. 206, ll. 13–15; DAARK f. 49, op. 1, d. 444, ll. 8–9; RGIA f. 1343, op. 57, d. 146, ll. 2–5; DAARK f. 27, op. 1, d. 1550, l. 6. Based on Notara's report that Crimean Greeks were purchasing documents attesting to noble status from the patriarch, the Senate required them to submit proof of service to the tsar and an oath of loyalty—more stringent criteria than those applied to the Tatars.

50. RGIA f. 1343, op. 57, d. 146, ll. 2–5; Cazac, "Familles de la Noblesse Roumaine," 211–226; DAARK f. 49, op. 1, d. 607, l. 32; DAARK f. 49, op. 1, d. 1409, ll. 9–10; DAARK f. 49, op. 1, d. 1975, ll. 7–18 and 29–32.

51. DAARK 49-1-607: 141–156; DAARK 49-1-6610: 97.

52. For biographical sketches of the forty Tatar nobles see O'Neill, "Mirza Sketches," *Beautiful Spaces,* http://dighist.fas.harvard.edu/projects/beautifulspaces/collections/show/4.

53. RGIA f. 1343, op. 57, d. 146, l. 1; RGIA f. 1343, op. 57, d. 64, ll. 157–164.

54. Riasanovsky, *Nicholas I*, 101. For the classic interpretation of "Official Nationality" see pages 73–183.

55. Quoted in Lincoln, *Nicholas I*, 122.

56. GARF f. 109, op. 61, d. 145, ll. 2–7.

57. DAARK f. 26, op. 4, d. 386, ll. 13–22; DAARK f. 26, op. 4, d. 414, ll. 5–6.

58. Savitskii, *Vedenie dvorianskoi rodoslovnoi knigi*, 26; Iablochkov, *Istoriia dvorianskago sosloviia*, 618.

59. DAARK f. 49, op. 1, d. 6620, ll. 1–24; DAARK f. 49, op. 1, d. 6621, ll. 1–15; DAARK f. 49, op. 1, d. 6626, ll. 1–36; Solov'ev, *Russkoe dvorianstvo*, 120–121; Dvoenosovoa, *Dvorianskaia rodoslovnaia kniga*, 50. The assembly had approved far more than two hundred cases, but the resources of the commission were limited.

60. *PSZ II*, vol. 15, no. 13,304 (March 27, 1840); DAARK f. 49, op. 1, d. 1617, ll. 1–5.

61. DAARK f. 49, op. 1, d. 1078, l. 33; DAARK f. 49, op. 1, d. 1591, ll. 20–21; DAARK f. 49, op. 1, d. 2161, ll. 1–2, 37–40 and 132.

62. Iablochkov, *Istoriia dvorianskago sosloviia*, 617–618; Kappeler, *Russian Empire*, 176–177.

63. On Orenburg's Muslim elite see RGIA f. 1343, op. 57, d. 206, ll. 1–21; RGIA f. 1343, op. 57, d. 213, ll. 1–10 and 23. On Lithuanian Tatars, see RGIA f. 1343, op. 57, d. 224, ll. 1–10.

64. DAARK f. 49, op. 1, d. 1014, ll. 1–30.

65. RGIA f. 994, op. 2, d. 473, l. 8. The language of testimonies to "noble" behavior is maddeningly formulaic, but once in a while a petition contains a refreshing variation, such as the Simferopol marshal's testimony regarding Ibrahim Mirza Machin: "He behaves well," swore Kachioni, "and in accordance with his status. He entertains no Masonic lies." See DAARK f. 49, op. 1, d. 389, l. 39.

66. Zhur'iari, "Poezdka," 108–111; Dombrovskii, "Istoriko-statisticheskii ocherk," 198; Bodaninskii, "Tatarskie 'Durbe' mavzolei," 199–200; O'Neill, "Decoding the Khan's Tomb," *Beautiful Spaces*, http://dighist.fas.harvard.edu/projects/beautifulspaces/neatline/show/tomb-of-mengli-giray.

67. The literature on provincial estates is voluminous. For a start, see Lovell, "Between Arcadia and Suburbia," 66–87; Roosevelt, "Tatiana's Garden," 335–349.

68. O'Neill, "Constructing Russian Identity in the Imperial Borderland: Architecture, Islam, and the Transformation of the Crimean Landscape," *Ab Imperio* 2 (2006): 163–192.

69. Ligne, *Prince de Ligne*, 27 and 36.

70. Vorontsov purchased land during this period from 226 individuals, spending the equivalent of over 37,000 silver rubles in the process. Edward Blore, an English architect, designed the palace. See Craven, *Journey*, especially her letters dated April 8 and 12, 1786; Markov, *Ocherki Kryma*, 25; Vorontsov, *Zapiski Gubernatora*, 177; Bragina and Vasil'eva, *Khoziaeva i gosti*, 110–118, 122.

71. Vorontsov, *Zapiski Gubernatora*, 177; Bragina and Vasil'eva, *Khoziaeva i gosti*, 110–118, 122, 126–127. On the use of architecture elsewhere see Morris, *Stones of Empire*, and Watenpaugh, *Image of an Ottoman City*.

72. DAARK f. 26, op. 4, d. 1396, ll. 1–13.

73. Wirtschafter, *From Serf to Russian Soldier*, 73; LeDonne, *Ruling Russia*, 341–342.

Chapter 3. Military Service and Social Mobility

1. N. Zakrevskii, "Sevastopol' 1831 god," *Morskoi Sbornik* 1862, no. 3: 56–61.

2. John Keep, Richard Hellie, Josh Sanborn, Elise Kimerling Wirtschafter, David Schimmelpennick van der Oye, and Bruce Menning have all made important English-language contributions to the field of military history. See also Eric Lohr and Marshall Poe's introductory essay in *Military and Society in Russia, 1450–1917*, edited by Eric Lohr and Marshall Poe, and the volume edited by Frederick W. Kagan and Robin Higham, *Military History of Tsarist Russia*, particularly Bruce W. Menning's chapter, "The Imperial Russian Army, 1725–1796." For an excellent introduction to modern work on Russian military history see the essays in *Reforming the Tsar's Army*, especially David M. McDonald's concluding essay, "The Military and Imperial Russian History."

3. Most soldiers served for twenty-five years (until 1793 they had served for life), although after 1834 indefinite leave could be granted to those who had served for twenty years and maintained an unblemished record.

4. Kappeler, *Russian Empire*, 129; von Hagen, "Limits of Reform," 34.

5. Menning, "Emergence," 130–161.

6. Baumann, "Subject Nationalities," 490.

7. Bagalei, "Kolonizatsiia Novorossiiskago kraia," 440–441.

8. Becattini, *Storia della Crimea*, 27; Thounmann, *Description de la Crimée*, 18, 21.

9. Seidamet, *La Crimée*, 17–18; Thounmann, *Description de la Crimée*, 22; Davies, "Foundations of Muscovite Military Power," 21.

10. Fisher, *Between Russians*, 24–25; Fisher, *Crimean Tatars*, 23; Fisher, "Şahin Giray," 350–351; Manz, "Clans of the Crimean Khanate," 294–295.

11. Fisher, "Şahin Giray," 360–361; Fisher, *Russian Annexation*, 120–127; RGVIA f. 52, op. 1, d. 295, ll. 5–8.

12. Menning, "Emergence," 135; Madariaga, *Russia*, 312.

13. Monetary payments could substitute for recruits on small estates and in other circumstances where poverty or low population density transformed recruitment into an institution of economic ruin. In part for this reason, non-Russian communities located within one hundred versts of the border from the Black Sea to the Baltic paid a monetary sum in place of each recruit from 1801 onward. Exemptions were also granted to some poll-tax payers, such as artisans in the Baltics and Finland, because of their economic value. See Beskrovny, *Russian Army*, 44–52; Kappeler, *Russian Empire*, 75–101; Wirtschafter, *From Serf to Russian Soldier*, 11–12; *PSZ II*, vol. 6, no. 4,677 (June 28, 1831).

14. Keep, *Soldiers of the Tsar*, 148 and 181; Fisher, "Şahin Giray," 341–364.

15. *PSZ I*, vol. 43, no. 15,945 (March 1, 1784).

16. *Bumagi Imperatritsy Ekateriny,* 300; Keep, *Soldiers of the Tsar,* 181–182.

17. RGVIA f. 52, op. 1, d. 336, ll. 17–18; Muftizade, "Ocherk voennoi sluzhby," 3.

18. RGVIA f. 52, op. 1, d. 332, ll. 179–180.

19. Masaev, *Tavricheskie tatarskie diviziony,* 6–7. All subsequent references to this source are to published documents from DAARK fond 799.

20. Masaev, *Tavricheskie tatarskie diviziony,* 29–30.

21. DAARK f. 49, op. 1, d. 5, ll. 6–8.

22. The land captains of the four Crimean districts received orders to maintain a close watch over the dismissed soldiers in order to discourage their participation in any criminal activity or "mischief" (*shalost*') in their villages. Masaev, *Tavricheskie tatarskie diviziony,* 108–115, 141–144.

23. There were captains with this name from the Şirin and Zuisk clans, but no surname is mentioned in any of the documents utilized here.

24. Masaev, *Tavricheskie tatarskie diviziony,* 262–263. On the Lithuanian Tatar light horse regiment see Vladimir Lapin, "Armiia imperii—imperiia v armii: organizatsiia i komplektovanie vooruzhennykh sil Rossii v XVI–nachale XX vv.," *Ab Imperio* 4 (2001): 117.

25. "Pis'ma Kakhovskago," 414.

26. Masaev, *Tavricheskie tatarskie diviziony,* 268–274, 297–301, 256–257. The repatriation of beşlis continued into 1794. When the four divisions that had remained loyal returned to Tavrida in early 1792, Catherine dissolved the regiment, maintaining two squadrons until March 29, 1796.

27. The clan connections of the other eleven could not be established with any certainty.

28. In October 1802, the Nogays were assigned the same status as Cossacks: freed from taxes but required to perform military service. Two Nogay horse regiments (each with five "hundreds") existed until May 13, 1805. See Galushko, *Kazach'i Voiska Rossii,* 16; and the relevant entries in the noble registers for 1833 and 1835 (RGIA f. 1343, op. 51, d. 486; RGIA f. 1343, op. 51, d. 489).

29. *PSZ I,* vol. 29, no. 22,374 (November 30, 1806); Markevich, "K stoletiiu otechestvennoi voiny," 10; "Notices," *TGV* 1851, no. 32–33; Mertvago, *Avtobiograficheskiia zapiski,* 199–200.

30. Markevich, "K stoletiiu otechestvennoi voiny," 5–9.

31. Markevich, "K stoletiiu otechestvennoi voiny," 19–25.

32. Markevich, "K stoletiiu otechestvennoi voiny," 10; *Le duc de Richelieu,* 242–243, 252; Gabaev, "Zakonodatel'nye akty," 145–146.

33. Mertvago, *Avtobiograficheskiia zapiski,* 200–201.

34. *Le duc de Richelieu,* 243; Markevich, "K stoletiiu otechestvennoi voiny," 11; Mertvago, *Avtobiograficheskiia zapiski,* 201.

35. Khodarkovsky, *Russia's Steppe Frontier,* 56–60.

36. Markevich, "K stoletiiu otechestvennoi voiny," 11–13.

37. Mertvago, *Avtobiograficheskiia zapiski,* 202–203; DAARK f. 49, op. 1, d. 237, ll. 1–3; *PSZ I,* vol. 30, no. 22,772 (January 24, 1808).

38. Gabaev, "Zakonodatel'nye akty," 127, 147–148; Iuritsyn, *Krymskii Konnyi,* 18; Markevich, "K stoletiiu," 33–34.

39. Masaev, "Krymskie tatary," chapter 3, part 3, 2–3, 7; Iuritsyn, *Krymskii Konnyi*, 19–20; Mikaberidze, *Russian Officer Corps*, lv–lvi.

40. Skal'kovskii, *Khronologicheskoe*, 205–206.

41. Iuritsyn, *Krymskii Konnyi*, 20–21; RGIA f. 1281, op. 11, d. 132, l. 106.

42. Bronevskii, *Obozrenie iuzhnago berega*, 113; Markevich, "K stoletiiu otechestvennoi voiny"; Muftizade, "Ocherk voennoi sluzhby," 13–14; Iuritsyn, *Krymskii Konnyi*, 21.

43. DAARK f. 49, op. 1, d. 607, ll. 5–6; Bezotosnyi, "Rossiiskii Titulovannyi Generalitet," *Otechestvennaia Istoriia* 2 (1998): 183. The generalitet consisted of the top four civil and military ranks.

44. *PSZ I,* vol. 34, no. 26,836 (May 7, 1817); Iuritsyn, *Krymskii Konnyi*, 21.

45. RGIA f. 1409, op. 1, d. 3041, ll. 2–3.

46. *PSZ II,* vol. 2, no. 1258 (July 20, 1827); Iuritsyn, *Krymskii Konnyi*, 22.

47. Iuritsyn, *Krymskii Konnyi*, 22–23.

48. Bitis, "Russian Army's Use," 546; Bitis, "Reserves Under Serfdom?" 191.

49. Masaev, "Krymskie tatary," chapter 4, part 2, page 3.

50. Masaev, "Krymskie tatary," chapter 4, part 2, 5.

51. *PSZ II,* vol. 6, no. 4,677 (June 28, 1831); DAARK f. 327, op. 1, d. 264, ll. 1–4; DAARK f. 327, op. 1, d. 280, ll. 1–6.

52. This komanda existed until 1890. For a discussion of the Crimean Tatars' aid to the Ottomans, see Williams, "*Hijra*," 79–108; Karpat, "Crimean Emigration," 275–306.

53. Gabaev, "Zakonodatel'nye akty," 140, 151–152; Beskrovny, 18.

54. GARF f. 109, op. 61, d. 145, ll. 10–13; DAARK f. 49, op. 1, d. 1174, ll. 1–2.

55. Druzhinina, *Severnoe Prichernomor'e*, 133, 185–193; RGIA f. 1281, op. 11, d. 132, ll. 54–64; Bolotina, "Glavnaia krepost'," 201–213.

56. Menning, "Emergence," 147.

57. Menning, "Emergence," 156.

58. DAARK f. 49, op. 1, d. 6493, ll. 1–8; DAARK f. 49, op. 1, d. 206.

59. DAARK f. 49, op. 1, d. 6546, ll. 1–50.

60. DAARK f. 49, op. 1, d. 504, ll. 1–4; DAARK f. 49, op. 1, d. 6561; DAARK f. 49, op. 1, d. 480, ll. 605, 749, 820, 989; DAARK f. 49, op. 1, d. 6597, ll. 100.

61. RGADA f. 286, op. 1, d. 120, ch. 30, ll. 341–342; RGIA f. 1343, op. 51, d. 488; RGIA f. 1343, op. 1, d. 488, ll. 28–30.

62. RGIA f. 1343, op. 51, d. 490, ll. 44–46; DAARK f. 49, op. 1, d. 607, ll. 21–22.

63. DAARK f. 49, op. 1, d. 6596, l. 18; RGIA f. 1343, op. 51, d. 486, ll. 50–51; RGIA f. 1343, op. 51, d. 488, ll. 12–14; DAARK f. 49, op. 1, d. 1408, ll. 1–11; DAARK f. 49, op. 1, d. 1975, ll. 1–52; DAARK f. 49, op. 1, d. 5539, ll. 1–25.

64. The Imperial Heraldry confirmed Kaya Bey's noble status in 1854. See DAARK f. 49, op. 1, d. 607, ll. 5–6; DAARK f. 49, op. 1, d. 6559, l. 37.

65. The Greek Cadet Corps was established in 1774 and renamed the Corps of Foreign Fellow Believers (*Korpus Chuzhesterannikh Edinoverstev*) a year later. It was initially set up to train a group of fifty Greek youths recruited to the Russian navy during the war of 1768–1774. Between 1774 and its dissolution in 1796 the corps trained 200 officers and was, according to Mikaberidze, "an effective train-

ing ground for offspring of petty Greek nobility, who entered the Russian service and achieved high positions in society" (xxv).

66. Mikaberidze, 341–343; RGVIA f. 228, op. 1, d. 54, l. 1.

67. Potemkin, "Rasporiazheniia," 315; Lashkov, "Vedomost' o vsekh seleniiakh," 137–154; RGVIA f. 228, op. 1, d. 54, l. 1; RGIA f. 1343, op. 51, d. 487, ll. 10–11; "Rudzevich," ESBE vol. 27 (1899), 211; "Rudzevich," RBS, vol. 25 (1918), 407–414.

Chapter 4. The New Domain

1. Kivelson, Cartographies, 9. As Kivelson and David Moon point out, too little work has been done on the meaning and role of the land or the natural world more broadly. The environmental turn has begun to move the field in that direction however. For discussions of the emerging field see Moon, Plough that Broke the Steppes: 13–16; Bruno, "Russian Environmental History."

2. For a discussion of the spread of cadastral mapping see Kain and Baigent, Cadastral Map.

3. Aleksei Karimov's groundbreaking work on the Russian cadaster was interrupted by his untimely death. His Dokuda topor i sokha khodili nevertheless remains invaluable. On survey work up to the Catherinian period see Malinovskii, Istoricheskii vzgliad na mezhevanie, and the classic work of German, Istoriia russkogo mezhevaniia.

4. For an excellent analysis of the logic of settlement see Sunderland, Taming the Wild Field.

5. Moon, "Russian Academy of Sciences Expeditions," 204–236; Gnucheva (sost.), Materialy dlia istorii ekspeditsii.

6. Gablits, Fizicheskoe opisanie Tavricheskoi oblasti. Within three years it was translated into French and German, and republished in abbreviated form in 1795. In his study of the cultural appropriation of Crimea, Andreas Schönle argues that this strategy enabled Gablits to transform Crimea "into a kind of palimpsest, in which the physical geography of the area lets other landscapes shine through." See Schönle, "Garden of the Empire," 7.

7. Grant, Historical Sketch, 7; Levashev, Kartina ili opisanie, 165; Pleshcheev, Obozrenie Rossiiskoi Imperii, 168. Pleshcheev (1752–1802) surveyed the Dardanelles and northern coast of Anatolia. He lifted the quote directly from page 8 of Gablits's Fizicheskoe Opisanie.

8. Gablits, Fizicheskoe opisanie, 9–12.

9. Sumarokov, Dosugi krymskogo sud'i, part 1, 180; Craven, Journey Through the Crimea, 218.

10. Thunmann, Description de la Crimée, 18; Skal'kovskii, "Zaniatie Kryma," 15; Lashkov, "Istoricheskii ocherk," part 1, 39–41; Sekirinskii, "Agrarnyi stroi," 140–149.

11. On the history of dachas in the more familiar late-imperial and Soviet sense see Lovell, Summerfolk.

12. PSZ I, vol. 16, no. 12,099 (March 22, 1764): 663–665. For the dominant Soviet-era analysis see Druzhinina, Severnoe Prichernomor'e: 53–69.

13. Lashkov, "Istoricheskii ocherk," part 3: 59–60; Lashkov, "Sbornik dokumentov," part 4: 145–158 ("vedomost' Akmechetskago uezda otmezhevannym i prektam naznachennym dacham kazennym i pomeshchich'im s pokazaniem chisla dush i desiatina zemli"). The register was completed during the period when all of Crimea was a single district within Novorossiia. The data on land types is drawn from Verner, *Pamiatnaia knizhka*, otdel 3, glava 1: 3.

14. Fisher, *Crimean Tatars*, 79. For the dacha registers see Lashkov, "Istoricheskii ocherk," part 3: 58–59.

15. RGIA f. 1307, op. 1, d. 9, l. 2; Mertvago, *Avtobiograficheskiia zapiski*, 181.

16. Lashkov, "Istoricheskii ocherk," part 3: 60–61.

17. *PSZ I*, vol. 22, no. 17,265 (November 9, 1794).

18. RGIA f. 1343, op. 57, d. 146, l. 36; *PSZ I*, vol. 22, no. 17,265 (November 9, 1794).

19. Lashkov, "Sbornik dokumentov," part 4: 134–135.

20. DAARK f. 799, op. 1, d. 445, ll. 3, 27; Lashkov, "Istoricheskii ocherk," part 3: 64; "O prosheniiakh deputatov," 16–17; RGIA f. 1374, op. 4, d. 231, l. 9. The commission, which was to be staffed by a surveyor, an assessor from the civil chamber, and two deputies from the higher land court, did not convene before Catherine's death on November 6.

21. Ligne, *Prince de Ligne*, 28. Tatars themselves were not "parceled out." The annexation manifesto decreed that they could not be enserfed or enslaved.

22. Mertvago, *Avtobiograficheskiia zapiski*, 182; *PSZ I*, vol. 24, no. 17,630 (December 10, 1796); DAARK f. 24, op. 1, d. 638, ll. 1–4; *AGM*, vol. 3: 520–523; Lashkov, "Sbornik dokumentov," part 5: 115–120. Kakhovskii received seventy-three complaints before the commission was established. By 1802 there were 607 complaints on the table.

23. *AGM*, vol. 3: 520–523; Lashkov, "Sbornik dokumentov," part 4: 122.

24. The Ottoman/Crimean version of freehold, *mülk*, was not terribly widespread. Such property could be bought, sold, or bequeathed and was exempt from most (if not all) taxes. The khan's holdings, or *miri*, included *mevat* (empty, unsettled lands which could be distributed as *timar*) as well as the salt lakes and forests and personal lands of the Giray clan. *Metruke* (lands reserved for common use according to Islamic law) and *waqf* (pious endowments) were widespread. The influence of Islamic law on the Crimean land regime dates to 1475, when the khanate became a vassal state of the Ottoman Empire. See Lashkov, "Istoricheskii ocherk," part 1: 35–81; Lashkov, "Sbornik dokumentov," part 4: 124–130.

25. İnalcık, *Ottoman Empire*, 107–110; İnalcık and Quataert, eds., *Economic and Social History*, 114–116.

26. Beyliks were hereditary within each clan, but were passed down from clan elder to clan elder rather than from father to son. See Lashkov, "Istoricheskii ocherk," part 2: 79–89.

27. Lashkov, "Istoricheskii ocherk," part 2: 99–115.

28. In comparison with the Russian government's encounter with the "Islamic model" of landholding in Central Asia in the second half of the nineteenth century, officials in late eighteenth-century Tavrida were operating in a remarkably information-scarce environment. See Pravilova, "Property of Empire."

29. Lashkov, "Istoricheskii ocherk," part 3: 68–69. Taranov (1759–1819) was the son of a poor noble from Kharkov. He earned the rank of lieutenant before retiring from military service in 1779. Beginning in 1784 he held a variety of appointed and elected posts in Tavrida, including provincial procurator and marshal of the nobility, and accumulated property valued at 150,000 rubles. His main estate and residence was at Bazarchik (near Simferopol), where he was buried in his English garden (*RBS*, vol. 20, 800).

30. *AGM*, vol. 3: 196–207.

31. RGIA f. 1307, op. 1, d. 4, ll. 26–27.

32. Michelsohnen also suggested that the land commission be abolished because it consisted of men who were themselves involved in land disputes and could therefore not be expected to come to objective opinions. See RGIA f. 1307, op. 1, d. 8, ll. 1–4; Bragina and Vasil'eva, *Puteshestvie*, 155–158.

33. In addition to Lopukhin, State Councilor Pavel Sumarokov, and three other appointed officials, the commission included two elected deputies each from among the landowners, mirzas, and Tatar peasants, plus three surveyors, a secretary, and two clerks from the Senate Chancellery. See *PSZ I*, vol. 27, no. 20,270 (May 19, 1802) and no. 20,276 (May 19, 1802); DAARK f. 24, op. 1, d. 638, l. 7.

34. *Arkhiv Gosudarstvennago Soveta*, vol. 3: 843.

35. RGIA f. 1409, op. 1, d. 2563, ll. 11, 140b-160b, and 200b.

36. DAARK f. 9, op. 1, d. 38, l. 21.

37. O'Neill, "Between Subversion and Submission," chapter 5; DAARK f. 24, op. 1, d. 459, ll. 1–11.

38. DAARK f. 24, op. 1, d. 638, ll. 15–20; RGIA f. 1305, op. 1, d. 3, ll. 1–20b; RGIA f. 1305, op. 1, d. 14, ll. 32–330b and 42–430b.

39. *PSZ I*, vol. 31, no. 24,349 (September 13, 1810); DAARK f. 24, op. 1, d. 638, l. 22. Destroying documents was among the most effective ways of nullifying a rival's claim. For example, a Tatar named Devlet Mirza destroyed firmans and commandeered Russian survey documents produced for the village of Usein Adzhi in order to squelch the claims of villagers—claims that had been upheld by the land commission. See RGIA f. 1409, op. 1, d. 2563, ll. 290b-30.

40. Shaw, "Mapmaking, Science and State Building," 409–429; Bagrow, *History of Russian cartography*; *PSZ I*, vol. 8, no. 5,793 (June 28, 1731); vol. 12, no. 9,361 (December 17, 1746); vol. 14, no. 10,352 (February 5, 1755); vol. 17, no. 12,474 (September 19, 1765).

41. Milov, *Issledovanie*, 16–21.

42. Ivanov, *Opyt istoricheskago izsledovaniia;* Wolfart, "Mapping the Early Modern State"; Home, "Scientific Survey and Land Settlement."

43. For a series of examples, see Dontsov, *Kartografirovanie zemel'*, 42–54. For the survey instructions see *PSZ I*, vol. 17, no. 12,659 (May 25, 1766); *PSZ I*, vol. 17, no. 12,474 (see the second "general rule"); Madariaga, *Russia*, 109–110.

44. Lashkov, "Istoricheskii ocherk," part 2: 111; Kharkhatai, "Istoricheskye sud'by," part 1: 214; Lashkov, "Sbornik dokumentov," part 3: 118–120; DAARK f. 24, op. 1, d. 457, ll. 69–70.

45. The grant added, because of Ibrahim's loyal service, lands south of a well-known tomb (*khan-kurgan*) up to the "big mountain" at the village of Iashlav. Lashkov, "Sbornik dokumentov," part 1: 85.

46. Lashkov, "Sbornik dokumentov," part 3: 100–107; RGIA f. 1341, op. 7, d. 695, ll. 46–55; RGADA f. 286, op. 2, d. 120, ch. 20, ll. 247–253.

47. Individual wills confirm that properties were cataloged according to both location and type, with the testators owning an average of over twenty-eight separate properties.

48. For examples see "O prosheniiakh deputatov": 13–15.

49. RGIA f. 1409, op. 1, d. 2563, ll. 21–22 and 23–230b.

50. Lashkov, "Sbornik dokumentov," part 4: 145–158.

51. The numbers include both instances in which an individual was the only one who owned land in a given location, and instances in which multiple individuals (and often Tatar peasant communities) owned land in a given location. Tatar peasants owned land in 584 (48 percent) of the villages listed on the registers: 357 were owned by some combination of Tatar and settler elites; fifty-two were owned by the state; the status of 214 was unknown; three villages were listed as waqf.

52. Lashkov, "Sbornik dokumentov," part 5: 84–154. This data is from a collection of four registers—one for each peninsular district—of settled places, compiled in 1805. The registers were prepared in order to facilitate the work of the land commission and are organized by volost'. They name each village and describe residents by ethnicity, number of households, male and female residents. The register lists the name and rank of all individuals and/or peasant communities who own land in the village.

53. By way of comparison, in Ufa province in 1795 there were 933 dachas, only 28 (3 percent) of which belonged to Muslims. See Lashkov, "Sbornik dokumentov," part 4: 145–158; Ivanov, *Opyt istoricheskago izsledovaniia*, 86–87; Gabdullin, *Ot sluzhilykh tatar k tatarskomu dvorianstvu*, 83.

54. RGIA f. 1350, op. 56, d. 406 [map].

55. *AGM*, vol. 3: 197, 209–212 and 520–523. For the Plan for the Distribution in New Russia Province of State Lands Towards Its Settlement, March 22, 1764, according to which indivisible and hereditary parcels ranging from 26 to 30 desiatinas were to be given to anyone who agreed to become a military settler, see Druzhinina, *Severnoe Prichernomor'e*, 59.

56. Lashkov, "Istoricheskii ocherk," part 3: 54–57; Bodarskii, *Naselenie Kryma*, 89.

57. Mertvago, *Avtobiograficheskiia zapiski*, 179; Mikhailovskii-Danilevskii, "Iz vospominanii," part 1: 94 and part 2: 342.

58. Bronevskii, *Obozrenie iuzhnago berega*, 184–185; Murav'ev-Apostol', *Puteshestvie*, 152.

59. Lashkov, "Sbornik dokumentov," part 3: 117–118 and 120–122.

60. "Ob orderakh kniazia Potemkina," 18–19; Markevich, "Materialy arkhiva," 98; Schönle, "Garden," 1.

61. *Krym i krymskie tatary*, 24–25; Haxthausen, *Russian Empire*, 127; Guthrie, *Tour*, 58.

62. Clarke, *Travels*, 153; Haxthausen, *Russian Empire*, 126; de Hell, *Travels in the Steppes*, 410.

63. Mikhailovskii-Danilevskii, "Iz vospominanii," part 1: 91; ITUAK iarlyks; Castelnau, *Essai sur l'histoire,* vol. 3, 261–262; *Crimea: Its Towns, Inhabitants,* 91. The significance of water remains a topic for investigation. For an excellent contemporary treatment (and compelling evidence that it went unaddressed for over a century) see Dingel'shtedt, "Zakon o vode."

64. Lashkov, "Sbornik dokumentov," part 3: 77, 96; *AGM,* vol. 3: 197, 209–212.

65. DAARK f. 24, op. 1, d. 457, l. 39–40.

66. DAARK f. 24, op. 1, d. 638, l. 20.

67. Bronevskii, *Obozrenie iuzhnago berega,* 60; de Hell, *Travels in the Steppes,* 371–372.

68. Dearborn, *Memoir,* 305; Oliphant, *Russian Shores,* 152; Guthrie, *Tour,* 210; *Crimea: Its Towns, Inhabitants,* 21–22; Gille, *Lettres,* 463.

69. Craven, 252–253; Guthrie, *Tour,* 117; Dearborn, *Memoir,* 307; Hommaire de Hell, 419–420; Marquis Gabriel de Castelnau, *Essai sur l'histoire ancienne et moderne de la nouvelle Russie,* vol. 3 (Paris, 1827), 264.

70. RGIA f. 1409, op. 1, d. 1856, ll. 3–6; Ford, "Reforestation," 350.

71. Mikhailovskii-Danilevskii, "Iz vospominanii," part 2: 343. Arakcheev stayed long enough to discover that the translations of Tatar petitions being used by the commission were inaccurate.

72. The decree was not a complete defeat for the Tatar population: henceforth dachas and properties for which Tatars possessed official documentation issued after 1794 could not be claimed by pomeshchiki or other would-be landowners. The Asiatic Department of the Ministry of Foreign Affairs bent over backwards to translate the full text into Tatar within two months. See *PSZ II,* vol. 2, no. 1,417 (September 28, 1827); RGIA f. 1341, op. 28, d. 525, ll. 26 and 35–36; DAARK f. 327, op. 1, d. 298, ll. 14–17; *PSZ II,* vol. 3, no. 2,444 (November 22, 1828).

73. Melitopol and Dneprovsk fell under the jurisdiction of the Ekaterinoslav survey department. *PSZ II,* vol. 4, no. 2,617 (January 24, 1829); DAARK f. 327, op. 1, d. 298, ll. 13–17; *PSZ II,* vol. 7, no. 5,639 (October 4, 1832); *PSZ II,* vol. 8, no. 5,994 (February 21, 1833); *PSZ II,* vol. 8, no. 5,995 (February 21, 1833).

74. Kivelson, *Cartographies,* 55. DAARK f. 377, op. 11, d. 155 [survey map for Sudak]; DAARK f. 377, op. 13, d. 1052 [survey map for Khalil Çelebi orchard]; DAARK f. 377, op. 20, d. 64, ll. 1–180b [survey book for Arginchik]; DAARK f. 377, op. 20, d. 23 [survey book for Achkora].

75. DAARK f. 377, op. 20, d. 871, ll. 1–13 [survey book for Iamichi]; DAARK f. 377, op. 11, d. 162 [survey map for Ay Serez].

76. Ivanov, *Opyt istoricheskago izsledovaniia.*

77. DAARK f. 377, op. 13, d. 170 [survey map for Bahçe Eli (Bakhche Eli)].

78. According to the Special Commission on Pious Endowments, in 1893 there were 245 waqf properties in Evpatoriia, 1,247 in Simferopol, 1,111 in Yalta, 509 in Feodosiia, and 159 in Perekop. Lashkov estimated that these figures would have to be at least doubled to approximate the number of pious endowments prior to 1783. See Lashkov, "Istoricheskii ocherk," part 3: 36–37; RGIA f.

1263, op. 1, d. 148, ll. 23–29; RGIA f. 1306, op. 1, d. 16, ll. 1–28; *Alfavitnye spiski,* 84–237.

79. Vasil'ev, "O nachale i uspekhov," 194.

Chapter 5. Intimacies of Exchange

1. LeDonne, "Geopolitics, Logistics, and Grain"; Patricia Herlihy, *Odessa: A History;* Charles King, *Odessa: Genius and Death.*

2. Levashev, *Kartina ili opisanie,* 164; Eton, *Survey,* 36–37, 44–45.

3. Kakhovksii, "Kratkoe primechanie," 593–594; *AGM,* vol. 3: 212; RGADA f. 1261, op. 1, d. 2541, ll. 1–4. A verst was the equivalent of 0.66 miles or 1.0068 kilometers.

4. İnalcık, *An Economic and Social History,* 196; Castelnau, *Essai sur l'histoire,* vol. 3: 257.

5. Markevich, "Materialy arkhiva kantseliarii," 88–103.

6. Lashkov, "O kameral'nom opisanii," 26–30; RGIA f. 1285, op. 3, d. 199, ll. 20; LeDonne, "Geopolitics, Logistics, and Grain," 1–41.

7. *PSZ I,* vol. 21, no. 15,757 (June 10, 1783).

8. *PSZ I,* vol. 22, no. 15,935 (February 22, 1784); DAMO f. 414, op. 1, d. 38, ll. 1–4; Lashkov, "O peresmotre Chernomorskago tarifa," 25–28.

9. Lashkov, "O peresmotre Chernomorskago tarifa," 29–39.

10. *PSZ I,* vol. 25, no. 18,373 (February 13, 1798); *PSZ I,* vol. 25, no. 18,374 (February 13, 1798); RGIA f. 1307, op. 1, d. 4, ll. 2–3.

11. *PSZ I,* vol. 25, no. 19,226 (December 21, 1799).

12. Eton, *Survey,* 5–6.

13. Eton, *Survey,* 9–11; Terristori, *Geographical, Statistical,* vii; Budishchev, *Atlas chernago moria.* The hydrographic department of the Admiralty followed with its own atlas in 1841, complete with twenty-six map folios and sixteen more detailed views of important harbors. See Manganari, *Atlas.*

14. Customs revenue at Feodosiia often spiked in the autumn. For example, in 1825, 72 percent of revenue came in the months of September through November. See DAARK f. 369, op. 1, d. 40, ll. 26–28ob, 40–42; DAARK f. 368, op. 1, d. 13, ll. 90, 101–127ob.

15. Eton, *Survey,* 37–38; Dearborn, *Memoir,* vol. 1, 309–310; Terristori, *Geographical, Statistical,* 31.

16. Terristori, *Geographical, Statistical,* 28; Eton, *Survey,* 35–36; Wilkinson, *Account,* 106.

17. Until 1774 the markets and ports of the Black Sea were oriented exclusively to Constantinople. As Castelnau put it, this "accustomed the Turks to habits and tastes for certain edibles that they now find impossible to do without." Castelnau, *Essai sur l'histoire,* vol. 2, 279; Druzhinina, *Severnoe Prichernomor'e,* 88; RGVIA f. 52, op. 1, d. 336, ch. 3, ll. 32–34; RGVIA f. 52, op. 1, d. 336, ch. 3, ll. 81; RGVIA f. 52, op. 1, d. 336, ch. 4, 12.

18. Anthoine de Saint-Joseph, *Essai historique,* 7–8, 230–231; Castelnau, *Essai sur l'histoire,* vol. 2, 277–278; DAARK f. 369, op. 1, d. 8, ll. 61–62.

19. Terristori, *Geographical, Statistical,* 42–43; *OVTR,* 1826. Each volume of the *OVTR* is composed of dozens of wide-format tables. Pagination is irregular and/or unavailable. For a visualization of the data see O'Neill, "(Ship) Traffic in the Black Sea," *Beautiful Spaces,* http://dighist.fas.harvard.edu/projects/beautifulspaces/exhibits/show/visualizations/traffic1827.

20. DAARK f. 221, op. 1, d. 75, ll. 1–20; Armstrong, "Coastal Shipping," 178; and the articles in Armstrong and Kunz, eds., *Coastal Shipping.*

21. *PSZ I,* vol. 24, no. 17,939 (April 29, 1797).

22. See for example the reports in *OVTR* 1826. A "last" was a unit for measuring the carrying capacity of a ship. Its definition changed between the seventeenth and nineteenth centuries, and depended on the commodity in question. A single last could range from 700 to 1,800 kilograms.

23. *PSZ I,* vol. 14, no. 10,653 (November 19, 1756); Dubrovin, *Prisoedinenie Kryma,* vol. 3: 47, 51; Dubrovin, *Prisoedinenie Kryma,* vol. 4: 593. Catherine II had earlier fixed the boundary of subjecthood at the Kuban so that she might deny responsibility for the actions of "any Tatars living on the far side of the river." See *PSZ I,* vol. 21, no. 15,901: 1082–1083 (article 3).

24. Lashkov, "Statistika," 140–141; Lashkov, *Kniaz' Grigorii,* 14; *PSZ,* vol. 28, no. 21,352 (June 18, 1804): 384–385. The decree stipulated that anyone caught lying about such communication would be sent to Siberia.

25. DAARK, f. 369, op. 1, d. 28, ll. 39–430b; DAARK f. 221, op. 1, d. 166, ll. 258–2590b; Eton, Survey, 43–44.

26. Taitbout de Marigny, *Three Voyages,* 11–12; "Obozrenie vostochnago berega," 87–88; DAARK f. 221, op. 1, d. 166, l. 152. Taitbout de Marigny helped build the schooner on which they transported the salt. The ship, the *Circassian,* was built at Alushta.

27. Wilkinson, *Account,* 69–70; DAARK f. 221, op. 1, d. 166, ll. 313–3140b; DAARK f. 369, op. 1, d. 28, ll. 9–140b.

28. DAARK f. 369, op. 1, d. 42, ll. 81–830b and 138–141.

29. DAARK f. 369, op. 1, d. 42, ll. 5–6.

30. DAARK f. 9, op. 1, d. 15, ll. 1–6.

31. DAARK f. 13, op. 1, d. 56, ll. 1–10b.

32. Taitbout, *Three Voyages,* 234. Taitbout de Marigny later served as Dutch consul at Odessa.

33. *PSZ I,* vol. 25, no. 18373 (February 13, 1798); *PSZ I,* vol. 44, shtat k no. 19228 (December 22, 1799); *PSZ I,* vol. 30, no. 23008 (May 8, 1808); Dearborn, *Memoir,* vol. 1: 309–310. The 1798 decree left the quarantines in place "for the protection of Our borders (*predely*) against the danger of contagion."

34. RGVIA f. 846, op. 16, d. 19059, ll. 1–4; DAARK f. 369, op. 1, d. 125, ll. 118–1190b; DAARK f. 221, op. 1, d. 167, ll. 12–340b; DAARK f. 221, op. 1, d. 166, l. 289; Terristori, *Geographical, Statistical,* 30.

35. Eton, *Survey,* 2–3; Dearborn, *Memoir,* vol. 1: 337–340; Terristori, *Geographical, Statistical,* 32–33, 37.

36. Skal'kovskii, "Iarmanki, ili sukhoputnye rynki Novorossiiskago-kraia," *Zhurnal ministerstva vnutrennykh del,* chast' 2 (March 1855): 78–79, 105–119. A great deal of Crimean salt made its way to Kriukov on the Dnepr, where it was traded for

grain before continuing further inland. I have included the market locations on the interactive map *Beautiful Spaces* (see the bibliographical note).

37. Skal'kovskii, "Iarmanki," 122–125.

38. Each market lasted nine days. See DAARK f. 27, op. 1, d. 3354, ll. 13–130b. The thirty-eight listy (pages) of the document are full of such announcements. For openings in 1830 see DAARK f. 27, op. 1, d. 3290, ll. 1–19.

39. Kerblay, "Les Foires commerciales," 427.

40. DAARK f. 26, op. 1, d. 8113. A "bucket," or *vedro*, is a liquid measure equivalent to 2.7 gallons or 12.3 liters.

41. Wilkinson, *Account*, 9–10; Heber, *Life*, 267, 225; Guthrie, *Tour*, 130; Pallas, *Travels*, vol. 2: 429.

42. Ballas, *Winemaking*, 13; Sumarokov, *Dosugi krymskogo sud'i*, part 1, 171–172, 180.

43. RGIA f. 1281, op. 11, d. 31, ll. 7, 83–84, 195, 234, 274, RGIA f. 1281, op. 11, d. 132, ll. 68, 142, and 180; Ballas, *Winemaking*, 26–28; Dearborn, *Memoir*, vol. 1 (Boston, 1819): 213–228; Holderness, *New Russia*, 138.

44. RGADA f. 1261, op. 1, d. 2553, ll. 1–3.

45. *VSOb* 66; *PSZ II*, vol. 1, no. 195 (March 16, 1826).

46. Ballas, *Winemaking*, 30–33; "O sostoianii raznykh otraslei" 12.

47. Aksakov, *Issledovaniia*, 292–293.

48. DAARK f. 27, op. 1, d. 1132, ll. 1–15; DAARK f. 27, op. 1, d. 2386, ll. 1–6, 41–42, and 98; DAARK f. 27, op. 1, d. 1147, ll. 1–2; *TGV* pribavlenie k no. 17 (April 29, 1838): 1.

49. *TGV*, no. 17 (29 April 1838): 4–6; *TGV*, no. 18: 6–7; *TGV*, no. 16: 4–5; *TGV*, pribavlenie k no. 8 (February 25, 1838): 1–2; Mikhailovskii-Danilevskii [1818], 90; Dearborn, *Memoir*, vol. 1: 323; Kelly O'Neill, "Crimean Town Revenues, 1837" (interactive visualization).

50. This particular claim to fame seems to have rotated among Evpatoriia, Bahçesaray, and Karasubazar. According to the annual governor's reports, in 1812 Evpatoriia generated seven times more revenue (19,780 rubles) than any other town in Tavrida. In 1817, Karasubazar's city revenues nearly reached 15,000 rubles, while Bahçesaray's amounted to 5,722 and Evpatoriia's to 8,611 rubles. See RGIA f. 1281, op. 1, d. 132, ll. 97; RGIA f. 1281, op. 1, d. 133, l. 63.

51. Sumarokov, *Dosugi krymskogo sud'i*, 115–116, 165; Haxthausen, *Russian Empire*, 107.

52. DAARK f. 369, op. 1, d. 28, ll. 15–150b; DAARK f. 221, op. 1, d. 167. RGIA f. 1285, op. 3, d. 199, l. 6. Documentation of the booming foreign trade is extensive in both published and archival form. As Kudriavtseva points out, counting Russian ships and enumerating their tonnage and cargo was in large part the raison d'être of the Russian consul in Constantinople.

53. DAARK f. 369, op. 1, d. 125, ll. 118–1180b; DAARK f. 221, op. 1, d. 167, ll. 12–340b; Prokhorov, "Gosudarstvennye uchrezhdeniia," 126; DAARK f. 369, op. 1, d. 41, ll. 7–8; Shavrov, 54; Wilkinson, *Account*, 64. A single merchant could easily make or break the fortunes of a small port: the port of Vannes was nearly done in by the poor luck of its biggest merchant in the mid-eighteenth century. See Le Bouëdec, "Small Ports," 110.

54. Dearborn, *Memoir,* vol. 1: 296–297.

55. RGIA f. 1281, op. 11, d. 131, ll. 35; RGIA f. 1281, op. 11, d. 132, l. 91; Arsen'ev, *Statisticheskie ocherki,* 348; *VSOb* vol. 11, part 2: 122, 135, 153–160; Kohl, 456; Clarke, *Travels in Various Countries,* 138; Holderness, *New Russia,* 217–218; Arsen'ev, *Statisticheskie ocherki,* 343–347; RGVIA f. 52 op. 1, d. 336, ch. 3: 1; Sekirinskii, "Agrarnyi stroi," 143; Montandon, *Guide du Voyageur,* 116.

56. *VSOb,* vol. 11, part 2 (1849): 136, 142–145; "O sostoianii raznykh otraslei sel'skago khoziastva," 76–77.

57. RGIA f. 1281, op. 11, d. 131, ll. 83–84 and 129; RGIA f. 1281, op. 1, d. 132, l. 143; "O sostoianii raznykh otraslei sel'skago khoziastva," 73.

58. Montandon, *Guide du Voyageur,* 72–75; Holderness, *New Russia,* 219–220. For an example of the battles joined over water sources, see *ITUAK* 20 (1894), 109.

59. Dubrova, "Gorod Aleshki," 217–222.

60. RGIA f. 1281, op. 11, d. 159, l. 120b.

61. RGIA f. 1281, op. 11, d. 160, ll. 7–10.

62. Bronevskii, *Obozrenie iuzhnago berega,* 179, 191–192; Vorontsov, *Zapiski Gubernatora,* 171.

63. Ianson, *Krym,* 26.

Conclusion

1. DAARK f. 327, op. 1, d. 228, ll. 1–6.

2. Aleksandrov, "O prebyvanii v Krymu," 187.

3. Krichinskii, *Ocherki russkoi politiki,* 12–13.

4. Aleksandrov, "O prebyvanii dervishei," 189–190; Krichinskii, *Ocherki russkoi politiki,* 13–14.

5. Bukharaev, "Sufism in Russia," 75; Voloshikhov, "Tekie 'Eni-dzhami'"; Smirnov, *Krymskoe khanstvo,* 441.

6. Frank, *Muslim Religious Institutions,* 260–267; Crews, "Muslim Heterodoxy," 9.

7. Roosevelt, *Country Estate,* 271.

8. Brumfield, *History,* 122–125; Bruess, *Religion, Identity and Empire,* 96; Gavril, "Khronologiko-istoricheskoe opisanie," 197–201; O'Neill, "Constructing Imperial Identity." Matthew Romaniello discusses the significance of the Church and churches throughout his study of empire building in Kazan in his *Elusive Empire,* particularly pages 38–42.

9. Feodosiia/Kefe alone held forty-one churches (eleven Orthodox and thirty Armenian Catholic), though only three of these still held services. See Lebedintsev, "Stoletie tserkovnoi zhizni," 206.

10. Potemkin, "Rasporiazheniia," 249–329. See for example Potemkin's orders of July 1, 1783 (262); May 31, 1783 (265); July 1, 1783 (272); October 16, 1783 (287).

11. Frank, *Muslim Religious Institutions,* 161; Potemkin, "Rasporiazheniia," 285.

12. Glushak (ed.), *Bogi Tavridy,* 120; Gavril, "Khronologiko-istoricheskoe opisanie," 201; RGIA f. 1281, op. 11, d. 131, ll. 127–134; DAARK f. 797, op. 2, d. 8142, ll. 2–9; Haxthausen, *Russian Empire,* 109. In 1778 some 30,000 Greek and

Armenian Christians left Crimea, enticed by Catherine II to resettle over the Russian border. This was an attempt to sap the economic vitality of the khanate and force the khan to rely on Russian support; an unintended consequence was the deterioration of Christian institutions in the region.

13. RGIA f. 1281, op. 11, d. 131, l. 120 (report for 1806); RGIA f. 1281, op. 11, d. 131, l. 164 (report for 1807); Skal'kovskii, "O nogaiskikh tatarakh," 161, 181, 189; Krikun, *Pam'iatniki*, 94.

14. Pallas, *Travels*, 266–267; Kolli, "O sud'be," 13–14; Kolli, "O sokhranenii," 380; Schnitzler, *Description de la Crimée*, 136.

15. Sinan was Chief Royal Architect of Sultan Suleyman I ("the Magnificent"). See Gülru Necipoglu, *The Age of Sinan: Architectural Culture in the Ottoman Empire* (Princeton: Princeton University Press, 2005).

16. Potemkin, "Rasporiazheniia," 285; Murzakevich, "Poezdka," 626–627. On the construction of the St. Vladimir Cathedral, which got under way only after the Crimean War, see Kozelsky, "Ruins into Relics."

17. RGIA f. 1286, op. 4, d. 102, l. 35; DAARK f. 327, op. 1, d. 286, ll. 16–27; RGADA f. 1261, op. 1, d. 2345; Malov, "O tatarskikh mechetiakh," 18; RGIA f. 1286, op. 4, d. 102, l. 35; Glushak, *Krym khristianskii*, 75.

18. Sumarokov, *Dosugi Krymskago sud'i*, 192–194; Kohl, *St. Petersburg, Moscow*, 448, 453; de Hell, *Travels in the Steppes*, 373.

19. Roosevelt, *Life on a Country Estate*, 174; Roosevelt, "Russian Estate Architecture," 66–72; Solov'ev, "Vo vkuse umnoi stariny," 12–14.

20. Oliphant, *Russian Shores*, 205; Montandon, *Guide du Voyageur*, 94. On coffeehouses as sources of rumor and objects of surveillance by the Ottoman state in the same time period, see Kırlı, "Kahvehaneler ve hafiyeler," 58–77.

21. *Crimea: Its Towns*, 48; Montandon, *Guide du Voyageur*, 79, 308–310; Murav'ev-Apostol, *Puteshestvie*, 191; Holderness, *New Russia*, 232–239; Oliphant, *Russian Shores*, 157.

22. DAARK f. 49, op. 1, d. 417; RGVIA f. 52, op. 1, d. 547, svod 232. The noble registers provide an incomplete picture of noble wealth and do not a give a complete picture of landownership; they do shed light on the way nobles presented themselves—and their qualifications—to the noble assembly.

23. Lashkov, "Istoricheskii ocherk," part 1, 76; DAARK f. 49, op. 1, d. 2161, l. 1.

24. DAARK f. 49, op. 1, d. 115, l. 18; DAARK f. 49, op. 1, d. 125, l. 15; DAARK f. 49, op. 1, d. 6558, ll. 3–4. None of these men were approved by the Heraldry. Only five mirzas entered the noble registers before 1820: Murtaza Çelebi, Temir Bey Biiarslanov, Ismail Bey Balatukov, Mehmetşa Bey Kantakuzin, and Batyr Aga Krımtay.

25. DAARK f. 49, op. 1, d. 5815, ll. 26–29; DAARK f. 49, op. 1, d. 2428, l. 32; DAARK f. 49, op. 1, d. 5507, ll. 15–16 and 31–36; DAARK f. 49, op. 1, d. 5510, ll. 13–16; DAARK f. 49, op. 1, d. 6559, l. 28; DAARK f. 49, op. 1, d. 6610, l. 97.

26. Kohut, "The Ukrainian Elite," 82–83; Krivosheia, "Prichislenie pol'skoi shliakhty," 17.

27. RGIA f. 1281, op. 2, d. 50, ll. 82–83.

28. Karpat, "Crimean Emigration"; Markevich, "Pereseleniia." On ship traffic in the 1860s see Ianson, *Krym*, 68 and 77.

29. Skal'kovskii, *Khronologicheskoe obozrenie*, 2, 17.

30. *PSZ I*, vol. 30, no. 22,772 (January 24, 1808).

31. *VSOb*, vol. 11, chast' 2: 11–12. Tavrida was first thought to occupy between 75,000 and 81,000 square versts (approximately 34,270 square miles or 22 million acres). Later measurements by the Academy of Sciences put the total area at 56,289 square versts (24,711 square miles). To put this another way, the Academy estimate put Tavrida at about the same size as modern-day West Virginia; previous estimates overestimated by an area the size of New Jersey.

32. Moon, "Russian Academy," 212; Ely, *This Meager Nature*, 39. For a complete listing and summaries of all Academy expeditions see Gnucheva (sost.), *Materialy dlia istorii ekspeditsii Akademii Nauk v XVIII i XIX vekakh*.

33. Pleshcheev, *Obozrenie Rossiiskiia Imperiia*. By 1793 Pleshcheev's work had gone through four editions and been translated into German and English.

34. LeDonne, "Territorial Reform of the Russian Empire, 1775–1796," parts 1 and 2. For the text of the statute see *PSZ I*, vol. 20, no. 14,392 (November 7, 1775). From the Petrine period forward the term *guberniia* described the main administrative unit. Prior to 1775 each guberniia consisted of several *oblasti* (provinces), which in turn consisted of districts (*uezdy*). Catherine's statute did away with the intermediary level, preserving the *oblast'* only in exceptional cases, and maintained the district as the subunit of the guberniia. Most gubernii underwent a dramatic reduction in territorial size. Many were grouped together in pairs and placed under the jurisdiction of a governor-general, but the 1775 statute confounds the distinction between oblast' and guberniia by using the term *namestnichestvo* as a synonym of guberniia throughout (see for example chapter 1, arts. 1–16).

35. *PSZ I*, vol. 21, no. 15,160 (May 19, 1771); LeDonne, "Territorial reform," part 1, 161.

36. Got'e, *Istoriia oblastnogo upravleniia*, 18; Seegel, *Mapping Europe's Borderlands*, 27.

37. Kivelson, *Cartographies of Tsardom*; Shaw, "Mapmaking," 420.

38. Kirilov, *Tsvetushchee sostoianie Vserossiiskago gosudarstva*. Kirilov completed the work in 1727.

39. Akerman, "Structuring of Political Territory in Early Printed Atlases," 141.

40. Postnikov, "Outline," 5–9. On the relevance of routes to Spanish spatial culture see Padrón, *Spacious Word*.

41. Benton, "Spatial Histories," 23–24. For a series of fascinating explorations of the function of travel in Russian literature see the collection of articles in the special section of *Russian Review* 70 (January 2011), "Travel, Home, and Russian Identity in the Nineteenth Century Literary Tradition."

42. *Pochtovyi dorozhnik*. The fascination with waterways spurred Nikolai Novikov, the famous satirist and journalist, to publish a volume entitled *Drevniaia Rossiiskaia Idrografiia (Ancient Russian Hydrography, Consisting of a Description of the Rivers, Streams, Lakes, and Wells of Muscovy, and the Towns and Boundaries Along Which They Are Located)* (Sanktpeterburg, 1773), originally compiled

circa 1680. The Russian State Library offers a high-quality digital copy: http://dlib .rsl.ru/viewer/01003335641#?page=1.

43. Murzakevich, "Atlas Chernago Moria," 722–725.

44. Nadezhdin, "Puteshestvie," 438; Demidov, *Travels*; Vsevolozhskii, *Puteshestvie*; Zelenetskii, "Voyage," 442–453.

45. Nadezhdin, "Puteshestvie," 438–441; Murzakevich, "Atlas Chernago Moria," 722–725.

46. *Putevoditel' po Krymu*, 2. Moskvich was a native of Yalta, born circa 1852. According to his own estimation his travel guides went through 223 editions and reached a circulation of some 825,000. See Zakharov, "Grigorii Moskvich."

47. *Tavricheskaia guberniia*, part 2; *Pamiatnaia kniga* (1867); Markov, *Ocherki Kryma*, ii, vii.

Bibliography

Archival Collections

RGIA

fond 797	Kantseliariia ober-prokurator Sinoda
fond 994	Mordvinovye
fond 1263	Komitet ministrov
fond 1281	Sovet ministerstva vnutrennykh del
fond 1285	Departament gosudarstvennykh khoziaistva
fond 1286	Departament politsii
fond 1305	Krymskaia komissiia
fond 1306	Tavricheskii komitet
fond 1307	Komitet dlia ustroeniia Novorossiiskoi gubernii
fond 1341	Pervyi departament Senata
fond 1343	Departament gerol'dii (Senata)
fond 1350	Tretii departament Senata
fond 1374	Kantseliarii general-prokurora
fond 1409	Sobstvennaia ego imperatorskogo velichestva kantseliarii

RGVIA

fond 52	Bumagi Potemkina
fond 228	Rudzevichy

RGADA

fond 1261   Arkhiv Vorontsovykh
fond 286   Gerol'dmeiskerskaia kontora

DAARK

fond 9   Feodosiiskii uezdnii zemskii sud
fond 13   Tavricheskii gubernskii prokuror
fond 24   Komissiia, uchrezhdennaia dlia razbora sporov po
             zemliam i dlia opredeleniia povinostei na krymskom
             poluostrove
fond 26   Kantseliariia Tavricheskogo gubernatora
fond 27   Tavricheskoe gubernskoe pravlenie
fond 49   Tavricheskoe gubernskoe dvorianskoe deputatskoe sobranie
fond 134   Perekopskoe dukhovnoe pravlenie
fond 221   Feodosiiskaia portovaia tamozhnia
fond 327   Kantseliarii Tavricheskogo gubernskogo predvoditelia
             dvorianstva
fond 368   Akmechetskii tamozhenii zastav
fond 369   Evpatoriiskaia portovaia tamozhnia
fond 377   Tavricheskaia gubernskaia chertezhnaia
fond 799   Tavricheskoe oblastnoe pravlenie

DAMO

fond 414   Ochakivs'ka portova mitnitsia

Published Documents and Document Collections

Adres-kalendar', ili obshchii shtat Rossiiskoi imperii na [1843–1849]. Sankt-peterburg: Imp. Akademiia nauk, 1843–1849.

Adres-kalendar': Obshchaia rospis' vsekh chinovnykh osob v gosudarstve, [1851–1857]. Sanktpeterburg: Imp. Akademiia nauk, 1851–1860.

Adres-kalendar': Obshchii shtat Rossiiskoi imperii na 1850 god. Sanktpeterburg: Imp. Akademiia nauk, 1850.

Alfavitnye spiski armiiano-grigorianskikh tserkvei i magometanskikh mechetei v Imperii. Sanktpeterburg: Departament dukhovnykh del inostrannykh ispovedanii MVD, 1886.

Arkhiv Gosudarstvennago Soveta. 12 volumes. Sanktpeterburg: Tip. Vtorago otdeleniia Sobstvennoi Ego Imperatorskago Velichestva kantseliarii, 1869–1904.

Arkhiv grafov Mordvinovykh. 10 vols. Sanktpeterburg: Tip. N. N. Skorokho-dova, 1901–1903.

Arkhiv Vorontsovykh. 40 vols. Moskva: Tip. A. I. Mamontova, 1870–1895.

Bossoli, Carlo. *The Beautiful Scenery and Chief Places of Interest Throughout the Crimea from Paintings.* London: Day & Son, 1856.

Bumagi Imperatritsy Ekateriny II khraniashchiiasia v gosudarstvennom archive Ministerstva Inostrannykh Del (gody s 1774 po 1788), chast' 4. *Sbornik Imperatorskago russkago istoricheskago obshchestva,* vol. 27. Sanktpeterburg: Imp. Akademiia nauk, 1880.

Catherine II, Empress of Russia. *Love and Conquest: Personal Correspondence of Catherine the Great and Prince Grigory Potemkin.* Translated by Douglas Smith. DeKalb: Northern Illinois University Press, 2004.

Demidov, Anatolii. *Album du Voyage dans la Russie méridionale et la Crimée, par la Hongrie, La Valachie et la Moldavie.* Paris, 1838.

"Doklad Imperatritse Ekaterine II-oi po vstupleniii Eia na Prestol, izobrazhaiushchii sistemu krymskikh tatar, ikh opastnost' dlia Rossii i pretenziiu na nikh." *ITUAK* 53 (1916): 190–193.

Dubrovin, N. F. *Prisoedinenie Kryma k Rossii: Reskripty, pis'ma, reliatsiia, i doneseniia.* 4 vols. Sanktpeterburg: Imp. Akademiia nauk, 1885.

Le duc de Richelieu. *Correspondance et documents, 1766–1822. Sbornik Imperatorskago russkago istoricheskago obshchestva,* vol. 54. St. Petersburg: Tip. Imp. Akademii Nauk, 1887.

Gabaev, G. "Zakonodatel'nye akty i drugie dokumenty o voennoi sluzhbe krymskikh tatar v riadakh voiskovykh chastei, predkov nyneshniago Krymskago Konnago Eia Velichestva Gosudaryni Imperatritsy Aleksandry Feodorovny polka." *ITUAK* 51 (1913): 135–152.

Kakhovskii, V. V. "Pis'ma Ekaterinoslavskago gubernatora Vasiliia Vasil'evicha Kakhovskago sostoiashchemu pri delakh Eia Velichestva Ekateriny II, tain. sov. V. S. Popovu, dlia doklada kniaziu Platoni Aleksandrovichu Zubovu (s 20 ianvaria 1792 po 24 iunia 1794 goda)." *ZOOID* 12 (1881): 330–427.

Kakhovskii, V. V. "Pis'my pravitelia Tavricheskoi oblasti Vasiliia Vasil'evicha Kokhovskago praviteliu kantseliarii V. S. Popovu, dlia doklada ego Svetlosti Kniaziu G. A. Potemkinu-Tavricheskomu." *ZOOID* 10 (1877): 235–360.

Kirilov, I. K. *Tsvetushchee sostoianie Vserossiiskago gosudarstva, v kakovoe nachal, privel i ostavil neizrechennymi trudami Petr Velikii [q.]* Moskva: v Universitetskoi Tipografii, 1831.

Lashkov, Fedor Fedorovich. "Sbornik dokumentov po istorii krymskotatarskago zemlevladeniia." Parts 1, 2, 3, 4, and 5. *ITUAK* 22 (1895): 82–115; 23 (1895): 118–129; 24 (1896): 72–137; 25 (1896): 89–158; 26 (1897): 24–154.

Masaev, M. V. *Tavricheskie tatarskie diviziony beshliskogo voiska (1784–1796): Dokumenty i materialy.* Simferopol': Dolia, 1999.

Mertvago, D. B. *Avtobiograficheskiia zapiski Dmitriia Borisovicha Mertvago 1760–1824.* Moskva: Izdanie Russkago Arkhiva, 1867.

Mesiatseslov i obshchii shtat Rossiiskoi imperii na [1831–1842]. Sanktpeterburg: Imp. Akademiia nauk, 1830–1842.

Mesiatseslov s rospis'iu chinovnykh osob v gosudarstve na leto ot Rozhdestva Khristova [1772–1829]. 57 vols. Sanktpeterburg: Imp. Akademiia nauk, 1772–1829.

"O prosheniiakh deputatov Tavricheskoi oblasti na Vysochaishee Imia v 1796 godu i Vysochaishem Ukaz 17 sentiabria 1796 goda." *ITUAK* 2 (1897): 9–19.

"Obozrenie vostochnago berega Chernago mor'ia." *Arkhiv Raevskikh,* vol. 3, 87–88.

Obzor vneshnei torgovli Rossii po Evropeiskoi i aziatskoi granitsam. Sankt Peterburg, Departament tamozhnykh sborov, 1802–1910.

Pamiatnaia kniga Tavricheskoi gubernii izdannaia Tavricheskim gubernskim statisticheskim komitetom, sostavlena pod redaktsiei Sekretaria statisticheskago komiteta K. V. Khanatskago. Simferopol', 1867.

Pamiatnaia knizhka Tavricheskoi gubernii na 1914 god. Simferopol': Tavricheskaia Gubernskaia Tipografiia, 1914.

The Papers of Grigorii Potemkin, Catalogs 1 and 2. Woodbridge, Conn.: Research Publications, 2000.

Pochtovyi dorozhnik, ili, opisanie vsekh pochtovykh dorog Rossiiskoi Imperii, Tsarstva Pol'skago, i drugikh prisoedinennykh oblastei: V trekh chastiakh, s prinadlezhashchimi k onomu tablistami, rospisaniiami, pochtovymi kartami i drugimi svedeniami. Sanktpeterburg: v Tip. Med. departamenta Ministerstva vnutrennykh del, 1824.

Pol'noe sobranoe zakonov Rossiiskoi Imperii. 45 vols. Sanktpeterburg: v Tip. Vtorago otdeleniia Sobstvennoi Ego Imperatorskago Velichestva kantseliarii, 1830.

Pol'noe sobranoe zakonov Rossiiskoi Imperii, sobranie vtoroe. 55 vols. Sanktpeterburg: v Tip. Vtorago otedeleniia Sobstvennoi Ego Imperatorskago Velichestva kantseliarii, 1830–1884.

Potemkin, G. A. "Rasporiazheniia svetleishago kniazia Grigoriia Aleksandrovicha Potemkina-Tavricheskago kasatel'no ustroeniia Tavricheskoi oblasti s 1781 po 1786-i god." *ZOOID* 12 (1881), 249–329.

Simferopoliu 200 let: Sbornik dokumentov i materialov. Kiev: Nauk "Dumka," 1984.

Tavricheskaia guberniia: Po svedeniiam 1864 goda. Spiski naselennykh mest Rossiiskoi Imperii, sostavlennye i izdavaemye Tsentral'nym statis-

ticheskim komitetom Ministerstva vnutrennykh del. Sanktpeterburg, vol. 41, 1865.

Uvarov, Aleksei Sergeevich. *Sobranie kart i risunkov k izledovaniam o drevnostiakh Iuzhnoi Rossii i beregov Chernago Moria.* Sanktpeterburg, 1851.

Vedomosti dukhovnym v Krymu vakufam, sostavlennyia vysochaishe uchrezhdennoiu Osoboiu Kommissieiu o vakufakh v 1893 godu. Simferopol': Tip. Tavricheskago Gubernskago Pravleniia, 1893.

Verner, K. A., ed. *Pamiatnaia knizhka Tavricheskoi gubernii.* Simferopol': Tip. Gazety "Krym," 1889.

Voenno-statisticheskoe obozrenie Rossiiskoi Imperii, t. 11, chast' 2. Sanktpeterburg, 1849.

Vorontsov, Graf Mikhail Semenovich. *Zapiski Gubernatora.* Odessa: Optimum, 2003.

Vysochaishie Reskripty Imperatritsy Ekateriny II i Ministerskaia perepiska po delam Krymskim; iz semeinago arkhiva grafa V. N. Panina. chast' 1. Moskva: Izdanie imperatorskago obshchestva istorii i drevnostei Rossiiskikh pri Moskovskom Universitete, 1872.

Zubov, P. A. "Ordera grafa (kniazia) Platona Aleksandrovicha Zubova praviteliu Tavricheskoi oblasti, 1795 god." *ITUAK* 24 (1896): 1–30.

Published Cartographic Materials

Bellin, Jacques Nicolas. *Carte réduite de la Mer Noire.* Paris, 1772.

Budishchev, K. *Atlas Chernago Moria.* Sankt Peterburg: v Morskoi tipografii, 1807.

L'Isle, Joseph de. *Charte derer von der Russisch-Keyser Armee im Jahr 1736. Russischer Atlas.* Sanktpeterburg: Akademiia nauk, 1745.

L'Isle, Joseph de. *Malaia Tatariia s pogranichnymi zemliami, lezhashchimi okolo Dnepra, Dona i Dontsa.* Sankt-Peterburg: Akademiia nauk, 1745.

L'Isle, Joseph de. *Verus Chersonesi Tauricae Seu Crimeae Conspectus. Russischer Atlas.* Sanktpeterburg: Akademiia nauk, 1745.

Manganari, Egor. *Atlas Chernago Moria.* Nikolaev: Pri Gidrograficheskom Chernomorskom depo, 1841.

Mercator, Gerhard. *Taurica Chersonesus.* Amsterdam: Ioannes Janssonius, 1607.

Ortelius, Abraham. *Russiae, Moscoviae et Tartariae.* Antwerp: Coppenium Diesth, 1570.

Vil'brekht, A. M. *Rossiiskoi atlas iz soroka chetyrekh kart.* Sanktpeterburg, Sochin. gravir. i pechat. pri Gornom Uchilishche, 1792.

Topographical Descriptions, Memoirs, and Travel Accounts

Anthoine de Saint-Joseph, Antoine-Ignace. *Essai historique sur le commerce et la navigation de la Mer-Noire; ou, Voyage et entreprises pour établir des rapports commerciaux et maritimes.* Paris, 1805.

Becattini, Francesco. *Storia della Crimea piccolo Tartaria ed alter Provincie circonvicine.* Venezia: Pressa Leonardo Rassaglia, 1785.

Bronevskii, Vladimir Bogdanovich. *Obozrenie iuzhnago berega Tavridy v 1815 godu.* Tula: Tip. Gubernskoe pravlenie, 1822.

Broniouij, Martini. *Martini Broniouij, de Biezdzfedea, bis in Tartariam nomine Stephani Primi Poloniae Regis legati, Tartariae description.* Coloniae Agrippinae, 1595.

Castelnau, G. de. *Essai sur l'histoire de la Nouvelle Russie: Statistique des provinces qui la composent.* 2nd ed. Paris, 1827.

Clarke, E. D. *Travels in Various Countries of Europe and Asia. Part the First: Russia Tahtary and Turkey.* 4th ed. London: Printed for T. Cadell and W. Davies by R. Watts, 1816.

Craven, Elizabeth. *A Journey Through the Crimea to Constantinople. In a series of Letters . . . to his Serene Highness the Margrave of Brandebourg, Ansbach and Bareith.* 2nd ed. London, G.G.J. and J. Robinson, 1789.

The Crimea: Its Towns, Inhabitants, and Social Customs. By a Lady Resident near the Alma. London: Partridge, Oakey, 1855.

Dearborn, H. A. S. *A Memoir of the Commerce and Navigation of the Black Sea, and the Trade and Maritime Geography of Turkey and Egypt,* vol. 1. Boston, 1819.

Demidov, M. Anatole de. *Travels in Southern Russia and the Crimea: Through Hungary, Wallachia and Moldavia during the Year 1837.* London: John Mitchell, Royal Library, Old Bond Street, 1855.

Eton, William. *A Survey of the Turkish Empire.* 2nd ed. London, 1799.

Gablits, Karl. *Fizicheskoe opisanie Tavricheskoi oblasti, po eia mestopolozheniiu i po vsem trem tsarstvam prirody.* Sankt Peterburg, 1785.

Gazley, John G. "The Reverend Arthur Young, 1769–1827: Traveller in Russia and Farmer in the Crimea." *Bulletin of the John Rylands Library* 38, no. 2 (1956): 360–405.

Gille, Floriant. *Lettres sur le Caucase et la Crimée: Ouvrage enrichi de trente vignettes dessinées d'après nature et d'une carte dressée au Dépôt topographique de la guerre à Saint-Pétersbourg.* Paris: Gide, 1859.

Gil'denshtedt, I. A. "Dnevnik puteshestviia v iuzhnuiu Rossiiu akademika S. Peterburgskoi Akademii Nauk Gil'denshtedta v 1773–1774 g." Translated by M. Shugurov. *ZOOID* 11 (1879): 180–203.

Grant, Anthony. *An Historical Sketch of the Crimea.* London: Bell & Daldy, 1855.

Guthrie, Maria. *A Tour, Performed in the Years 1795–6, Through the Taurida, or Crimea, the Antient Kingdom of Bosphorus, the Once-Powerful Republic of Tauric Cherson, and All the Other Countries on the North Shore of the Euxine, Ceded to Russia by the Peace of Kainardgi and Jassy.* London: T. Cadell, Jun. and W. Davies, in the Strand, 1802.

Haxthausen, Baron von. *The Russian Empire: Its People, Institutions, and Resources.* Translated by Robert Faire. London: Frank Cass, 1968.

Heber, Reginald, and Amelia Shipley Heber, *The Life of Reginald Heber, DD, Lord Bishop of Calcutta.* London: John Murray, 1830.

Holderness, Mary. *New Russia: Journey from Riga to the Crimea, by Way of Kiev; with Some Account of the Colonization, and the Manners and Customs of the Colonists of New Russia. To Which are Added, Notes Related to the Crim Tatars.* London: Sherwood, Jones, 1823.

Hommaire de Hell, Xavier. *Travels in the Steppes of the Caspian Sea, the Crimea, the Caucasus, &c.* London: Chapman and Hall, 1847.

Kakhovksii, M. V. "Kratkoe primechanie o poluostrove Tavricheskom Grafa M. V. Kakhovskago." *Russkii Arkhiv* 4 (1873): 592–607.

Kohl, J. G. *Russia: St. Petersburg, Moscow, Kharkoff, Riga, Odessa, the German Provinces of the Baltic, the Steppes, the Crimea, and the Interior of the Empire.* New York: Arno Press, 1970.

Ligne, Charles Joseph (prince) de. *The Prince de Ligne: His Memoirs, Letters, and Miscellaneous Papers,* vol. 2. Translated by Katharine Prescott Wormeley. Boston: Hardy, Pratt, 1899.

Manstein, Christopher Herman. *Contemporary Memoirs of Russia from the Year 1727 to 1744.* London, 1856.

Mikhailovskii-Danilevskii, Aleksandr Ivanovich. "Iz vospominanii Mikhailovskago-Danilevskago: Puteshestvie s imperatorom Aleksandrom I po iuzhnoi Rossii v 1818-m godu." Parts 1 and 2, *Russkaia Starina* 1897 (July): 69–102; 1897 (August): 333–356.

Milner, Rev. Thomas. *The Crimea, Its Ancient and Modern History: The Khans, the Sultans, and the Czars.* London: Longman, Brown, Green and Longman, 1855.

Montandon, C. H. *Guide du Voyageur en Crimée.* Odessa: Imprimerie de la ville, 1834.

Murav'ev-Apostol, Ivan Matveevich. *Puteshestvie po Tavride v 1820 god.* Sanktpeterburg, Tip. Sostoiashchei pri osobennoi kantseliarii ministerstva vnutrennikh del, 1823.

Murzakevich, Nikolai. "Poezdka v Krym v 1836 godu." *Zhurnal ministerstva narodnago prosveshcheniia* 3 (1837): 625–696.

Nadezhdin, N. "Puteshestvie chrez iuzhnuiu Rossiiu, Krym i Odessu . . . N. S. Vsevolozhskago." *ZOOID* 1 (1844): 438–441.

Oliphant, Laurence. *The Russian Shores of the Black Sea in the Autumn of 1852 with a Voyage down the Volga, and a Tour Through the Country of the Don Cossacks.* London: Redfield, 1854.

Pallas, Peter Simon. *Travels Through the Southern Provinces of the Russian Empire, in the Years 1793 and 1794.* 2nd ed. London: John Stockdale, 1812.

Parkinson, John. *A Tour of Russia, Siberia and the Crimea 1792–1794.* London: Cass, 1971.

Peyssonnel, M. de (Charles). *Traité sur le commerce de la Mer Noire.* Paris, 1787.

"Podennaia zapiska puteshestviiu ego siiatel'stva kniazia Vasil'ia Mikhailovich Dolgorukova v Krymskii poluostrov, vo vremia kampanii 1773 goda." *ZOOID* 8 (1872): 182–187.

Putevoditel' po Krymu. Odessa: Izd. kn. magazina A. E. Kekhribardzhi, 1872.

Schnitzler, Johann Heinrich. *Description de la Crimée, surtout au point de vue de ses lignes de communication.* Paris: Veuve Berger-Levrault et Fils, 1855.

Seymour, Henry. *Russia on the Black Sea and the Sea of Azov, Being a Narrative of Travels in the Crimean and Bordering Provinces with Notices of the Naval, Military and Commercial Resources of Those Countries.* London: J. Murray, 1855.

Sumarokov, Pavel Ivanovich. *Dosugi Krymskago sud'i, ili vtoroe puteshestvie v Tavridu.* Sankt Peterburg: Imperatorskaia tipografiia, 1803–1805.

Taitbout de Marigny, Edouard. *Three Voyages in the Black Sea to the Coast of Circassia: Including Descriptions of the Ports, and the Importance of Their Trade: With Sketches of the Manners, Customs, Religion.* London: J. Murray, 1827.

Telfer, John Buchan. *The Crimea and Transcaucasia: Being the Narrative of a Journey in the Kouban, in Gouria, Georgia, Armenia, Ossety, Imeritia, Swannety, and Mingrelia, and in the Tauric Range.* London: Henry King, 1876.

Terristori. *A Geographical, Statistical and Commercial Account of the Russian Ports of the Black Sea, the Sea of Asoph and the Danube: Also an Official Report of the European Commerce of Russia in 1835.* London, 1837.

Thunmann, Hans Erich. *Description de la Crimée.* Strasbourg: chez J.G. Treuttel, 1786.

Tott, François. *Memoirs of Baron de Tott. Containing the State of the Turkish Empire and the Crimea, During the Late War with Russia. With Numerous Anecdotes, Facts, and Observations, on the Manners and Customs of the Turks and Tartars. The second edition. To Which Are Subjoined, the Strictures of M. de Peyssonnel. Translated from the French.* 2 vols. London, 1786.

Vsevolozhskii, N. S. *Puteshestvie, chrez Iuzhnuiu Rossiiu, Krym i Odessu, v Konstantinopol', Maluiu Aziiu, Severnuiu Afriku, Mal'tu, Sitsiliiu, Italiiu, Iuzhnuiu Frantsiiu i Parizh, v 1836 i 1837 godakh.* Moskva: v Tip. Avgusta Semena, 1839.

Wilkinson, Charles. *An Account of the Navigation and Commerce of the Black Sea Collected from Original Sources.* London: Printed by W. Wilson, 1807.

Zelenetskii, K. "Voyage dans la Russie méridionale et la Crimée." *ZOOID* 1 (1844): 442–453.

Secondary Sources

"Abrikosovoe derevo, posazhennoe Imperatritseiu Ekaterinoiu II." *ZOOID* 1 (1844): 607–608.

Aksakov, I. S. *Issledovaniia o torgovliena ukrainskikh iarmarkakh.* St. Petersburg, v Tip. Imp. Akademii Nauk, 1858.

Akerman, James. "The Structuring of Political Territory in Early Printed Atlases." *Imago Mundi* 47 (1995): 138–154.

Aleksandrov, Ivan F. "K istorii uchrezhdeniia Tavricheskago Magometanskago Dukhovnago Pravleniia." *ITUAK* 54 (1918): 316–355.

Aleksandrov, Ivan F. "O musul'manskom dukhovenstve i upravlenii dukhovnymi delami musul'man v Krymu posle ego prisoedineniia k Rossii." *ITUAK* 51 (1914), 207–220.

Aleksandrov, Ivan F. "O prebyvanii v Krymu anatoliiskikh dervishei s chudesnoi vodoi protiv saranchi." *ITUAK* 55 (1918): 186–191.

Aleksandrov, Ivan F. "Sheikh Imam Mansur, propovednik gazavata na Kavkaze v kontse XVIII veka." *ITUAK* 56 (1919): 1–38.

Andreev, A. R. *Istoriia Kryma: Kratkoe opisanie proshlogo Krymskogo poluostrova.* Moskva: Izd-vo Mezhregional'nyi tsentr otraslevoi informatiki Gosatomnadzora Rossii, 1997.

Armstrong, John, and Andreas Kunz, eds. *Coastal Shipping and the European Economy, 1750–1980.* Mainz: Verlag Philipp von Zabern, 2002.

Armstrong, John. "Coastal Shipping: The Neglected Sector of Nineteenth-Century British Transport History." *International Journal of Maritime History* 6, no. 1 (June 1994): 175–188.

Arsenev, Konstantin. *Statisticheskie ocherki Rossii.* St. Petersburg: Tip. Imp. Akademii Nauk, 1858.

Ascherson, Neal. *Black Sea.* 1st American ed. New York: Hill and Wang, 1995.

"Astronomicheskoe polozhenie gorodov v Krymu." *ZOOID* 8 (1872): 257–264.

Azamatov, Danil'. "The Muftis of the Orenburg Spiritual Assembly in the 18th and 19th Centuries: The Struggle for Power in Russia's Muslim Institution." In *Muslim Culture in Russia and Central Asia from the 18th to the Early 20th Centuries*, vol. 2, edited by Anke von Kugelgen, Michael Kemper and Allen J. Frank, 355–384. Berlin: Klaus Schwarz Verlag, 1998.

Azamatov, Danil'. "Russian Administration and Islam in Bashkiria (18th–19th Centuries)." In *Muslim Culture in Russia and Central Asia from the 18th to the Early 20th Centuries*, vol. 1, edited by Michael Kemper, Anke von Kugelgen, and Dmitriy Yermakov, 96–111. Berlin: Klaus Schwarz Verlag, 1996.

Bagalei, D. I. "Kolonizatsiia Novorossiiskago kraia i pervyia shagi ego po puti kul'tury." *Kievskaia Starina* 25 (May/June, 1889): 438–484.

Bagrow, Leo. *A History of Russian Cartography up to 1800*. Wolfe Island, Ont.: Walker Press, 1975.

Ballas, Mikhail. *Vinodelie v Rossii (istoriko-statisticheskij ocherk)*. S. Peterburg: Tip. V. Kirshbauma, 1895.

Baron, Nick. "New Spatial Histories of Twentieth-Century Russia and the Soviet Union: Surveying the Landscape." *Jahrbücher für Geschichte Osteuropas* 55, no. 3 (2007): 374–400.

Bartlett, Roger. "The Russian Nobility and the Baltic German Nobility in the Eighteenth Century." *Cahiers du Monde russe et soviétique* 34, no. 1–2 (1993): 233–244.

Barrett, Thomas. *At the Edge of Empire: The Terek Cossacks and the North Caucasus Frontier, 1700–1860*. Boulder, Colo.: Westview Press, 1999.

Baskakov, N. A. *Russkie familii tiurkskogo proizkhozhdeniia*. Moskva: Mishel, 1993.

Bassin, Mark. "Geographies of Imperial Identity." In *The Cambridge History of Russia*, vol. 2, edited by Dominic Lieven, 45–63. Cambridge: Cambridge University Press, 2006.

Bassin, Mark. *Imperial Visions: Nationalist Imagination and Geographical Expansion in the Russian Far East, 1840–1865*. Cambridge: Cambridge University Press, 1999.

Bassin, Mark. "Inventing Siberia: Visions of the Russian East in the Early Nineteenth Century." *American Historical Review* 96, no. 3 (1991): 763–794.

Baumann, Robert F. "Subject Nationalities in the Military Service of Imperial Russia: The Case of the Bashkirs." *Slavic Review* 46, no. 3/4 (Autumn–Winter 1987): 489–502.

Bennigsen, Alexandre. "Un mouvement populaire au Caucase au XVIII siècle: La "Guerre Sainte" du *sheikh* Mansur (1785–1791)." *Cahiers du Monde russe et soviétique* 5, no. 2: 159–205.

Benton, Lauren. *Law and Colonial Cultures: Legal Regimes in World History, 1400–1900.* Cambridge: Cambridge University Press, 2002.

Benton, Lauren. "Spatial Histories of Empire." *Itinerario* 30, no. 3 (September 2006): 19–34.

Berdinskikh, Viktor Arkadievich. "Prikhodskoe dukhovenstvo Rossii i razvitie kraevedeniia v XIX veke." *Voprosy istorii,* no. 10 (October 1998): 134–138.

Berdinskikh, Viktor Arkadievich. *Uezdnye istoriki: Russkaiaprovintsial'naia istoriografiia.* Moskva: Novoe literaturnoe obozrenie, 2003.

Beskrovny, L. G. *The Russian Army and Fleet in the Nineteenth Century: Handbook of Armaments, Personnel and Policy.* Translated by David R. Jones. Gulf Breeze, Fla.: Academic International Press, 1996.

Bezotosnyi, Viktor Mikhailovich. "Rossiiskii titulovannyi generalitet v voinakh protiv Napoleonovskoi Frantsii v 1812–1815 godakh." *Otechestvennaia Istoriia,* no. 2 (1998): 178–189.

Bitis, Alexander. "Reserves Under Serfdom? Nicholas I's Attempts to Solve the Russian Army's Manpower Crisis of 1831–1832." *Jahrbücher für Geschichte Osteuropas* 51 (2003): 185–196.

Bitis, Alexander. "The Russian Army's Use of Balkan Irregulars During the 1828–1829 Russo-Turkish War." *Jahrbücher für Geschichte Osteuropas* 50 (2002): 537–557.

Bodaninskii, U. "Tatarskie 'Durbe' mavzolei v Krymu." *Izvestiia Tavricheskogo obshchestva istorii, arkheologii i etnografii* 1, no. 58 (1927): 195–201.

Bodarskii, Ia. E. *Naselenie Kryma v kontse XVIII–kontse XX vekov.* Moskva: Rossiiskaia Akademiia nauk, 2003.

Bolotina, N. Iu. "Glavnaia krepost' dolzhna byt' Sevastopol': Dokumenty o sozdanii bazy Chernomorskogo flota. 1784–1793 gg." *Istoricheskii Arkhiv* 1997, no. 2: 201–213.

Bragina, Tat'iana, and Natal'ia Vasil'eva. *Khoziaeva i gosti dvorianskikh imenij Kryma.* Moskva: Globus, 2002.

Bruess, Gregory L. *Religion, Identity and Empire: A Greek Archbishop in the Russia of Catherine the Great.* New York: Columbia University Press, 1997.

Brumfield, William. *A History of Russian Architecture.* Cambridge: Cambridge University Press, 1993.

Bruno, Andy. "Russian Environmental History: Directions and Potentials." *Kritika* 8, no. 3 (2007): 635–650.

Buckler, Julie A. *Mapping St. Petersburg: Imperial Text and Cityshape.* Princeton: Princeton University Press, 2005.

Bukharaev, Ravil. "Sufism in Russia: Nostalgia for Revelation." In *Sufism in Europe and North America,* edited by David Westerland, 64–94. London: Routledge Curzon, 2004.

Bukhteev, M. "Opyt statisticheskago opisaniia Novorossiiskago kraia, A. Skal'kovskago." *ZOOID* 3 (1853): 466–507.

Burbank, Jane, and Frederick Cooper, eds. *Empires in World History: Power and the Politics of Difference.* Princeton: Princeton University Press, 2010.

Burbank, Jane, Anatolii Remnev, and Mark von Hagen, eds. *Russian Empire: Space, People, Power, 1700–1930.* Bloomington: Indiana University Press, 2007.

Cazac, Matei. "Familles de la noblesse Roumaine au service de la Russie XV–XIX Siècles." *Cahiers du Monde russe et soviétique* 34, no. 1–2 (1993): 211–226.

Confino, Michael. "À propos de la notion de service dans la noblesse Russe aux XVIII et XIX siècles." *Cahiers du Monde russe et soviétique* 34, no. 1–2 (1993): 47–58.

Cresswell, Tim. *Place: A Short Introduction.* Malden, Mass.: Blackwell, 2004.

Crews, Robert D. "Empire and the Confessional State: Islam and Religious Politics in Nineteenth-Century Russia." *The American Historical Review* 108, no. 1 (2003): 50–83.

Crews, Robert D. *For Prophet and Tsar: Islam and Empire in Russia and Central Asia.* Cambridge: Harvard University Press, 2006.

Crews, Robert D. "Islamic Law, Imperial Order: Muslims, Jews, and the Russian State." *Ab Imperio* 2004, no. 3 (2004): 467–490.

David-Fox, Michael, Peter Holquist, and Alexander M. Martin. "The Imperial Turn." *Kritika* 7, no. 4 (2006): 705–712.

Davies, Brian. "The Foundations of Muscovite Military Power, 1453–1613." In *The Military History of Tsarist Russia,* edited by Frederick W. Kagan and Robin Higham, 11–30. New York: Palgrave, 2002.

Deringil, Selim. *The Well-Protected Domains: Ideology and Legitimation of Power in the Ottoman Empire, 1876–1909.* London: I. B. Tauris, 1998.

Desaive, Dilek. "Deux inventaires d'archives Ottomanes et leur contribution à l'histoire de la Crimée." *Cahiers du Monde russe et soviétique* 15, no. 3–4 (1974): 415–421.

DeWeese, Devin. "The Politics of Sacred Lineages in 19th-Century Central Asia: Descent Groups Linked to Khwaja Ahmad Yasavi in Shrine Documents and Genealogical Documents." *Journal of Middle Eastern Studies* 31 (1999): 507–530.

Dickinson, Sara. "Russia's First 'Orient': Characterizing the Crimea in 1787." *Kritika* 3, no. 1 (2002): 3–25.

Dickson, P. "Monarchy and Bureaucracy in Late Eighteenth-Century Austria." *English Historical Review* 110, no. 436 (1995): 323–367.

Dingel'shtedt, N. "Zakon o vode dlia Kryma." *Zhurnal iuridicheskago obshchestva pri Imperatorskom S. Peterburgskom Universitete,* kniga 8 (October 1895): 59–124.

Dolbilov, Mikhail D., and A. I. Miller, eds. *Zapadnye okrainy Rossiiskoi imperii.* Moskva: Novoe literaturnoe obozrenie, 2007.

Dolgorukii, K. I. "Stikhi na Mishenskuiu dolina." *Vestnik Evropy* 53, no. 19 (October 1810): 209.

Dombrovskii, F. "Istoriko-statisticheskii ocherk g. Bakchesaraia." *Novorossiiskii kalendar'* (1849): 380–396.

Dontsov, A. V. *Kartografirovanie zemel' Rossii: Istoriia, nauchnye osnovy, sostoianie, perspektivy.* Moskva: Kartgeotsentr-Geodezizdat, 1999.

Druzhinina, E. I. *Severnoe Prichernomor'e v 1775–1800 gg.* Moskva: Akademiia nauk SSSR, 1959.

Dubrova, P. "Gorod Aleshki." *ZOOID* 3 (1853): 217–222.

Dvoenosovoa, G. A. *Dvorianskaia rodoslovnaia kniga Kazanskoi gubernii 1785–1917 gg.* Kazan, 2004.

Eliade, Mircea. *The Myth of the Eternal Return.* Princeton: Princeton University Press, 1974.

Eliseeva, O. I. *Geopoliticheskie proekty G. A. Potemkina.* Moskva: Institut rosssiiskoi istorii RAN, 2000.

Ely, Christopher. *This Meager Nature: Landscape and National Identity in Imperial Russia.* Northern Illinois University Press, 2009.

Enikeev, Said Murza. *Ocherk istorii tatarskogo dvorianstva.* Ufa: Gilem, 1999.

Entsiklopedicheskii slovar'. 43 vols. Sanktpeterburg: F.A. Brokgauz, I.A. Efron, 1890–1907.

Ergene, Boğaç. *Local Court, Provincial Society and Justice in the Ottoman Empire: Legal Practice and Dispute Resolution in Çankırı and Kastamonu (1652–1744).* Leiden: Brill, 2003.

Evtuhov, Catherine. *Portrait of a Russian Province: Economy, Society, and Civilization in Nineteenth-Century Nizhnii Novgorod.* Pittsburgh: University of Pittsburgh Press, 2011.

Evtuhov, Catherine. "Voices from the Regions: Kraevedenie Meets the Grand Narrative." *Kritika* 13, no. 4 (Fall 2012): 877–887.

Faizova, Irina Viktorovna. *"Manifest o volnosti" i sluzhba dvorianstva v XVIII stoletii.* Moskva: Nauka, 1999.

Fedorchenko, V. *Dvorianskie rody, proslavivshie otechestvo: Entsiklopediia dvorianskikh rodov.* Moskva: Olma-Press, 2003.

Figueirôa-Rêgo, Joáo de. "Family Genealogical Records: Cleansing and Social Reception (Portugal—16th to 18th century)." e-*Journal of Portuguese History* 6, no. 1 (2008): 1–11.

Fisher, Alan W. *Between Russians, Ottomans and Turks: Crimea and Crimean Tatars*. Istanbul: Isis Press, 1998.

Fisher, Alan W. *The Crimean Tatars*. Stanford, Calif.: Hoover Institution Press, 1978.

Fisher, Alan W. "Enlightened Despotism and Islam Under Catherine II." *Slavic Review* 27, no. 4 (1968): 542–553.

Fisher, Alan W. *The Russian Annexation of the Crimea, 1772–1783*. Cambridge: Cambridge University Press, 1970.

Fisher, Alan W. "Şahin Giray, the Reformer Khan, and the Russian Annexation of the Crimea." *Jahrbücher für Geschichte Osteuropas* 15, no. 3 (1967): 341–364.

"Floods in the Crimea." *New York Times* (August 1, 1897). http://search .proquest.com.ezp-prod1.hul.harvard.edu/docview/95521706 ?accountid=11311.

Florovskii, A. "Neskol'ko faktov iz istorii russkoi kolonizatsii Novorossii v nachale XIX v." *ZOOID* 33: 25–40.

Ford, Caroline. "Reforestation, Landscape Conservation, and the Anxieties of Empire in French Colonial Algeria." *American Historical Review* 113, no. 2 (2008): 341–362.

Frank, Allen J. *Muslim Religious Institutions in Imperial Russia: The Islamic World of Novouzensk District and the Kazakh Inner Horde, 1780–1910*. Leiden: Brill, 2001.

Gabdullin, Il'dus Rashitovich. *Ot sluzhilykh tatar k tatarskomu dvorianstvu*. Moskva: R. Sh. Kudashev, 2006.

Gaiman, V. D. "Iz Feodosiiskoi stariny." *ITUAK* 53 (1916): 96–110.

Galushko, Iu. *Kazach'i Voiska Rossii: Kratkii istoriko-khronologicheskii spravochnik kazach'ikh voisk do 1914 goda*. Moskva: Russkii mir, 1993.

Gavril, Arkhiepiskop Ekaterinoslavskii, Khersonskii i Tavricheskii. "Khronologiko-istoricheskoe opisanie tserkvei Eparkhii Khersonskoi i Tavricheskoi." *ZOOID* 2 (1848), 140–210.

Geraci, Robert P. *Window on the East: National and Imperial Identities in Late Tsarist Russia*. Ithaca, N.Y.: Cornell University Press, 2001.

German, I. E. *Istoriia russkogo mezhevaniia (kurs)*. Moskva, 1907.

Givens, Robert D. "Eighteenth-Century Nobiliary Career Patterns and Provincial Government." In *Russian Officialdom: The Bureaucratization of Russian Society from the Seventeenth to the Twentieth Century*, edited by Walter McKenzie Pintner and Don Karl Rowney, 106–129. Chapel Hill: University of North Carolina Press, 1980.

Glushak, A. S., ed. *Bogi Tavridy: Istoriia religii narodov Kryma*. Sevastopol, [s.n.], 1997.

Glushak, A. S. *Krym khristianskij*. Sevastopol', 1996.

Gnucheva, V. N., sost. *Materialy dlia istorii ekspeditsii Akademii Nauk v XVIII i XIX vekakh*. Leningrad: Izd. Akademii Nauk SSSR, 1940.

Gorizontov, Leonid. "The 'Great Circle' of Interior Russia: Representations of the Imperial Center in the Nineteenth and Early Twentieth Centuries." In *Russian Empire: Space, People, Power, 1700–1930*, edited by Jane Burbank, Mark von Hagen, and Anatolyi Remnev, 67–93. Bloomington: Indiana University Press, 2007.

"Gorod Aleshki." *ZOOID* 3 (1853): 217–224.

Got'e, Iu. *Istoriia oblastnogo upravleniia v Rossii ot Petra I do Ekateriny II*, vol. 1. Moskva, 1913.

Gryzlova, B. V. *Gubernii Rossiiskoi Imperii: Istoriia i rukovoditeli, 1708–1917*. Moskva: Obedinennaia redaktsiia MVD Rossii, 2013.

Gvosdev, Nikolas K. *Imperial Policies and Perspectives Towards Georgia, 1760–1819*. Basingstoke, U.K.: Macmillan, 2000.

Herlihy, Patricia. *Odessa: A History, 1794–1914*. Monograph Series (Harvard Ukrainian Research Institute). Cambridge: Distributed by Harvard University Press for the Harvard Ukrainian Research Institute, 1986.

Home, Robert. "Scientific Survey and Land Settlement in British Colonialism, with Particular Reference to Land Tenure Reform in the Middle East, 1920–1950." *Planning Perspectives* 21 (January 2006): 1–22.

Iablochkov, Mikhail T. *Istoriia dvorianskago sosloviia v Rossii*. Sanktpeterburg, 1876.

Ibneeva, Guzel' V. *Puteshestviia Ekateriny II: Opyt "osvoeniia" imperskogo prostranstva*. Kazan: Kazanskii gosuniversitet, 2006.

İnalcık, Halil, and Donald Quataert, eds. *An Economic and Social History of the Ottoman Empire*. 1st paperback ed. Cambridge: Cambridge University Press, 1997.

İnalcık, Halil. "The Khan and the Tribal Aristocracy: The Crimean Khanate Under Sahib Giray I." *Studies in Ottoman Social and Economic History*. London: Varorium Reprints, 1985: 445–456.

İnalcık, Halil. *The Ottoman Empire: The Classical Age, 1300–1600*. Translated by Norman Itzkowitz and Colin Imber. New Rochelle, N.Y.: Aristide D. Caratzas, 1989.

"Istoricheskaia spravka ob obrazovanii v Tavricheskoi gubernii tatarskikh dvorianskikh rodov." *ZOOID* 23 (1901), chast' 3: 41–43.

Iuritsyn, V. T., ed. *Krymskii Konnyi Ee Velichestva Gosudaryni Imperatritsy Aleksandry Feodorovny Polk, 1784–1922*. San Francisco: Globus, 1978.

Ivanov, Petr Ivanovich. *Opyt istoricheskago izsledovaniia o mezhevanii zemel' v Rossii.* Moskva: Selivanovskii, 1846.

Jersild, Austin. *Orientalism and Empire: North Caucasus Mountain Peoples and the Georgian Frontier, 1845–1917.* Montreal: McGill-Queen's University Press, 2002.

Jones, Robert. *The Emancipation of the Russian Nobility, 1762–1785.* Princeton: Princeton University Press, 1993.

Kagan, Frederick W., and Robin Higham, eds. *The Military History of Tsarist Russia.* New York: Palgrave, 2002.

Kain, Roger J. P., and Elizabeth Baigent. *The Cadastral Map in the Service of the State: A History of Property Mapping.* Chicago: University of Chicago Press, 1992.

Kappeler, Andreas. *The Russian Empire: A Multiethnic History.* Harlow, England: Longman, 2001.

Kardases, Vasiles. *Diaspora Merchants in the Black Sea: The Greeks in Southern Russia, 1775–1861.* Lanham, Md.: Lexington Books, 2001.

Karimov, Aleksei. *Dokuda topor i sokha khodili: Ocherki istorii zemel'nogo i lesnogo kadastra v Rossii XVI–nachala XX veka.* Moskva: Nauka, 2007.

Karpat, Kemal H. "The Crimean Emigration of 1856–1862 and the Settlement and Urban Development of Dobruca." In *Passé Turco-Tatar,* edited by Chantal Lemercier-Quelquejay, 275–306. Paris: Éditions Peeters, 1986.

Keppen, Petr. *O drevnostiakh iuzhnago berega Kryma i gor Tavricheskikh.* Sankt Peterburg: Pechatano pri Imperatorskoi Akademii Nauk, 1837.

Kerblay, Basile. "Les Foires commerciales et le marché interieur en Russie dans la première moitié du XIX siècle." *Cahiers du Monde russe et soviétique* 7, no. 3 (1966): 414–435.

Khairedinova, Zarema Zudievna. "Vozniknovenie i razvitie Tavricheskogo magometanskogo dukhovnogo pravleniia (konets XVIII–nachalo XX vv.)." Dissertation (Candidatura), Tavrida National University, Simferopol', 2003.

Kharkhatai, F. "Istoricheskye sud'by krymskikh tatar." Parts 1 and 2. *Vestnik Evropy* 2 (June 1866): 182–236; 2 (June 1867): 142–174.

Khodarkovsky, Michael. "'Not by Word Alone': Missionary Policies and Religious Conversion in Early Modern Russia." *Comparative Studies in Society and History* 38, no. 2 (1996): 267–293.

Khodarkovsky, Michael. *Russia's Steppe Frontier: The Making of a Colonial Empire, 1500–1800.* Bloomington: Indiana University Press, 2002.

Khodarkovsky, Michael. *Where Two Worlds Met: The Russian State and the Kalmyk Nomads, 1600–1771.* Ithaca, N.Y.: Cornell University Press, 1992.

King, Charles. *Odessa: Genius and Death in a City of Dreams*. New York: W.W. Norton, 2011.

Kırımlı, Hakan. "Crimean Tatars, Nogays, and Scottish Missionaries: The Story of Kattı Giray and Other Baptized Descendants of the Crimean Khans." *Cahiers du Monde russe* 45, no. 1–2 (2004): 67–81.

Kırımlı, Hakan. *National Movements and National Identity Among the Crimean Tatars, 1905–1916*. Leiden: E. J. Brill, 1996.

Kırlı, Cengiz. "Kahvehaneler ve hafiyeler: 19. yüzyıl ortalarında Osmanlı'da sosyal control." *Toplum ve Bilim* 83 (1999/2000): 58–77.

Kivelson, Valerie. *Cartographies of Tsardom: The Land and Its Meanings in Seventeenth-Century Russia*. Ithaca, N.Y.: Cornell University Press, 2006.

Kohut, Zenon E. *Russian Centralism and Ukrainian Autonomy: Imperial Absorption of the Hetmanate, 1760s–1830s*. Cambridge: Harvard Ukrainian Research Institute, 1988.

Kohut, Zenon E. "The Ukrainian Elite in the Eighteenth Century and Its Integration into the Russian Nobility." In *The Nobility in Russia and Eastern Europe*, edited by Ivo Banac and Paul Bushkovitch, 65–97. New Haven: Yale Concilium on International and Area Studies, 1983.

Kolli, L. "O sokhranenii i vozobnovlenii v Krymu pamianikov drevnosti, i ob izdaniii opisaniia i risunkov o nykh." *ZOOID* 8: 363–403.

Kolli, L. "O sud'be nekotorykh istoricheskikh zdanii v Starom Krymu i Feodosii." *ITUAK* 35: 10–17.

Korelin, A. P. "The Institution of Marshals of the Nobility: On the Social and Political Position of the Nobility." *Soviet Studies in History* 17, no. 4 (1979): 3–35.

Korf, Baron S. A. *Dvorianstvo i ego soslovnoe upravlenie za stoletie 1762–1855 godov*. S. Peterburg: Tip. Trenke i Fiusno, 1906.

Kozelsky, Mara. *Christianizing Crimea: Shaping Sacred Space in the Russian Empire and Beyond*. DeKalb: Northern Illinois University Press, 2010.

Kozelsky, Mara. "Ruins into Relics: The Monument to Saint Vladimir on the Excavations of Chersonesos." *Russian Review* 63, no. 4 (2004): 655–672.

Krichinskii, Arslan. *Ocherki russkoi politiki na okrainakh*, t. 1. *K istorii religioznykh pritesnenii krymskikh tatar*. Baku: Soiuz musul'manskoi trudovoi intelligentsia, 1919.

Krikun, Iukhim. *Pam'iatniki krymskotatarskoi arkhitekturi (XIII–XX stoletiia)*. Simferopol': "Tavrida," 2001.

Krivosheia, I. I. "Prichislenie pol'skoi shliakhty k rossiiskomu dvorianstvu v kontse XVIII–v pervoi polovine XIX vekov (na primere Umanskogo uezda Kievskoi gubernii)." In *Problemy priznaniia i utverzhdeniia v pravakh rossiiskogo dvorianstva vysshykh soslovii narodov Rossiiskoi Imperii i inostrannykh dvorian,* edited by O. M. Karamyshev, 12–17. Sankt Peterburg: SPb-skor Dvorianskoe Sobranie, 1997.

Krym i krymskie tatary (po povodu stoletiia prisoedineniia Kryma k Rossiiu). Kiev: Tip. Kievskogo gosudarstvennogo pravleniia, 1885.

Kurtiev, Refat. *Kalendarnye obriady krymskikh tatar.* Simferopol': Krymuchpedgiz, 1996.

Lashkov, Fedor Fedorovich. "Arkhivnyia dannyia o beilikakh v krymskom khanstve." *Opyt iz trudov 6-go arkheologichnogo s"ezda v Odesse v 1884 g.,* t. 4, 96–110. Odessa: 1889.

Lashkov, Fedor Fedorovich. "Istoricheskii ocherk krymsko-tatarskago zemlevladeniia." Parts 1, 2, 3, and 4. *ITUAK* 22 (1895): 35–81; 23 (1895): 71–117; 24 (1896): 35–71; 25 (1896): 29–88.

Lashkov, Fedor Fedorovich, "K voprosu o kolichestve naseleniia Tavricheskoi gubernii v nachale XIX stoletiia." *ITUAK* 53 (1916): 158–176.

Lashkov, Fedor Fedorovich. *Kniaz' Grigorii A. Potemkin-Tavricheskii kak deiatel' Kryma.* Simferopol': Tip. Gordeevskogo, 1890.

Lashkov, Fedor Fedorovich. "O kameral'nom opisanii Kryma 1784 g." *ITUAK* 2 (1897): 20–30.

Lashkov, Fedor Fedorovich. "O peresmotre Chernomorskago tarifa 1782 g." *ITUAK* 1 (1897): 25–39.

Lashkov, Fedor Fedorovich. "Statistika. Statisticheskiia svedeniia o Kryme, soobshchennyia kaimakanami v 1783 godu." *ZOOID* 14 (1886): 91–156.

Lazzerini, Edward J. "The Crimea Under Russian Rule: 1783 to the Great Reforms." In *Russian Colonial Expansion to 1917,* edited by Michael Rywkin, 123–138. London: Mansell Publishing, 1988.

Lazzerini, Edward J. "Local Accommodation and Resistance to Colonialism in Nineteenth-Century Crimea," in *Russia's Orient: Imperial Borderlands and Peoples, 1700–1917,* edited by Daniel R. Brower and Edward J. Lazzerini, 169–187. Bloomington: Indiana University Press, 1997.

Le Bouëdec, Gérard. "Small Ports from the Sixteenth to the Early Twentieth Century and the Local Economy of the French Atlantic Coast." *International Journal of Maritime History* 21, no. 2 (December 2009): 103–126.

Lebedintsev, Protoierei A. "Stoletie tserkovnoi zhizni Kryma 1783–1883." *ZOOID* 13: 200–219.

LeDonne, John P. "Administrative Regionalization in the Russian Empire, 1802–1826." *Cahiers du Monde russe* 43, no. 1 (2002): 5–33.

LeDonne, John P. "Building an Infrastructure of Empire in Russia's Eastern Theater, 1650s–1840s." *Cahiers du Monde russe* 47, no. 3 (2006): 581–610.

LeDonne, John P. "Frontier Governors General, 1775–1825: Territorial or Functional Administration?" *Cahiers du Monde russe* 42, no. 1 (2001): 5–30.

LeDonne, John P. "Geopolitics, Logistics, and Grain: Russia's Ambitions in the Black Sea Basin, 1737–1834." *The International History Review* 28, no. 1 (2006): 1–41.

LeDonne, John P. *Ruling Russia: Politics and Administration in the Age of Absolutism, 1762–1796*. Studies of the Harriman Institute. Princeton: Princeton University Press, 1984.

LeDonne, John P. "The Territorial Reform of the Russian Empire, 1775–1796 [I. Central Russia, 1775–1784]." *Cahiers du Monde russe et soviétique* 23, no. 2 (1982): 147–183.

LeDonne, John P. "The Territorial Reform of the Russian Empire, 1775–1796 [II. The Borderlands, 1777–1796]." *Cahiers du Monde russe et soviétique* 24, no. 4 (1983): 411–457.

Levashev, Pavel. *Kartina ili opisanie vsekh nashestvii na Rossiiu Tatar i Turkov, i ikh tut branei, grabitel'stv i opustoshenii, nachavshikhsia v polovine desiatago veka i pochti bezpreryvno chrez vosem sot let prodolzhavshikhsia*. Sanktpeterburg, 1792.

Lieven, D. C. B. *Empire: The Russian Empire and Its Rivals*. New Haven: Yale University Press, 2001.

Lincoln, W. Bruce. *Nicholas I: Emperor and Autocrat of All the Russias*. DeKalb: Northern Illinois University Press, 1989.

Lindsay, James E. *Daily Life in the Medieval Islamic World*. Westport, Conn.: Greenwood Press, 2005.

Lohr, Eric. *Russian Citizenship: From Empire to Soviet Union*. Cambridge: Harvard University Press, 2012.

Lohr, Eric, and Marshall Poe, eds. *The Military and Society in Russia 1450–1917*. Leiden: Brill, 2002.

Lovell, Stephen. "Between Arcadia and Suburbia: Dachas in Late Imperial Russia." *Slavic Review* 61, no. 1 (2002): 66–87.

Lovell, Stephen. *Summerfolk: A History of the Dacha, 1710–2000*. Ithaca, N.Y.: Cornell University Press, 2003.

Madariaga, Isabel de. *Russia in the Age of Catherine the Great*. New Haven: Yale University Press, 1981.

Magocsi, Paul R. *This Blessed Land: Crimea and the Crimean Tatars*. Toronto: Distributed by the University of Toronto Press for the Chair of Ukrainian Studies, University of Toronto, 2014.

Malinovskii, F. L. *Istoricheskii vzgliad na mezhevanie v Rossii do 1765 goda*. S. Peterburg, v Tip. A. Sycheva, 1844.

Malov, E. "O tatarskikh mechetiakh v Rossii." Parts 1 and 2. *Pravoslavnyi sobesednik* 12 (1867): 285–320; 13 (1868), chast' 1: 1–45.

Mani, Lata. *Contentious Traditions: The Debate on Sati in Colonial India.* Berkeley: University of California, 1998.

Manz, Beatrice Forbes. "The Clans of the Crimean Khanate, 1466–1532." *Harvard Ukrainian Studies* 2, no. 3 (1978): 282–307.

Marasinova, E. N. *Psikhologiia elity rossiiskogo dvorianstva poslednei treti XVIII veka: Po materialam perepiski.* Moskva: Rosspen, 1999.

Markevich, Arsenii. "K istorii khanskago bakhchisarajskago dvortsa." *ITUAK* 23 (1895): 130–176.

Markevich, Arsenii. "K stoletiiu otechestvennoi voiny. Tavricheskaia guberniia v sviazi s epokhoi 1806–1815 godov." *ITUAK* 49 (1913): 1–100.

Markevich, Arsenii. *K voprosu o polozhenii protiv-musul'manskoi missii v Tavride.* Simferopol': Tavricheskaia gubernskaia tipografiia, 1911.

Markevich, Arsenii. "Materialy arkhiva kantseliarii Tavricheskago gubernatora, otnosiashchiesia k puteshestviiu Imperatritsy Ekateriny II v Krym v 1787 g." *ITUAK* 11 (1891): 77–143.

Markevich, Arsenii. "Opyt ukazatelia sochinenii." *ITUAK* 28 (1898): 92–185.

Markevich, Arsenii. "Opyt ukazatelia knig i statei." *ITUAK* 32–33 (1902): 47–128.

Markevich, Arsenii. "Pereseleniia krymskikh tatar v Turtsiiu v sviazi s dvizheniem naseleniia v Krymu." *Izvestiia Akademii Nauk SSSR* (1928): 375–405; (1929): 1–16.

Markevich, Arsenii. *Taurica, ITUAK* 20 (1894): 1–394.

Markov, Evgenii. *Ocherki Kryma: Kartiny krymskoi zhizni, istorii, i prirody.* S.-Peterburg: Tip. Tovarishchestva M. O. Vul'f, 1884.

Martin, Virginia. "Kazakh Oath-Taking in Colonial Courtrooms: Legal Culture and Russian Empire-Building." *Kritika* 5, no. 3 (2004): 483–514.

Martin, Virginia. *Law and Custom in the Steppe: The Kazakhs of the Middle Horde and Russian Colonialism in the Nineteenth Century.* Richmond, U.K.: Curzon, 2001.

Masaev, M. V. "Krymskie tatary v vooruzhennykh silakh Rossii (konets XVIII–nachalo XX vv.)." Dissertation (Candidatura), Tavrida National University, Simferopol', 2003.

Menning, Bruce W. "The Emergence of a Military-Administrative Elite in the Don Cossack Land, 1708–1836." In *Russian Officialdom: The Bureaucratization of Russian Society from the Seventeenth to the Twentieth Century,* edited by Walter McKenzie Pintner and Don Karl Rowney, 130–161. Chapel Hill: University of North Carolina Press, 1980.

"Mery o privedenii v izvestnost' Novorossiiskago i Kavkazskago kraia." *ZOOID* 10 (1877): 225–229.

Mikaberidze, Alexander. *The Russian Officer Corps in the Revolutionary and Napoleonic Wars, 1792–1815.* Staplehurst, U.K.: Spellmount, 2005.

Milov, L. V. *Issledovanie ob "Ekonomicheskikh primechaniiakh" k general'nomu mezhevaniiu: K istorii russkogo krest'ianstva i sel'skogo khoziaistva vtoroi poloviny XVIII v.* Moskva: Izd-vo Moskovskogo universiteta, 1965.

Moon, David. "The Russian Academy of Sciences Expeditions to the Steppes in the Late Eighteenth Century." *Slavonic and East European Review* 88, no. 1/2 (2010): 204–236.

Morris, Jan. *Stones of Empire: The Buildings of the Raj.* Oxford: Oxford University Press, 1983.

Morrison, Alexander. "Metropole, Colony, and Imperial Citizenship in the Russian Empire." *Kritika* 13, no. 2 (2012): 327–364.

Muftizade, Izmail. "Ocherk voennoi sluzhby krymskikh tatar s 1783 po 1889 god." *ITUAK* 30 (1899): 1–25.

Murzakevich, Nikolai. "Atlas Chernago Moria." *ZOOID* 2 (1848): 722–725.

Nepomniashchii, A. A. *Arsenii Markevich: Stranitsy istorii Krymskogo kraevedeniia.* Simferopol': Biznes Inform, 2005.

Nepomniashchii, A. A. *Muzeinoe delo v Krymu i ego starateli (XIX–nachalo XX veka): Biobibliograficheskoe issledovanie.* Simferopol': Tavricheskii natsional'nyi un-t im. V. I. Vernadskoho, 2000.

Nepomniashchii, A. A. "Novye istochniki o razvitii istoricheskogo kraevedeniya Kryma." *Otechestvennye arkhivy,* no. 4 (July 1998): 25–28.

Nepomniashchii, A. A. *Zapiski puteshestvennikov i putevoditeli v razvitii istoricheskogo kraevedeniia Kryma (posledniaia tret' XVIII–nachalo XX veka).* Kiev: Instytut ukrains'koi arkheohrafii ta dzhereloznavstva im Hrushevs'koi NAN Ukrainy, 1999.

Nolde, Boris. *La formation de l'empire Russe, tome premier.* Paris: Institut d'Études Slaves, 1952.

"O prosheniiakh deputatov Tavricheskoi oblasti na Vysochaishee Imia v 1796 godu." *ITUAK* 2 (1897): 9–19.

"O sostoianii raznykh otraslei sel'skago khozaistva v iuzhnoi Rossii v 1848 godu." *Zhurnal ministerstva gosudarstvennago imushchestva* (1849): 1–57.

O'Neill, Kelly. *Beautiful Spaces: An Experiment in Narrative Mapping and Crimean History* [digital history project]. http://dighist.fas.harvard.edu/projects/beautifulspaces/.

O'Neill, Kelly. "Between Subversion and Submission: The Integration of the Crimean Khanate into the Russian Empire, 1783–1853." Ph.D. diss., Harvard University, 2006.

O'Neill, Kelly. "Constructing Russian Identity in the Imperial Borderland: Architecture, Islam, and the Transformation of the Crimean Landscape." *Ab Imperio* 2 (2006): 163–192.

O'Neill, Kelly. "Rethinking Elite Integration: Crimean Murzas and the Evolution of Russian Nobility." *Cahiers du Monde russe* 51, no. 2–3 (2010): 397–417.

"Ob orderakh kniazia Potemkina i grafa Zubova." *ITUAK* 3 (1897): 1–35.

"Otryvok povestvovaniia o Novorossijskom krae, iz original'nykh istoch-nikov pocherknutyi." *ZOOID* 3 (1853): 79–129.

Padrón, Ricardo. *The Spacious Word: Cartography, Literature, and Empire in Early Modern Spain.* Chicago: University of Chicago Press, 2004.

Panchenko, A. M. "Potemkinskie derevni kak kul'turnyi mif." In *Iz istorii russkoi kul'tury,* t. 4 *(XVIII–nachalo XIX veka),* 685–700. Moskva: Shkola "Iazyki russkoi kul'tury." 1996.

Papernyi, Vladimir. *Kul'tura "Dva."* Ann Arbor, Mich.: Ardis, 1985.

Pearson, Michael. "Littoral Society: The Concept and the Problems." *Journal of World History* 17, no. 4 (December 2006): 353–373.

Pleshcheev, Sergei Ivanovich. *Obozrenie Rossiiskiia Imperiia v nyneshnem eia novoustroennom sostoianii.* Sankt Peterburg, 1787.

Polonskaia, I. "Pervye desiat' let Simferopoliia." *ITUAK* 55 (1918): 135–141.

Pomeranz, William E. "Justice from Underground: The History of the Underground Advokatura." *Russian Review* 52, no. 3 (1993): 321–340.

Postnikov, Alexei. "Outline of the History of Russian Cartography." In *Regions: A Prism to View the Slavic-Eurasian World,* edited by Kimitaka Matsuzato, 5–9. Sapporo: Slavic Research Center, Hokkaido University, 2000.

Pravilova, Ekaterina. *Finansy Imperii: Den'gi i vlast' v politike Rossii na natsional'nykh okrainakh, 1801–1917.* Moskva: Novoe izdatel'stvo, 2006.

Pravilova, Ekaterina. "The Property of Empire: Islamic Law and Russian Agrarian Policy in Transcaucasia and Turkestan." *Kritika* 12, no. 2 (2011): 353–386.

Prokhorov, D. A. "Gosudarstvennye uchrezhdeniia Tavricheskoi oblasti v kontse 18 veka." *Kul'tura narodov Prichernomor'ia* 1998 (4), 123–138.

"Protokol otkrytiia Tavricheskoi Uchenoi Arkhivnoi Kommissii v g. Simferopole." *ITUAK* 1 (1897): 1–14.

Pushkin, Alexander. *The Bakchesarian Fountain.* Translated by William D. Lewis. Philadelphia: C. Sherman, 1849.

Raeff, Marc. "The 18th-Century Nobility and the Search for a New Political Culture in Russia." *Kritika* 1, no. 4 (2000): 769–782.

Raeff, Marc. "In the Imperial Manner." In *Catherine the Great: A Profile,* edited by Marc Raeff, 197–236. New York: Hill and Wang, 1972.

Ransel, David L. "Bureaucracy and Patronage: The View from an Eighteenth-Century Russian Letter-Writer." In *The Rich, the Well Born, and the*

Powerful: Elites and Upper Classes in History, edited by Frederic Cople Jaher, 154–178. Urbana: University of Illinois Press, 1973.

Remnev, Anatolii. "Siberia and the Russian Far East in the Imperial Geography of Power." In *Russian Empire: Space, People, Power, 1700–1930*, edited by Jane Burbank, Anatolii Remnev, and Mark von Hagen, 425–454. Bloomington: Indiana University Press, 2007.

Riasanovsky, Nicholas. *Nicholas I and Official Nationality in Russia, 1825–1855*. Berkeley: University of California, 1969.

Romaniello, Matthew P. *The Elusive Empire Kazan and the Creation of Russia, 1552–1671*. Madison: University of Wisconsin Press, 2012.

Roosevelt, Priscilla R. "Tatiana's Garden: Noble Sensibilities and Estate Park Design in the Romantic Era." *Slavic Review* 49, no. 3 (1990): 335–349.

Rostovtzeff, Michael Ivanovitch. *Iranians and Greeks in South Russia*. Oxford: Clarendon Press, 1922.

Rudnev, S. "Lichnii sostav pervykh sudov v Tavricheskoi gubernii: Doreformennago-Tavricheskago grazhdanskago i ugolovnago suda i uchrezhdennago po ustavam Imperatora Aleksandra II Simferopol'skago okruzhnago suda." *ITUAK* 52 (1915): 225–233.

Russkii Biograficheskii Slovar', 27 volumes. Sanktpeterburg: Izdanie Imperatorskago Russkago istoricheskago obshchestva, 1896–1918.

Ruzhitskaia, I. V. "Sudebnoe zakonodatel'stvo Nikolaia I (rabota nad ugolovnym i grazhdanskim ulozheniiami)," *Otechestvennaia istoriia* 4 (2001), 41–57.

Sarandinaki, M. "Tavrida." *Vestnik Evropy* 164, no. 2 (January 1829): 116–126.

Savitskii, I. V. *Vedenie dvorianskoi rodoslovnoi knigi v Olonetskoi gubernii, 1791–1841 gg.*

"Sbornik sobytii v Novorossiiskom krae." *ZOOID* 7 (1868): 297–305.

Schimmelpennick van der Oye, David, and Bruce Menning, eds. *Reforming the Tsar's Army: Military Innovation in Imperial Russia from Peter the Great to the Revolution*. Washington, D.C.: Woodrow Wilson Center Press, 2004.

Schönle, Andreas. "Garden of the Empire: Catherine's Appropriation of the Crimea." *Slavic Review* 60 (2001), no. 1: 1–23.

Seed, Patricia. *Ceremonies of Possession in Europe's Conquest of the New World, 1492–1640*. Cambridge: Cambridge University Press, 1995.

Seegel, Steven. *Mapping Europe's Borderlands: Russian Cartography in the Age of Empire*. Chicago: University of Chicago Press, 2012.

Seidamet, Djafer. *La Crimée: Passé, présent, revendications des Tatars de Crimée*. Lausanne: Impr. G. Vaney-Burnier, 1921.

Sekirinskii, S. A. "Agrarnyi stroi krymskikh tatar v XVI–XVIII vv." *Materialy po arkheologii, istorii, i etnografii Tavrii* 2 (1991): 140–149.

Sevastianova, A. A. *Russkaia provintsial'naia istoriografiia vtoroi poloviny XVIII veka*. Moskva: Arkheograficheskaiia komissiia Rossiiskoi Akademii Nauk, 1998.

Shaw, Denis J. B. "Mapmaking, Science, and State Building in Russia Before Peter the Great." *Journal of Historical Geography* 31 (2005): 409–429.

Skal'kovskii, Apollon. *Khronologicheskoe obozrenie istorii Novorossiiskogo kraia, 1730–1823*. Odessa: Gorodskaia tipografiia, 1838.

Skal'kovskii, Apollon. "O nogaiskikh tatarakh zhivushchikh v Tavricheskoi gubernii." Parts 1 and 2. *Zhurnal ministerstva narodnago prosveshcheniia* 11 (1843): 105–130; 12 (1843): 147–190.

Skal'kovskii, Apollon. *Opyt statisticheskago opisaniia Novorossiiskago kraiia*. Odessa, 1850.

Skal'kovskii, Apollon. "Zaniatie Kryma v 1783 godu: Materialy dlia Istorii Novorossiiskago kraia." *Zhurnal ministerstva narodnago prosveshcheniia* 2 (1841): 1–44.

Slezkine, Yuri. *Arctic Mirrors: Russia and the Small Peoples of the North*. Ithaca, N.Y.: Cornell University Press, 1994.

Smirnov, V. D. *Krymskoe Khanstvo pod verkhovenstvom Otomanskoi porty do nachala XVIII veka*. Sankt-Peterburg, 1887.

Smith-Peter, Susan. "Bringing the Provinces into Focus: Subnational Spaces in the Recent Historiography of Russia." *Kritika* 12, no. 4 (2011): 835–848.

Smith-Peter, Susan. "How to Write a Region: Local and Regional Historiography." *Kritika* 5, no. 3 (2004): 527–542.

Smolin, V. "K voprosu o nazvanii Chernago moria v drevnosti." *ITUAK* 53 (1916): 90–95.

Solov'ev, K. A. *"Vo vkuse umnoi stariny . . ." Usadebnyi byt rossiiskogo dvorianstva II poloviny XVIII–I poloviny XIX vekov*. Sankt-Peterburg: Nestor, 1998.

Solov'ev, V. I. *Russkoe Dvorianstvo i ego vydaiushchiesia predstaviteli*. Rostov-na-Donu: Feniks, 2000.

Sosnogorov, M. A., ed. *Putevoditel' po Krymu*. Kiev, 2010.

Steinwedel, Charles. "Making Social Groups, One Person at a Time." In *Documenting Individual Identity*, edited by Jane Caplan and John Torpey, 67–82. Princeton: Princeton University Press, 2001.

Sunderland, Willard. "Empire Without Imperialism? Ambiguities of Colonization in Tsarist Russia." *Ab Imperio* 2 (2003): 101–114.

Sunderland, Willard. "Imperial Space: Territorial Thought and Practice in the Eighteenth Century." In *Russian Empire: Space, People, Power, 1700–1930*, edited by Jane Burbank, Mark von Hagen, and Anatolyi Remnev, 33–66. Bloomington: Indiana University Press, 2007.

Sunderland, Willard. *Taming the Wild Field: Colonization and Empire on the Russian Steppe*. Ithaca, N.Y.: Cornell University Press, 2004.

Thaden, Edward C. *Russia's Western Borderlands, 1710–1870*. Princeton: Princeton University Press, 1984.

Tompkins, Stuart R. "The Russian Bible Society: A Case of Religious Xenophobia." *American Slavic and East European Review* 7, no. 3 (1948): 251–268.

"Topograficheskoe opisanie dostavshimsia po mirnomu traktatu ot Otomanskoi porty vo vladenie Rossiiskoi Imperii zemliam, 1774 goda." *ZOOID* 7 (1868): 166–198.

Turhan, Ömer. "XIX Yüzyılda Kırım, Kafkasya ve Civarında Misyonerlik Faaliyetleri." *Belleten* 64, no. 241 (2000): 925–947.

Vasil'ev, Ilarion. "O nachale i uspekhov mezhevaniia v Rossii." *Vestnik Evropy* 122, no. 3 (1822): 185–201.

Veinstein, Gilles. "Missionnaires jésuites et agents français en Crimée au début du XVIIIe siècle." *Cahiers du Monde russe et soviétique* 10, no. 3–4 (1969): 414–458.

Velychenko, Stephen. "Identities, Loyalties and Service in Imperial Russia: Who Administered the Borderlands?" *Russian Review* 54, no. 2 (1995): 188–208.

Voloshikhov, Ivan. "Tekie 'Eni-dzhami' dervishei-molchal'nikov v Simferopole." *ITUAK* 54 (1918): 356–359.

Vozgrin, V. E. *Istoricheskie sud'by krymskikh tatar*. Moskva: Mysl', 1992.

Watenpaugh, Heghnar Zeitlian. *The Image of an Ottoman City: Imperial Architecture and Urban Experience in Aleppo in the 16th and 17th Centuries*. Leiden: Brill, 2004.

Werth, Paul W. *At the Margins of Orthodoxy: Mission, Governance and Confessional Politics in Russia's Volga-Kama Region, 1827–1905*. Ithaca, N.Y.: Cornell University Press, 2002.

Werth, Paul. *The Tsar's Foreign Faiths: Toleration and the Fate of Religious Freedom in Imperial Russia*. Oxford: Oxford University Press, 2014.

Williams, Brian Glyn. *The Crimean Tatars: The Diaspora Experience and the Forging of a Nation*. Leiden: Brill, 2001.

Williams, Brian Glyn. "*Hijra* and Forced Migration from Nineteenth-Century Russia to the Ottoman Empire: A Critical Analysis of the Great Crimean Tatar Emigration of 1860–1861." *Cahiers du Monde russe* 41, no. 1 (2000): 79–108.

Wirtschafter, Elise Kimerling. *From Serf to Russian Soldier*. Princeton: Princeton University Press, 1990.

Withers, Charles. "Place and the 'Spatial Turn' in Geography and in History." *Journal of the History of Ideas* 70, no. 4 (2009): 637–658.

Wolfart, Philip. "Mapping the Early Modern State: The Work of Ignaz Ambros Amman, 1782–1812." *Journal of Historical Geography* 34 (2008): 1–23.

Wortman, Richard S. *The Development of a Russian Legal Consciousness.* Chicago: University of Chicago Press, 1976.

Wortman, Richard S. "Russian Monarchy and the Rule of Law: New Considerations of the Court Reform of 1864." *Kritika* 6, no. 1 (2005): 145–170.

Wortman, Richard S. *Scenarios of Power: Myth and Ceremony in Russian Monarchy.* 2 vols. Studies of the Harriman Institute. Princeton: Princeton University Press, 1995.

Zakharov, Pavel Pavlovich. "Grigorii Moskvich: Izdatel', puteshestvennik, organizator turisma v Rossii." http://www.mountain.ru/article/article _display1.php?article_id=6565.

Zakrevskii, N. "Sevastopol' 1831 god (zapiski vracha morskoi sluzhby)." *Morskoi Sbornik* 1862, no. 3: 56–61.

Zhur'iari, I. "Poezdka v blizhaishiia orestnosti Bakhchisaraia." *ITUAK* 9 (1890): 108–111.

Ziablovskii, E. F. *Geografiia Rossiiskoi Imperii.* St. Petersburg: Tip. Imp. Akademii Nauk, 1831.

Zorin, Andrei. *Kormia dvuglavogo orla: Literatura i gosudarstvennaia ideologiia v Rossii v poslednei treti XVIII-pervoi treti XIX veka.* Moscow: Novoe literaturnoe obozrenie, 2001.

Index